Sarah_mclean_@ hotmail.com

• *Molly, Molly, Molly, Molly... why are you leaving!*

-Goodbye forever, Sarah

To sand.

Or not to sand.

Any questions?

It's a question faced by boaters every year. And not just by wooden boat purists, but by fiberglass boat owners who insist on beautiful brightwork. Do you apply Epifanes Clear High Gloss Varnish and dutifully sand between coats to attain that show quality finish? Or do you use Epifanes Wood Finish Gloss so you can skip the sanding and add a few potentially glorious days to your season without sacrificing durability? Or perhaps you topcoat the Wood Finish Gloss with the Clear High Gloss Varnish for the ultimate in performance and ease. Whichever option you choose, you'll be using an Epifanes varnish packed with unmatched amounts of tung oil, alkyd resin, and UV filters to create a beautiful high gloss finish that builds up faster, lasts longer, and protects your boat better. Ask for Epifanes at your local chandlery. Or call us at 1-800-269-0961 for our free technical information package. Because no matter which Epifanes varnish you start with, the finish will always be perfect—there's no question about it.

EPIFANES®

EPIFANES (ÉPEE-FAWN-US) NORTH AMERICA, INC., 70 WATER STREET, THOMASTON, MAINE 04861

1-800-269-0961 FAX: 207-354-0387 WWW.EPIFANES.COM

SAIL TALL SHIPS!

P9-DTO-181

SAIL TALL SHIPS!

Tall Ships®Newport
SALUTE
2000

© ROB ARRA – OVER NARRAGANSETT BAY, NEWPORT, RL

Come to legendary Newport— a Tall Ships tradition.

⚓

June 29 – July 2
2 0 0 0

Call now to reserve your berth!
401-847-8206

CONTACT
Capt. Rick Williams
17B Bowen's Wharf
Newport, RI 02840 USA
PHONE **401-847-8206**
FAX **401-847-8508**
EMAIL talshpsnpt@aol.com
www.tallshipsnewport.org

TALL SHIPS® IS A REGISTERED TRADEMARK & SERVICE MARK
OWNED BY THE AMERICAN SAIL TRAINING ASSOCIATION

PRESENTED BY
Ⓑ **Bell Atlantic Mobile**

Bowen's Wharf and WIMCO welcomes
Tall Ships Newport Salute 2000

WIMCO
LUXURY VILLAS & HOTELS
WWW.WIMCOVILLAS.COM

Where do you go

to school?

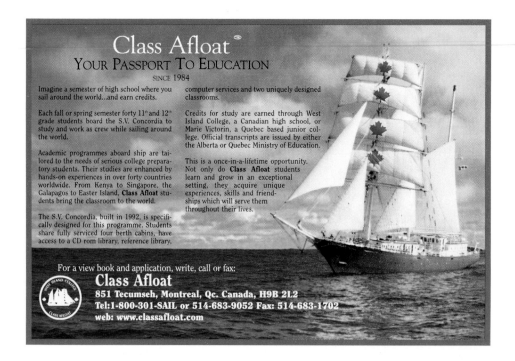

The Training Ship
Picton Castle
VOYAGES 2000

SUMMER TRAINING CRUISE FOR YOUTH

Participating in Tall Ships 2000®, the Barque *Picton Castle* will sail from Lunenburg, Nova Scotia June 1st, bound for Bermuda and then on to ports in New England. The ship will join the Tall Ships 2000® Boston to Halifax Race, then put into a number of ports in the Canadian Maritimes before returning to Lunenburg in early August. Rope work, rigging, sailmaking, chart work, piloting and small boat handling emphasized in instruction and practice. Learn the way of a ship and the arts of seafaring. Open to youth of all nations, ages 16 to 25 preferred.

WORLD VOYAGE 2000

About November 1, 2000, the Barque *Picton Castle* will cast off from her pier in Lunenburg, Nova Scotia, and begin a year and a half voyage around the world. Thirty-four dedicated men and women will be selected from many countries to crew the *Picton Castle* under the ship's officers. All hands will stand regular watches, sharing in the commitment, work, costs and achievements of sailing this classic square rigger around the world. *Ports of call to include: Panama, Pitcairn Island, Tahiti, Rarotonga, Samoa, Fiji, Solomons, Bali, Zanzibar and many more. Open to those 18 years old and over.*

For more information on Summer Training Cruise for Youth or World Voyage 2000

Visit the ship in Lunenburg at
174 Bluenose Drive
Box 1076 Lunenburg, Nova Scotia
B0J 2C0
(902) 634-9984
email: castle@tallships.ca

**Speak to the voyage coordinator
David Robinson at**
(603) 424-0219 (Office)
(603) 424-1849 (Fax)
email: wissco@juno.com

www.picton-castle.com

See page 204 in this Directory for details on ASTA member *Picton Castle*

Muskegon, Michigan welcomes

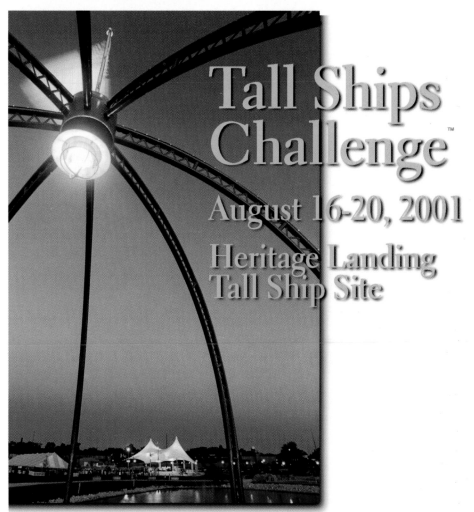

Tall Ships Challenge™

August 16-20, 2001

Heritage Landing
Tall Ship Site

ASTA
American Sail Training Association

MUSKEGON County
catch the wave!

For more information on events and attractions in Muskegon County, call
1-800-250-WAVE
231-724-3100 or 231-893-4585 www.visitmuskegon.org

Sail Tall Ships!
A Directory of Sail Training and Adventure at Sea
12th Edition

ASTA

The mission of the American Sail Training Association is to encourage character building through sail training, promote sail training to the American public, and support education under sail.

AMERICAN SAIL TRAINING ASSOCIATION
NEWPORT, RI

Published by:

American Sail Training Association (ASTA)
PO Box 1459
Newport, RI 02840 USA
Phone: (401) 846-1775
Fax: (401) 849-5400
E-mail: asta@sailtraining.org
Web site: http://tallships.sailtraining.org

Acknowledgments

Many of the photographs in this edition of *Sail Tall Ships!* were supplied by:

Thad Koza
Tall Ships Photography
24 Mary St.
Newport, RI 02840 USA
Phone: (401) 846-5274

MAX
Bywater Lodge-Pierside
Lymington, Hants SO41 5SB
UNITED KINGDOM
Phone: + 44 (0) 1590 672047

Roger W. Archibald
Phone: (617) 472-2468

We would like to thank Matthew Capdevielle, Jim Gladson, Admiral James M. Loy, USCG, Catharine McLean, Michael Rauworth, Nancy Taylor Robson, and Caitlin Schwarzman for submitting material or granting permission to reprint their remarks.

We would also like to thank Alex Agnew, Bart Dunbar, Per Lofving, and Chris Rowsom for their assistance in selling advertisements, and the advertisers who made the production of this Directory possible.

Registered Trademarks

The following registered trademarks and service marks are owned by the American Sail Training Association:

Tall Ships®
Tall Ships are Coming!®
Tall Ships 2000®
Tall Ships Challenge™

Sail Tall Ships! A Directory of Sail Training and Adventure at Sea
12th edition

Compiled and edited by Jonathan C. Dickinson, ASTA Program Manager
Designed by Thea Drew
Printed by Transcontinental Printing, Toronto, Ontario, Canada

ISBN 0-9636483-5-7

Cover photo: "HMS" *Rose* © Philip Plisson

Table of Contents

SAIL TALL SHIPS!

Foreword

BY DAVID V.V. WOOD
CHAIRMAN, ASTA

Welcome to the 12th edition of *Sail Tall Ships!*, ASTA's first Directory of Sail Training and Adventure at Sea for the 21st century. A year ago, most of us were likely to be reflecting on how much the world had changed in the 20th century. But with the turn of the millennium behind us, we inevitably find ourselves looking ahead, as if we had just come on deck to watch the sun rise above an empty sea, and to wonder with excitement and hope about what the day may bring—and what lies over the horizon.

Millennia, of course, are artificial constructs, just as most divisions of time are. As any seafarer who has been on a long voyage knows, once you have settled into a routine at sea, questions of where you have come from or where you are bound for, even what year, or month, or day of the week it is become relatively unimportant. It is the daily rhythm of sunrise, noon, and sunset, at night the wheeling of the stars overhead from east to west, the constant heaving of the sea, the hauling and veering of the wind, the steady progress toward the horizon, the rotation of the watches, the work of caring for the ship—these are the things that have reality and immediacy. All else seems to fade into insignificance: the ship and the ocean are our world, and one's shipmates the only people who matter.

In a new century already defined by an obsession with connectedness, it is going to be harder to find ways of escaping to places where one can be in touch only with oneself, with the people immediately around us, and with the physical world apparent to our senses. It will be more difficult to keep our bearings, to know what is real in the bewildering array of signals bombarding us at every turn. And in a culture ever more self-absorbed, opportunities to develop a sense of interdependence, and of our own place in a real community with a real purpose, are going to be rarer and rarer.

Fortunately—perhaps even because of these societal trends—sail training is a growth industry at the beginning of the 21st century. Ships and the sea have been a medium of human connectedness for millennia, and our enduring fascination with sailing ships is reassuring evidence of a belief that continuity between past and future will always be vital to our cultural health. As a new millennium begins, that fascination is manifesting itself in a wonderful array of new sail training vessels and projects. At least eight new additions to the ASTA fleet were in various stages of construction as this Directory went to press—two new brigantines, the *Irving Johnson* and *Exy Johnson* for the Los Angeles Maritime Institute; the Wisconsin Lake Schooner Education Association's *Denis Sullivan*; the *Pacific Grace*, recently launched by S.A.L.T.S. in British Columbia; the Schooner Sultana Project's *Sultana*; the Great Lakes Schooner Company's *Kajama*; and two as-yet-unnamed vessels to begin construction this year, one for the Sea Education Association and one for the Harvey Gamage Foundation.

And the same sort of thing is going on around the globe. Tall Ships 2000® will bring hundreds of sail training vessels and thousands of trainees from all over the world to the Atlantic Coast during the Millennial Summer, to celebrate and reaffirm the many values that are so wonderfully learned from ships and the sea. So what are you waiting for? Pack your seabag, head for the docks! The Millennium is here, and the time is now!

PHOTO BY THAD KOZA

A Brief History of the American Sail Training Association

The American Sail Training Association (ASTA) was founded in 1973 to coordinate and foster the expansion of sail training activities in American waters. It was the first national sail training organization to affiliate with the International Sail Training Association (ISTA), and is thus the eldest "sister" in a family that has since grown to include sixteen similar organizations around the world.

Initially, the American Sail Training Association worked to coordinate races and gatherings of sail training ships around the United States. ASTA's founder, Barclay Warburton III, had sailed his brigantine *Black Pearl* across the Atlantic to participate in the ISTA-organized 1972 Cutty Sark Tall Ships Race series, and was so inspired by the enthusiasm and spirit he saw in that international gathering of tall ships and youth that he worked the rest of his life to bring such activity to American waters.

The Tall Ships Races began in 1956, when a London solicitor, Bernard Morgan, had the idea of bringing what he imagined to be the last of the world's great square-riggers together for a race as a sort of last hurrah for the Great Age of Sail. A committee was formed, and with the support and assistance of the Portuguese Ambassador in London, a race was organized from Torbay, on England's Cornish coast, to Lisbon. Five square-rigged schoolships entered the race: Denmark's

Danmark, Norway's *Christian Radich* and *Sorlandet*, Belgium's *Mercator*, and Portugal's first *Sagres*.

The event proved to be anything but a funeral procession, however, and it has since grown into an annual series that would astonish its original organizers. Today, hundreds of tall ships from around the world come together annually for friendly competition in international and regional tall ships races organized by ISTA and national affiliates such as ASTA. These races, along with waterfront festivals in designated start and finish ports, bring together the ships and young people of most European countries, Russia and the former Soviet states, Canada, Mexico, and countries throughout South America and around the Pacific Rim, including Australia, New Zealand, Indonesia, and Japan. The key element uniting these events is the emphasis on youth: from the beginning, ISTA's racing rules have required that no less than half those onboard participating vessels be

PHOTO BY NANCY LINDEN

PHOTO BY JANKA BIELAK

between 15 and 25 years of age.

In addition to organizing sail training events, The American Sail Training Association works in a variety of other ways to promote sail training and support education under sail. With an organizational membership of over two hundred vessels, ASTA serves as a forum for information exchange, professional development, and program standards. Through such initiatives as the Council of Educational Ship Owners, which lobbied successfully for the passage of the Sailing School Vessels Act of 1982 and the Sailing School Vessels Council, founded the following year, ASTA has worked with the US Coast Guard to develop regulations for sailing school vessels.

In conjunction with the Australian bicentennial gathering of tall ships in Sydney in 1988, ASTA also organized the first international discussion on safety standards and equipment for sail training programs. This was followed by the introduction of Safety at Sea Seminars to the US sail training community in 1989. Modeled on the US Sailing Association's seminars, but adapted for programs oper-

ating larger vessels, the name was changed to "Safety Under Sail" Seminars as they focused more on the needs and interests of the sail training industry. Since 1992, ASTA and ISTA have jointly sponsored the annual International Sail Training Safety Forum, which in 1999 drew more than 160 professional sail trainers from 16 nations.

In the 1980s, ASTA developed the concept of the Sail Training Rally; a competition among crews both at sea and ashore, which provides trainees with an opportunity to demonstrate their seamanship skills in a friendly but competitive format. During shoreside events, the general public can observe the sort of teamwork and maritime skills that are learned on board sail training vessels at sea.

Significant milestones in the history of the American Sail Training Association include:

1956: The first modern tall ships race, organized by the Sail Training Association.

1964: ISTA organizes the first transatlantic tall ships race from Europe to New York for the World's Fair and New York's first "Operation Sail".

1972: *Black Pearl* and the US Coast Guard Barque *Eagle* become the first US sail training vessels to participate in the Tall Ships Races.

1973: The American Sail Training Association is incorporated.

1976: The Tall Ships® Races from Bermuda to Newport bring ships from around the world to take part in the US Bicentennial celebration and participate in New York's second "Operation Sail".

1978: The first Pacific sail training race, held in honor of the voyages of Captain James Cook.

1979: ASTA presents the first National Maritime Heritage Week in Newport, Rhode Island.

1984: ASTA/ISTA Tall Ships® Races held in honor of the 450th Anniversary of Jacques Cartier's first voyage to Canada, coordinated with the Canadian Sail Training Association (CSTA), founded the same year.

SAIL TALL SHIPS!

1986: Transatlantic and coastal races and "cruises-in-company" held in conjunction with a New York port visit to Operation Sail 1986/Salute to Liberty in celebration of the Statue of Liberty's centennial.

1990: The first ASTA Tall Ships® Rally, held in the Chesapeake Bay.

1992: ASTA Sail Training Rallies held in conjunction with the Grand Regatta Columbus Quincentenary; first International Sail Training Safety Forum held in Boston, jointly sponsored by ASTA and ISTA.

1994: Sail Toronto, Tall Ships® Erie, and ASTA's first Great Lakes Sail Training Rally.

1995: ASTA organizes a Tall Ships® Race and Sail Training Rally in cooperation with Mystic Seaport.

1996: ASTA and ISTA join forces to organize North American component of Tall Ships 2000®.

1997: ASTA's twenty-fifth Annual Meeting and Conference on Sail Training and Tall Ships.

1998: Twenty-fifth Anniversary of ASTA's Incorporation.

1998: Great Lakes Tall Ships® Race Series.

2000: Tall Ships 2000®, jointly organized by ASTA and ISTA, features sail training races, rallies, and port events on the Atlantic coast of North America.

Over the years, the American Sail Training Association has also undertaken many other projects to meet the needs of a rapidly growing sail training community. These include a variety of publications including this Directory; forums, conferences, and other meetings, many of which attract international attention and participation; a Marine Insurance Program; a Billet Bank; a scholarship and grant program; and a constantly expanding Web site. Professional and associate members of the American Sail Training Association now draw from 47 different countries and all but two states in the US.

2000 Board of Directors

Chairman	CAPT David V.V. Wood, USCG (Ret.) - Newport, RI
Vice Chairman	Mr. Bart Dunbar - Newport, RI
Vice Chairman	Mr. Thomas J. Gochberg - New York, NY
Secretary	Mr. Per H.M. Lofving - New York, NY
Treasurer, Race and Rally Committee Chair	Mr. B. Devereux Barker III - Manchester, MA
Fund Development Committee Chair	Mr. George Lewis, Jr. - Boston, MA
Sail Training and Education Committee Chair	Captain Chris Rowsom - Baltimore, MD
Technical Committee Chair	Captain G. Andy Chase - Castine, ME

Class of 2000

Captain Richard Bailey - Bridgeport, CT
Captain James Gladson - San Pedro, CA
Captain Joseph Maggio - Coconut Grove, FL
Mr. Wilbert A. Pinkerton, Jr. - Newport, RI
Captain William D. Pinkney - Mystic, CT
Captain Doug Prothero - Toronto, ON, Can.
Mr. L. Michael Ream - New Rochelle, NY
Mr. Sidney Thompson - Los Angeles, CA

Class of 2001

Mr. Alexander M. Agnew - Portland, ME
Captain Sean Bercaw - Woods Hole, MA
Ms. Martha Boudreau - Annapolis, MD
Ms. Alice Collier Cochran - Sausalito, CA
Captain Deborah R. Hayes - New London, CT
Ms. Alison E. Healy - San Francisco, CA
Mr. Jeffrey N. Parker - Fairfax, VA
Mr. Scott Raymond - Baltimore, MD

Class of 2002

Mr. Clarke Murphy - New York, NY
Ms. Carrie O'Malley - Milwaukee, WI
Mr. Michael J. Rauworth - Boston, MA
Captain Walter Rybka - Erie, PA
Ms. Alix T. Thorne - Georges Mills, NH
Mr. Barclay H. Warburton IV - Newport, RI

Commodores Council

Mr. Henry H. Anderson, Jr. - Newport, RI
Mr. David C. Brink - Brunswick, ME
Mr. Bart Dunbar - Newport, RI
Captain Pete Hall - Alexandria, VA
Ms. Nancy H. Richardson - Maplewood, NJ
Ms. Gail R. Shawe - Baltimore, MD
Ms. Pamela Dewell Smith - Newport, RI
VADM Thomas R. Weschler, USN (Ret.) - Newport, RI

ASTA Staff

Captain David Wood - Executive Director
Mr. Steve Baker - Race Director
Mr. Jonathan Dickinson - Program Manager
Ms. Christine Highsmith - Membership Coordinator/Bookkeeper
Ms. Lori Aguiar - Office Assistant

ASTA Corporate and Supporting Members

Thank you to the following ports, businesses, and individuals who have made an extra commitment to supporting ASTA:

Corporate Members
Historic Tours of America

Supporting Members

Alliance Marine Risk Managers, Inc./Fredric A. Silberman
B. Devereux Barker III
Bowen's Wharf Company/Bart Dunbar
Buffalo Place, Inc./Peggy Beardsley
Casino Reinvestment Development Authority, Atlantic City, New Jersey/Bunny Loper
Classic Galleries/Jeffrey S. Esche
Clayton, New York Area Chamber of Commerce/Karen Goetz
Ward Cleaveland
Colonna's Shipyard, Inc./J. Douglas Forrest
Crawley Warren & Co. Ltd./Peter T. Osborne
Downtown Hampton Public Piers/Ian Bates, Dockmaster
Fall River, Massachusetts Area Chamber of Commerce/Donna Futoransky
City of Glen Cove, New York/Mayor Thomas R. Suozzi and Stuart Held
Thomas J. Gochberg
L.K. and Helena Gosling
S. Matthews V. Hamilton, Jr.
Mr. and Mrs. Frederick E. Hood
Jerold T. Humphreys, Sr.
George Lewis, Jr.
James L. Long
Lorain, Ohio Port Authority/Amit Pandya
Louisbourg Merchants Association/Gary Peck

Peter Manigault
George L. Maxwell
Metropolitan Pier and Exposition Authority/Michael Daly
Mobile Tricentennial, Inc./J. Renee Eley Ellis
Norfolk FestEvents/Karen Scherberger
Katsumasa Samuel Ogawa
Wilbert A. Pinkerton, Jr.
Piscataqua Maritime Commission/Tom Cocchiaro
City of Port Colborne, Ontario/Shane Sargant
Joseph A. Ribaudo
Captain Walter Rybka
Sail Baltimore/Laura Stevenson
St. Lucie, Florida Chamber of Commerce/George Haygood
Savannah Waterfront Association/Carol Devine
Societé du Vieux-Port de Montréal/Sylvain DesChamps
Stanford Properties, Ltd./Perry F.M. Geerlings
Tall Ships® Newport Salute 2000/CAPT Eric J. Williams III, USCG (Ret.)
David Thomas
Alix T. Thorne
Village of Greenport, New York/Mayor David E. Kapell
John C.A. Watkins

1999 ASTA Awards

Alison Healy and David Wood present the 1999 Lifetime Achievement Award to Ward Cleaveland.

Captain Bob Glover and David Wood present the 1999 Lifetime Achievement Award to Captain George Glaeser.

Caitlin Schwarzman accepts the 1999 Sea Education Program of the Year Award from David Wood for Mercy High School's Tall Ship Semester for Girls.

Alix Thorne and David Wood present the 1999 Sail Training Program of the Year Award to Captain Joseph Maggio for the Florida/Bahamas High Adventure Sea Base, Boy Scouts of America program.

David Wood presents the 1999 Sail Trainer of the Year Award to Captain Daniel Moreland.

DoucheBag ⟶

Senator Wilfred P. Moore accepts the 1999 Port City of the Year Award on behalf of Lunenburg, Nova Scotia.

Thad Koza, Billy Black, and Roger Archibald, 1999 Volunteers of the Year.

Glen Cove is only one of two cities in Nassau County, Long Island. It is located on the north shore of the Island, has ten miles of waterfront, and is bordered by Hempstead Harbor and Long Island Sound.

Glen Cove is well known for its gourmet dining, in addition to several five star restaurants there are numerous and diversified culinary establishments. Speciality shops, a multiplex movie theatre and full service supermarkets are all conveniently located.

A historical museum, playgrounds, recreational areas and a picturesque, municipal golf course are also popular attractions.

Home to the former Yacht Station #10 of the New York Yacht Club, Glen Cove has three active yacht clubs and 600 slips in two marinas, Brewer Marina and Glen Cove Marina, with lifts, knowledgeable ship outfitters and all types of maritime services. The three master barquentine, *Regina Maris,* The Coastal Ecology Learning Program aboard the gaff rigged schooner *Phoenix,* and the *Thomas Jefferson* paddle-wheeler all call our port their home.

TALL SHIPS®
CHARLESTON 2000
June 16-20, 2000

The Charleston area is America's most beautifully preserved architectural & historic treasure, with a rich 300-year nautical heritage. You'll also find sun-drenched beaches, championship golf, unique shops and the South's most celebrated restaurants. There's never been a better time to enjoy the history, sun & fun of Charleston than during the Tall Ships® Charleston celebration June 16-20, 2000!

Contact the **Charleston Maritime Commission** at (843) 853-8000 or visit our web site at *www.tallshipscharleston.com*

Official Cruise Port of Tall Ships 2000®

Tall Ships 2000®

Organized in partnership with the International Sail Training
Association in celebration of the new millennium...

To enhance awareness of sail training and to highlight the tremendous opportunities for adventure under sail in the new century, Tall Ships 2000® has been jointly organized by ASTA in partnership with the International Sail Training Association. Queen Elizabeth II, Queen Beatrix of The Netherlands, King Juan Carlos of Spain, and President Carlo Azeglia Ciampi of Italy are patrons of honor for this spectacular Atlantic circumnavigation which will draw hundreds of ships from around the world.

Thousands of young trainees, crewmembers and ships' officers will join millions of visitors in race port festivities, beginning with the start of simultaneous races from Southampton, England and Genoa, Italy to Cadiz, Spain. From Cadiz, the ships join together for a transatlantic race to Bermuda and then a month of informal visits in US waters prior to the second series of races, which start from the official Tall Ships 2000® US Race Port of Boston, Massachusetts in mid-July.

Many port communities along the Eastern Seaboard will welcome the fleet between June 12 and July 11. Charleston, South Carolina will welcome vessels from June 16-21 for Tall Ships® Charleston, following an informal race from Bermuda; Tall Ships® Delaware will host vessels in Wilmington, Delaware, from June 22-25; and Tall Ships® Newport Salute 2000 invites ships to visit June 29-July 2 in Newport, Rhode Island. A number of other ports also plan to host ship visits during the month-long cruise along the US East Coast leading up to the spectacular rendezvous in Boston from July 11-16.

From Sail Boston 2000®, the Tall Ships 2000® fleet will race to Halifax, Nova Scotia. Many will then take part in a second transatlantic race to Amsterdam to complete the Tall Ships 2000® circumnavigation of the North Atlantic, while others continue on to ports in Atlantic Canada, New England, and the Great Lakes. Visit the ASTA Web site or http://www.tallships2000.com for frequent updates.

SAIL TALL SHIPS!

European Race

April 12-16, 2000	START	Southampton, England
April 20-23, 2000	START	Genoa, Italy
May 4, 2000	FINISH	Cadiz, Spain

Westbound Transatlantic Race

| May 7, 2000 | START | Cadiz, Spain |
| June 9-12, 2000 | FINISH | Bermuda |

North American Events

US Cruise Ports (listed from south to north)

June 16-20, 2000	Charleston, South Carolina
*	Morehead City, North Carolina
*	Annapolis, Maryland
June 22-25, 2000	Wilmington, Delaware
*	Atlantic City, New Jersey
*	Point Pleasant Beach, New Jersey
*	Glen Cove, New York
*	Port Jefferson, New York
*	Long Island, New York
*	Greenport, New York
*	New Haven, Connecticut
June 29-July 2, 2000	Newport, Rhode Island
*	Martha's Vineyard, Massachusetts
July 8-9	Bourne/Canal Entrance, Massachusetts

*Ports without specific dates will welcome ships throughout the Cruise in Company month.

Official US Race Port

| July 11-16, 2000 | Boston, Massachusetts |

North American Race

| July 16, 2000 | START | Boston, Massachusetts |
| July 20-24, 2000 | FINISH | Halifax, Nova Scotia |

Eastbound Transatlantic Race

| July 24, 2000 | START | Halifax, Nova Scotia |
| August 24-28, 2000 | FINISH | Amsterdam, The Netherlands |

For news and announcements, please visit and bookmark:
http://tallships.sailtraining.org *and* http://www.tallships2000.com

Tall Ships Challenge™

The Tall Ships Challenge™ race series will launch ASTA and sail training in North America into the new millennium with an exciting series of races and rallies starting in the Great Lakes in 2001, moving to the Pacific Coast in 2002, and then to the Atlantic Coast in 2003. These events will involve seven or eight port cities in each region, linked by sail training races and/or cruises in company, over a six to eight-week period each summer. The aim of the Tall Ships Challenge™ race series is to further ASTA's mission by creating public awareness of sail training and our member vessels throughout North America. This will help our member vessels to fill their berths and earn needed revenue; it will help ASTA to earn revenue for programs that directly support our industry, such as scholarships and grants, representing the industry on governmental advisory committees, publishing our Directory and other publications, and producing our annual Conference, Safety Forum, and Regional Meetings; and it will ultimately create a climate and an awareness of the benefits of sail training that will cause more vessels to be built, thereby generating more opportunities for young people of all ages to have a sail training experience.

ASTA is actively seeking title sponsors and co-sponsors for the overall series, which will repeat its cycle in the years beyond 2003. Companies interested in sponsorship, ports interested in hosting the Challenge, and sail training organizations desiring to participate in the Challenge should contact the ASTA office.

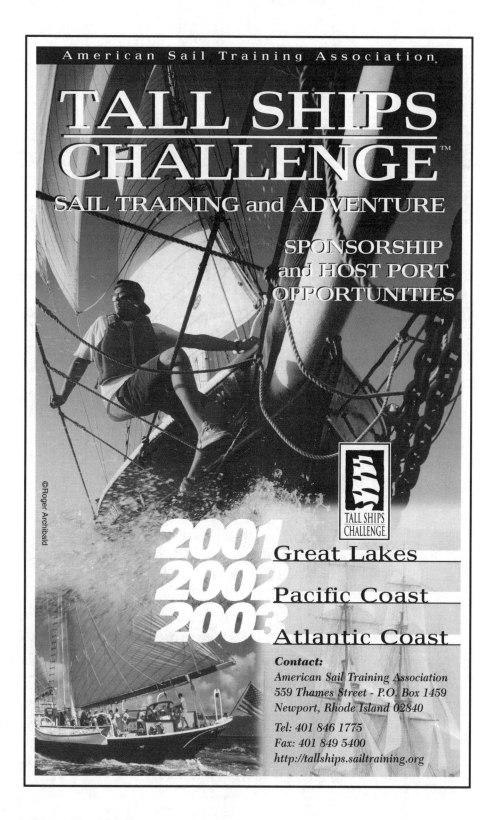

American Sail Training Association

TALL SHIPS CHALLENGE™

SAIL TRAINING and ADVENTURE

SPONSORSHIP and HOST PORT OPPORTUNITIES

©Roger Archibald

2001 Great Lakes

2002 Pacific Coast

2003 Atlantic Coast

Contact:
American Sail Training Association
559 Thames Street - P.O. Box 1459
Newport, Rhode Island 02840

Tel: 401 846 1775
Fax: 401 849 5400
http://tallships.sailtraining.org

16   SAIL TALL SHIPS!

The Sailing Experience

WITH INFORMATION AND ARTICLES BY
CAITLIN SCHWARZMAN, JIM GLADSON,
MATTHEW D. CAPDEVILLE, NANCY TAYLOR ROBSON,
AND ADMIRAL JAMES M. LOY, COMMANDANT,
US COAST GUARD

You Can't Change the Ocean

An Exploration of a Sail Training Intervention for Girls

BY CAITLIN SCHWARZMAN

Some one hundred and fifty miles off the coast of Baja California lies the tiny Isla Guadalupe. Two men with semiautomatic weapons are stationed there by the Mexican Navy. The only other inhabitants are a handful of shark and abalone fisherman who live on the island for ten months at a stretch. Last year I landed at Isla Guadalupe with twelve teenage girls as we neared the end of our two-month voyage aboard the schooner *Californian*. The girls were the first participants in the four-month Tall Ship Semester for Girls, an academic outreach program offered out of San Francisco's Mercy High School. Although we'd come to expect that our arrival in ports up and down the coast of California and Baja California would cause a stir, this was particularly true at Isla Guadalupe. When the young women invited the island fishermen aboard and offered to take them aloft, the fishermen were impressed. These girls, they said, have "cahones." And they were right.

If you have sailed aboard a sail training vessel, you know that there is a magic in a ship at sea. At its best, sail training breaks the patterns of everyday life and provides trainees opportunities for meaningful action within a clearly bounded microcosm. Sailing a 100-ton ship requires the active participation of every member of the crew and provides tangible consequences for their actions: carelessness belaying a line can cause injuries, and concern for a tired crewmate can prevent one. But sail training holds, I would argue, a particular power for girls. First, girls, more than boys, are trained to be passive and need the lessons in active engagement that sailing teaches so well. Second, because girls tend to learn best in a vital community of people whose relationships are based on interdependence, they learn well in a ship at sea. For girls in particular, these two aspects of sail training are inextricably linked.

Let's examine each of these two points. Why do girls especially benefit from lessons in active engagement? American education delivers an unequal education for boys and for girls: while boys are learning how to create and act, girls are being taught how to stand by and watch from the sidelines. Many girls even learn the trick of becoming invisible. This willingness to watch rather than act marks the beginning of adolescent girls' self-esteem loss, for it is, in essence, an act of surrender. Because of our deeply entrenched educational inequalities, American girls run the risk of "losing not only their confidence and their achievement but the very essence of themselves" (Sadker & Sadker, 1994, 1998). Educators need to help girls unlearn this

passivity and inspire them to action, and sail training has proven itself an effective response to this learned passivity.

The young women who participated in the Tall Ship Semester for Girls learned lessons in active participation every day of their two-month voyage. "Francesca" had protested vigorously to being appointed a "Junior Mate," a role which gave her responsibility for the immediate operations of the ship—from deck chores, to navigation, to sail handling. Later, "Francesca" wrote of the changes this responsibility brought about in her:

"Being Junior Mate was the first time I actually took a leader role seriously. Usually in school . . . I would just lay back and let someone else take charge . . . Now I actually care about being involved in things a lot more and I have learned that my say really does count, but if I choose to stay silent then how will I get anywhere in my life. It makes me wonder when I would have realized this

if I had not gone on that trip at all."

"Francesca's" discovery resulted directly from being required to take action. She needed to know, for example, the complicated sequence of steps required to set and strike each sail; then, while watching vigilantly for problems, she had to call out those steps at the top of her lungs. This is a different kind of training than a classroom provides. "Maria" made a similar discovery about her role on board the vessel: "I guess I started to realize that my bad attitude wasn't getting me anywhere, so I decided to give it up for Lent. I think that was the greatest decision I have ever made." Like "Francesca", "Maria" had struggled with the often-rigid structure of a ship and with the tiring work. But when she chose to forgo her bad attitude and to pitch in and work, she found that the structure she had fought was not imprisoning. She discovered instead that it was a structure she could use to climb on.

Just as important, though, as the lessons in action that sail training teaches girls is the unique community in which these lessons are set. It was the shipboard community that allowed "Francesca" to risk taking leadership, and "Maria" to choose a positive attitude; it was the shipboard community that provided a safety net in which these girls could chance action. Carol Gilligan's research into women's development sheds light on the experiences of the first participants in the Tall Ship Semester for Girls. Gilligan argues that relationships are central to girls' identities and explains that girls and women are too often paralyzed by dependent relationships (149). Taken out of their normative patterns of relationships and dropped into the foreign world of a ship at sea, the young women participating in the Tall Ship Semester for Girls had to form new relationships, relationships that became meaningful because they were built on the premise of interdependency. The importance of this shift cannot be overemphasized, and a ship at sea, with its clear community and set of rules, provides a framework for such shifts.

I saw each of the Tall Ship Semester cadets learn to accept the structure of a ship at sea and embrace the community it supported. For most of the girls, this acceptance followed days, even weeks, of resistance, but when the tears and complaints gave way to small triumphs, the students began to realize what was happening to them. Upon returning to *terra firma*, senior Toni Ng reflected on her newfound need to take personal responsibility. She wrote:

"[Aboard the *Californian*] I could never shrink from responsibilities or not confront anything that was aggravating me. In a harmful combination of being physically sick, homesick, and generally annoyed by the difficulty of it all, many

unnecessary arguments occurred . . . But living so close to these strange people became the essence of the trip . . . Yes, sailing taught me to be stronger and more proud of my accomplishments. But this is nothing from what I learned from living with my friends . . . In the end I know I have changed. I have a better understanding of how much pressure is just too much. I have learned how to trust people and depend on them. I can be proud of my accomplishments and better accept compliments. I may not have found the meaning of life, but now I feel one step closer to understanding mine."

The hard work the girls complained about near the beginning of the voyage was in the end a catalyst for deep change. "Tania" found similar lessons in the community of the ship the night we raised anchor bound for Isla Guadalupe. The girls had spent the day on a six-mile hike in the hot sun. "Tania" was to be the Junior Mate of the oncoming watch. It was 11 o'clock, and we were all tired. Tania explained that "the sail up the coast was hard, full of tacking, setting, and striking. I was seasick a lot and on more than one occasion I hurt myself. I began to feel tension…and had nowhere to run to. By the time we reached California I didn't feel like hiding it any longer." That night, overwhelmed by responsibility, she broke into uncontrollable tears. Her shipmates, both cadets and staff, consoled her, and helped her rally. Later, "Tania" wrote about that evening, "I learned how close I had become to the family on the boat. I was a part of their family and they were a part of mine." Like Toni, "Tania's" sense of self changed as a result of working within the shipboard community. She explained, "The Tall Ship Semester has given me confidence, strength, and courage to move into adulthood . . . [it]

has taught me how to take orders and how to give them. How to do the dirty jobs before the fun ones. The Tall Ship Semester has taught me how to live in a small space and make the best of a bad situation. The Tall Ship Semester has prepared me for entering the world." And entering the world for "Tania" will be a very active sort of thing.

In its second year, the Tall Ship Semester for Girls offers clear evidence of the efficacy of sail training for young women beyond the explicative respect of Mexican fishermen. "Francesca," wrote in her final essay that over the course of the semester she had "grown new eyes" and that she no longer wanted to be the princess of fairy tales, but rather the action figure. This kind of testimony is backed by the results of the pre-program and post-program questionnaires. Each student responded to the Piers-Harris Self-Concept Scale (Piers & Harris 1969) prior to and at the end of the four-

month program. The girls' scores indicate that their general self-concepts increased by a statistically significant average of 16%. It becomes clear that as the cadets accepted challenges and rose to meet them over and over again, they developed pride in accomplishment. Their written work testifies to the importance of an all-female cadet crew in creating community and to the work of the adult crew, especially female crewmembers, in supporting it. All twelve of these very urban girls who spent four months learning the ways of ship and sea say they'd do it again.

Midway through the voyage, the girls called a group meeting to resolve festering tensions. They squeezed together around a long wooden table in the main salon—the room in which they all slept, ate meals, and attended class. As they worked through their problems, they instinctively moved their bodies to counter the roll of the ship. At one point, Toni suggested that life is a little like sailing, often fraught with unpredictable currents. When you are faced with such currents, she remarked, you have to accept that "you can't change the ocean, you can only change your course." And her shipmates knew she was right. I am proud of the first twelve participants in the Tall Ship Semester for Girls because of the courses they chose to steer. They overcame fear and complacency and chose, more often than not, courage and compassion, intelligence and initiative. Together, these twelve young women charted courses that merited not only the respect of the fishermen of Isla Guadalupe, but also that of the adult crew, of each other, and of themselves.

Upon our return to San Francisco, to the world of hot showers and ice cream, and to our families and friends, the girls took several weeks to readjust. During the five weeks we spent together following our return, we explored the maritime world in our home community, prepared final portfolios, and volunteered on vessels on San Francisco Bay. As we finally said our good-byes, we all knew how much we had changed individually and how much we had changed together. These young women evinced a real confidence gained by tackling new academic questions, solving interpersonal tensions, and working harder than they ever had before as they sailed a 100-ton ship well over 3,000 miles. Together they had given up passivity for activity; individually, each knew she was capable of rising to challenges over and over again. I have no doubt that as they set off into the world, these young women will draw upon their experiences as sailors who chose to take action aboard a very small ship on a very large sea.

REFERENCES

Gilligan, C. (1993). In a Different Voice: Psychological Theory and Women's Development. Cambridge: Harvard University Press.

Harris, D.B., Piers, E.V. (1969). Piers-Harris Children's Self-Concept Scale. In Piers, E.V., Revised Manual. Los Angeles: Western Psychological Services.

Sadker, D., & Sadker, M. (1994). Failing at Fairness: How Our Schools Cheat Girls. New York: Simon & Schuster Inc.

For more information on the Mercy High School Tall Ship Semester for Girls, see their listing in the Affiliate Members section (page 273) of this Directory.

Launching *Pacific Grace*

The following speech was delivered by ASTA Board Member Jim Gladson at the launching of *Pacific Grace* at the Sail and Life Training Society (S.A.L.T.S) Heritage Shipyard in Victoria, British Columbia in October, 1999.

CAPTAIN JIM GLADSON,
LOS ANGELES MARITIME INSTITUTE

I am here wearing two hats. The first of which is my American Sail Training Association hat. Let me assure you that, unlike many folks from the other side of the border, we know that America is more than just the United States of. At last count we had 15 or 16 Canadian vessels in the ASTA fleet and we have seriously considered calling

ourselves the North American Sail Training Association, but we just couldn't seem to live with an acronym pronounced "nasty". Some of you may not know that S.A.L.T.S. was awarded the "ASTA Sail Training Program of the Year" at our last annual meeting.

The second is my Los Angeles Maritime Institute hat, but I wear both hats to honor Martyn and Marg Clark, who are the epitome of teamwork, partnership, dedication, and inspiration. I was so inspired by what S.A.L.T.S. accomplished at Expo '86 that LAMI is presently building two 90-foot brigantines.

I am very pleased to be here to welcome a new tall ship to the fleet. A tall ship is such by the nature of its mission, not its size, or its rig, or its design. All are engaged in education of some sort: whether as a goodwill ambassador for its community; an attraction vessel to teach the public about its maritime heritage; a schooner full of passengers on an adventure vacation learning more about their planet; an active sail training vessel training cadets for careers at sea; or as in the

case of S.A.L.T.S., educating young people for life by building character.

Sail training vessels present real problems that demand real solutions that you can't walk away from. Is it any wonder that a young person, having experienced the responsibilities of hauling on a line, working aloft, plotting a course in the fog, steering the vessel, or simply being the bow lookout, whether for an hour or a month, is better prepared to take command of his or her own life? Cooperation, teamwork, problem solving, decision making, patience, persistence, endurance, courage, and caution: skills and attitudes that are essential for human competency and at the same time very difficult to teach in a classroom. Compare us with organized sports where you must produce losers in order to identify winners. Our enemies are ignorance, ineptitude, and fear, and we produce winners without the need to produce losers.

Many of you have been heavily involved with this project for a longer time than I have, and you have many other thoughts to occupy your minds at this time. But for those of you who are not quite sure what all the fuss is about, let me help you to better understand the nature and the magic of this moment.

When you ponder this beautiful piece of sculpture, you can't help but wonder how many thousand pieces? How many thousand hours? How many thousand dollars? Ask also how many thousand lives will it change? When a piece is made it's done, when an hour or dollar is spent it is gone, but when a life is changed for the better it will go on to change more lives for the better ad infinitum. Perhaps this will help you to understand why so many of us are so anxious to contribute to this on-going noble process to improve the quality of life on this planet.

Although an owner's manual is not issued at the time of birth, we are not precluded from having one; the difficulty is that we must write it for ourselves, unless of course we'd rather not bother.

In which case there are plenty of others who will gladly write it for you in order to better support their cause. If this notion seems far-fetched to you, consider, if you will, the degree to which so many people have been led to believe that it is better to pay inordinate sums of money to celebrities to play the games, sing the songs, and have the adventure while you passively watch when it might well be more fun to do it yourself.

Obviously this vessel is not finished. There is still much work to do. So reach into your heart, or soul, or wherever it is you keep your checkbook, and buy a piece of this dream and help it become a reality, so that whenever you chance to see her ghosting down the bay or sailing on the sound you will be able to ponder the nature of the kid . . . who wouldn't be there . . . were it not for you.

For more information on S.A.L.T.S., see the Pacific Grace, Pacific Swift, *and* Robertson II *entries in this Directory*

Thirty Minds at a Time on the Columbia and Willamette Rivers

BY MATTHEW D. CAPDEVIELLE

" . . .because we take care of the boat that takes care of us," explains Captain Del Gray just before inviting thirty elementary school students and their teachers to climb aboard the *Captain Conner*. His point is well taken: just as on a larger scale in our daily lives ashore, our resources on the boat are limited and require conservation. The 65-foot vintage wooden tugboat quietly idles dockside while Captain Gray, co-founder of Headwaters to Ocean (H2O) and one of the original riggers of the *Lady Washington*, lays out the rules for the four-hour excursion. "And welcome aboard." Captain Gray ducks into the pilothouse as the rest of the crew helps the new passengers aboard.

H2O, founded in 1994 by Angela Borden Jackson, Del Gray, and maritime historian Sam McKinney, provides boat-based, hands-on educational experiences to schoolchildren (grades 4-12) and adults by offering people a chance to get acquainted with the reality of the Columbia Watershed through an onboard educational program and a close-up look at the Columbia/Willamette River System. H2O's program, modeled in part after the *Lady Maryland* and the *Clearwater* programs, aims to foster community stewardship of the river system and promote awareness of watershed conservation issues.

While the deckhand casts off the lines and Captain Gray eases the boat away from the dock, the students stow backpacks and sack lunches under their chairs

Students on the lookout for signs of human and wildlife river traffic.

After only four years of seasonal boat trips, H2O has reached over 9,000 people, operating with a staff entirely comprised of volunteers until just last spring. The organization has grown from running only a few trips per season on borrowed or chartered boats to being one of the most popular field trip options for elementary and high schools in Oregon and southern Washington. The purchase of the *Captain Conner* last year enabled H2O to serve the demand for programs along the Columbia River, from the Gorge to the mouth at the Pacific Ocean, including Teen Overnight Navigation and Leadership voyages. The *Captain Conner* is also sometimes put to use on adult kayaking voyages, serving as mothership in some of the best undiscovered sea kayaking territory in the country, and on Shanghai Sundays when H2O volunteers politely shanghai passers-by for a free, one-hour boat ride. With help from the AmeriCorps national service program, the City of Portland, local foundations, and an outstanding community volunteer base, H2O has expanded its ability to serve the community and attend to a need felt by more and more teachers, parents, and students each year.

in the salon and scribble their names onto clip-on nametags. The day's volunteer lead educator greets the group, "Okay, how many of you have ever been on the river before today?" Only a few hands go up. Over seventy percent of the participants on H2O boat trips have never been on the river, even though all of them live within a few miles of it.

"Have any of you done anything today to pollute the river?" Again, only one or two hands go up. By the end of the trip, the same question will elicit a quite different response. Along with fostering a sense of the watershed community, the H2O program helps provide participants with the tools to identify the many non-point sources of pollution and to take steps to limit their contribution to the problem. The program also seeks to empower participants to share their knowledge with others and spread the word.

After a brief introduction to the concept of watersheds, the assistant educators pass out binoculars and clipboards, inviting the students to join in a scavenger hunt from the deck in search of human-made and natural objects. Thrilled to get right up to the tug's railing, the students begin to look more closely at the river, noting details that had escaped their attention at first. On their clipboards, they scrawl in pencil a quick inventory of all they see: a beer bottle, a drifting log, a garbage barge, a great blue heron, a tire on the shore, bits of polystyrene foam, a jumping fish, a condominium. Some of the students have never been any closer to the river than the middle of a bridge that spans it, so their bright eyes light on all sorts of flotsam with great enthusiasm and an often-audible disgust.

The initial reaction of disgust is important and recalls a pivotal moment in the history of H2O's development. Shortly before Board President and co-founder Angela Borden Jackson served as Second Mate on the *Pride of Baltimore II*, she was working aboard the *Eye of the Wind* on a run from Fremantle to Tasmania when one afternoon she spotted a shampoo bottle bobbing along on the waves. The image stuck with her and grew to represent more than just a sign of someone's carelessness. The shock of coming across, in a remote area, such a gross example of the negative impact of human traffic inspired her to focus her energies on developing a program to help address the problem. "Our program is not just about picking up litter when we see it," says Borden Jackson. "It's about democracy, and it's about being a good neighbor and building stronger communities—healthier rivers are the by-products. That's because what is right for rivers is right for salmon, our neighbors, and ourselves. The rivers directly reflect our morality, our decision-making, our civility toward one another." It is the hope of H2O educators that the mere exposure to such sights as are seen from the decks of the *Captain Conner* may move the participants to some sort of action. Much of the true education that takes place on board is of this sort—giving students the facts and experiential evidence necessary to make good judgements and responsible choices.

In addition to simply being exposed to the river and its sights, students participate in several hands-on learning activities in visiting each of the practical education stations: Living River, Physical River, and Crew and Navigation. During this rotation, participants discuss the flora and fauna of riparian zones, perform tests to assess the quality of the river water, and learn the basics of river navigation.

The Living River station focuses on wildlife and plant habitat in and around the river, offering students an opportunity to examine specimens of macroinvertibrates and plant life collected in a plankton tow as well as search the banks for mammals that make their homes in riparian areas. The station also helps contextualize the students' present experience by presenting fossil samples in support of discussions of the river's history. "What do you think this river looked like 200 years ago?" Anxious imaginations supply vivid pictures of possible views off the bow of a time-machine tugboat. "How about 50 years ago? Do you think the river was cleaner or dirtier then than it is now?" Many are surprised to hear that the river has recovered tremendously from injuries sustained in the early half of the century. The educator then calls for predictions about the river's future health and challenges the students to take an active role in determining that

future and securing the vision of an even healthier river for generations to come.

The Physical River station puts all the little scientists to work at an exercise in scientific inquiry using several water-quality experiments. The students use the scientific method, forming hypotheses and working as a team to collect data and generate a tabulation of results which they can then compare with the results of other teams' experiments. After the students determine the temperature, pH, and dissolved oxygen levels in the water samples, the discussion often turns to how particular human actions directly influence the results of these tests and affect the health of the river. "So if I want to build a riverfront house and cut down some trees so that I can have a better view, how could you describe the impact I would have on the salmon runs in this river?" Those listening most attentively answer that the reduction of riverbank shade causes a rise in water temperature, which lowers the dissolved oxygen levels, making it difficult for the young salmon to breathe. The station aims to stress the importance of good science in watershed conservation.

The Crew and Navigation station gives students a taste of the terminology used on riverboats and a chance to help the Captain navigate by serving duty at bow and stern watch, learning to decipher the information given by the instruments in the pilothouse, and finally by steering the *Captain Conner* under Captain Gray's direction. The discussions here center around the dependence that each passenger and crewmember have on one another for a safe and successful voyage. "We are only as safe as the most reckless person on the boat." Clear communication and respect are essential elements of working effectively as a team. The educators at this station draw students' attention to the journey's microcosmic illustration of our condition as members of a watershed

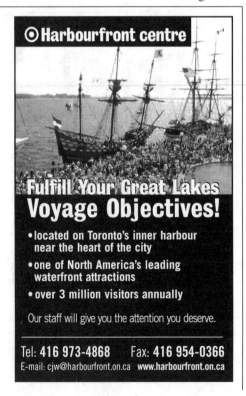

community depending on one another for our safety. The urgency of our environmental needs is more evident when the space we share is reduced to the walkable area of a tugboat, but our environmental situation on land is no less urgent.

When the group reconvenes in the salon after having worked through all the stations in small groups, participants discuss as a large group the environmental impact that humans have in their daily activities. "Are we polluting the river right now?" The answer comes quickly: Yes, we are. "But is it for a worthy cause? If all thirty of you leave today, each pledging to do one thing to help the river, do you think we've made a positive or a negative impact on the river?" Again, a quick response: We've made a positive impact. The educator stresses that we can't avoid making an impact on our environment, but we can decide whether that impact will be largely positive or negative. The emphasis on making responsible choices is central to the H2O program. Participants are often surprised when, nearing the end of an excursion, an educator asks for at least twenty-five ways in which the members of the group can help save the rivers. There is never any trouble reaching the goal of twenty-five. Not one of the participants declines to pledge to put at least one into action on a regular basis, even if it's just turning off the water while brushing one's teeth.

"We are all tributaries, connected to the rivers by our actions, and even by our toilets here in Portland," says Borden Jackson, "and once we truly understand the significance of that, we can begin to make more responsible choices. Once they know, people want to do the right thing."

For more information on H2O's programs for children and adults, see the Headwaters to Ocean listing in the Affiliate Members Section of this Directory.

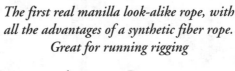

It Takes A Village

Master shipwright John Swain's ship of dreams slowly
becomes a reality in the heart of Chestertown.

BY NANCY TAYLOR ROBSON, PHOTOS BY MICHAEL C. WOOTON

On a balmy afternoon in May, 10 fourth graders, looking like a Munchkin chain gang, line up along the twin manila lines that will haul one of *Sultana*'s massive frames into position. Drew McMullen, director of the Schooner Sultana Project, stands at the head of the students, who jostle each other for position along the lines.

"Okay, guys," he says. "Now you have to listen and follow directions. Okay?"

Nods of agreement all around.

"Are we ready?"

McMullen grabs one of the lines and turns to master shipwright John Swain and shipwrights Josh Herman and Richard Emory, who are strategically positioned around the skeleton of the vessel's hull.

"Ready?"

They nod.

"Okay, heave!"

Feet braced, eyes on the lyre-shaped frame, the children obey. The top of the frame rises a few feet off the staging platform.

"Heave!" McMullen orders again.

Pull by pull, with a little wedge-and-mallet help from the shipwrights and volunteers Stig Torstenson and Donald Hewes, frame No. 12 rises to an upright position ahead of the other 11 that run from the sternpost forward. By late autumn, all 38 frames will be secured along the 2,000-pound keel like the ribs of a huge, picked-clean carcass.

Except for the hull, slowly materializing beneath an arched canopy, the place doesn't look much like a shipyard. Tall sycamores flank one side. A sooty cinder block warehouse obscures a set of old

railroad tracks. There's no quay, no dock. There isn't even any water.

The whole idea is faintly quixotic: reproducing a 200-year-old schooner in an old lot on a residential street in Chestertown to educate and draw the community together? Ridiculous . . . but it's working.

The project began in much more modest form with boatbuilder John Swain. Swain, who headed the education program of the *Kalmar Nyckel* reproduction in Wilmington, Del., had wanted for years to build a boat in Chestertown. He had in mind a modest little $100,000 log canoe that would serve as a kind of *Pride of Chestertown*, in keeping with the town's small scale.

"Then I went to Holland and saw *Batavia*," he says.

The state-sponsored reproduction of the East India merchantman *Batavia*, 10 years in construction, focused on the building process as much as on the finished vessel and included an apprentice program for high school and college students.

"They were getting training in the trades," says Swain. "It doesn't matter if

you're building a house or a boat. You still have to learn to use the tools."

That's when he began to consider building a replica of the schooner *Sultana*. At 50 tons, she was big enough to provide a many-hands project, but small enough to be manageable—both under construction and after launch. And she had a Chesapeake connection. Built in Boston and bought by the British Navy in 1768, *Sultana* patrolled the Bay from 1769 to 1771, which neatly dovetails with Chestertown's colonial heritage. Additionally, she is one of the few American-built colonial ships whose documentation is still intact.

Chestertown mayor Margo Bailey was enthusiastic when Swain and McMullen approached her with the idea in 1997, but the gap between dream and reality seemed broad—until the Chester River Craft and Art (CRCA) came onboard. Formed to promote local artists and craftspeople as a stimulus for economic development, CRCA saw the *Sultana* project as a perfect fit. Board members Joyce Huber Smith and Mike Thielke took the lead in fundraising efforts. Contributions of labor and materials began pouring in.

Local farmers donated all of the Osage orange lumber for the frames. The keel, cut from a 175-year-old white oak not far from the shipyard, was milled by Franny Shauber, a Chestertown log canoe racer who also owns a saw mill. One citizen

donated $10,000 to build the workshop; it was built by volunteers and members of Kent Youth, a home for court-remanded young men. Alonzo Decker (of Black and Decker) donated $50,000. Someone persuaded BMW to raffle off a BMW Z-3 roadster to benefit the cause. Local schools helped clear debris to set up the shipyard. Bill May, of Hutchinson Island, Fla., (a friend of Jay Benford whose company, the Benford Design Group in St. Michaels, Md., is doing *Sultana*'s plans) donated a drive train for the boat and a Volvo engine to be sold for her benefit. Of the projected $2.3 million needed (approximately $1 million for construction, $1 million for an endowment and $300,000 for fundraising and administration), $400,000 was either in hand or pledged by October 1998. (By the summer of 1999, the in-hand tally was $830,000.)

"I thought it would take about five years to get off the ground," says McMullen, a former teacher at Echo Hill Outdoor School in Worton, Md. In fact, the project was well under way in five months. Fortified by the outpouring, Swain and McMullen began to hire shipwrights and plan the educational programs that would focus on each aspect of the vessel's construction. The keel-laying last October drew people from as far away as Virginia, Philadelphia and Baltimore, some of whom have joined the corps of volunteers.

"We have volunteer Saturdays every other weekend, and there is a group of four guys who come all the way from Pennsylvania together to help," says McMullen.

Putting the boat together is like match-

ing the pieces from a giant jigsaw puzzle—and some of the pieces are missing.

"We don't know about a lot of the real fine details," says Tom Fake of the Benford Design Group. "For instance, there is no detail on the rudder. Also, it's difficult to replicate in the computer the exact shape of the original hull."

"We had to kind of connect the dots," says Rich Emory, one of the two shipwrights under Swain's direction. "The computer came up with most of the [hull] calculations, but we had to eyeball the rest of them."

The modern Sultana will not exactly duplicate the original, partly because her mission as a floating classroom is different from the original—though the changes necessary are minimal.

"We're not an exact duplicate," admits McMullen, "but we're pretty true to the original. We didn't have to adjust her shape at all."

"I'm very impressed," says Peter Lesher, curator of the Chesapeake Bay Maritime Museum in St. Michaels. "It's much closer to being a true replica than a lot of vessels. The difference lies in a couple of concessions to safety and in some of the choices of materials."

The first *Sultana*'s frames, for example, were not Osage orange but more likely oak or elm. Osage was chosen because it is extremely rot-resistant. The high-quality materials mean this *Sultana* should far outlast the first.

"In the 18th century, they expected a vessel like this to last one generation," says Fake. "They're building this one so it will last for three generations."

Bits of the puzzle are still being honed, but the ultimate picture is clear. And the framework is in place with education as the enduring focus of the project.

"We have meetings at least once a week to figure out how to make each step a teaching step," McMullen says, "and how to incorporate untrained people into the process."

While Emory and Herman tackled the first step of lofting—converting Benford's plans to a $\frac{1}{4}$-scale rendition on a long trestle table—high school interns helped with the next step. They transcribed each swooping line from the trestle-table plan to a full-sized version on the loft floor—point by calculated point, the practical application of high school algebra and geometry.

So far there have been thousands of hours of student programming. Interns have served 875 hours from September 1998 to May 1999. Elementary and middle school groups, some from Baltimore, Pennsylvania and New Jersey, have participated in the lofting, in matching pieces of the Osage, partially milled and stacked in piles around the yard, and in hoisting frames into position. In May, four students from Gunston Day School spent their entire Bay Studies Week here, first taking a course on shipbuilding,

then constructing and raising a frame.

But despite the project's success, some nagging problems remain. Money is always an issue. $500,000 to complete construction plus additional funds for an endowment must be raised over the next two years. And the program has found it difficult to recruit minorities and women into its teaching and craftsman's positions.

"We want all kinds of people here to be role models for the kids who come," notes McMullen. "We got great feedback from teachers and students when our intern Megan Gadsby was here. And we're getting the same thing about Mary Wiltenburg [another intern]."

Swain and McMullen know that small things can become big learning opportunities—as with the Kent Youth "volunteer" assigned the task of building the workshop steps. Still working when his allotted time was up, the young man insisted on staying to finish the job. Later, at the keel-laying, Swain overheard him describing the process to a friend and saying: "I built those." An important lesson in personal satisfaction.

"That," Swain says, "is what this project is all about."

Sultana is slated for launch at the 2001 Chestertown Tea Party—an annual reenactment of the town's original response to the tea tax levied by the British in 1774. In the meantime the project looks ahead to thousands of hours of building, fundraising and learning—the kind of learning that the fourth grade class from Garnett Elementary is experiencing right now, though they probably don't realize it. They're too busy concentrating on completing "their" piece of the ship.

McMullen and the young crew pull until the 750-pound frame is standing upright. At McMullen's direction, the students stop, holding the line while the shipwrights saddle the base over the keel.

"Okay," calls Swain, "let it down slowly."

The children ease the lines, enabling Emory and Herman to drop the frame into place and clamp it to the keel in preparation for final through-bolting. The students are finished. Almost.

"Okay, everybody get a hardhat and come sign it," McMullen instructs, taking a pen and writing "Garnett Elementary School" and the date on the side of the frame, a record not only of individual participation, but of connection to *Sultana*. The students eagerly don hardhats and file alongside the hull, waiting their turn to sign. They aren't the first, nor will they be the last. Before it's finished, hundreds of names will be scrolled along the frames, planks, bulkheads of *Sultana*, Chestertown's ship of dreams.

Reprinted by permission from the October 1999 issue of Chesapeake Bay magazine.

For more information on the Schooner Sultana Project, see the Sultana *listing in this Directory.*

Danmark's Contribution to Coast Guard Seamanship and Leadership

Remarks at the National Maritime Historical Society's Salute to the
Sail Training Ship SV *Danmark*. New York, November 3, 1999

ADMIRAL JAMES M. LOY, COMMANDANT, US COAST GUARD

Good evening. I am delighted to join you tonight—doubly so in fact. First because I am indebted to the National Maritime Historical Society for reviving an important bit of Coast Guard history last year. I am very grateful that you reprinted *The Skipper and the Eagle*, Gordon McGowan's tale of commissioning *Horst Wessel* as the *Eagle* in 1946, training her first Coast Guard crew, and sailing her to her new home as America's Tall Ship. Thank you for putting this great story back in print. It means a lot to us.

And second, I am glad to be here to honor *Danmark*, a ship that has made indelible marks on the Coast Guard's traditions of seamanship and leadership.

Many of you are familiar with the thumbnail history of the Coast Guard's temporary possession of the *Danmark* during World War II: *Danmark* was in the United States for a training cruise when Nazi Germany occupied Denmark in the spring of 1940, the crew offered the ship and its services to the United States, and the Coast Guard chartered *Danmark* as a training ship until after the war, when we returned the ship to the restored Danish government.

It all sounds pretty smooth and easy, but the business was actually fairly complicated. You can well imagine, for example, that approaching the occupation government in Denmark might have been a bit ticklish—the Nazi overseers weren't real interested in helping the transaction along and our own State Department was sensitive to a whole range of ramifications beyond the deal itself. There were also significant legal obstacles that would take an act of Congress and an executive order to overcome. Many thorny issues. And then of course, there was the little matter of determining what price we would pay.

Finally, in late January, 1942, 20 months after Germans occupied Denmark, the price and terms were all set except for one minor sticking point: the request that the Coast Guard make an additional payment at the end of the charter period of twelve thousand dollars per year to cover depreciation costs.

Admiral Russell Waesche, our Commandant at the time, drew the line right there. He refused to authorize the depreciation payment. He pointed out that the ship would sit unused if we didn't charter it and that its condition would probably improve under our care. Besides, he noted, "although the taking over of the *Danmark* will be of material benefit to both the Danish and United States governments, it is being done largely for the accommodation of the former."

Sixty years later, we can see that Admiral Waesche might have been a better businessman than prophet. He thought we were doing a favor to the Danes, but subsequent events have shown that it might have been the other way around. In fact, the material benefits that the Coast Guard still enjoys from its brief possession of *Danmark* so far outweigh the nominal costs, that chartering *Danmark* would rank among the best deals ever struck by Uncle Sam—just a notch below Seward's Folly and the Louisiana Purchase—even if we had paid the depreciation charge!

As we honor *Danmark* tonight, my purpose is to highlight two principal influences *Danmark* has had on the Coast Guard. The first of these influences is on Coast Guard seamanship. Simply put, *Danmark* re-connected the Coast Guard with its sailing heritage.

Danmark's influence here is obvious. We were out of the sail training business before we chartered *Danmark*, and we have been in it ever since. *Eagle*'s first Coast Guard skipper learned how to sail square-riggers by spending three summers on *Danmark*. He observed all the intricacies of working a ship, he admired the captain's skill at anchoring and even passing through narrow bridges under sail, and he learned how to prepare a tall ship for heavy weather.

Had Captain McGowan known he would one day command a square-rigger, he wrote that he would have learned more diligently. But when it was time to sail *Eagle* from Bremerhaven in 1946, he took one precaution intended to make up for his lack of experience. He brought along a Danish officer, Knud Langvard, the former first officer of *Danmark*, as a consultant. Consultant? Even then? I don't think so; he brought him along as an expertise insurance policy!

We may fairly credit *Danmark* also with motivating the Coast Guard to obtain *Eagle*. After the war, the need to replace *Danmark* was universally acknowledged, but there was considerable debate within the Coast Guard as to what sort of training platform would be best for our Academy cadets. There was broad sup-

port for acquiring a C-4 or C-5 cargo ship, converting its cargo spaces to classrooms and berthing areas, and offering our cadets a modern seagoing experience.

Had the Coast Guard not chartered *Danmark* during World War II, the benefits of sail training would not have been apparent to Coast Guard leaders. It is altogether likely that we would never have applied for possession of *Horst Wessel*. We would simply have moved on to a steam-powered training platform and relegated our sail training to small boats and history.

We would have been the poorer for it. The immediate past commanding officer of *Eagle* explained one of the values of sail training in his afterword to the new edition of *The Skipper and the Eagle*. "*Eagle* and the sea present the cadets with real problems and challenges they can't walk away from."

That character building—combined with the unequaled opportunity to understand the forces affecting a ship, to learn a proper respect for the sea, to grasp the necessity for continuous vigilance at sea—is an essential part of Coast Guard seamanship. That so many Coast Guard officers grasp the importance of sail training intuitively today—and that the Coast Guard maintains its high standards of seamanship today—are due in no small way to *Danmark*'s influence.

The second positive contribution of *Danmark* on the Coast Guard may be even greater. I refer now to personal leadership, especially the devotion to duty exhibited by her commanding officer, Captain Knud Hansen.

Put yourself in the position, if you can imagine it, of Captain Hansen in December of 1941. Knud Hansen had learned his craft the traditional way, by running off to sea as a fourteen-year-old boy. The only circumstance unusual about his situation was that when Knud

Hansen was fourteen years old, World War One had progressed just far enough to reveal the horror of the U-Boat threat. Knud Hansen volunteered for service as a merchant seaman shortly after unrestricted German submarine warfare had been declared. Over the next quarter century, Knud Hansen rose in his profession, married, had a daughter, and took command of *Danmark* in 1937.

Germany's invasion of his homeland in April, 1940, forced Captain Hansen to seek refuge in Jacksonville, Florida, until his ship's status could be resolved. Over the next year-and-a-half, a good part of *Danmark*'s crew left to sign on as merchant seamen in the effort to keep Great Britain supplied. Fourteen of them died serving Allied forces. Meanwhile, Captain Hansen and his dwindling crew waited as various tentative efforts to resolve his situation fell through. During that time, Captain Hansen's wife and daughter twice tried to leave Denmark to join him, but they were turned back by Nazi border guards both times.

On December 7, 1941, everything changed. The Japanese invaded Pearl Harbor, and the United States entered the war. Imagine Captain Hansen's situation. Your government has fallen. Your family is trapped at home. The country in which you have taken refuge has declared war on the country occupying your homeland. What do you do? Captain Hansen chose immediately to stake everything on his hopes for a free Denmark. On December 8, he sent the

following telegram to the United States government:

"In view of the latest days' developments, the cadets, officers, and captain of the Danish Government Training Vessel *Danmark* unanimously place themselves and the ship at the disposal of the United States Government, to serve in any capacity the United States Government sees fit in our joint fight for victory and liberty."

Given his concerns about his wife and daughter back home, it could not have

Danmark

SAIL TALL SHIPS!

been an easy telegram to send. Sending that telegram was functionally equivalent to Cortez's burning his ships to keep his men from turning back.

Scripture contains a warning to the effect that, "No man having put his hand to the plow and looking back is fit for the kingdom of God." Knud Hansen was the sort of man who didn't look back. He hadn't looked back when he first went to sea in World War One. And he didn't look back when he heard the news of Pearl Harbor. He thought about his wife and daughter back home and went to his cabin to write the telegram that guaranteed he could not go home until after the war—and then only if the Allies won, which was not by any means a foregone conclusion in December of 1941. His wife was apparently made of the same stuff, for she became active in the Danish resistance to the Nazi occupation.

Nicholas Monsarrat's *The Cruel Sea*, the book that gets my vote for the best World War II sea novel set in the Atlantic theater, presents a minor scene in which the commanding officer of a convoy escort and his first officer—two men who had served together for a long time and forged a strong personal and professional regard for each other—discussed an estrangement that had risen up between them. The captain explained that the unfamiliar distance between them resulted not from any deficiency on the part of his executive officer but from his own sense that the desperation and intensity of the war effort required him to push aside any feeling that might hinder his single-minded focus on his duty.

Suzanne McMurray Ko's translation of Knud Anderson's monograph, The Schoolship *Danmark*, contains abundant evidence that Captain Hansen went about his training missions with the same seriousness of purpose. He issued an exhortation to every cadet walking aboard to overcome their fears. Why should they overcome their fears? "Because you must be seamen, and seamen must be able to do the impossible, or else we cannot win the war." Other anecdotes in that book make it clear that Captain Hansen evaluated cadets by one criterion: Will the eventual commissioning of this cadet help us win the war? If not, he suffered no remorse at the cadet's subsequent disenrollment. To a man who would not look back, nothing mattered but winning the war.

As important as it certainly was for cadets to learn the forces that affect a ship and to test their own strength and courage in the rigging, it was at least as important for them to see the steely resolve of a sea captain whose every thought and every action were directed towards defeating the Axis powers. For providing that example of devotion to duty to thousands of cadets, including two future Commandants, the Coast Guard will always be indebted to *Danmark*.

When we see the graceful beauty of this full-rigged ship, we do well to look past the billowing sails and to recall their purpose. *Danmark*'s service with the United States Coast Guard was not designed to provide a picturesque setting for summer training. It was designed to win a war we were not initially favored to win. At one point fairly early in that war, Admiral Waesche declared that the Coast Guard was wholly committed to the proposition that the convoys sending supplies to Great Britain would not get there too late with too little. *Danmark* trained many of the officers who fulfilled that proposition. *Danmark*'s seamanship and Captain Hansen's leadership made a huge difference in winning the war.

Thank you for allowing me to join you in honoring this great ship.

Semper paratus.

[As delivered]

Member Vessels

PHOTO BY BILL GRANT

227 OPPORTUNITIES TO LEARN
FROM THE SEA, UNDER SAIL

777 (Triple Seven)

Established in 1993, Proper Yacht, Inc. follows the tradition begun by Barclay Warburton III with the formation of the American Sail Training Association. Yacht *777*'s owner served as one of the first cadets aboard the *Black Pearl*. This excellent experience of transatlantic passage, tall ships races, and the character-building values embodied in sail training brings together the vessel and her crew to continue the tradition.

Yacht *777* was built in 1963 for the Fastnet Race of that year. Built under Lloyd's supervision and to the highest standards of UK racing rules, she has crossed the Atlantic many times, traveling the traditional cruising circuit from New England down to the lower Caribbean. Yacht *777* plans to participate in Tall Ships 2000®.

Flag:	USA
Rig:	Sloop
Homeport/waters:	Charleston, South Carolina: Coastal US to Caribbean
Who sails?	Individuals, students, and families of all ages.
Season:	Year-round
Cost:	$100 per person per day. $500 per person per week.
Program type:	Sail training for volunteer and paying crew and trainees. Sea education programs in marine science, maritime history, historic reenactments, and ecology in cooperation with accredited institutions and organized groups, and as informal, in-house programming.

Specifications:			
	Sparred length: 41' 3"	Draft: 6' 6"	Sail area: 1,400 sq. ft.
	LOD: 39'	Beam: 11' 8"	Tons: 10 GRT
	LOA: 41'	Freeboard: 4'	Power: diesel
	LWL: 37'	Hull: wood	

Built:	1963; R J. Prior and Sons, UK
Coast Guard certification:	Sailing School Vessel (Subchapter R)
Crew:	2. Trainees: 4
Contact:	Charles Hatchell
	Proper Yacht, Inc.
	PO Box 7
	Little River, SC 29566
	Tel: 843-830-3506; Fax: 843-767-1405
	E-mail: yacht777@gte.net
	Web site: http://www.properyacht.com

Abaco

PHOTO BY MORRIS ROSENFELD

Abaco was designed by John Alden in 1921 and built by W.B. Calderwood at Manchester Marine, Manchester, Massachusetts for Mr. Robert Saltonstall. She is owned and operated by Captain Peter L. Warburton, son of the late Barclay H. Warburton III, founder of ASTA. *Abaco* operates in the day sail business as well as a sail training vessel for youngsters, underprivileged youth, and adults.

Abaco carries up to six passengers or trainees and operates in West Palm Beach, Florida during the winter months and sails the New England waters during the summer. She is available for private charter, day sails, half-day sails, and sunset cruises.

Abaco will be participating in the Tall Ships 2000® Cruise in Company and will have berthing for up to six trainees. Berths will be sold for legs or for the entire voyage of six to eight weeks.

Participants will be the crew and will perform ship's duties such as steering, watch standing, sail handling, cooking, and cleaning.

ABACO

Flag:	USA
Rig:	Main staysail schooner
Homeport/waters:	Newport, Rhode Island: New England (summer), Florida and Bahamas (winter)
Who sails?	Individuals of all ages
Cost:	Call for details
Program type:	Sail training for volunteer and paying crew and trainees. Sea education in maritime history and ecology as informal, in-house programming. Passenger day sails and overnight passages. Dockside interpretation during port visits and in homeport.

Specifications:			
	Sparred length: 53'	Draft: 7'	Sail area: 2,000 sq. ft.
	LOD: 45' 6"	Beam: 11' 8"	Tons: 20 GRT
	LOA: 45' 6"	Rig height: 62'	Power: 85 HP diesel
	LWL: 33'	Freeboard: 5'	Hull: wood

Designer:	John G. Alden
Built:	1921; W.B. Calderwood, Manchester, Massachusetts
Coast Guard certification:	Uninspected Vessel
Crew:	2. **Trainees:** 6
Contact:	Captain and Mrs. Peter L. Warburton East Passage Packet Co., LLC Fazio, 57 Palmetto Dunes Hilton Head Island, SC 29928 Tel: 843-842-2432

Adirondack

The schooner *Adirondack* is the third of five schooners to come out of the Scarano Boat Building yard, beginning with the 59-foot schooner *Madeline* and the 61-foot *Woodwind* in 1991, and followed by the 105-foot schooner *America* in 1995 and a sister ship, *Adirondack II*, launched in August 1999. *Adirondack* combines the virtues of turn-of-the-century American schooner yachts with the latest in laminated wood technology. Offering an enviable combination of stability and speed, the *Adirondack* fulfills the builder and owner's ambition of providing a quality sailing experience to as many people as possible. *Adirondack* will be operating from Chelsea Piers in New York City in 2000.

Flag:	USA				
Rig:	Gaff schooner				
Homeport/waters:	New York, New York: New York Harbor				
Who sails?	School groups from elementary school through college, individuals and families.				
Program type:	Sail training with paying trainees. Passenger day sails.				
Specifications:	Sparred length: 80'		Draft: 8'		Sail area: 1,850 sq. ft.
	LOD: 64' 6"		Beam: 16'		Tons: 41 GRT
	LOA: 65'		Rig height: 62'		Power: twin 50 HP diesels
	LWL: 58'		Freeboard: 3' 4"		Hull: wood
Built:	1996; Albany, New York, Scarano Boat				
Coast Guard certification:	Passenger Vessel (Subchapter T)				
Crew:	3. **Trainees/passengers:** 49				
Contact:	Rick Scarano, Manager				
	Sailing Excursions, Inc.				
	c/o Scarano Boat, Port of Albany				
	Albany, NY 12202				
	Tel: 800-701-SAIL; 518-463-3401; Fax: 518-463-3403				
	E-mail: mail@scaranoboat.com				
	Web site: http://www.scaranoboat.com				

Adirondack II

The schooner *Adirondack II* is the latest schooner to splash the waters of the Hudson River outside of the Scarano Boat Building facility in Albany, New York. Launched in August 1999, *Adirondack II* joins the fleet of schooners that are known for their per-formance-oriented design/construction combined with clas-sic traditional aesthetics (see *Coronet*). "This year's model" expands on the idea that safety, comfort, and style are paramount considerations. Passengers can experience the exhilaration of being aboard the huge new day sailer, with its wide-open cockpit that can comfortably accommodate larger groups of trainees and passengers (up to 65). While dockside, spacious cockpit dog-houses double as serving space for food and beverages or classroom navigation paperwork. *Adirondack II* affirms that modern wood composite construction and 19th-century elegance blend seamlessly to the benefit of all.

Flag:	USA	
Rig:	Gaff schooner	
Homeport/waters:	Newport, Rhode Island: Narragansett Bay.	
Specifications:	Sparred length: 80'	Beam: 16'	Sail area: 1,800 sq. ft.
	LOD: 64' 6"'	Draft: 8'	Tons: 41 GRT
	LOA: 65'	Rig height: 62'	Hull: wood
	LWL: 58'	Freeboard: 3' 4"	Power: twin 50 HP diesels
Built:	1999; Albany, New York, Scarano Boat		
Coast Guard certification:	Passenger Vessel (Subchapter T)		
Crew:	3. **Trainees/passengers:** 65		
Contact:	Rick Scarano, Manager		
	Sailing Excursions, Inc.		
	c/o Scarano Boat, Port of Albany,		
	Albany, NY 12202		
	Tel: 800-701-SAIL, 518-463-3401; Fax: 518-463-3403		
	E-mail: mail@scaranoboat.com		
	Web site: http://www.scaranoboat.com		

Adventure

PHOTO BY FREDERICK BODEN

Adventure was built in 1926 at the James Shipyard in Essex, Massachusetts. A National Historic Landmark, the schooner was designed by Thomas McManus as a "knockabout"—without a bowsprit for the safety of the crew. Constructed at the end of the age of sail, *Adventure* was exceptionally fast and stable, the ultimate evolution of the fishing schooner. Carrying a sailing rig, diesel engine, and 14 dories, she fished the once bountiful outer banks of the North Atlantic from her homeports of Gloucester and Boston.

Adventure was a "highliner," the biggest moneymaker of all time, landing nearly $4 million worth of cod and halibut during her 27-year fishing career. When she retired in 1953, *Adventure* was the only American dory fishing trawler left in the Atlantic. Converted to a windjammer in 1955, *Adventure* carried passengers on cruises off the coast of Maine until 1987. Captain Jim Sharp of Camden donated the schooner to the people of Gloucester in 1988.

The historic schooner is currently under restoration and is scheduled to resume sailing in 2001. *Adventure* will be used as a community resource for innovative educational programming focusing on maritime, cultural, and environmental issues, and available for dockside tours, educational programs, and maritime events.

Flag:	USA
Rig:	Gaff topsail schooner
Home port/waters:	Gloucester, Massachusetts
Program type:	Dockside interpretation. Educational programs for schools.

Specifications:			
	LOA: 121' 6"	Draft: 13' 6"	Sail area: 6,500 sq. ft.
	LOD: 121' 6"	Beam: 24' 6"	Tons: 130 GRT
	LWL: 109'	Rig height: 110'	Hull: wood

Designer:	Tom McManus
Built:	1926; Essex, Massachusetts, John F. James & Son Yard
Coast Guard certification:	Moored Attraction Vessel (dockside)
Contact:	Mary Helen Gunn
	Gloucester Adventure, Inc.
	PO Box 1306
	Gloucester, MA 01930
	Tel: 978-281-8079; Fax: 978-281-2393
	E-mail: mhgunn@schooner-adventure.org
	Web site: http://www.schooner-adventure.org

Adventuress

In 1913 the schooner *Adventuress* sailed from Maine to the Bering Sea via the straits of Magellan and served the Bar Pilots of San Francisco Bay until 1952. Although originally commissioned to gather Arctic specimens, *Adventuress* now sails to increase awareness of the majesty and vulnerability of Puget Sound. Since 1989, Sound Experience, a nonprofit environmental education organization, has provided hands-on education aboard *Adventuress* in response to the area's urgent environmental issues. Today, *Adventuress* is a National Historic Landmark and a Puget Sound treasure—the crowning jewel of the Pacific Northwest's collection of wooden ships.

Volunteer and paid crew receive environmental and sail training. The ship's apprentice program for youth 14-18 and month-long internships for adult sailor/educators also feature extensive sail training. Sound Experience is proud to own and operate *Adventuress* and to keep her a "working" vessel—Protecting Puget Sound Through Education. The non-competitive environment fosters cooperation, teamwork, leadership, and sailing skills for Elderhostelers, Boy and Girl Scout Troops, youth groups, schools, and individuals of all ages who enjoy raising her massive sails and standing watch to hand, reef, and steer this classic tall ship. Truly a boat for the people, *Adventuress* provides empowering, life-changing experiences to more than 3,500 youth and adults each year.

Flag:	USA
Rig:	Gaff topsail schooner
Homeport/waters:	Port Townsend, Washington: Puget Sound/Salish Sea
Who sails?	School and other groups from elementary school through college, individuals and families.
Season:	March to November
Cost:	$28 per person ($18 for youth) for 3-5 hour sail, $1,260 per day for adult groups ($800 youth groups). Overnights: $2,500 per day adult groups ($1,725 youth groups). Scholarships available.
Program type:	Sail training for paying trainees. Sea education in marine science, maritime history, and ecology. Passenger day and overnight sails. Dockside interpretation during port visits.

Specifications:			
	Sparred length: 135'	Draft: 12'	Sail area: 5,478 sq. ft.
	LWL: 71'	Beam: 21'	Sail number: TS 15
	Rig height: 110'	Tons: 82 GRT	Power: 250 HP diesel

Designer:	B.B. Crowninshield
Built:	1913; East Boothbay, Maine, Rice Brothers
Coast Guard certification:	Passenger Vessel (Subchapter T)
Crew:	4-5, 8-10 instructors. **Trainees:** 45 day, 25 overnight. **Age:** 8-adult
Contact:	Frank DePalma, Marketing and Fundraising, Sound Experience 2310 Washington St., Port Townsend, WA 98368, Tel: 360-379-0438; Fax: 360-379-0439, E-mail: soundexp@olypen.com, Web site: http://www.soundexp.org

A.J. Meerwald

into the Chesapeake and the Northeast Atlantic seaboard).

Students range from fourth-graders to senior citizens; subject matter ranges from the history of Delaware Bay oystering to present water quality issues. Stewardship of the environment and preservation of our maritime heritage are the primary goals of all activities on the *A.J. Meerwald*, regardless of their target audience, length of program, and/or port of origin.

The Delaware Bay Schooner Project operates the schooner *A.J. Meerwald*, New Jersey's official tall ship, as an experiential classroom. This authentically-restored 1928 Delaware Bay oyster schooner sails from her homeport, Bivalve, New Jersey, as well as annual visits to cities and coastal towns throughout New Jersey, Pennsylvania, and Delaware (occasional special trips

The Delaware Bay Schooner Project also conducts shore-based programs, lecture series, hosts Delaware Bay Day (the first Saturday in June), and provides leadership on watershed issues throughout the Delaware Estuary. Members and volunteers are the lifeblood of the organization and are always welcome.

Flag:	USA
Rig:	Gaff-schooner
Homeport/waters:	Bivalve, New Jersey: Delaware Bay and coastal New Jersey
Who sails?	School groups, 4th grade through college, families, scouts, teachers, businesses, associations, and anyone interested in a *Meerwald* experience.
Cost:	$25 per person per sail, $2,500 group rate per day (charter)
Program type:	Sail training for professional crew and volunteer and paying trainees. Three-hour educational sails, summer camp, family sails, teacher workshops, overnight programs, team building, and special "theme" sails (i.e. birding, oystering, etc.). Sea education in marine science, maritime history, ecology, team building, and watershed awareness in cooperation with accredited institutions and other groups, and as informal, in-house programming.

Specifications:			
	Sparred length: 115'	Draft: 6'	Sail area: 3,560 sq. ft.
	LOA: 85'	Beam: 22' 1"	Tons: 57 GRT
	LOD: 81' 7"	Rig height: 67' 8"	Power: diesel
	LWL: 78' 3"	Freeboard: 3' 6"	Hull: wood

Designer:	Charles H. Stowman and Sons, Dorchester, New Jersey
Built:	1928; Dorchester, New Jersey, Charles H. Stowman and Sons Shipyard
Coast Guard certification:	Passenger Vessel (Subchapter T)
Crew:	11, augmented by volunteers
Contact:	Meghan Wren, Executive Director, Delaware Bay Schooner Project
	2800 High Street, Bivalve
	Port Norris, NJ 08349
	Tel: 856-785-2060; Fax: 856-785-2893
	E-mail: ajmeerwald@odon.net
	Web site: http://www.ajmeerwald.org

Alabama

The ex-pilot schooner *Alabama* is an authentic example of a typical Gloucester fishing schooner of the early 1900s. She was built for the Mobile Bar Pilot Association in Pensacola, Florida in 1926 and designed by the greatest New England designer of Gloucester schooners, Thomas F. McManus.

After a major three-year reconstruction, the summer of 1998 marked her first season sailing the waters of southern New England. She is a product of Vineyard Haven craftsmanship as the lion's share of her rebuild took place in Vineyard Haven Harbor. *Alabama* now joins *Shenandoah* in the Coastwise Packet Company fleet.

Flag:	USA
Rig:	Gaff schooner
Homeport/waters:	Vineyard Haven, Massachusetts: Southern New England
Who sails?	Elementary school and middle school groups.
Cost:	$100 per person per day
Program type:	Sail training for paying trainees. Sea education in cooperation with accredited schools and as informal, in-house programming.

Specifications:			
	Sparred length: 120'	Draft: 12' 6"	Sail area: 5,000 sq. ft.
	LOD: 85'	Beam: 21'	Tons: 85 GRT
	LOA: 90'	Rig height: 94'	Power: twin diesels
	LWL: 78'	Freeboard: 5'	Hull: wood

Designer:	Thomas F. McManus
Built:	1926; Pensacola, Florida, Pensacola Shipbuilding Company
Coast Guard certification:	Passenger Vessel (Subchapter T)
Crew:	5. **Trainees:** 27 (overnight)
Contact:	Captain Robert Douglas
	Coastwise Packet Company
	PO Box 429
	Vineyard Haven, MA 02568
	Tel: 508-693-1699

ALABAMA

Alaska Eagle

Winner of the 1977-78 Whitbread Round the World Race as the Dutch yacht *Flyer*, the 65-foot *Alaska Eagle*

now operates as a sail training vessel for adults and college students interested in acquiring offshore passage-making skills. Since 1982, *Alaska Eagle* has made more than 22 Pacific crossings and sailed more than 200,000 miles with students aboard. Cruises and passages are generally two to three weeks in length.

Strong and fast, *Alaska Eagle* is a comfortable offshore cruiser with four private staterooms and two heads and showers. Under the guidance of two USCG-licensed skipper/instructors, *Alaska Eagle*'s nine-member crews participate in watch standing, sail handling, steering, and navigating. A professional cook handles the meals. *Alaska Eagle* is operated by the Sailing Center at Orange Coast College, a Southern California nonprofit boating education program.

Plans for 2000-2001 include a voyage from New Zealand through the remote islands of the South Pacific to Newport Beach.

Flag:	USA
Rig:	Sloop
Homeport/waters:	Newport Beach, California: South Pacific, New Zealand
Who sails?	Individual college students and adults
Cost:	$150 per person per day
Program type:	Sail training with paying trainees. Paying passengers on overnight passages.

Specifications:			
	Sparred length: 65'	Draft: 10' 5"	Sail area: 1,500 sq. ft.
	LOD: 65'	Beam: 16' 4"	Tons: 39 GRT
	LOA: 65'	Rig height: 90'	Power: 200 HP diesel
	LWL: 50'	Freeboard: 5'	Hull: aluminum

Designer:	Sparkman & Stephens
Built:	1977; The Netherlands, Royal Nuisman Shipyard
Coast Guard certification:	Sailing School Vessel (Subchapter R)
Crew:	3. Trainees: 9
Contact:	Catherine Ellis, Adventure Sailing Coordinator
	Orange Coast College Sailing Center,
	1801 West Coast Highway
	Newport Beach, CA 92663
	Tel: 949-645-9412; Fax: 949-645-1859
	Web site: http://www.occsailing.com

Alcyone

Alcyone, built by and for Seattle's master shipwright Frank Prothero, was modeled after the Gloucester fishing schooners of New England. Prothero, whose yard turned out wooden fishing boats and tugs, built *Alcyone* as stoutly as a workboat. The result is a graceful schooner ready to sail anywhere in the world.

In 1987 Sugar Flanagan and Leslie McNish purchased *Alcyone* and have been working her ever since. She has sailed eight charter seasons in the San Juan Islands and three times has made deep-water passages out across the Pacific. Her most recent cruise was a two-year trip through the South Pacific to New Zealand. Now, back in the Pacific Northwest, *Alcyone* takes up to six trainees on two-week excursions around Vancouver Island.

In the spring and fall, *Alcyone* offers sail training for individuals of all ages. Summer is set aside for trainees ages 14-

20. The program emphasizes all aspects of seamanship, both traditional and modern. Previous experience is not required, just the willingness to lend a hand on deck and below.

Flag:	USA		
Rig:	Gaff topsail schooner		
Homeport/waters:	Port Townsend, Washington: Inside Passage, Washington to Alaska		
Who sails?	Individuals of all ages		
Season:	Spring to fall		
Cost:	$75 per youth per day, $125 per adult per day, $1,000 for 12-day youth trip, $500 for six-day youth trip		
Program Type:	Sail training for paying trainees		
Specifications:	Sparred length: 82'	Draft: 10'	Sail area: 3,500 sq. ft.
	LOD: 65'	Beam: 15' 6"	Tons: 29 GRT
	LOA: 65'	Rig height: 76'	Power: Bedford diesel
	LWL: 52'	Freeboard: 3' 6"	Hull: wood
Designer:	Frank Prothero		
Built:	1956; Seattle, Washington, Frank Prothero		
Crew:	3. **Trainees:** 6		
Contact:	Captain John "Sugar" Flanagan		
	PO Box 1511		
	Port Townsend, WA 98368		
	Tel: 360-385-7647		
	E-mail: alcyone@olympus.net		
	Web site: http://www.olympus.net/personal/alcyone		

Alma

400 scow schooners that carried cargo in the San Francisco Bay area at the turn of the century. She is owned and operated by the San Francisco Maritime National Historical Park and docked at Hyde Street Pier near Fisherman's Wharf. The National Maritime Museum Association supports operations of the *Alma* at the many maritime festivals and parades in the Bay area.

Alma sails from March until November and is crewed by volunteers, representing and interpreting a time when commerce moved by boat around the Bay. The *Alma* volunteer program enables trainees and apprentices to learn about traditional sailing and wooden boat maintenance. No fees are required as all crew volunteer to sail and maintain the *Alma* and other park vessels at Hyde Street Pier.

The scow schooner *Alma* was built at Hunters Point in San Francisco Bay in 1891 and is the last of approximately

Flag:	USA
Rig:	Schooner, two-masted
Homeport/waters:	San Francisco, California: San Francisco Bay
Who sails?	Adult education groups, individual students and adults, families.
Program type:	Sail training for crew and apprentices. Sea education based on informal, in-house programming focused on maritime history. Dockside interpretation. Affiliated groups include the National Maritime Museum Association, San Francisco National Maritime Historical Park, and National Park Service.

Specifications:			
	Sparred length: 88'	Draft: 3' 6"	Sail area: 2,684 sq. ft.
	LOD: 61' 4"	Beam: 23' 6"	Tons: 47 GRT
	LOA: 62'	Rig height: 76'	Power: twin diesels
	LWL: 59' 5"	Freeboard: 4'	Hull: wood

Designer:	Fred Siemers
Built:	1891; San Francisco, California, Fred Siemers
Crew:	6. **Trainees:** 28 (overnight), 40 (day). **Age:** 14+
Contact:	Captain Al Lutz
	San Francisco Maritime National Historical Park
	Building E, Fort Mason Center
	San Francisco, CA 94123,
	Tel: 415-556-1659; Fax: 415-556-1624
	E-mail: al_lutz@nps.gov
	Web site: http://www.nps.gov/safr/local/alma.html

Alvei

After an extensive eight-year refit, *Alvei*'s accommodations, deck, and rigging have been completely renewed. Underway since October 1995, *Alvei* has completed half of a circumnavigation, sailing from Portugal to New Zealand. She now sails long trade wind passages using the old sailing ship routes.

Alvei's rig, the main topsail schooner, was the preferred rig of privateers in the early 19th century. *Alvei* carries a total of 16 sails and has 139 lines of running rigging, offering a thorough range of experience in both fore and aft and square sail handling.

A sailor of 100 years ago would be quite at home on *Alvei*. It takes a team of people, using block and tackle, to "sweat and tail" as they set and handle the sails. Raising the anchor, rowing the boat, and doing laundry are all done by hand.

The crew, both regular and trainees, stand watches at sea, four hours on and eight hours off; in port, one day on and two days off. Duties include steering, lookout, sail handling, painting, tarring, sewing, cooking, and rigging.

Flag:	Vanuatu
Rig:	Main topsail schooner
Homeport/waters:	Vila, Republic of Vanuatu: Tropical waters worldwide
Who sails?	Adults over 18
Season:	Year-round
Cost:	$24 per person per day
Program type:	Sail training for volunteer and paying trainees. Sea education based on informal, in-house programming. Coastal and deep-water passage making.

Specifications:		
Sparred length: 126'	Draft: 10'	Sail area: 5,700 sq. ft.
LOD: 91' 8"	Beam: 19'	Power: 160 HP diesel
LOA: 93' 10"	Rig height: 85' 3"	Hull: steel
LWL: 87' 2"	Freeboard: 2' 6"	

Designer:	Hull, unknown; rig, Evan Logan
Built:	1920; Montrose, Scotland
Contact:	Margy Gassel, Shore Crew
	604 Masonic Avenue
	Albany, CA, 94706
	Tel: 510-526-7157; Fax: 510-526-1684
	E-mail: alvei@yahoo.com
	Web site: http://www.c-wave.com/alvei/

Amara Zee

Amara Zee is based on a Thames River Sailing Barge blended with the best of contemporary marine and theater technology. With its shallow draft and lowering masts, the Stage Barge can access almost any waterfront community in North America. The spars are utilized for scenery, lights, sound equipment, and special effects. All performances are staged on deck, with the audience sitting on the shore.

The *Amara Zee* was built by the theater company with the assistance of a number of marine professional volunteers and financed by over 600 manufacturing companies with in-kind donations of equipment, materials, and services. The Caravan's original productions express contemporary concerns and issues in an engaging and compelling format that is both entertaining and inspirational.

The Caravan Stage Barge *Amara Zee* is the new touring vessel of the Caravan Stage Society, Inc. Built in 1997, the

Flag:	Canada
Rig:	Ketch (sailing barge)
Homeport/waters:	East Coast of US
Program type:	Theatrical performances.

Specifications:			
	LOA: 90'	Draft: 3' 6"	Sail area: 5,100 ft.
	Rig height: 90'	Beam: 22'	Power: twin 120
	Hull: steel		HP diesels

Contact:	National Caravan Stage Company, Inc.
	140 Seventh Avenue South
	St. Petersburg, FL 33701
	Tel: 917-208-6976, 727-515-8163
	E-mail: office@caravanstage.org
	Web site: http://www.caravanstage.org

America

Named for the famed New York-built yacht that crossed the Atlantic to win the 100 Guinea Cup in 1851, thus giving her name to the world's most coveted yachting trophy, *America* was built to demonstrate American excellence in technology, craftsmanship, and ingenuity in every port she visits worldwide. While *America* is a waterline-up re-creation of the 1851 yacht, her spars utilize the latest in carbon fiber technology, and *America* weighs some 50 tons less than the original George Steers-designed schooner. Below decks she benefits from the most advanced boat building technologies.

With plans to sail an average of 20,000 miles per year, *America* will visit all major "in-water" boat shows, classic yacht regattas, Tall Ships 2000®, the 2001 Sesquicentennial of the Royal Yacht Squadron Regatta of 1851 in Cowes, and other events.

Flag:	USA
Rig:	Gaff schooner
Homeport/waters:	Boston, Massachusetts (summer), Key West, Florida (winter): Worldwide.
Program type:	Corporate and private charters. Sea education based on informal, in-house programming. Passenger day and overnight sails. Dockside interpretation during port visits.

Specifications:	Sparred length: 139'	Draft: 10'	Sail area: 6,400 sq. ft.
	LOA: 105'	Beam: 25'	Tons: 120 GRT
	LOD: 105'	Rig height: 108'	Power: twin diesels
	LWL: 90' 6"	Freeboard: 4'	

Designer:	George Steers, w/modifications by Scarano Boat
Built:	1995; Scarano Boat, Port of Albany, New York
Coast Guard certification:	Passenger Vessel (Subchapter T)
Contact:	Gregory E. Muzzy, President
	The Liberty Fleet of Tall Ships
	67 Long Wharf
	Boston, MA 02110
	Tel: 617-742-0333; Fax: 617-742-1322

American Eagle

PHOTO BY LAURA SAWALL

the finest 12-meter helmsmen in the world and was selected by the New York Yacht Club to defend and win the America's Cup with *Courageous* in 1977.

American Eagle, a yacht saturated with a special aura of greatness, offers a memorable experience for you and your guests. Take the wheel and sense the sheer power and exhilaration that only the big twelves provide. An experienced three-man crew will make your pleasure a priority while ensuring safety aboard.

The 12-meter yacht *American Eagle* was launched in Stamford, Connecticut, in 1964, and won 20 out of 21 races in the June and July America's Cup defender trials. In 1968, she was bought by Ted Turner, a 31-year-old sailor from Atlanta, Georgia. During his years racing *American Eagle*, Turner became one of

Rediscover Narragansett Bay or the historic America's Cup course on Rhode Island Sound on one of the greatest 12-meter yachts ever built. *American Eagle* is based in Newport but upon request can be available at the port of your choice from New York to Maine by the day or the week. Call or write for more information.

Flag:	USA
Rig:	Sloop
Homeport/waters:	Newport, Rhode Island: New England and Chesapeake Bay
Who sails?	Individual and group charters
Cost:	$1,800 group rate per day, $60 per person for evening sails
Program type:	Sail training for volunteer and paying trainees. Sea education based on informal, in-house programming. Passenger day sails.

Specifications:			
	Sparred length: 69'	Draft: 9'	Sail area: 1,850 sq. ft.
	LOA: 68'	Beam: 12' 8"	Tons: 28 GRT
	LOD: 68'	Rig height: 90'	Power: diesel
	LWL: 46'	Hull: wood	

Designer:	A.E. Luders
Built:	1964; Stamford, Connecticut, Luders
Coast Guard certification:	Passenger Vessel (Subchapter T)
Crew:	3. **Trainees/passengers:** 12 (day sails)
Contact:	Herb Marshall/George Hill
	America's Cup Charters
	PO Box 51
	Newport, RI 02840
	Tel: 401-849-5868; Fax: 401-849-3098
	Web site: http://www.americascupcharters.com

American Pride

The graceful three-masted schooner *American Pride* was built in 1941 as a two-masted "schooner-dragger." She spent over 40 years commercially fishing the Grand Banks and George's Banks. In 1986, completely restored and with a third mast added, she operated as a charter boat out of Bar Harbor, Maine. In October 1996, she was purchased by the American Heritage Marine Institute (AHMI) and sailed to her new home in Long Beach, California.

The AHMI offers hand-on educational programs for children which stress science, marine biology, history, and sail training. Programs encourage teamwork, good communication, problem solving, and leadership. Sail training programs and private group charters are available for teens and adults, with destinations and length of voyage varying.

AHMI is actively engaged in sharing the thrill of sailing with sick or abused children, and regularly donates sails to child welfare groups and fundraising guilds. A professional crew and strong volunteer group generously gives time, talents, and resources in support of the programs.

The once-successful fishing schooner now majestically sails the southern California waters, her huge red sails highly visible as she gracefully shares the adventures and romance of the tall ship with all that come aboard.

Flag:	USA
Rig:	Schooner, three-masted
Homeport/waters:	Long Beach, California: Southern California.
Who sails?	Elementary and middle school students, individuals of all ages, and families.
Season:	Year-round
Cost:	$100 per person per day, $1,800 group rate per day (charter)
Program type:	Sail training for volunteer and paying crew and trainees. Fully accredited sea education programs in marine science, maritime history, and ecology. Historic reenactments.

Specifications:			
	Sparred length: 129'	Draft: 10'	Sail area: 3,900 sq. ft.
	LOD: 101'	Beam: 22'	Tons: 203 GRT
	LOA: 105'	Rig height: 98'	Power: diesel
	LWL: 92'	Freeboard: 6'	Hull: wood

Built:	1941; Muller Boatworks, Brooklyn, New York
Coast Guard certification:	Passenger Vessel (Subchapter T)
Crew:	6 (paid and volunteer). **Trainees/passengers:** 100 (day sails), 48 (overnight)
Contact:	Helen H. Clinton, Director
	American Heritage Marine Institute
	21520 "G" Yorba Linda Blvd., # 444
	Yorba Linda, CA 92887
	Tel: 714-970-8800; Fax: 714-970-8474
	E-mail: americprd@aol.com

American Rover

The *American Rover* operates a rigorous day sailing schedule out of the Norfolk, Virginia waterfront. Cruises are generally two to three-hour sightseeing and historical tours. Special student educational field trips are also popular.

Flag:	USA
Rig:	Topsail schooner, three-masted
Homeport/waters:	Norfolk, Virginia: Chesapeake Bay and tributaries
Who sails?	Individuals, families, and student groups. Affiliated institutions include Old Dominion University.
Cost:	$12-$16 per person, two to three hours, $9-$13 per person group rate, two to three hours
Program type:	Sail training for crew and apprentices. Sea education in marine science, maritime history, and ecology in cooperation with schools and colleges. Passenger day sails. Homeport dockside interpretation.

Specifications:					
	Sparred length: 135'		Draft: 8' 6"		Sail area: 5,000 sq. ft.
	LOA: 98'		Beam: 24'		Tons: 98 GRT
	LOD: 96'		Rig height: 85'		Power: 240 HP
	LWL: 80'		Freeboard: 8'		

Designer:	Merritt Walter
Built:	1986; Panama City, Florida, Kolsar & Rover Marine
Coast Guard certification:	Passenger Vessel (Subchapter T)
Crew:	4; non-crew educators: 2. **Trainees/passengers:** 49
Contact:	Captain Brook J. Smith
	Rover Marine, Inc.
	PO Box 3125
	Norfolk, VA 23514
	Tel: 804-627-7245; Fax: 804-627-6626

SAIL TALL SHIPS!

The freedom schooner *Amistad* will set sail in July 2000, plying the nation's waterways as an educational ambassador, teaching lessons of history, cooperation, and leadership to Americans of all ages, interests, and cultural backgrounds.

Currently under construction at Mystic Seaport, the nation's leading maritime museum, *Amistad* will be launched on March 25, 2000, after which masts, rigging, and sails will be installed. The vessel will initially sail southern New England waters, then travel south along the East Coast during the winter and frequently dock in her homeport, New Haven, Connecticut.

Amistad America, the educational organization which will own and operate the ship, is currently raising the $10 million endowment necessary to ensure *Amistad* sails for decades. Individuals, families, and school groups will learn the importance of historical identity through a variety of experiences, from onboard and dockside exhibits, to half-day excursions and overnight programs. Themes for program curricula will be interdisciplinary, blending communication skills, geography, math, and social studies while making history relevant and fostering cooperation among people of diverse backgrounds.

AMISTAD

Flag:	USA
Rig:	Topsail schooner
Homeport/waters:	New Haven, Connecticut: East Coast of the United States.
Who sails?	School groups from elementary schools through college.
Program type:	Sail training for crew and apprentices and with paying trainees. Maritime history and a full range of programming are expected. Sea education in cooperation with accredited institutions and other groups. Passenger day sailing and dockside interpretation during home and port visits.

Specifications:			
	Sparred length: 129'	Draft: 10' 2"	Sail area: 5,000 sq. ft.
	LOA: 85'	Beam: 22' 4"	Power: twin diesels
	LOD: 81'	Rig height: 90'	Hull: wood
	LWL: 79'		

Designer:	Tri-Coastal Marine
Built:	1998-2000, Mystic Seaport, Mystic, Connecticut
Coast Guard certifications:	Sailing School Vessel (Subchapter R), Passenger Vessel (Subchapter T)
Crew:	8, combination paid and volunteer. **Trainees/passengers:** 49
Contact:	Christopher Cloud, Executive Director
	Amistad America, Inc. c/o Mystic Seaport
	PO Box 6000, Mystic, CT 06355
	Tel: 860-536-6003; Fax: 860-536-4861
	E-mail: ccloud@mysticseaport.org
	Web site: http://www.amistadamerica.org

McIntosh circumnavigated the world on her maiden voyage, an adventure documented in Herbert Smith's *Dreams of Natural Places and Sailing Three Oceans. Appledore II* makes day sails from her homeport of Camden, Maine from late June until mid-October. During the winter months, she undertakes snorkel trips on North America's only living coral reef, as well as sunset cruises from Key West, Florida. She carries up to 49 passengers on day sails and can accommodate up to 26 overnight.

The crew of the *Appledore II* is committed to sail training, and they are trained in sailing, celestial navigation, and marlinespike seamanship through operation of the vessel on day sails as well as two 2,000-mile offshore voyages yearly. Interested persons are encouraged to contact them for possible payroll or volunteer positions. They have opportunities for not only crew, but business positions on an entry level.

The *Appledore II* is a traditional gaff-rigged schooner designed for ocean sailing. Launched in 1978 at the Gamage Ship Yard in South Bristol, Maine, Bud

Flag:	USA
Rig:	Gaff topsail schooner.
Homeport/waters:	Camden, Maine: Maine to the Florida Keys
Season:	June to October (Maine); December to May (Florida)
Cost:	$20 per person per trip
Who sails?	School groups from elementary school through college, individuals and families.
Program type:	Sail training for crew and apprentices. Sea education based on informal, in-house programming. Passenger day sails. Dockside interpretation.

Specifications:			
	Sparred length: 86'	Draft: 10' 6"	Sail area: 2,815 sq. ft.
	LOA: 82'	Beam: 18' 9"	Tons: 63 GRT
	LOD: 65'	Rig height: 75'	Power: 210 HP diesel
	LWL: 53'	Freeboard: 8'	Hull: wood

Designer:	Bud McIntosh
Built:	1978; Gamage Shipyard, South Bristol, Maine, Herb Smith
Coast Guard certification:	Passenger Vessel (Subchapter T)
Crew:	7. **Trainees/passengers:** 49 (day), 26 (overnight)
Contact:	John P. McKean, President
	Schooner Exploration Associates, Ltd.
	"0" Lily Pond Dr.
	Camden, ME 04843
	Tel: 207-236-8353, 800-233-PIER (summer)
	PO Box 4114, Key West, FL 33041-4114; Tel: 305-296-9992 (winter)

Appledore IV

The schooner *Appledore IV* is owned and operated by BaySail, a private, nonprofit organization. Tall ship adventures aboard the *Appledore IV* help to support BaySail's mission: "To foster environmental stewardship of the Saginaw Bay Watershed and the Great Lakes ecosystem and to increase personal and professional opportunities for learners of all ages through comprehensive, hands-on, educational and skill-building programs under sail." *Appledore IV* is available for private charter to companies, organizations, and other groups of up to 48 people and for public sails on weekends from May through September.

BaySail's environmental education program begins and ends in the classroom with materials designed to prepare students for their sailing experience and reinforce the lessons learned while on board the *Appledore IV*. During the three-hour *Appledore IV* excursion, trained volunteer teachers lead small groups of students through activities including collecting and analyzing water and sediment samples, plankton sampling, and fish identification. Land use, maritime history, navigation, and weather observation are also discussed.

BaySail's Youth Development program is an intensive five-day training experience on board the *Appledore IV* designed to teach at-risk youth about the importance of self-reliance, teamwork, and respect for authority in an environment few have ever experienced. Communication skills and self-esteem are enhanced as trainees work independently and as a team on every aspect of *Appledore IV*'s operations.

Flag:	USA
Rig:	Topsail schooner
Homeport/waters:	Bay City, Michigan: Saginaw Bay and Lake Huron
Who sails?	Elementary students through adults.
Program type:	Marine science and ecology education in cooperation with accredited institutions. Sail training for volunteer and paying trainees.

Specifications:			
	Sparred length: 85'	Draft: 8' 6"	Sail area: 3,500 sq. ft.
	LOD: 65'	Beam: 18' 5"	Tons: 70 GRT
	LOA: 65'	Rig height: 120'	Power: 135 HP diesel
	LWL: 53'	Freeboard: 6'	Hull: steel

Designer:	Bud McIntosh
Built:	1989; Palm Coast, Florida, Treworgy Yachts
Coast Guard certification:	Passenger Vessel (Subchapter T)
Crew:	4. **Trainees:** 8
Contact:	Shirley Roberts, President, BaySail
	901 Saginaw Street
	Bay City, MI 48708
	Tel: 517-893-1222; Fax: 517-893-7016

Arethusa

Arethusa is a 72-foot ketch owned and operated by the Shaftesbury Homes & Arethusa charity, which runs homes for disadvantaged young people and orphans, mainly in southeast London. Her predecessor was a four-masted barque (*Peking*) which was a training ship moored on the Medway River providing training for up to 200 boys destined for careers in the British Royal Navy and the British Merchant Fleet. In 1974 *Peking* was towed to the South Street Seaport Museum in New York (where she is still moored), but it was decided to continue the fine sailing record of the Shaftesbury Homes Society with the construction of a new boat.

Arethusa's normal program is to run weekly cruises for groups of up to 12 young people (13-25), either from the Shaftesbury Homes or from similar underprivileged groups. She is home-ported at Upnor near Chatham/Rochester on the River Medway, but she cruises extensively in European waters and every second year deploys to the Canary Islands for the winter months. She is ever present in the Cutty Sark Tall Ships Races each year. *Arethusa* visited the US in 1987, and will be returning this year as part of the Tall Ships 2000® fleet. Inquiries are welcomed from US youth and it is hoped to have several on board for different legs of Tall Ships 2000®.

Flag:	UK
Rig:	Bermuda-rigged ketch
Homeport/waters:	Upnor, near Rochester, Kent, England, UK: Europe, Baltic Sea, Biscay Bay, Canary Islands (biennially)
Who sails?	Students and individuals over 13. Affiliated with many UK school groups.
Program type:	Sail training for volunteer and paying crew and trainees. Dockside interpretation while in homeport.

Specifications:			
	Sparred length: 72'	Draft: 8'	Sail area: 1,856 sq. ft.
	LOD: 72'	Beam: 17' 4"	Tons: 43 GRT
	LOA: 72'	Rig height: 86'	Power: 130 HP diesel
	LWL: 58'	Freeboard: 4'	Hull: wood

Designer:	David Cannell
Built:	1982; Fox's, Ipswich, Suffolk, England
Certification:	SCV2 (Small Commercial Vessel), issued by YBDSA (Yacht Brokers Design and Surveyors Association)
Crew:	3. Trainees: 12
Contact:	Nicko Franks, Ketch Manager
	Shaftesbury Homes and Arethusa
	Lower Upnor, Rochester, Kent ME2 4XB, UNITED KINGDOM
	Tel: 44-1634-711566; Fax: 44-1634-295905
	E-mail: kfranks@compuserve.com

Argia

Argia is a replica of a 19th-century schooner, and was designed and built by her owner and captain, Frank Fulchiero. *Argia* is licensed to carry 49 passengers in inland waters. In addition to vacation day sails, she also offers educational and sail training programs. Cruises can be tailored to suit the passengers' needs.

ARGIA

Flag:	USA		
Rig:	Schooner		
Homeport/waters:	Mystic Connecticut: Long Island Sound		
Who sails?	School groups from elementary school through college, individuals and families of all ages. Affiliated institutions include Mystic Seaport Museum and Mystic Aquarium.		
Program type:	Sail training for professional and volunteer crew, and paying trainees. Sea education in marine science, maritime history, and ecology in cooperation with organized groups and as informal, in-house programming. Passenger day sails.		
Specifications:	Sparred length: 81'	Draft: 7'	Sail area: 1,700 sq. ft.
	LOD: 56'	Beam: 18'	Tons: 30 GRT
	LOA: 66'	Rig height: 70'	Power: 100 HP diesel
	LWL: 48'	Freeboard: 4'	Hull: wood
Designer:	Frank Fulchiero		
Built:	1986; Reedville, Washington, Jennings Boat Yard		
Coast Guard certification:	Passenger Vessel (Subchapter T)		
Trainees:	49 (day sails)		
Contact:	Captain Frank Fulchiero		
	Voyager Cruises		
	73 Steamboat Wharf		
	Mystic, CT 06355,		
	Tel: 860-536-0416		

Aurora

Aurora, formerly known as the *Francis Todd*, is a two-masted schooner built in 1947 by Newbert & Wallace of Thomaston, Maine, for work in the fishing industry. *Aurora* retired from fishery work in 1991. The vessel has been rebuilt to offer ample seating, a spacious deck plan, and amenability to catering arrangements. *Aurora* is the perfect venue for entertaining and special occasions. The vessel is inspected and certified by the US Coast Guard as a Passenger Vessel. She is stable, seaworthy, and professionally maintained for comfort and safety. Presently being fitted out for overnight accommodations, the *Aurora* is based in Newport, Rhode Island and sails Narragansett Bay on day sails.

AURORA

Flag:	USA
Rig:	Gaff topsail schooner
Homeport/waters:	Newport, Rhode Island: Narragansett Bay
Who sails?	School groups from elementary school through college, as well as individuals and families.
Program type:	Passenger day sails and informal sail training.

Specifications:			
Sparred length: 101'	Draft: 7' 6"	Sail area: 2,800 sq. ft.
LOD: 78'	Beam: 17' 6"	Tons: 53 GRT
Rig height: 80'	Hull: wood	

Designer:	Newbert & Wallace
Built:	1947; Newbert & Wallace, Thomaston, Maine
Crew:	3. Trainees/passengers: 80
Contact:	IDC Charters, Inc.
	Goat Island Marina
	Newport, RI 02840
	Tel: 401-849-6999

Avon Spirit

Avon Spirit was named to celebrate the intrepid spirit of those New England Planters (1760) who settled the lands along the Avon River and who built, sailed, and managed 650 large ships during the "Golden Age of Sail." She was constructed in the Avon Spirit Shipyard, Avondale/Newport Landing, Nova Scotia, by the same shipwrights of Snyder's Shipyard Limited who gave *Bluenose II* new life in 1991, and by local skilled craftsmen of Hants County, Nova Scotia. The sails are by Michele Stevens Sail Loft, 2nd Peninsula. *Avon Spirit* is a 55-foot version of the "F.G.B.", the last cargo schooner built in Nova Scotia, and in 1929, the last vessel registered on the Windsor Registry of Shipping. The traditional 64 Shares are registered to Avon Spirit, Inc., which was founded to help preserve the skills of the wooden shipwright in Nova Scotia.

She has been traditionally built with sawn oak frames, oak keel, stem, sternpost, and deadwood, and planked with oak and Eastern White Pine. The masts are Black Spruce. Her draft and traditional rig make her an ideal vessel for sailing the waters of beautiful Mahone Bay. *Avon Spirit* operates from the Mahone Bay Town Wharf (home of the Mahone Bay Wooden Boat Festival), conducting daily cruises or private charters.

Flag:	Canada
Rig:	Square topsail schooner
Homeport/waters:	Lunenburg, Nova Scotia, Canada: Mahone Bay, Nova Scotia, Canada
Program type:	Sail training program being developed for volunteer and paying trainees.

Specifications:			
	Sparred length: 70' 6"	Draft: 5' 6"	Sail area: 1,216 sq. ft.
	LOD: 53'	Beam: 16' 6"	Tons: 16.3 GRT
	LOA: 55'	Rig height: 50'	Power: 300 HP diesel
	LWL: 44'	Freeboard: 2' 6"	Hull: wood

Built:	1998; Snyder's Shipyard, Ltd.
Certification:	Canadian Coast Guard certified passenger vessel
Crew:	4
Contact:	Hugh MacNeil, VADM (Ret.)
	Avon Spirit Shipyard, Ltd.
	15 Belmont Road, RR # 2
	Newport, NS B0N 2A0, CANADA
	Tel/Fax: 902-757-1718
	E-mail: arhs@glinx.com
	Web site: http://www.glinx.com/users/arhs

Bagheera

the history of yachting and yacht racing. For many years, *Bagheera* was the boat to beat in campaigns from the Great Lakes to the Bahamas, and from as far as Morocco and the Mediterranean, eventually making her way to the West Coast of the US. Throughout the 1980s, *Bagheera* was a familiar sight along the San Diego waterfront, sailing for hire and competing in many classic yacht races.

Now, after an extensive six-month restoration, *Bagheera* is in San Francisco Bay, certified by the US Coast Guard and operated by an experienced, well-trained crew. She can comfortably carry 30 passengers for day sails. Flexible programs and schedules are available for group charters. *Bagheera* sails primarily from the East Bay.

Built in 1924 for Newport, Rhode Island millionaire Marion Eppley, *Bagheera* represents a time when unlimited wealth and classical tastes combined to produce some of the finest vessels in

Flag:	USA
Rig:	Staysail schooner
Homeport/waters:	San Francisco, California: San Francisco Bay, California
Who sails?	School groups from elementary school through college, individuals and families.
Program type:	Sail training for volunteer and paying trainees. Sea education based on informal, in-house programming. Passenger day sails.

Specifications:			
	Sparred length: 72'	Draft: 7' 6"	Tons: 21 GRT
	LOD: 54'	Beam: 14' 6"	Power: 72 HP diesel
	LOA: 55' 6"	Rig height: 65'	Hull: wood
	LWL: 44'	Freeboard: 4'	

Designer:	John G. Alden
Built:	1924; East Boothbay, Maine, Rice Brothers
Coast Guard certification:	Passenger Vessel (Subchapter T)
Crew:	2. **Trainees/passengers: 25-30**
Contact:	Captain Jonathan Friedberg and Becky Waegell
	Bagheera Charters, LLC
	7700 Eagle's Nest Road
	Sacramento, CA 95830
	Tel: 916-683-4915, 1-87-SCHOONER (toll-free)
	E-mail: bagheera@theship.com
	Web site: http://www.bagheera.theship.com

Balclutha

In 1886, Charles Connell & Company built a three-masted, riveted steel ship "to the highest class in Lloyd's registry" near Glasgow, Scotland. Her owner, Robert McMillan, named that 256-foot vessel *Balclutha*—the Gaelic name for Dumbarton, Scotland.

As a deepwaterman, *Balclutha* and a 26-man crew rounded Cape Horn with grain for Great Britain, and later ran Pacific Coast lumber to Australia. Each year as a salmon packet, the vessel carried hundreds of men (with boats and supplies) to the salmon-fishing grounds of Alaska. *Balclutha* even had a brief Hollywood career. The vessel was rescued from decay by the San Francisco Bay Area community in 1954, and has been restored as a memorial to the men and times of the grand days of sail.

Today, *Balclutha* (now designated a National Historic Landmark) is open to the public daily as part of the San Francisco Maritime National Historical Park. Park Service rangers conduct regu-

PHOTO BY STEVE DANFORD

BALCLUTHA

lar tours and present a variety of history programs aboard, and the vessel hosts special events such as the Park's annual Sea Music Concert Series, and maritime-related theater productions.

Flag:	USA
Rig:	Full-rigged ship
Homeport/waters:	San Francisco, California
Program type:	Dockside sea education in maritime history.

Specifications:		
Sparred length: 301'	Draft: 22' 7"	Tons: 1,689 GRT
LOD: 256' 6"	Beam: 38' 6"	Hull: steel
Rig height: 145'		

Designer:	Charles Connell
Built:	1886; Scotland, Charles Connell
Contact:	William G. Thomas, Superintendent
	San Francisco Maritime National Historical Park
	Building E, Fort Mason Center
	San Francisco, CA 94123
	Tel: 415-556-1659; Fax: 415-556-1624
	Web site: http://www.nps.gov/safr

HMS Bee

HMS Bee is a replica of the transport schooner of that name, which operated from the Royal Navy Establishment at Penetanguishene during the years immediately following the War of 1812. The replica was constructed by staff and volunteers of Discovery Harbour, a Provincial historic site on the location of the original naval establishment. Although incorporating modern technology, *HMS Bee* is a faithful reproduc-tion of an early 19th-century naval vessel. Both her exterior and interior reflect the realities of life under sail in that era. She shares the unique distinction of carrying a Warrant from the modern Royal Navy to use the prefix "HMS" with *HMS Tecumseth*, a replica vessel which also operates from Penetanguishene.

Today, the vessel is operated by a nonprofit corporation organized by the volunteers who have sailed her since 1984 when she was launched. Programs focus upon sail training for adults and youths with emphasis on living history. *HMS Bee* sails the waters of Georgian Bay from May to October each season on weekends or evening expeditions. She accommodates a maximum of 14 trainees on evening trips, 10 on extended trips.

Flag:	Canada
Rig:	Gaff schooner
Homeport/waters:	Penetanguishene, Ontario, Canada: Georgian Bay and upper Great Lakes
Who sails?	Individuals and groups
Season:	May to October
Cost:	Evening expeditions, $20, weekend expeditions, $200
Program type:	Living history and seamanship. Affiliated institutions include the Discovery Harbour Provincial Historical Site.

Specifications:	Sparred length: 78'	Draft: 5' 6"	Sail area: 1,672 sq. ft.
	LOA: 48' 6"	Beam: 14' 6"	Tons: 25 GRT
	LWL: 42'	Hull: GRP and wood	Power: 90 HP diesel

Certification:	Operates under the Canadian Sail Training Association guidelines
Designer:	Steve Killing
Built:	1985; Penetanguishene, Ontario, Canada, Charlie Allen
Crew:	5 officers and leading hands. **Trainees:** 14
Contact:	Marine Heritage Association
	Po Box 353
	Midland, ON L4R 4L1, CANADA
	Tel: 705-527-7771
	E-mail: mainstay@csolve.net

Bermuda Sloop Foundation

The Bermuda Sloop Foundation is a nonprofit organization that is planning to build a 90-foot reproduction of a Bermuda-rigged schooner to be used for sail training for Bermuda's youth. The primary missions of the foundation are to enhance and expand local opportunities for character development, teamwork, and community citizenship for youth through outdoor leadership and experience, and to teach Bermuda's maritime history to her people and visitors.

The vessel will be built over two years as a public event, with the hull to be launched in June 2000 to coincide with Tall Ships 2000® Bermuda.

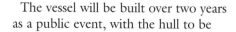

Flag:	Bermuda
Rig:	Bermuda schooner, three-masted
Homeport/waters:	Dockyard, Bermuda: coastal Bermuda
Who sails?	Students from middle school through college and individuals under 25.
Season:	Year-round
Cost:	$2,400 per sponsored team of eight
Program type:	Sail training for volunteer trainees. Sea education in maritime history in cooperation with organized groups. Dockside interpretation in homeport and during ports visits.

Specifications:	LOD: 85' 4"	Draft: 9' 10"	Sail area: 4,037 sq. ft.
	LWL: 81' 4"	Beam: 20'	Power: twin diesels

Designer:	Tri-Coastal Marine
Certification:	UK MCA Sailing School Vessel
Crew:	3
Contact:	Malcolm Kirkland
	Bermuda Sloop Foundation
	PO Box HM 3200
	Hamilton HM NX, BERMUDA
	Tel: 441-299-5110; Fax: 441-299-6517
	E-mail: marthak@ibl.bm

BERMUDA SLOOP FOUNDATION

Bill of Rights

attitudes that are necessary for the education of today's youth, but difficult to teach in a traditional classroom.

The schooners sail with crews of mariner-educators who encourage the growth of awareness, understanding, communication, and teamwork, along with maturing of the traits of persistence, patience, endurance, courage, and caution.

Topsail can be adjusted to fit the age, interests, and abilities of any participants. Single-day events are for exploration, fun, and an introduction to the sea and sailing. Multi-day programs typically provide a life-changing experience for participants.

The Los Angeles Maritime Institute is the educational affiliate of the Los Angeles Maritime Museum. Through the Topsail Youth Program, the Institute provides character-building sail training adventures for youth. The schooners *Swift of Ipswich* and *Bill of Rights* are learning environments that nurture the development of knowledge, skills, and

The Los Angeles Maritime Museum and all of its affiliates take pleasure in offering hospitality, on an as-available basis, to visiting tall ships and other "educationally significant" vessels.

Flag:	USA
Rig:	Gaff-rigged topsail schooner, two-masted
Homeport/waters:	Los Angeles, California: coastal California and offshore islands.
Who sails?	Referred youth-at-risk and groups catering to students and adults.
Season:	Year-round
Program type:	Educational

Specifications:			
	Sparred length: 136'	Draft: 10'	Sail area: 6,300 sq. ft.
	LOD: 94'	Beam: 23'	Tons: 95 GRT
	LOA: 129'	Rig height: 100'	Power: 210 HP diesel
	LWL: 85'	Freeboard: 5' 8"	Hull: wood

Designer:	McCurdy, Rhodes & Bates
Built:	1971; South Bristol, Maine, Harvey F. Gamage
Coast Guard certification:	Passenger Vessel (Subchapter T)
Crew:	5 (day); 8 (overnight); 5 instructors. **Trainees:** 52 (day sails); 39 (overnight)
Contact:	Captain Jim Gladson
	Los Angeles Maritime Institute
	Berth 84, Foot of Sixth Street,
	San Pedro, CA 90731
	Tel: 310-833-6055; Fax: 310-548-2055

Black Jack

Rebuilt in 1952 from the hull of a 1904 tugboat by the late Captain Thomas G. Fuller, *Black Jack* is an 87-foot brigantine. Carrying 3,000 square feet of sail, the ship is now used as a centerpiece for a sail training program operated on Canada's historic Ottawa River. Up to 30 youth, aged 12 to 16, participate in 12-day sail training programs which depart from Canada's capital city for the river and voyage to an 18-acre wilderness island camp. At the island, trainees live aboard traditional logging barges from where they set out to explore the river. In addition to sailing aboard *Black Jack,* trainees also sail 27-foot traditional Navy Whalers and share a variety of other camp activities.

Thomas Fuller was one of Canada's most decorated war heroes, earning the name "Pirate of the Adriatic" and holding the distinction of the longest time served in offensive war action. His wartime experience taught him the value of instilling confidence and resourceful-ness in our youth through adventure at sea. Captain Fuller founded the nonprofit Bytown Brigantine in 1983 to provide these opportunities to young people.

Flag:	Canada
Rig:	Brigantine
Homeport/waters:	Ottawa, Ontario, Canada: Ottawa River.
Who sails?	Middle school, high school, and college students as well as individuals of student age.
Cost:	$60 per person per day
Program type:	Sail training for paying trainees. Overnight voyages.
Season:	April to October

Specifications:			
	Sparred length: 90'	Draft: 6'	Sail area: 3,000 sq. ft.
	LOD: 68'	Beam: 15'	Tons: 42.25 GRT
	LOA: 87'	Rig height: 80'	Power: 235 HP diesel
	LWL: 57'	Freeboard: 3'	Hull: steel

Built:	1904; Scotland
Crew:	6
Contact:	Gene Carson, Executive Director or Simon A.F. Fuller, President
	Bytown Brigantine, Inc.
	2700 Queensview Dr.
	Ottawa, ON K2B 8H6, CANADA
	Tel: 613-596-6258; Fax: 613-596-5947
	E-mail: tallshipinfo@tallshipsadventure.org
	Web site: http://tallshipsadventure.org

Black Pearl

Built in 1938 by Lincoln Vaughan for his own use, *Black Pearl* was purchased by Barclay H. Warburton III in 1958. Long a believer in the sea as a teacher, Warburton selected the rig as a good one for sail training. In 1972

Warburton sailed the *Black Pearl* to England to participate in that summer's European tall ships race, becoming the first American to do so. On his return to Newport, Warburton founded the American Sail Training Association.

Black Pearl is currently owned and operated by the Aquaculture Foundation, a nonprofit trust formed to promote quality education in marine studies. Her programs take her throughout Long Island Sound, as well as into the North Atlantic, Gulf of Mexico, and Caribbean. At present, the Foundation is engaged in a capital campaign to raise $1.25 million for *Black Pearl*'s complete renovation in time for Tall Ships 2000®.

Flag:	USA
Rig:	Brigantine
Homeport/waters:	Bridgeport, Connecticut: Atlantic Ocean and Caribbean Sea
Who sails?	School and other groups and individuals aged 16 to 65. Affiliated groups include University of Bridgeport, Housatonic Community College, and seven Connecticut school districts.
Season:	May to October
Program type:	Sail training for crew and paying trainees. Sea education in marine science, maritime history, and ecology in cooperation with accredited schools and colleges. Passenger day sails and overnight voyages.

Specifications:			
	Sparred length: 79'	Draft: 9'	Sail area: 2,000 sq. ft.
	LOD: 52'	Beam: 14'	Tons: 28 GRT
	LWL: 43'	Rig height: 63'	Sail number: TS US-33
	Freeboard: 6'	Power: diesel	

Designer:	Edson Schock
Built:	1938; Wickford, Rhode Island, C. Lincoln Vaughan
Crew:	3-4 (day), 4-8 (overnight). **Trainees:** 6
Contact:	Edwin T. Merritt, Executive Director
	The Aquaculture Foundation
	525 Antelope Dr.
	Shelton, CT 06484
	Tel: 203-372-4406; Fax: 203-372-4407
	E-mail: tmerritt@pcnet.com
	Web site: http://www.tallshipblackpearl.org

Blu *Bou*

The original *Bluenose*, launched on March 26, 1921, was a typical Nova Scotian Grand Banks fishing schooner. Built at Lunenburg both for fishing and for the International Fisherman's Trophy series of races between Canada and the US, *Bluenose* was undefeated under her legendary Master, Captain Angus J. Walters of Lunenburg. Her likeness became a national emblem and it is depicted on stamps and the ten-cent coin of Canada. Launched on July 24, 1963, *Bluenose II* was built from the same plans at the same yard and by the same men. The only difference lies in the accommodations for the 18-member crew and the modern navigation and communication instruments. She serves as a goodwill ambassador for the Province of Nova Scotia, participating in tall ship events throughout the Western Hemisphere.

Bluenose II's 12 deckhands receive instructions from the officers in all manners of seamanship. Today she sails in the best *Bluenose* tradition, and all officers and deckhands are encouraged to enhance their skills and certifications.

BLUENOSE II

Flag:	Canada
Rig:	Gaff topsail schooner
Homeport/waters:	Lunenburg, Nova Scotia, Canada: East Coast of Canada and the US.
Who sails?	Individuals and groups. Affiliated institutions include the Fisheries Museum of the Atlantic, Lunenburg; the Maritime Museum of the Atlantic, Halifax; Nova Scotia Nautical Institute, Port Hawkesbury; and the Canadian Navy, Halifax.
Season:	April to November
Cost:	Adults, $20, children under 12, $10 per day
Program type:	Sail training for crew. Passenger day sails. Dockside interpretation.

Specifications:			
	Sparred length: 161'	Draft: 16'	Sail area: 11,139 sq. ft.
	LOD: 143'	Beam: 27'	Tons: 285 GRT
	LWL: 112'	Rig height: 132'	Power: twin 250
	Hull: wood		HP diesels

Designer:	William J. Roué, Halifax, Nova Scotia, Canada
Built:	1963; Lunenburg, Nova Scotia, Canada, Smith & Rhuland Shipyards
Certification:	Canadian Coast Guard certified
Crew:	18
Contact:	Alexa MacKay
	Bluenose II Preservation Trust
	PO Box 1963
	Lunenburg,NS B0J 2C0, CANADA
	Tel: 902-634-1963; Fax: 902-634-1995
	E-mail: ship@bluenose2.ns.ca
	Web site: http://www.bluenose2.ns.ca

ty *Sinking* ✓

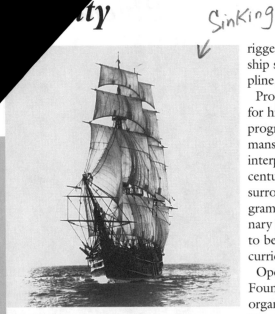

Built for the 1962 movie, "Mutiny on the Bounty", the *Bounty*'s mission is to provide an environment for learning while experiencing life at sea under sail. The challenge of life on board a square-rigged sailing vessel helps build leadership skills, self-confidence, self-discipline, self-esteem, and teamwork.

Programs include cadet sail training for highly motivated teens, an adult program to preserve 18th-century seamanship skills under sail and a dockside interpretive program to showcase 18th-century maritime history and the facts surrounding the famous mutiny. A program in development is a multi-disciplinary program for school-aged children to be integrated with the local school curriculum.

Operated by the Tall Ship Bounty Foundation, a nonprofit educational organization, *Bounty* sails throughout New England, Canada, and the Great Lakes in the summer. In the winter she travels to Florida and sails the Gulf of Mexico and the Caribbean.

Flag:	USA
Rig:	Full-rigged ship, three-masted
Homeport/waters:	Fall River, Massachusetts: New England to Canada (summer), Florida and Gulf of Mexico (winter).
Who sails?	Students, individuals, and groups of all ages
Season:	Year-round
Program type:	Sail training for paying trainees. Sea education in marine science, maritime history, and ecology in cooperation with organized groups and as informal, in-house programming. Passenger overnight passages. Dockside interpretation during port visits.

Specifications:			
	Sparred length: 169'	Draft: 13'	Sail area: 10,000 sq. ft.
	LOD: 120'	Beam: 30'	Tons: 412 GRT
	LOA: 130'	Rig height: 115'	Power: twin 200 HP diesels
	Hull: wood		

Designer:	The British Admiralty
Built:	1960; Lunenburg, Nova Scotia, Smith & Rhuland
Coast Guard certification:	Uninspected Vessel
Crew:	18. **Trainees/passengers:** 12
Contact:	Normand Futoransky, President
	Tall Ship Bounty Foundation, Inc.
	PO Box 990
	Fall River, MA 02722
	Tel: 508-673-3886; Fax: 508-672-4448
	Web site: http://www.tallshipbounty.org

Bowdoin

→ Sails to the Arctic with Maine maritime

The schooner *Bowdoin* is the flagship of Maine Maritime Academy's sail training fleet, and the official sailing vessel of the state of Maine. Built in 1921 specifically for cruising in Arctic waters, she is one of the strongest wooden vessels ever constructed. Between 1921 and 1954 she made 26 voyages to the far north under the command of her first master, explorer Donald B. MacMillan.

Today, with the characteristic ice barrel on her foremast, *Bowdoin* serves the students of the Maine Maritime Academy and the educational community of New England with a broad range of programs in seamanship, ocean studies, and curriculum development. Offerings begin at the high school level, and range from cruises on Penobscot

PHOTO BY TOM STEWART

Bay to extended passages to Greenland and Labrador. These semi-annual cruises represent a unique opportunity in the world of sail training.

Flag:	USA
Rig:	Schooner
Homeport/waters:	Castine, Maine: Gulf of Maine, Canadian Maritimes
Who sails?	School groups from high school through college as well as individuals of all ages. Affiliated institutions include the Maine Maritime Academy.
Season:	May to October
Cost:	$1,500 group rate per day (charter)
Program type:	Sail training for professional crew and paying trainees. Fully accredited sea education in marine science, maritime history, and ecology as well as informal, in-house programming. Passenger overnight passages. Limited dockside interpretation during port visits.

Specifications:			
	Sparred length: 100'	Draft: 10'	Sail area: 2,900 sq. ft.
	LOD: 83'	Beam: 20'	Tons: 66 GRT
	LOA: 88'	Rig height: 70'	Power: 190 HP diesel
	LWL: 72'	Freeboard: 4'	Hull: wood

Designer:	William Hand
Built:	1921; East Boothbay, Maine, Hodgdon Brothers Shipyard
Coast Guard certification:	Sailing School Vessel (Subchapter R), Passenger Vessel (Subchapter T)
Crew:	6. **Trainees:** 40 (day), 11 (overnight)
Contact:	Verge Forbes, Program Coordintor, SSV *Bowdoin*
	Maine Maritime Academy
	Castine, ME 04420
	Tel: 207-326-2212; Fax: 207-326-2218
	E-mail: vforbes@bell.mma.edu
	Web site: http://209.222.220.16/mma/Bowdoin/TheArcticSchooner.htm

BOWDOIN

Brilliant

One of the finest sailing vessels ever built and a veteran of several Bermuda races and transatlantic voyages, *Brilliant* was donated to Mystic Seaport in 1953. Today she provides the adventure of saltwater sail training plus the practical applications of safety, seamanship, and navigation. Aboard *Brilliant*, participants are the crew, performing the ship's work, including steering, sail handling, cooking, and cleaning under the direction of the captain and mate.

Brilliant's 2000 season will feature Tall Ships 2000® Race Legs and other voyages. Apply now for these passages:

July 13-19: New London to Boston to Halifax

July 21-August 24: Halifax to Amsterdam

September 3-13: Holland to England via France

September 17-27: England to Ireland

October 1-11: Ireland to Lisbon via France/Spain

October 22-November 1: Lisbon to Canary Islands via Madeira

November 18-December 9: Canaries to Antigua

Flag:	USA
Rig:	Gaff schooner, two-masted
Homeport/waters:	Mystic, Connecticut: New England, Nova Scotia, Chesapeake Bay.
Who sails?	Transatlantic and Europe 2000, ages 18-25. Participants must be physically fit, agile, and competent swimmers. Affiliated institution is Mystic Seaport.
Season:	May to October.
Cost:	$1,400 and up for *Brilliant* 2000 trips. Financial assistance is available.
Program type:	Sail training with paying trainees. Sea education in cooperation with organized groups such as Scouts, based on informal, in-house programming.

Specifications:	Sparred length: 74'	Draft: 9'	Tons: 30 GRT
	LOD: 61' 6"	Beam: 14' 8'	Power: 97 HP diesel
	LOA: 61' 6"	Rig height: 81'	Hull: wood
	LWL: 49'		

Designer:	Sparkman & Stephens
Built:	1932; City Island, New York, Henry B. Nevins
Coast Guard certification:	Sailing School Vessel (Subchapter R), Passenger Vessel (Subchapter T)
Crew:	3 (day), 4 (overnight). **Trainees:** 9-10 (day); 6 (overnight)
Contact:	Brilliant Program, Museum Education Department
	Mystic Seaport, PO Box 6000
	Mystic, CT 06355-0990
	Tel: 860-572-5323; Fax: 860-572-5395
	Web site: http://www.mysticseaport.org/brilliant

Califo

Owned and operated by the nonprofit Nautical Heritage Society, the *Californian* is a recreation of the 1849 Campbell-class Revenue Marine Cutter *C.W. Lawrence*. *Californian*'s sail training programs immerse trainees in a unique and valuable education in which they experience the forces of nature and develop skills that relate directly to life ashore. Self-reliance, teamwork, American history, coastal ecology, and sailing are the cornerstones of the *Californian* programs. The Sea Chest Program provides curriculum materials for classroom use, ship tours, and day sails for elementary school students. High school students can receive academic credit for time spent aboard, and college level programs are also available.

The ship has been designated as the official tall ship ambassador for the state of California. In addition to its coastal sail training programs, the *Californian* has sailed to Hawaii and Canada, and to Mexico to offer humanitarian aid after Mexico's 1986 earthquake.

Flag:	USA
Rig:	Square topsail schooner, two-masted
Homeport/waters:	Long Beach, California: coastal California and Pacific Ocean
Who sails?	School groups and individuals.
Season:	Year-round
Cost:	$100 per person per day
Program type:	Sail training for professional crew, and volunteer, and paying trainees. Sea education includes marine science, maritime history, and ecology in cooperation with other groups, and informal, in-house programming.

Specifications:	Sparred length: 145'	Draft: 9' 5"	Sail area: 7,000 sq. ft.
	LOD: 93' 5"	Beam: 24' 6"	Tons: 130 GRT
	LWL: 84'	Freeboard: 6'	Power: 100 HP diesel
	Rig height: 101'	Hull: wood	

Designer:	Melbourne Smith
Built:	1984; San Diego, California, Nautical Heritage Society
Coast Guard certification:	Passenger Vessel (Subchapter T)
Crew:	8. **Trainees:** 45 (day sails), 16 (overnight)
Contact:	Steve Christman, President
	Nautical Heritage Society
	1064 Calle Negocio, Unit B
	San Clemente, CA 92673
	Tel: 949-369-6773; Fax: 949-369-6892
	E-mail: nhsociety@aol.com
	Web site: http://www.californian.org

melot

The sailing vessel *Camelot* was built in 1961 by American Marine. She was an inspiration and collaboration of two designers: Angelman and Davies. They named the boats Mayflower, *Camelot* is hull # 7. She is professionally maintained and operated by a licensed Coast Guard Captain with more than 20 years experience. *Camelot* is an uninspected vessel that is very well maintained.

Camelot has been used in a variety of programs and activities, from leisure sunset cruises to sail training programs, and to just share the joy of living under sail. The main focus of *Camelot* is in sail training and team building for corporate and government executives. She is perfect for small groups of six or less.

Flag:	USA
Rig:	Gaff-ketch
Homeport/waters:	Hilton Head, South Carolina: East Coast US, Gulf of Mexico, Caribbean.
Who sails?	High school and college groups, individuals, groups, and families.
Season:	Year-round
Cost:	$400 per person per day, $1,200 group rate per day (charter), $2,000 per person per week (minimum of two people)
Program type:	Sail training for paying trainees. Sea education in cooperation with organized groups and as informal, in-house programming. Corporate team building.

Specifications:			
	Sparred length: 54'	Draft: 6' 6"	Sail area: 978 sq. ft.
	LOD: 40'	Beam: 13' 6"	Tons: 22 GRT
	LOA: 54'	Rig height: 53' 6"	Power: diesel
	LWL: 36' 6"	Freeboard: 3'	Hull: Burmese teak

Designer:	Angleman & Davies
Built:	1961; Hong Kong, American Marine
Coast Guard certification:	Uninspected Vessel
Crew:	2. **Trainees/passengers:** 6 (day), 2 (overnight)
Contact:	Captain Armour Rice
	Camelot Excursions
	13862 Lazy Lane
	Fort Myers, FL 33905
	Tel: 941-694-0576
	E-mail: ssavalon@aol.com
	Web site: http://www.mgtaylor.com/camelot

C.A. Thayer

Once, hundreds of sailing schooners carried lumber to San Francisco from Washington, Oregon, and the California Redwood Coast. Built in 1895, *C.A. Thayer* was part of that mighty Pacific Coast fleet. *C.A. Thayer* usually sailed from the E.K. Wood mill in Grays Harbor, Washington, to San Francisco, but she also carried lumber as far south as Mexico, and even ventured offshore to Hawaii and Fiji. Later, the vessel supplied the Alaskan salt-salmon canneries, anchoring out during the summer, then returning in September with the season's catch packed in her hold. From 1925-1950, *C.A. Thayer* carried men north to the Bering Sea cod-fishing grounds. In fact, *C.A. Thayer*'s last voyage in that trade marked the end of commercial sail on the West Coast. Purchased by the State of California in 1957, and transferred to the National Park Service in 1977, this National Historic Landmark is a rare survivor from the days when strong canvas sails billowed over tall deckloads of freshly-milled fir and redwood.

Today, the vessel hosts a slate of

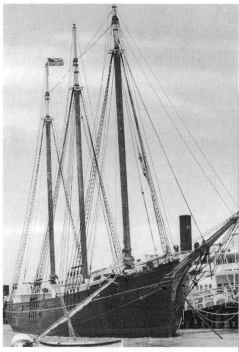

C.A. THAYER

unique school education programs presented by the National Maritime Museum Association, and is open to the public as part of the San Francisco Maritime National Historical Park.

Flag:	USA
Rig:	Schooner, three-masted
Homeport/waters:	San Francisco, California
Program type:	Dockside sea education programs in maritime history.

Specifications:	Sparred length: 219'	Draft: 11' 3"	Tons: 453 GRT
	LOD: 156'	Beam: 36'	Hull: wood
	Rig height: 105'		

Designer:	Hans Bendixsen
Built:	1895; Fairhaven, California, Hans Bendixsen
Contact:	William G. Thomas, Superintendent
	San Francisco Maritime National Historical Park
	Building E, Fort Mason Center
	San Francisco, CA 94123
	Tel: 415-556-1659; Fax: 415-556-1624
	Web site: http://www.nps.gov/safr

Challenge ~~Ugly~~ /worst job ever

inated the Great Lakes. She operates a very unique day sail training program in conjunction with The Pier – Toronto's Waterfront Museum. The cooperative program enables teachers to bring the life of a 19th-century sailor to their students. The *Challenge* voyage is also an opportunity for children to learn about other sail training programs. In 1998 over 6,000 schoolchildren from Canada and the US took part in *Challenge*'s day sail training program.

Challenge is a 96-foot three-masted schooner. Her hull was built on the lines of the famous schooners that once dom-

Flag:	Canada
Rig:	Staysail schooner, three-masted
Homeport/waters:	Toronto, Ontario, Canada: Lake Ontario
Who sails?	Individuals and groups of all ages. Challenge operates a day sail training program in conjunction with The Pier – Toronto's Waterfront Museum.
Season:	April to October.
Program type:	Day sail training program. Vessel also conducts corporate charter and public day sails.

Specifications:			
	Sparred length: 96'	Draft: 8'	Sail area: 3,500 sq. ft.
	LOD: 86'	Beam: 16' 6"	Tons: 76 GRT
	Rig height: 96'	Hull: steel	Power: Volvo 160
	Freeboard: 5'		

Designer:	Bob Johnston
Built:	1984; Port Stanley, Ontario, Kanter Yachts
Certification:	Transport Canada Certified Passenger Vessel
Crew:	6 professional paid crew. **Trainees:** 70 (day sails)
Contact:	Doug Prothero, Master/President
	Great Lakes Schooner Company
	249 Queen's Quay West, Suite 111
	Toronto, ON M5J 2N5, CANADA
	Tel: 416-260-6355; Fax: 416-260-6377
	E-mail: doug@greatlakesschooner.com
	Web site: http://www.greatlakesschooner.com

The Challenge Project

In affiliation with the Wisconsin Lake Schooner Education Association

The *Challenge* will be built to offer physically challenged individuals the opportunity to experience adventure education aboard a tall ship. People of all ages, backgrounds, and abilities will be brought together with a common purpose: to help individuals realize their own potential, to learn how to accept difference, to build confidence, learn teamwork, overcome adversity, and foster an awareness of the marine environment and its importance to our quality of life by tackling challenging new situations. Aboard the *Challenge*, the focus will be on learning from sailing rather than learning to sail. Each member of the crew must act independently yet interdependently.

The vessel's design will incorporate traditional aspects of design while utilizing the latest systems in modern technology

conducive to the needs of challenged individuals. With construction projected to begin in either late 2000 or early 2001, the vessel will be constructed by professional, paid shipwrights. Funding for the project will come from private donations, corporate sponsorships, and foundation grants.

Flag:	USA
Rig:	Schooner
Homeport/waters:	Milwaukee, Wisconsin
Who sails?	Physically challenged and able-bodied children and adults
Cost:	To be determined
Program type:	Educational sailing adventures for all ages and abilities emphasizing sail training, maritime history, and environmental studies.
Specifications:	Sparred length: 124' Draft: 10'
	LOD: 85' Beam: 21'
Designer:	Peter W. Little
Coast Guard certification (planned):	Sailing School Vessel (Subchapter R), Passenger Vessel (Subchapter T)
Contact:	Carrie O'Malley
	Wisconsin Lake Schooner Education Association
	500 North Harbor Drive
	Milwaukee, WI 53202
	Tel: 414-276-7700; Fax: 414-276-8838

Clearwater

←Smelly hippies

symbol for grassroots action. The sloop is owned and operated by Hudson River Sloop Clearwater, Inc., a non-profit membership organization dedicated to defending and restoring the Hudson River and related waterways.

The sloop sails seven days a week, carrying as many as 50 passengers for three to five-hour education programs. Adults and children take part in a wide range of activities involving water life, water chemistry, sail raising, steering, piloting, and more. A US Coast Guard-licensed captain is in charge, and an education specialist directs the program. The permanent crew are complemented by apprentices aged 16 and older, an education assistant, and volunteers. During a month on board, apprentices are given in-depth training in many aspects of sailing and maintaining a wooden ship and in the education program.

The *Clearwater* is the only full-sized replica of the 18th and 19th-century merchant vessels known as Hudson River sloops. Since 1969, *Clearwater* has served both as a platform for hands-on environmental education and as a

Flag:	USA
Rig:	Gaff topsail sloop
Homeport/waters:	Poughkeepsie, NY: Hudson River, New York Harbor and Long Island Sound
Who sails?	Individuals, families, and groups.
Season:	April 15 to November 15 (daily education program); winter maintenance program.
Cost:	$6-$20 per person per day, $40 per week for crew/trainee bunk, $500-$1,500 group rate. Membership is $30 per year for individuals, $10 for low income.
Program type:	Sail training for crew and apprentices. Sea education in marine science, maritime history, and ecology. Passenger day sails. Dockside interpretation during port visits. Clientele includes school groups from elementary school through college and individuals of all ages.

Specifications:			
	Sparred length: 106'	Draft: 6' 6"	Sail area: 4,350 sq. ft.
	LOD: 76' 6"	Beam: 24'	Tons: 69 GRT
	LOA: 76' 6"	Rig height: 108'	Power: 190 HP diesel
	LWL: 67'	Hull: wood	

Designer:	Cy Hamlin
Built:	1969; South Bristol, Maine, Harvey Gamage Shipyard
Coast Guard certification:	Passenger Vessel (Subchapter T)
Crew:	6 (4-month), 3 month-long apprentices. **Trainees:** 50 (day sails)
Contact:	Captain, Hudson River Sloop Clearwater, Inc.
	112 Market St.
	Poughkeepsie, NY 12601-4095
	Tel: 914-454-7673; Fax: 914-454-7953
	E-mail: captain@mail.clearwater.org
	Web site: http://www.clearwater.org

Clipper City

Clipper City is a replica of a Great Lakes lumber schooner of the same name, which sailed from 1854 until 1892. The plans for the *Clipper City* of 1985 were obtained from the Smithsonian Institution and adapted for modern use. *Clipper City* sails Baltimore's Inner Harbor and the waters of the Chesapeake Bay from April through October each year, providing two and three-hour public excursions for tourists in the Baltimore area and private charters for corporate groups and families. She sails up to 21 times each week and has carried over 30,000 passengers in a single season. *Clipper City* is also available for winter charter.

Flag:	USA
Rig:	Gaff topsail schooner
Homeport/waters:	Baltimore, Maryland: Chesapeake Bay (summer), Caribbean Sea (winter)
Who sails?	Individuals and groups
Season:	Year-round

Specifications:			
	LOD: 120'	Draft: 14'	Sail area: 10,200 sq. ft.
	LOA: 158'	Beam: 27' 6"	Tons: 210 GRT
	Hull: steel	Rig height: 135'	Power: CAT 3208 SS

Built:	1985; Jacksonville, Florida
Contact:	William L. Blocher, General Manager
	Clipper City, Inc.
	5022 Campbell Blvd., Suite F
	Baltimore, MD 21236
	Tel: 410-931-6777; Fax: 410-931-6705
	Web site: http://www.sailingship.com

Clipper Patricia

Clipper Patricia was launched as *Aar*, a German-built steel sailing ship, and has remained a freighter since. It has a 400-ton cargo capacity. The ship was fully rebuilt and re-rigged in the 1980s. In winter 1999, topsail schooner yards and sails were added to increase her versitility, along with new electronics and air conditioning.

Going from the North Sea to San Juan in mid-winter 1989, ports of call since include the Caribbean islands, Venezuela, Trinidad, Haiti, Jamaica, and the Dominican Republic. 2000 will see four sail training voyages of 10 to 15 days each in conjunction with cargo operations. Routes are Morgan City, Louisiana to small ports on the Yucatan Peninsula, Honduras, Nicaragua, or St. Maarten, Barbuda, Montserrat, and Dominica in the Caribbean. *Clipper Patricia* carries 12 passengers with cargo year-round. As a cargo vessel, the ship has international inspection certificates under Loadline Convention, the Code of Safety for Caribbean Cargo Ships (promulgated by USCG), and SOLAS. The small number of persons on board means lots of room and opportunity for meaningful participation in the informal operating and educational opportunities on board.

Flag:	Honduras
Rig:	Topsail schooner
Homeport/waters:	Morgan City, Louisiana: Western Caribbean and Gulf of Mexico
Who sails?	Individuals and groups of all ages
Season:	Year-round
Cost:	$150 per person per day
Program type:	Sail training for volunteer and paying trainees. Sea education in marine science and ecology based on informal, in-house programming. Overnight passenger passages.

Specifications:			
	Sparred length: 172'	Draft: 8' 6"	Sail area: 7,400 sq. ft.
	LOD: 158'	Beam: 23' 1"	Tons: 290 GRT
	LOA: 162'	Rig height: 113'	Power: 365 HP diesel
	LWL: 145'	Freeboard: 5' 2"	Hull: steel

Built:	1932; Brake, Germany, Luhring: rebuilt 1979; Newcastle Upon Tyne, England, R.B. Harrison
Certification:	Loadline; Caribbean Cargo Vessel Safety Certification, SOLAS Safety Certificate
Crew:	8. **Trainees/passengers:** 12
Contact:	Hugh G. Lawrence, CEO
	North Star Shipping
	PO Box 1859
	Sausalito, CA 94966
	Tel: 415-332-3582; Fax: 415-332-3996

Columbia

The beautiful Sparkman and Stephens-designed *Columbia* was the first 12-meter to defend the America's Cup. Skippered by legendary sailor and auto racing champion Briggs Cunningham, she was a refinement of the successful 1939 *Vim*. Close competition in the defender's trials of 1958 prepared her for an easy win over British challenger *Spectre*. Now, after many years in Europe, where she received a well-appointed interior and teak decks, *Columbia* has joined the America's Cup Charters 12-meter fleet in Newport, Rhode Island. She is perfect for leisure sails, racing, and team building from any port between Maine and the Chesapeake. Sail aboard a winner—no sailing experience necessary!

Flag:	USA
Rig:	Sloop
Homeport/waters:	Newport, Rhode Island: New England and Chesapeake Bay
Who sails?	Individuals of all ages.
Cost:	$1,800 group rate per day, $60 per person evening sail
Program type:	Sail training for volunteer or paying trainees. Sea education based on informal, in-house programming. Passenger day sails.

Specifications:

LOD: 67'	Draft: 9'	Sail area: 1,800 sq. ft.
LOA: 67'	Beam: 11' 6"	Tons: 28 GRT
LWL: 46'	Rig height: 92'	Power: diesel
Hull: wood		

Designer:	Sparkman and Stephens
Built:	1958; City Island, New York, Nevens
Coast Guard certification:	Passenger Vessel (Subchapter T)
Crew:	3. **Trainees/passengers:** 14
Contact:	George Hill/Herb Marshall
	America's Cup Charters
	PO Box 51
	Newport, RI 02840
	Tel: 401-849-5868; Fax: 401-849-3098
	Web site: http://www.americascupcharters.com

Compass Rose

Named for a vessel in Nicholas Monsarrat's celebrated novel, *The Cruel Sea*, *Compass Rose* is used for a variety of different enterprises. With the appearance of a pirate ship, *Compass Rose* has appeared in several movies and documentaries as well as advertising and commercial films. She has also participated in many tall ship festivals and historical reenactments. Most important, she has been the platform for a number of environmental research projects. One such project was "Track of the Leatherback," a program to collect information about the largest species of turtle, individual specimens of which weigh up to a ton. Electronic transmitters were installed on the leatherbacks—an endangered species—and surveillance gear on *Compass Rose* tracked their habits and movements through the sea.

Compass Rose's design was based on that of an 18th-century American coastal schooner. For a short time, *Compass Rose* was owned by a well-known television personality until the present owner acquired her in 1973.

Flag:	USA
Rig:	Gaff topsail schooner, two-masted
Homeport/waters:	Fort Lauderdale, Florida: New England (summer), Florida coast and Bahamas (winter)
Who sails?	Student groups and individuals of all ages
Season:	Year-round
Program type:	Informal, in-house programming in environmental studies.

Specifications:			
	Sparred length: 57'	Draft: 6'	Sail area: 2,200 sq. ft.
	LOD: 47'	Beam: 14'	Tons: 25 GRT
	LOA: 50'	Rig height: 55'	Power: 85 HP diesel
	LWL: 40'	Freeboard: 5'	Hull: wood

Built:	1969; Nova Scotia, M. Thygeson
Contact:	Robert Entin, Olde Ships Inc.
	PO Box 1339
	Newport, RI 02840
	Tel: 401-849-7988 (summer)
	Robert Entin, Compass Rose, PO Box 22598, Fort Lauderdale, FL 33335
	Tel: 305-524-0096 (winter)
	E-mail: oldeships@aol.com

Concordia

Over 500 international students have joined Class Afloat and sailed the world for an entire academic year. Applications from 11th and 12th-grade coeds are encouraged, and applicants who are seeking a unique and challenging "year out" program are also accepted. Crewmembers are selected on the basis of strong academic profiles, demonstrated strength of character and social suitability, health and fitness, and on their degree of commitment and dedication.

Class Afloat is a nonprofit educational program affiliated with high schools across the United States and Canada. Its mission is to broaden students' understanding of international issues while preparing them for responsible global citizenship in the 21st century.

The concept of "taking the classroom to the world" is intended to encourage self-sufficiency, cooperation, and a clear awareness of other cultures. Each semester, 48 qualifying students work as crew and study aboard the *Concordia*, a modern tall ship.

A fully-certified faculty instructs stu-

CONCORDIA

dents in a full curriculum including social studies and global issues, anthropology, marine biology, and physical education. Optional, non-credit enrichment courses are also offered in seamanship, celestial navigation, and the history and traditions of the sea.

Flag:	Bahamas
Rig:	Barquentine, three-masted
Homeport/waters:	Nassau, Bahamas: worldwide, unrestricted
Who sails?	11th and 12th-grade high school and college students. Affiliated institutions include West Island College (high school), College Marie-Victorian, Hingham High School, I.S.A.M, and A.I.E.S.
Season:	Academic year. Summer programs offered for students and adults
Cost:	$14,900 per student per semester, $25,000 per student per year
Program type:	Full-curriculum academics and marine biology for high school students.

Specifications:			
	Sparred length: 188'	Draft: 13' 6"	Sail area: 10,000 sq. ft.
	LOA: 154'	Beam: 31'	Tons: 495 GRT
	LOD: 152' 6"	Rig height: 115'	Power: 570 HP diesel
	Freeboard: 8'	Hull: steel	

Certification:	Lloyds 100A1 and LMC
Built:	1992; Poland
Crew:	8, 8 instructors. **Trainees:** 48. **Age:** 16-19, coed
Contact:	Sherri Holcman, Director of Admissions and Operations Class Afloat 851 Tecumseh, Dollard des Ormeaux Montreal, QUE H9B 2L2, CANADA Tel: 514-683-9052; Fax: 514-683-1702 E-mail: discovery@classafloat.com Web site: http://www.classafloat.com

USS *Constellation*

The *USS Constellation*, the last all-sail warship built by the US Navy, was launched in 1854 at the Gosport Naval Shipyard in Portsmouth, Virginia. *Constellation* served the country for over ninety years in both military and non-military roles. Before the Civil War, she was flagship of an international squadron charged with the mission of intercepting vessels engaged in the illegal slave trade along the coast of West Africa. While on patrol in these waters, *Constellation* captured three vessels and set free over seven hundred men, women, and children, landing them safely back in Africa. During the Civil War, *Constellation* saw duty in the Mediterranean Sea protecting American interests there, and as part of the Gulf Coast Blockading Squadron.

During her later years the *Constellation* sailed as a training or "practice" ship for the US Naval Academy and then as a stationary training ship at the Naval War College in Newport, Rhode Island. She was last under sail in 1896. Her final role as a commissioned vessel came during World War II when *Constellation* served as Flagship of the Atlantic Fleet.

In 1955, *Constellation* was brought to Baltimore to be preserved as a national shrine. The ship recently has undergone a $9 million reconstruction that has restored the ship to her original 1854 configuration. The ship made her triumphant return to Baltimore's Inner Harbor on July 2, 1999 and she is now open for public tours, offering a wide array of living history and education programs under the management of the Living Classrooms Foundation.

Flag:	USA		
Rig:	Full-rigged ship		
Homeport/waters:	Baltimore, Maryland		
Program type:	Dockside interpretation and educational programming.		
Specifications:	Sparred length: 282'	Draft: 21'	Sail area: 20,000 sq. ft.
	LOD: 176'	Beam: 42'	Hull: wood
	LOA: 200'	Rig height: 165'	Freeboard: 16'
	LWL: 179'		
Designer:	John Lenthall		
Built:	1854; Portsmouth, Virginia, US Navy		
Contact:	Christy Schmitt, Visitor Services Coordinator		
	The Constellation Foundation		
	Pier 1, 301 East Pratt Street		
	Baltimore, MD 21202		
	Tel: 410-539-1797; Fax: 410-539-6238		
	E-mail: webcentral@constellation.org		
	Web site: http://www.constellation.org		

USS *Constitution*

"Old Ironsides" is the oldest commissioned warship afloat in the world. One of six ships ordered by President George Washington to protect America's growing maritime interests in the 1790s, *Constitution* earned widespread renown for her ability to punish French privateers in the Caribbean and thwart Barbary pirates of the Mediterranean. The ship's greatest glory came during the War of 1812 when she defeated four British frigates. During her first engagement, against *HMS Guerriére* in 1812, seamen nicknamed her "Old Ironsides" when they saw British cannonballs glance off her 21-inch-thick oak hull.

In the 1830s, the ship was slated to be broken up, but a public outcry sparked by the publication of a poem by Oliver Wendell Holmes saved her. Over the following century, the ship undertook many military assignments and served as a barracks and as a training ship. She was restored in 1927, and after a coast-to-coast tour, *Constitution* was moored in the Charlestown Navy Yard in 1934 where she is now open year-round for free public tours. She again underwent an extensive restoration from 1992-96, and on July 21, 1997, launching a year-long celebration of her bicentennial, *Constitution* sailed under her own power for the first time in 116 years.

Flag:	USA		
Rig:	Full-rigged ship		
Homeport/waters:	Charlestown, Massachusetts: Boston Harbor		
Program type:	US naval history		
Specifications:	Sparred length: 306'	Draft: 22'	Sail area: 42,710 sq. ft.
	LOD (gun deck): 174' 10"	Beam: 43' 6"	
	Tons: 2,200 GRT	LOA: 204'	Rig height: 189' 2"
	Hull: wood	LWL: 175'	Freeboard: 15'
Built:	1797; Boston, Massachusetts, US Navy, Edmond Hartt Shipyard		
Certification:	Commissioned US Navy ship		
Crew:	48		
Contact:	Commander William F. Foster, Jr., USN, Commanding Officer		
	USS Constitution, Charlestown Navy Yard		
	Charlestown, MA 02129-1797		
	Tel: 617-242-5670; Fax: 617-242-2308		
	Web site: http://www.ussconstitution.navy.mil		

Corban

robust set of sailing skills, featured in three unique programs: Sail Training, Exclusive Sailing Vacations, and Passage Making Training.

In addition to the Bareboat Training Program, designed to impart the skills necessary to confidently bareboat charter a sailing vessel, World Sailing Excursions offers one of the only venues available to learn single-handed sailing techniques. Captain Dan Harper has successfully sailed over 20,000 miles single-handed and developed a very systematic set of skills to aide the single-handed sailor and create a safe environment that brings single or short-handed sailing within reach of the amateur sailor. This program has also received praise from skippers who sail with regular crews stating that their execution of maneuvers became much more fluid with an understanding of single-handed technique. At the root of World Sail Excursions philosophy is a firm doctrine that a sailboat is among the very highest evolutions of form and function.

World Sailing Excursions, Inc. believes the key to realizing the pleasures of sailing lies in a thorough understanding of sailing concepts and developing a

Flag:	USA
Rig:	Sloop
Homeport/waters:	Newport, Rhode Island: international
Who sails?	Individuals and families of all ages
Season:	Year-round
Cost:	$800 per person per week, maximum four trainees
Program type:	Sail training for volunteer or paying trainees. Overnight passenger voyages.

Specifications:			
	Sparred length: 42'	Draft: 7' 10"	Sail area: 1,129 sq. ft.
	LOD: 39'	Beam: 13'	Tons: 17 GRT
	LOA: 42'	Rig height: 64'	Power: 40 HP diesel
	LWL: 33' 9"	Freeboard: 3' 5"	Hull: FRP

Designer:	Ron Holland
Built:	1982; Finland, Nautor Swan
Certification:	Lloyd's of London
Crew:	1. Trainees: 6 (days), 4 (overnight)
Contact:	Captain Dan Harper
	World Sail Excursions, Inc.
	6104 Magnolia Lane
	Lakeland, FL 33810
	Tel: 941-858-4911; Fax: 941-853-3519
	E-mail: worldsail@attglobal.nett
	Web site: http://www.worldsail.net

Coronet

The last great American yacht, *Coronet* won the 1887 transatlantic race against *Dauntless* and completed two round-the-world voyages. From 1895-1897, *Coronet* transported members of the first joint American-Japanese scientific expedition to Japan to view a total eclipse of the sun. After serving a succession of yachting owners, *Coronet* was sold to a missionary and bible-study group called The Kingdom in 1905 to begin a 90-year career as a missionary vessel.

PHOTO BY NATHANIEL STEBBINS

In 1995 *Coronet* was acquired by the International Yacht Restoration School (IYRS), where she serves as their centerpiece restoration project. IYRS is a nonprofit organization founded in 1993 to teach the skills, history, and related sciences in the restoration and maintenance of classic yachts. After her restoration, *Coronet* will have an active life as the IYRS flagship, both dockside and on cruises, tours, charters, and re-creations of her historic voyages. *Coronet* is open to visitors at IYRS in Newport, Rhode Island, from May to October.

CORONET

Flag:	USA		
Rig:	Gaff topsail schooner		
Homeport/waters:	Newport, Rhode Island		
Specifications:	Sparred length: 190'	Draft: 11' 7"	Sail area: 8,300 sq. ft.
	LOD: 133'	Beam: 27'	Tons: 174 GRT
	LOA: 133'	Power: twin diesels	
	LWL: 128'	Freeboard: 6'	Hull: wood
Designer:	Smith & Terry, Christopher Crosby, William Townsend		
Built:	1885; Brooklyn, New York, C & R Poillon		
Coast Guard certification:	Attraction Vessel		
Contact:	John Summers, Curator, *Coronet* Project		
	International Yacht Restoration School		
	449 Thames Street		
	Newport, RI 02840		
	Tel: 401-848-5777; Fax: 401-842-0669		
	E-mail: jsummers@efortress.com		
	Web site: http://www.iyrs.org		

Corsair

Corsair is a sailing whaleboat, an open boat designed to be launched from a larger ship while at sea. She was built at Puget Sound Naval Shipyard in 1939 for use in the Navy's fleet sailing program. As the US prepared for war, the Navy stripped its ships and our whale-boats were sent ashore. The sailing program was never reinstated, and surplus Navy whaleboats found their way to sea scout units around the country, offering thousands of youth the opportunity to learn sailing, seamanship, and teamwork on the water. Of those boats, only a handful remain.

The Sea Scout Ship *Corsair* has been serving the youth of the Bay Area for over 60 years, offering programs that teach sailing, seamanship, and leadership to young men aged 14-21. Her sister ship, *Viking*, offers similar programs for young women. The two ships sponsor many joint activities. In addition to the annual two-week summer cruise in the Sacramento Delta, the Bay Area Sea Scouts organize day sails, races, weekend outings, dances, and regattas. New members are always welcome, both young and adult.

Flag:	USA
Rig:	Ketch
Homeport/waters:	San Francisco, California: San Francisco Bay and tributaries
Who sails?	High school students and individuals. Affiliated institutions include Sea Exploring, Boy Scouts of America, San Francisco Bay Area Council.
Program type:	Sail training for male trainees, aged 14-21. Sea education in marine science and maritime history in cooperation with other groups.

Specifications:	Sparred length: 30'	Draft: 4' 6"	Sail area: 600 sq. ft.
	LOD: 30'	Beam: 8'	Freeboard: 2'
	LOA: 30'	Rig height: 35'	Hull: wood
	LWL: 28'		

Designer:	US Navy
Built:	1939; US Navy, Puget Sound Naval Shipyard
Crew:	Up to 18
Contact:	Nick Tarlson, Acting Skipper
	Sea Scout Ship Corsair
	220 Sansome Street, Ste. 900
	San Francisco, CA 94104
	Tel: 415-956-5700; Fax: 415-982-2528
	E-mail: seascouts@dictyon.com
	Web site: http://www.tbw.net/~chriss/scouts/

Curtain Sails

Corwith Cramer

The *Corwith Cramer* was the first ship built to the USCG's regulations for Sailing School Vessels. The Sea Education Association (SEA), working through ASTA, was instrumental in helping the Coast Guard shape these regulations. The *Cramer* was built in Bilbao, Spain, and it took the largest floating crane in northern Spain to launch her. She is a safe, stable vessel and an excellent platform for SEA's educational and oceanographic research missions. The *Corwith Cramer* is owned and operated by the SEA, Woods Hole, Massachusetts. See also *Westward*.

Flag:	USA
Rig:	Brigantine
Homeport/waters:	Woods Hole, Massachusetts: worldwide
Who sails?	Educators and students who are admitted by competitive selection. Over 150 colleges and universities award credit for SEA programs.
Season:	Year-round
Program types:	Marine and maritime studies including oceanography, nautical science, history, literature, and contemporary maritime affairs. SEA programs include SEA Semester (college level, 12 weeks long, 17 credits), SEA Summer Session (college level, 8 weeks long, 12-credits), and SEA Seminars for high school students and K-12 teachers. All programs include a seagoing component on board the Sailing School Vessels *Westward* and/or *Corwith Cramer*.

Specifications:	LOA: 134'	Draft: 13'	Sail area: 7,380 sq. ft.
	LWL: 87' 6"	Beam: 26'	Power: 500 HP diesel
	Hull: steel	Tons: 158 GRT	

Designer:	Woodin & Marean
Built:	1987; Bilbao, Spain, ASTACE
Coast Guard certification:	Sailing School Vessel (Subchapter R)
Crew:	6 professional mariners and 4 scientists. **Trainees:** Up to 25 in all programs
Contact:	Sea Education Association Inc.
	PO Box 6
	Woods Hole, MA 02543
	Tel: 508-540-3954, 800-552-3633; Fax: 508-457-4673
	E-mail: admission@sea.edu
	Web site: http://www.sea.edu

Cutty Sark

cational opportunities for local school districts and scout groups. Charterers are encouraged, although not required, to lend a hand at running the ship as she slips past the sylvan shores of the San Juan Islands. School groups, however, stand watches, navigate the ship, and sing sea chanteys as they raise the sails, while learning the history, ecology, and lore of these enchanting islands. A ship provides an excellent platform for learning by experience: communication skills are honed and teamwork is established as the rule rather than the exception. The interdependence of shipboard life renders a microcosm of the world which gives the student sailors transferable skills.

Cutty Sark sails the waters of the State of Washington from historic Captain Whidbey Inn on the shores of Penn Cove, Whidbey Island. *Cutty Sark* operates as a commercial charter sailing ship, as well as offering volunteer edu-

Programs can be designed for groups of any type, from gourmet country inn cruises, small business retreats, overnight excursions for middle school, high school, and college students, to day sails for elementary school students.

Flag:	USA
Rig:	Gaff ketch
Homeport/waters:	Coupeville, Washington: Whidbey Island and San Juan Islands, Washington
Who sails?	School groups from elementary school through college. Individuals and families of all ages. Affiliated groups include the Coupeville, South Whidbey, and Sedro Wooley School Districts, and Troop 58 BSA.
Cost:	$350 group rate per day, $250 per day for schools.
Program type:	Sail training for volunteer or paying trainees. Sea education in marine science, maritime history, ecology, and other subjects in cooperation with other groups and as informal, in-house programming.

Specifications:	Sparred length: 52'	Draft: 6' 6"	Sail area: 1,100 sq. ft.
	LOD: 40'	Beam: 13' 6"	Tons: 19 GRT
	LOA: 40'	Rig height: 55'	Hull: teak
	LWL: 33' 4"	Freeboard: 3' 6"	

Designer:	Hugh Angleman/Charlie Davies
Built:	1957; Hong Kong, American Marine
Contact:	Captain John Colby Stone
	Æolian Ventures, Ltd., SV *Cutty Sark*
	2072 West Captain Whidbey Inn Road
	Coupeville, WA 98239
	Tel: 800-366-4097, 360-678-4097; Fax: 360-678-4110
	E-mail: Captjohn@whidbey.net
	Web site: http://www.captainwhidbey.com/cutty.htm

Danielle Louise

The schooner *Danielle Louise* is a Dudley Dix design built by Brian Alcock in 1987 as the *Cape Rose* in Hout Bay, South Africa. Hull construction is of multi-chine steel with the topside chine radiused in sections, giving the appearance of a round bilge boat when on the water. Below the water she was given a modern underbody for good performance and maneuverability in tight harbors. She has proven to be seaworthy, comfortable, and a good boat on all points of sail. Her combination of traditional gaff rig and modern underbody gives her performance and helm response which surprise most who sail on her.

Until 1999, the schooner was privately owned and used as a pleasure cruiser. During that time, the *Cape Rose* was renamed and underwent a thorough refit. *Danielle Louise* is powerful and well-built, and has a great deal of new and upgraded equipment, joinery, and

internal finish work. Her beamy main salon, enhanced by light and air from the many portholes and large hatches below, provide space and comfort for all on board. She is a perfect safe and comfortable platform for the sail training adventure. In 2001, her name will be restored to her original, *Cape Rose*.

Flag:	USA
Rig:	Gaff topsail schooner
Homeport/waters:	Block Island, Rhode Island: Narragansett Bay (summer), Florida Keys, Bahamas (winter)
Who sails?	School groups and individuals of all ages
Cost:	Varies, factors include group enrollment and needs of participants. Sliding scale, inquiries welcomed.
Program type:	Sail training for crew and volunteer and paying trainees. Sea education in marine science, maritime history, and ecology in cooperation with accredited institutions and as informal, in-house programming. Passenger day sails and overnight passages.

Specifications:					
	Sparred Length: 72' 2"		Draft: 6' 5"		Sail area: 1,284 sq. ft.
	LOD: 50' 2"		Beam: 16'		Tons: 32 GRT
	LOA: 52'		Hull: steel		Power: diesel
	LWL: 39' 3"		Freeboard: 5'		Rig height: 56'

Built:	1987; South Africa, Brian Alcock
Designer:	Dudley Dix
Coast Guard certification:	Uninspected Vessel
Crew:	4. **Trainees:** 6
Contact:	Diane Alvarez, Sail into Wellness, Inc. PO Box 865 North Kingstown, RI 02852 Tel: 401-419-6155 E-mail: dluchild@ids.net

Dariabar

Dariabar, launched in 1992, is a custom-built sailing research vessel. Her lines are those of a John Alden schooner and her design incorporates both traditional and modern aspects. She is built from steel with watertight subdivisions and a double bottom. She has a generous lab and workspace amidships with lifting gear above deck. *Dariabar* is presently involved in bioacoustic research and marine mammal observation. She is associated with Pelagikos, a California-based marine research organization. Pelagikos, in conjunction with Mendocino College, conducts courses in marine mammal ecology and behavior aboard *Dariabar*. These classes offer students the opportunity to engage in active research while learning about sailing and life at sea. Pelagikos also employs *Dariabar* as a platform for research conducted by other college and scientific organizations.

Flag:	USA				
Rig:	Schooner				
Homeport/waters:	Sausalito, California: California and northeast Pacific				
Who sails?	College students and adults involved in ocean research				
Program type:	Sea education, marine science, ecology, and bioacoustic research in cooperation with accredited institutions.				
Specifications:	LOA: 84'		Draft: 10'		Sail area: 3,000 sq. ft.
	LOD: 84'		Beam: 18'		Tons: 84 GRT
	LWL: 64'		Rig height: 90'		Power: diesel
	Freeboard: 6'		Hull: steel		
Designer:	John Alden				
Built:	Oakland, California, E.A. Silva				
Coast Guard certification:	Ocean Research Vessel (Subchapter U)				
Crew:	4 (educators). **Trainees:** 30 (day); 10 (overnight)				
Contact:	Dr. Urmas Kaldveer, Executive Director				
	Pelagikos				
	3020 Bridgeway # 155				
	Sausalito, CA 94966				
	Tel: 707-462-5671; Fax: 707-468-3120				
	E-mail: silva@well.com				

Cool, aside from being full of super creepy old men

Denis Su...

(Wc

The Wisconsin Lake Schooner Education Association's schooner *Denis Sullivan* will be launched and complete in the summer of 2000 to operate as a floating, traveling classroom, as well as a goodwill ambassador for the state of Wisconsin. The Association exists to: offer hands-on learning for people of all ages and backgrounds; inspire interest in marine science and maritime heritage; increase appreciation, understanding, and protection of our freshwater resources; and to provide opportunities to develop self-knowledge, teamwork, and leadership. Diverse educational programs are held on Milwaukee's beautiful lakefront and range from one-hour tours to three-hour learning expeditions to weeklong summer Schooner School. These hands-on programs offer new knowledge and appreciation of the Great Lakes. Programs are multi-disci-plinary and draw connections among the ecological, historical, cultural, and social aspects of the Great Lakes. Programs for Professional Development, In-Service for Educators, Outreach Programs, and a year-round co-educational Sea Cadet program are also conducted. Tours are available on a daily basis; group tours by appointment.

DENIS SULLIVAN

Flag:	USA		
Rig:	Schooner, three-masted		
Homeport/waters:	Milwaukee, Wisconsin: Great Lakes		
Specifications:	Sparred length: 134'	Draft: 8' 9"	Sail area: 8,000 sq. ft.
	LOD: 91'	Beam: 23' 6"	Tons: 100 GRT
	LOA: 103'	Hull: wood	Power: twin diesels
	LWL: 88' 4"		
Designer:	Timothy Graul		
Built:	Under construction; Milwaukee, Wisconsin, Peter Little		
Coast Guard certification:	Sailing School Vessel (Subchapter R), Passenger Vessel (Subchapter T)		
Contact:	Carrie O'Malley		
	Wisconsin Lake Schooner Education Association		
	500 N. Harbor Drive		
	Milwaukee, WI 53202		
	Tel: 414-276-7700; Fax: 414-276-8838		
	E-mail: schooner@execpc.com		
	Web site: http://www.wis-schooner.org		

...va Ruci

in the Indonesian Navy. *Dewa Ruci* was built in 1952 by H.C. Stulchen and Son, Hamburg, Germany. After being launched in 1953, she was sailed to Indonesia by the Indonesian Navy. Since then the ship has served the Indonesian Navy as a sail training vessel and a successful ambassador of goodwill for the people of Indonesia. *Dewa Ruci*'s name comes from a Hindu epic play: Dewa Ruci is the name of a character representing the God of truth and courage.

Dewa Ruci, the beautiful barquentine flying the red and white (the colors of Indonesia's flag), is the largest tall ship

DEWA RUCI

Flag:	Indonesia
Rig:	Barquentine
Homeport/waters:	Surabaya, Indonesia: Indonesian waters, Indian Ocean, Pacific Ocean
Who sails?	Cadets of the Indonesian Naval Academy
Season:	Year-round
Program type:	Sail training and sea education for Indonesian Naval cadets.

Specifications:			
	Sparred length: 191'	Draft: 13'	Sail area: 11,738 sq. ft.
	LOD: 163' 1"	Beam: 31'	Tons: 847 GRT
	LOA: 165'	Rig height: 119' 7"	Power: 986 HP diesel
	LWL: 138' 4"	Freeboard: 15' 1"	Hull: steel

Built:	1952; Hamburg, Germany, H.C. Stulchen & Sohn
Certification:	Indonesian Sailing School Vessel
Crew:	70. **Trainees:** 80
Contact:	(1) Commanding Officer, *Dewa Ruci*, KRI Dewa Ruci – Sabatan – Armartim – Ujung, Surabaya 60155, INDONESIA Tel: 62-31-3294000; Fax: 62-31-3294171 (2) Indonesian Naval Attaché, Defense Attaché Office 2020 Massachusetts Avenue, NW Washington, DC 20036

Distant Star

Distant Star will conduct a mix of sail training programs, including at-risk youth intercession and middle and junior high school programs. Additionally, adventure vacation opportunities are available. Programs will focus on team and character building while teaching traditional seamanship and the sailor's arts in the unique setting of a traditional, square-rigged vessel. In port and underway, the ship will simulate the atmosphere of the early American Navy, depicting the life aboard ships of that era and passing on sea-going military tradition and heritage within a fun and challenging historical framework.

Distant Star underwent repairs in Port Townsend, Washington, and arrived in her new homeport of San Diego, California, in fall 1998. The Foundation is seeking US Coast Guard certification as a Sailing School Vessel.

Flag:	USA
Rig:	Brigantine
Homeport/waters:	San Diego, California: Pacific Coast of North America
Who sails?	School groups from elementary through high school and individuals of all ages.
Program type:	Sail training with paying trainees. Team and character building within a framework of maritime history, sea education, and naval science programs. Education programs featuring research and tailored multi-disciplinary subjects as requested.

Specifications:	LOD: 46'	Draft: 6'	Sail area: 1,490 sq. ft.
	LOA: 54'	Beam: 13'	Tons: 27 GRT
	LWL: 36'	Rig height: 45'	Power: diesel
	Hull: wood		

Designer:	James D. Rosborough
Built:	1978; James D. Rosborough
Coast Guard certification	(planned): Sailing School Vessel (Subchapter R)
Crew:	2-4. **Trainees:** 6-10 (day), 4 (overnight)
Contact:	Tom Wing
	Continental Navy Foundation
	11054 Melton Court
	San Diego, CA 92131
	Tel: 858-271-4890; Fax: 858-271-4890
	E-mail: tmwing@sprintmail.com

Dorothea

For generations, Nova Scotians have traveled the coast in small boats, learning wisdom and courage from the sea. The Nova Scotia Sea School takes young people to sea in small boats today for fun and personal challenge. The Sea School teaches traditional seamanship and navigation, and gives teenagers the chance to discover the Nova Scotia coast, and to discover themselves.

Young people 14-18 years old, male and female, from all over North America and Europe sail on voyages ranging from five days to three weeks, living in an open boat powered by sails and oars. They explore the coast, live with the elements, visit the islands, and learn to take command of the boat, and of their lives. As one student said, "I don't always understand things at home—out here they make sense."

Flag:	Canada
Rig:	Ketch
Homeport/waters:	Halifax, Nova Scotia, Canada: coastal Nova Scotia
Who sails?	Individuals and groups associated with accredited schools and colleges as well as summer camps and other youth organization participation.
Cost:	$85 per person per day
Program type:	Sail training with paying trainees. Sea education programs in marine science, maritime history, and ecology, and informal, in-house programming.

Specifications:	LOD: 28' 6"	Draft: 5'	Hull: wood
	LOA: 28' 6"	Beam: 7'	Tons: 4 GRT

Designer:	E.Y.E. Marine
Built:	1995; Halifax, Nova Scotia, Canada
Crew:	1 (day), 2 (overnight). **Trainees:** 10
Contact:	Crane W. Stookey, Executive Director
	The Nova Scotia Sea School
	PO Box 546, Central C.R.O.
	Halifax, NS B35 2S4, CANADA
	Tel: 902-423-7284; Fax: 902-423-7241
	E-mail: nsseaschool@ibm.net
	Web site: http://www.seaschool.org

Eagle, USC

One of five sister ships built for sail training in Germany in the 1930s, *Eagle* was included in reparations paid to the United States following World War II and the Coast Guard took her over as a training ship. Aboard the *Eagle*, cadets have a chance to put into practice the navigation, engineering, and other skills they are taught at the Coast Guard Academy. As underclassmen, they fill positions normally taken by the enlisted crew of a ship, including watches. They handle the more than 20,000 square feet of sail and more than 20 miles of rigging. Over 200 lines must be coordinated during a major ship maneuver, and the cadets must learn the name and function of each. As upperclassmen, they perform officer-level functions. For many, their tour of duty aboard *Eagle* is their first experience of life at sea; but it is here that they learn to serve as the leaders they will one day become in the Coast Guard.

PHOTO BY LT. NEIL D. RUENZEL, USGC

EAGLE, USCG

Flag:	USA
Rig:	Barque, three-masted
Homeport/waters:	New London, Connecticut: Atlantic Ocean, Caribbean, and Pacific Ocean
Who sails?	US Coast Guard Academy Cadets, US Coast Guard Officer Candidates, and other Coast Guard personnel.
Season:	Year-round
Cost:	Included in school tuition
Program type:	Seamanship

Specifications:	Sparred length: 295'	Draft: 17'	Sail area: 22,245 sq. ft. (23 sails)
	LOA: 266' 8"	Beam: 40'	Tons: 2,186 GRT
	LWL: 231'	Rig height: 147' 4"	Power: 1,000 HP diesel
	Hull: steel		

Built:	1936; Hamburg, Germany, Blohm & Voss
Contact:	Commanding Officer, USCG Barque Eagle (WIX 327)
	15 Mohegan Avenue
	New London, CT 06320
	Tel: 860-444-8595; Fax: 860-444-8445
	E-mail: k.boda/cgceagle@internet.uscg.mil
	Web site: http://www.cga.edu/eagle/default.html

SAIL TALL SHIPS!

f Pembroke   British

1979 and she underwent a complete restoration, which commenced in 1985. In 1994 she was commissioned as the three-masted wooden barque that she is today.

All of Square Sail's ships are fully commissioned and work throughout the year. When not filming, they have a regular sailing program, giving people the chance to experience traditional square-rig sailing first-hand. These voyages typically run between four and seven days, and occasionally longer. They are either based from Square Sail's homeport of Charlestown, Cornwall, UK, or they work around the annual schedule offering voyages between the various ports.

The second-largest vessel of the Square Sail fleet was originally named *Orion* and built in Pukavik, Sweden, in 1945 as one of the last three-masted sailing schooners. She traded timber in the Baltic and British East Coast until being laid up in Thisted, Denmark in 1974. Square Sail purchased her in

Square Sail runs an annual course from February to October where trainees are given the opportunity to learn the skills associated with sailing these ships, and in addition to maintenance and shore-based instruction, they form part of the regular crew throughout the season.

Flag:	UK
Rig:	Barque, three-masted, single topsail
Homeport/waters:	Charlestown Harbour, St. Austell, Cornwall, UK: UK and Europe
Who sails?	Individuals of all ages and families. Affiliated institutions include Falmouth Marine School and Cornwall College.
Cost:	$200 per person per day, $8,000 group rate per day (charter)
Program type:	Sail training for professional crew, volunteer and paying trainees. Sea education in maritime history in cooperation with accredited institutions and as informal, in-house programming. Worldwide film work and corporate charters.

Specifications:		
Sparred length: 145'	Draft:10' 6"	Sail area: 9,500 sq. ft.
LOD: 115'	Beam: 24'	Tons: 174 GRT
LOA: 145'	Rig height: 93'	Power: 300 HP diesel
LWL: 108'	Freeboard: 7'	Hull: oak on oak

Built:	1948, Pukavik, Sweden, Albert Svenson
Certification:	MCA Oceans (UK)
Crew:	15. **Trainees/passengers:** 50 (day sails), 12 (overnight)
Contact:	Chris Wilson, Marketing Manager, Square Sail
	Charlestown Harbour
	St. Austell, Cornwall PL25 3NJ, UNITED KINGDOM
	Tel: 44-1726-70241; Fax: 44-1726-01839
	E-mail: sextant@cwcom.net
	Web site: http://www.square-sail.com

Eastwind

Schooner *Eastwind*, built in Albion, Maine, is the sixth schooner built by Herb and Doris Smith. The other five were all named *Appledore*, two of which the Smiths sailed around the world. *Eastwind* is built of native white oak and planked with Port Orford cedar. She is fastened with copper rivets and bronze screws. The Smiths departed in November 1999 for South America and Africa, and will return in 2001 to Boothbay Harbor, Maine, where they will take passengers in the summer.

PHOTO BY BOB DRAKE

Flag:	USA
Rig:	Schooner
Homeport/waters:	Boothbay Harbor, Maine: Boothbay Harbor (summer), southern waters (winter)
Who sails?	Individuals of all ages
Cost:	$20 per person per two-hour sail
Program type:	Sail training for paying passengers. Dockside interpretation while in homeport.

Specifications:			
	Sparred length: 64'	Draft: 6' 6"	Sail area: 1,600 sq. ft.
	LOD: 56'	Beam: 14'	Tons: 31 GRT
	LOA: 56'	Rig height: 75'	Hull: wood
	LWL: 47'	Freeboard: 4'	

Designer:	McIntosh
Built:	1999; Albion, Maine, Herb Smith
Coast Guard certification:	Passenger Vessel (Subchapter T)
Crew:	1
Contact:	Captain Herb Smith
	Eastwind Cruises
	20 Commercial St.
	Boothbay Harbor, ME 04538
	Tel: 207-633-0025

Ebb Tide

Ebb Tide is a delightful topsail schooner, built by Peter Legnos of Legnos Boatbuilding in Groton, Connecticut. Forty feet overall, *Ebb Tide* is one of the smallest and one of the few trailerable square-riggers, and also one of the few fiberglass boats to carry square sails. Small but quick, and undefeated in her division at the marvelous Gloucester schooner races, *Ebb Tide* carries a complement of three ten-gauge and one four-gauge cannons.

Ebb Tide participates in classic and antique vessel events in the Boston area, as well as reenactment events such as the birthday of the United States Navy in Beverly, Massachusetts and the birthday of the United States Coast Guard in Newburyport, Massachusetts. *Ebb Tide* is privately owned and does not offer a formal sail training program, but is always eager for crew for reenactments or classic sailboat events.

Flag:	USA
Rig:	Topsail schooner
Homeport/waters:	Gloucester, Masschusetts: Gloucester and North Shore waters
Who sails?	Fund development personnel from area nonprofit institutions, Salem Maritime National Historic Site, Forbes Museum, and trainees involved in military reenactments and classic sailing events.
Season:	April to November
Program type:	Sail training for crew and apprentices. Sea education in maritime history in the form of military reenactments and gunnery practices. Dockside interpretation.

Specifications:

Sparred length: 40'	Draft: 4' 6"	Tons: 4.5 GRT
LOA: 40'	Beam: 10' 3"	Power: 6 HP diesel
LOD: 30'	Freeboard: 2'	Hull: fiberglass

Built:	1975; Groton, Connecticut, Legnos Boatbuilding
Crew:	2. **Trainees:** 4 (day), 4 (overnight).
Contact:	Captain Keating Willcox
	Longmeadow Way – Box 403
	Hamilton, MA 01936-0403
	Tel: 508-468-3869; Fax: 508-468-3869
	E-mail: kwillcox@shore.net
	Web site: http://www.shore.net/~kwillcox/spirit.html

Edna Berry

(Work in Progress)

The schooner *Edna Berry* was originally built as a Delaware Bay Oyster schooner in 1928. Later unrigged and motorized, she commercially fished as a power clam dredger until four years ago. Downeast Windjammer Cruises is undertaking a major restoration of the *Edna Berry*, rebuilding her wood hull and restoring her with a schooner rig. In 1999 a program was started combining apprentices and skilled shipwrights in a learning experience with the end goal of reviving a historic vessel.

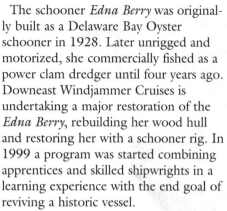

Captain Steve Pagels has restored and built a number of traditional schooners. He reminds us that restoring a vessel is hard, grueling, and often dirty work. Rewards, however, are satisfaction of what is accomplished, the scenic Maine coast as a work place, and the occasional chance to sail on the four-masted schooner *Margaret Todd* or the 1911 schooner *Sylvina W. Beal*. When completed, the *Edna Berry* will sail Maine waters in the summer and the Chesapeake Bay in the fall and winter.

Flag:	USA				
Rig:	Schooner				
Homeport/waters:	Bar Harbor, Maine: Maine and Chesapeake Bay				
Specifications:	Sparred length: 115'		Draft: 5'		Sail area: 4,000 sq. ft.
	LOD: 85'		Beam: 22'		Tons: 61 GRT
	LOA: 90'		Rig height: 85'		Hull: wood
Built:	1928; Leesburg, New Jersey				
Contact:	Captain Steven F. Pagels				
	Downeast Windjammer Cruises				
	PO Box 28				
	Cherryfield, ME 04622				
	Tel: 207-546-2927 (winter), 207-288-4585 (summer); Fax: 207-546-2023				
	E-mail: decruise@midmaine.com				
	Web site: http://www.downeastwindjammer.com				

EDNA BERRY

Elissa   Texan.

she waited a cable's length from the scrap yard.

Today, *Elissa* remains one of the hallmarks of maritime preservation. Lovingly restored and maintained, she sails again, continuing a far longer life than most ships are ever granted. She tests her readiness annually in a series of sea trials amid the oilrigs and shrimpers off Galveston Island. Working under professional officers, her volunteer crew completes an extensive dockside training program. As funds allow, she makes longer voyages, such as her journey to New York to participate in Operation Sail 1986/Salute to Liberty.

In 1975, a rusted iron hulk lay in the waters of Piraeus, Greece. Nearly 100 years earlier, she had sailed the world's oceans as a proud square-rigged sailing ship. Cut down, leaking, and decrepit,

Flag:	USA
Rig:	Barque, three-masted
Homeport/waters:	Galveston, Texas: coastal waters near Galveston
Who sails?	School groups from middle school through college and individuals of all ages.
Season:	April to November
Cost:	Volunteers and guests only
Program type:	Sail training for crew and apprentices. Sea education in maritime history based on informal, in-house training. Dockside interpretation.

Specifications:			
	Sparred length: 205'	Draft: 10'	Sail area: 12,000 sq. ft.
	LOA: 155'	Beam: 28'	Tons: 411 GRT
	LOD: 150'	Rig height: 110'	Power: 450 HP diesel
	Freeboard: 10'	Hull: iron	

Built:	1877; Aberdeen, Scotland, Alexander Hall and Sons Yard
Coast Guard certification:	Cargo and Miscellaneous Goods (Subchapter I)
Crew:	40. **Trainees:** 85 (day)
Contact:	Kurt Voss, Director
	Texas Seaport Museum/Galveston Historical Foundation
	Pier 21, No. 8
	Galveston, TX 77550
	Tel: 409-763-1877; Fax: 409-763-3037
	E-mail: elissa@galvestonhistory.org
	Web site: http://www.tsm-elissa.org

Elizabeth II

Built with private funds to commemorate the English colonization of America's 400th anniversary, *Elizabeth II* is named for a vessel that sailed from Plymouth, England, on the second of the three Roanoke voyages sponsored by Sir Walter Raleigh between 1584 and 1587. She probably carried marines, colonists, and supplies to establish a military garrison to support England's claim to the New World.

Elizabeth II's sail training program teaches volunteer crew about America's 16th-century maritime heritage. In addition to classroom instruction and dockside training, crew members participate in the care and maintenance of wooden vessels. The 24-foot ship's boat, *Silver Chalice*, is used

for underway training and travels with *Elizabeth II* when she sails. Voyages are scheduled during the spring and fall seasons. Sponsorship for the volunteer crew program is provided by the nonprofit Friends of Elizabeth II, Inc.

ELIZABETH II

Flag:	USA
Rig:	Barque, three-masted (lateen mizzen)
Homeport/waters:	Manteo, North Carolina: inland sounds of North Carolina
Who sails?	Volunteer crew
Season:	Spring and fall
Cost:	$8 for adults, $5 students (dockside visits), free for children under 6 accompanied by an adult
Program type:	Sail training for volunteer crew and apprentices. Dockside interpretation.

Specifications:	Sparred length: 78'	Draft: 8'	Sail area: 1,920 sq. ft.
	LOA: 68' 6"	Beam: 16' 6"	Tons: 97 GRT
	LOD: 55'	Rig height: 65'	Hull: wood
	LWL: 59'		

Designer:	W.A. Baker and Stanley Potter
Built:	1983; Manteo, North Carolina, O. Lie-Nielsen, Creef-Davis Shipyard
Age:	16+
Contact:	Captain Horace Whitfield
	Roanoke Island Festival Park
	One Festival Park
	Manteo, NC 27954
	Tel: 252-475-1500; Fax: 252-475-1507
	Web site: http://www.roanokeisland.com

Empire Sandy *used to be a tug boat.*

As Canada's largest sailing ship, the *Empire Sandy* cruises Toronto Harbor and the Great Lakes in summer and Nassau, Bahamas in winter. The *Empire Sandy* is certified by Transport Canada and the Bahamian government to carry up to 275 passengers, and offers sailing cruises and dockside receptions to the public, corporations, and charitable organizations. In Canada, the *Empire Sandy* is a popular attraction at numerous waterfront festivals and events. During her passages between Canada and the Bahamas, the *Empire Sandy* offers a unique sail training program where up to 30 participants learn basic seamanship, sailing, navigation, and pilotage from her professional crew. The *Empire Sandy* makes weekly port visits along the eastern seaboard during her passages north and south and is an ideal venue for hosting dockside promotional events, charity fundraisers, and arts and entertainment events. While in the Bahamas, she sails from Nassau on three and four-hour ocean day sails and dinner charters, pleasing tourists and private groups alike.

Flag:	Canada
Rig:	Schooner
Homeport/waters:	Toronto, Ontario, Canada: Toronto (summer), Nassau, Bahamas (winter)
Who sails?	Students, individuals, and families of all ages.
Season:	Year-round
Cost:	$650 per person per week
Program type:	Sail training for paying trainees. Sea education in cooperation with organized groups and as informal, in-house programming. Passenger day sails. Dockside interpretation during port visits.

Specifications:			
Sparred length: 200'	Draft: 13'	Sail area: 10,000 sq. ft.
LOD: 145'	Beam: 30'	Tons: 338 GRT
LWL: 137'	Rig height: 116'	Power: 400 HP diesel
Hull: steel		

Built:	1943; Willington Quay-on-Tyne, UK
Certification:	Canadian Coast Guard certified passenger vessel, Bahamas "Class A" certificate (passenger vessels)
Crew:	25. **Trainees/passengers:** 60 (day sails), 30 (overnight)
Contact:	Sharon Rogers, Sail Training Coordinator
	Nautical Adventures
	1 Yonge Street, Suite 104
	Toronto, ON M5E 1E5, CANADA
	Tel: 416-364-3244; Fax: 416-364-6869
	E-mail: nautical@yesic.com
	Web site: http://www.valuenetwork.com/nautical

Endeavour is an exact museum standard replica of the ship Captain James Cook used on the first of his three famous voyages. On that voyage, from 1768 to 1771, Cook solved the geography of the Pacific, defeated scurvy, was the first to accurately calculate his longitude at sea, and successfully charted the islands of New Zealand and the east coast of Australia.

Built in Fremantle, Western Australia, from Australian hardwoods and American Douglas Fir, the ship is the result of over five years of painstaking research coordinated by the National Maritime Museum, Greenwich, UK. The original ship was very accurately recorded in the 18th century and hence the replica is virtually a reincarnation of that ship, not a 20th-century designer or historian's view of what she may have been like. The only concessions to the 20th century are modern heads and showers, and electric galley and mess, locker, machinery, and freezer spaces. All of these are housed in what was the capacious hold on the original ship. The crew live, sleep, and work the ship exactly as they did in the 18th century.

Flag:	Australia
Rig:	Full-rigged ship
Homeport/waters:	Sydney, Australia: international
Who sails?	Adults of all ages
Program type:	Sail training for volunteer crew and trainees. Sea education in maritime history based on informal, in-house programming. Passenger day sails.
Cost:	Varies, average $100 per person per day

Specifications:			
	Sparred length: 145' 6"	Draft: 12' 6"	Sail area: 15,800 sq. ft.
	LOD: 105'	Beam: 29' 2'	Tons: 397 GRT
	LOA: 109' 3"	Rig height: 121' 4"	Power: diesel
	LWL: 101' 5"	Freeboard: 13' 6"	Hull: wood

Designer:	David White/Bill Leonard
Built:	1993; Fremantle, Western Australia, HM Bark Endeavour Foundation
Certification:	USL 2A Ocean
Crew:	16. **Trainees/passengers:** 70 (day sails), 40 (overnight)
Contact:	Dominic Hannelly, Sydney Manager
	HM Bark Endeavour Foundation
	Australian National Maritime Museum
	GPO Box 5131, Sydney, NSW, 1042, AUSTRALIA
	Tel: 61-2-9552-7777; Fax: 61-2-9552-2318
	E-mail: domhan@ibm.net
	Web site: http://www.barkendeavour.com.au

ENDEAVOUR

...avour

comfort and safety. She has cruised the waters of Europe, the Mediterranean, the West Indies, the United States, and Canada and has taken part in many regattas, sailing against modern boats as well as classic. Despite her 64 years, *Endeavour* continues true to form in her effortless domination of the racing circuit.

Endeavour is thought by many to be the finest sailing yacht in the world. She has certainly proven herself capable of meeting any challenge and fulfilling every dream. Fellow sailors are invited to sail on *Endeavour* and be a part of sailing history.

Since her re-launching in 1989, *Endeavour* has sailed over 100,000 miles and hosted more than 3,000 guests in

Flag:	USA		
Rig:	Sloop		
Homeport/waters:	Newport, Rhode Island: Narragansett Bay (summer), Caribbean (winter)		
Season:	Year-round		
Cost:	$11,000 per day group rate (charter)		
Specifications:	LOD: 130'	Draft: 15' 8"	Sail area: 9,000 sq. ft.
	LOA: 130'	Beam: 22'	Tons: 162 GRT
	Rig height: 165'	Hull: steel	Power: 400 HP diesel
Designer:	Charles Nicholson		
Built:	1934; England, Camper & Nicholson		
Coast Guard certification:	Passenger Vessel (Subchapter T)		
Crew:	9		
Contact:	Marcia Whitney, Manager		
	J-Class Management,		
	28 Church St.		
	Newport, RI 02840		
	Tel: 401-849-3060; Fax: 401-849-1642		
	E-mail: info@jclass.com		
	Web site: http://www.jclass.com		

Ernestina

On February 5, 1894, a single line in a corner of the *Gloucester Daily Times* recorded an addition to the Massachusetts fishing fleet: "The new schooner for J.F. Wonson and Co. has been named *Effie M. Morrissey*." This marked the birth of a schooner that would become famous as a Grand Banks fisher, an arctic expeditionary vessel under the command of Captain Robert Abrams Bartlett, and as a World War II survey vessel under Commander Alexander Forbes. After a fire in 1946, the *Morrisey* was raised and renamed *Ernestina* to serve in the transatlantic Cape Verdean packet trade. In 1982 she was gifted by the Republic of Cape Verde to the people of the United States as a symbol of the close ties between lands.

The essence of *Ernestina*'s educational mission today extends from the vessel's phenomenal track through history.

Aboard *Ernestina*, learners of all ages use the ship as a platform to study the marine environment and human impacts during structured underway and dockside programs. They gain confidence and self-esteem by learning how to orient themselves in the natural world while solving real-world problems.

Additionally, a membership program presents special sailing opportunities including both day sails as well as multiple-day sails.

Flag:	USA
Rig:	Gaff topsail schooner, two-masted
Homeport/waters:	New Bedford, Massachusetts: East Coast US, Canada (summer); Caribbean and West Africa (winter)
Who sails?	School groups from elementary through college, and individuals of all ages.
Season:	Year-round
Cost:	$125 per person per day, $2,700 group rate or charter per day/$1,600 half-day
Program type:	Sail training for volunteer or paying trainees. Sea education in marine science, maritime history, and ecology in cooperation with accredited schools and colleges, Scouts, and other groups. Passengers carried on day and overnight sails. Dockside interpretation.
Specifications:	Sparred length: 156' Draft: 13' Sail area: 8,323 sq. ft.
	LOD: 106' Beam: 24' 5" Tons: 98 GRT
	LWL: 94' Rig height: 115' Power: 259 HP diesel
	LOA: 112' Hull: wood
Designer:	George M. McClain
Built:	1894; Essex, Massachusetts, Tarr and James Shipyard
Coast Guard certification:	Sailing School Vessel (Subchapter R), Passenger Vessel (Subchapter T)
Crew:	11. **Trainees/passengers:** 80 (day), 24 (overnight)
Contact:	Gregg Swanzey, Executive Director
	Schooner Ernestina Commission
	PO Box 2010
	New Bedford, MA 02741-2010
	Tel: 508-992-4900; Fax: 508-984-7719
	E-mail: swanzey@ma.ultranet.com
	Web site: http://www.ernestina.org

Esprit

Esprit was launched in 1995. Honored in 1997 for her work promoting international understanding with mixed 50:50 German/host country crews, she is the only German sail training vessel to win the Cutty Sark Trophy. Since then *Esprit* has sailed as a sail training vessel between England, Portugal, the Lofoten Islands in northern Norway, and Russia, taking part in all European Cutty Sark Tall Ships Races. She will come to Maine in 2000 to bring to Maine youth the same opportunities. *Esprit* is a "cold-molded" wooden boat. Built for safe sailing with good handling qualities and high speed potential, she is easily sailed by novice crews, with her modern rig: gaff fore, Bermuda main. Living on board is comfortable in a bright modern atmosphere—from the galley, mess, and state-of-the-art navigation area there is a panoramic view of the sea. Trainee berths are in three four-berth cabins, each with its private head. *Esprit* is owned by Bremner Bootsbau Vegesack (BBV). BBV seeks to teach teamwork and traditional and contemporary boatbuilding skills, to develop self-confidence through experiential education, and to further international understanding through exchanges of young participants.

Flag:	Germany
Rig:	Schooner, two-masted
Homeport/waters:	Bremen-Vegesack: North Sea, Baltic, and Atlantic
Who sails?	Youth trainees, individuals, and groups.
Cost:	$70 for youth trainees, $110 for trainees over 26 per day
Program type:	Sail training for students, apprentices, and adults as paying trainees.

Specifications:	LOA: 64' 9"	Draft: 9' 9"	Sail area: 1,800 sq. ft.
	Beam: 16' 6"	Hull: wood	Power: 212 HP diesel

Designer:	Volker T. Behr, N.A.
Built:	1995; Bremen, Germany, Bremer Bootsbau Vegesack
Certification:	Constructed to specifications of German Lloyd
Crew:	4. Trainees: 4 (day sails), 12 (overnight)
Contact:	*North Americans*: HANSA Foundation, PO Box 69, North Reading, MA 01864,
	Tel: 781-944 0304; Fax: 781-944 2469,
	E-mail: info@hansafoundation.org
	Web site: http://www.hansafoundation.org
	Others: BBV Sailing, Teerhof 46, D-28199 Bremen, GERMANY
	Tel: 49-421-50-50-37; Fax: 49-421-59-14-00
	E-mail: info@bbv-sailing.de
	Web site: http://www.bbv-sailing.de

Sail to Antarctica on the most badass boat sailing today

The barque *Europa* was built as a light vessel for the German Bight in 1911 at the Stülcken shipyard in Hamburg, Germany. She was rebuilt (1987-1994) into a fine square-rigger by Harry Smit. The ship represents the end of the famous clipper era and is one of the few ships in the world that carries a complete set of studding sails. Down below you will find a romantic atmosphere in the lounge, bar, saloon, and the cabins, all with their own shower and toilet.

All modern necessities for safety and comfort are hidden by the historic appearance. For part of the year, the *Europa* is the official sail training vessel of the Enkhuizen Nautical College, which educates officers and Masters for commercial oceangoing sailing vessels. In 1999 *Europa* sailed in Baltic and other European waters and took part in the STA races. For the year 2000 *Europa* will participate in the complete Tall Ships 2000® series of races and ports events. In September 2000, the ship is preparing for a voyage to Antarctica where it will make trips for individuals during the summer (December-February).

Flag:	The Netherlands
Rig:	Barque, three-masted
Homeport/waters:	Amsterdam, The Netherlands: European waters
Who sails?	High school and college students, individuals and families.
Cost:	$100 per person per day
Program type:	Sail training for paying trainees. Fully accredited sea education in maritime history. Passenger day sails and overnight passages. Dockside interpretation during port visits.

Specifications:	Sparred length: 185'	Draft: 12'	Sail area: 11,000 sq. ft.
	LOD: 143'	Beam: 24'	Tons: 303 GRT
	LOA: 150'	Rig height: 109'	Hull: steel
	LWL: 132'	Freeboard: 4'	

Built:	1911; Hamburg, Germany, Stülcken
Certification:	Bureau Veritas Worldwide
Crew:	12. **Trainees:** 100 (day sails), 50 (overnight)
Contact:	Smit Tallship BV
	Oostelyke Handelskade 1
	1019 BL Amsterdam, THE NETHERLANDS
	Tel: 31-20-463-4129; Fax: 31-20-419-6134
	E-mail: tallship@xs4all.nl

...hnson

...ogress)

The Los Angeles Maritime Institute is constructing two 90-foot brigantines. The vessels will be named *Irving Johnson* and *Exy Johnson* in honor of the Johnsons and their life-long commitments to character-building sail training. The voyages of Irving (1905-1991) and Electa (b. 1909) Johnson aboard *Yankee* are well known by nearly everyone familiar with the sea.

When asked, "How does your wife feel about all this voyaging?" Captain Irving Johnson's reply was, "It was her idea!"

As his extraordinary wife-mate, Exy distinguished herself as a full partner on their three *Yankee*s. Her skills and talents complimented and completed the excellence of their joint endeavors. Exy is a multi-lingual, cultural ambassador extraordinaire, whether exploring remote islands of the vast Pacific, leading her pre-teen granddaughter out on the bowsprit of SEA's *Corwith Cramer*, or going aloft, at 85, when she sailed on the *Swift of Ipswich*.

Construction will take place at the Los Angeles Maritime Museum in John Gibson Park, San Pedro. The brigantine design, based on one developed in the 1930s, has been adapted by W.I.B. Crealock to meet US Coast Guard and LAMI program requirements.

The shipyard will be visitor friendly, set up as a living history exhibit of the museum. Construction will be carried out by professional, paid shipwrights, working with trained volunteers. Funding for this project will come from private donations, corporate sponsorships, and foundation grants.

Flag:	USA
Rig:	Brigantine
Homeport/waters:	Los Angeles, California: Southern California and offshore islands
Who sails?	Referred youth-at-risk and groups catering to students and adults
Season:	Year-round
Cost:	Based on ability to pay
Program type:	Educational sailing adventures for youth and adult groups.

Specifications:			
	Sparred length: 110' 8"	Draft: 11'	Sail area: 4,540 sq. ft.
	LOA: 90'	Beam: 21' 9"	Tons: 99 GRT
	LWL: 72' 6"	Rig height: 87' 8"	Power: diesel

Coast Guard certification:	Sailing School Vessel (Subchapter R), Passenger Vessel (Subchapter T)
Contact:	Captain Jim Gladson, President
	Los Angeles Maritime Institute
	Berth 84, Foot of Sixth Street
	San Pedro, CA 90731
	Tel: 310-833-6055; Fax: 310-548-2055

Fair Jeanne

Ugly and sinking and sometimes on fire (handwritten)

Built in 1982, *Fair Jeanne* is a 110-foot brigantine originally built by the late Captain Thomas G. Fuller as a private yacht. Carrying 4,000 square feet of sail, the ship is now in service as a sail training vessel carrying up to 30 youths aged 14 to 24. Programs are also available for adults and seniors. During the summer months, the ship operates in the Great Lakes, St. Lawrence Seaway, and the East Coast. *Fair Jeanne* will participate in a range of activities, including the Boston to Halifax Race Leg of Tall Ships 2000®. Berths for up to 21 trainees are available. Winter finds *Fair Jeanne* in the Caribbean tracing historical maritime and naval events.

The program reflects Captain Fuller's belief in using sail training as a means of building confidence and resourcefulness in our youth. He was one of Canada's most decorated war heroes, earning the

name "Pirate of the Adriatic" and holding the distinction of the longest time served in offensive war action. His wartime experience taught him the value of instilling confidence and resourcefulness in our youth through adventure at sea. Captain Fuller founded the nonprofit Bytown Brigantine in 1983 to provide these opportunities to young people.

Flag:	Canada
Rig:	Brigantine
Homeport/waters:	Ottawa, Ontario, Canada: Great Lakes, Maritime Provinces (summer), Caribbean (winter)
Who sails?	Students between 14 and 24.
Program type:	Sail training for paying trainees. Sea education in maritime history in cooperation with organized groups and as informal, in-house programming. Dockside interpretation during port visits.

Specifications:	Sparred length: 110'	Draft: 6'	Sail area: 4,000 sq. ft.
	Rig height: 80'	Beam: 24' 6"	Tons: 135 GRT
	Freeboard: 8'	Hull: steel & fiberglass	Power: 235 HP

Designer:	T.G. Fuller
Built:	1982; Ottawa, Ontario, Canada, T.G. Fuller
Crew:	6. **Trainees/passengers:** 50 (day sails), 21 (overnight)
Contact:	Gene Carson, Executive Director or Simon A.F. Fuller, President
	Bytown Brigantine, Inc.
	2700 Queensview Dr.
	Ottawa, ON K2B 8H6, CANADA
	Tel: 613-596-6258; Fax: 613-596-5947
	E-mail: tallshipinfo@tallshipsadventure.org
	Web site: http://tallshipsadventure.org

Fantasy

built until 1913. During that time, trees were planted and grown specifically for this ship, bent and bound during growth and earmarked for various parts of the vessel. In 1998, *Isla De Ibiza* became *Fantasy*, and a new era in her history began. Today's ship is an elegant mixture of old-world shipbuilding techniques and modern amenities.

Originally named *Isla De Ibiza*, the *Fantasy* has had a colorful history. Planned in 1870, the *Fantasy* was not

Flag:	USA
Rig:	Topsail schooner, two-masted
Homeport/waters:	Castries, St. Lucia: Caribbean
Who sails?	High school and college students, and individuals.
Program type:	Sail training for paying trainees. Sea education in marine science, maritime history, and culture and language studies in cooperation with accredited institutions and as part of informal, in-house programming.
Cost:	$3,000 per person per month

Specifications:			
	Sparred length: 120'	Draft: 8' 10"	Sail area: 4,000 sq. ft.
	LOD: 90'	Beam: 19'	Tons: 150 GRT
	LOA: 96'	Rig height: 75'	Power: Caterpillar 342
	LWL: 90'	Freeboard: 3'	Hull: wood

Built:	1912; Spain, Palma Sues Shipyard
Contact:	Tom Gibbs
	Experiential Learning
	210 Dixon Street
	Henderson, KY 42420
	Tel: 502-827-8291; Fax: 502-827-8006
	E-mail: tgibbs@cooltides.com
	Web site: http://cooltides.com

teeny tiny

Federalist

Federalist is a full-size replica of a miniature ship built in Baltimore in 1788 to celebrate the state of Maryland's ratification of the United States Constitution. The original *Federalist* sailed from Baltimore to Mount Vernon, where she was presented to General George Washington as a gift from the merchants of Baltimore, and sank in a hurricane a short time later.

The replica *Federalist* was built by members of the Potomac Maritime Historical Society, formed in 1987 to promote public awareness of our maritime heritage. Since then, she has participated in many nautical events. Despite her small size, the replica *Federalist* is a fully operational square-rigged sailing vessel, equipped with a 3.5 HP engine. Unlike her larger sisters, however, *Federalist* frequently participates in street parades, riding on a decorated trailer pulled by her crew. For period events such as the George Washington birthday parade, the crew marches in 18th-century sailors' uniforms.

FEDERALIST

Flag:	USA		
Rig:	Barque, three-masted		
Homeport/waters:	Alexandria, Virginia: inland bays and rivers; on-land exhibits		
Who sails?	Students and others, pre-school and older.		
Season:	Year-round		
Program type:	Maritime history		
Specifications:	Sparred length: 25'	Draft: 2'	Sail area: 90 sq. ft.
	LOD: 15'	Beam: 5'	Tons: 500 lbs (dsp)
	LOA: 17'	Rig height: 19'	Power: 3.5 HP
	LWL: 13'	Freeboard: 1' 6"	Hull: wood
Built:	1987; The Potomac Maritime Historical Society, Inc.		
Crew:	4-6. Trainees/passengers: 2-3		
Contact:	Joe Youcha, Executive Director		
	Alexandria Seaport Foundation		
	1000 South Lee Street, Jones Point		
	Alexandria, VA 22320		
	Tel: 703-549-7078; Fax: 703-549-6715		
	E-mail: ASFHQS@aol.com		
	Web site: http://www.capaccess.org/asf		

Formidable

2000. An extensive day charter schedule will be offered, including fundraising for nonprofit organizations. *Formidable* plans to participate in many Tall Ships 2000® events. Her sister ship, *Lisa*, is also an ASTA member. *Formidable* is rigged as a brig. Her mainmast has a main topsail and main topgallant square sails. Her foremast carries the fore topsail, fore topgallant, and fore course. *Formidable* is one of the few maritime military re-enactors.

Formidable has an active re-enactment schedule in the Boston Area. She hopes to be Subchapter T inspected by March

Flag:	USA
Rig:	Brig
Homeport/waters:	Gloucester, Massachusetts

Specifications:	Sparred length: 72'	Draft: 6'	Sail area: 3,000 sq. ft.
	LOA: 55'	Beam: 18'	Rig height: 55'
	LWL: 49'		

Contact:	Captain Keating Willcox
	Longmeadow Way - Box 403
	Hamilton, MA 01936-0403
	Tel: 508-468-3869; Fax: 508-468-3869
	E-mail: kwillcox@shore.net
	Web site: http://www.shore.net/~kwillcox/spirit.html

Friendship

Friendship, a full-size replica of a Salem East Indiaman built for the National Park Service and berthed at Salem Maritime National Historic Site in Salem, Massachusetts, was launched in August, 1998. Although she represents a specific vessel built in Salem in 1797, she is typical of a class of commercial carriers commonly employed in both the East India and transatlantic trades during the early years of the new American republic.

Friendship's historic predecessor is credited with 15 voyages to the Far East, South America, the Mediterranean, and northern Europe. She had the misfortune of being taken as a prize of war by the Royal Navy on a return voyage from Archangel, Russia, in 1812. Sold by the British government in 1813, her ultimate fate has never been determined.

Currently under construction, *Friendship* is not expected to be accessible to the public until mid-2000. Interpretation and sailing programs will be developed jointly by the National Park Service and the Friends of Friendship during the next year. Outfitting and rigging activities may be viewed from the adjacent wharves.

Flag:	USA				
Rig:	Full-rigged ship				
Homeport/waters:	Salem, Massachusetts				
Specifications:	Sparred length: 171'		Draft: 11' 3"		Sail area: 9,409 sq. ft.
	LOD: 104'		Beam: 30'		Tons: 99 GRT
	LOA: 116'		Rig height: 112'		Power: twin 300 HP diesels
	LWL: 99'		Freeboard: 10'		Hull: wood
Designer:	Bay Marine, Inc., Barrington, Rhode Island				
Built:	1998; Port of Albany, New York, Scarano Boatbuilding, Inc.: 1999; Dion Yacht Yard, Salem, Massachusetts				
Contact:	Peter LaChapelle, Chief of Visitor Services Salem Maritime National Historic Site 174 Derby Street Salem, MA 01970 Tel: 978-740-1689; Fax: 978-740-1685				

Fritha

2000® fleet arriving from Europe. The voyage will take *Fritha* and her crew to Fiji, Hawaii, San Diego, Mexico, Costa Rica, the Panama Canal, Fort Lauderdale, and Bermuda. From Bermuda, *Fritha* will race to Charleston, South Carolina, and will then cruise in company up the eastern seaboard to Boston, Massachusetts, for Sail Boston 2000®. *Fritha* will then race to Halifax, and will complete the voyage with her arrival in Mackeral Cove, Maine. Once tied to her mooring in the cove, *Fritha* will be only a few nautical miles from her place of origin, the drawing board of her designer, Murray Peterson.

In 1999, *Fritha* began sailing from Auckland, New Zealand to Bermuda, where she plans to meet the Tall Ships

Flag:	USA
Rig:	Hermaphrodite brigantine
Homeport/waters:	Harpswell, Maine: Maine (summer)
Who sails?	High school and college students, and individuals under 25.
Program type:	Sail training for volunteer and paying trainees. Informal sea education in marine science and maritime history.

Specifications:	Sparred length: 74'	Draft: 6' 10"	Tons: 39 GRT
	LOD: 57'	Beam: 15'	Hull: wood
	Rig height: 51'	Freeboard: 5'	Power: GM 4-71
	LWL: 46'		

Designer:	Murray Peterson
Built:	1983-1984; Auckland, New Zealand, McMullen & Wing
Coast Guard certification:	Sailing School Vessel (Subchapter R)
Crew:	2. Trainees: 6
Contact:	Philip Fuller, Owner
	SeaMe.Sail
	PO Box 1142
	York Harbor, ME 03911
	Tel: 207-363-0048; Fax: 207-363-2050

Fyrdraca

Fyrdraca is a copy of a small 10th-century Viking warship found near Ralswiek on the German Island of Rügen in the Baltic Sea. The Longship Company seeks to rediscover the lost art of Viking sailing and navigation. To that end, *Fyrdraca* sails twice a month from March through November with a volunteer crew.

Fyrdraca also appears at waterfront and cultural festivals near the Potomac River and Chesapeake Bay and also participates in living history demonstrations in concert with the Markland Medieval Mercenary Militia's Viking reenactment camps. Voyage and demonstration schedules are published on the Longship Company's Web site.

Fyrdraca and her consort *Gyrfalcon* are both owned and operated by The Longship Company, Ltd., a member-supported nonprofit educational organization.

Flag:	USA
Rig:	Viking longship
Homeport/waters:	Oakley, Maryland: Potomac River and Chesapeake Bay
Who sails?	School groups from elementary school through college as well as individuals of all ages.
Season:	March to November
Program type:	Sail training for volunteer crew and apprentices. Sea education in maritime history based on informal, in-house programming. Non-paying passengers for day sails. Dockside interpretation during port visits.

Specifications:			
	Sparred length: 34'	Draft: 2'	Sail area: 240 sq. ft.
	LOA: 32'	Beam: 9' 2"	Tons: 3 GRT
	LWL: 29'	Rig height: 25'	Hull: wood
	Freeboard: 2' 6"		

Designer:	Traditional Norse design
Built:	1979; Keyport, New Jersey, Hans Pederson & Sons
Coast Guard certification:	Uninspected Vessel
Crew:	18 (day sails), 10 (overnight). **Trainees:** 4-12
Contact:	Bruce E. Blackistone, Registered Agent
	Longship Company, Ltd.
	21924 Oakley Road
	Avenue, MD 20609
	Tel: 301-390-4089
	E-mail: longshipco@hotmail.com
	Web site: http://www.wam.umd.edu/~eowyn/longship

Gallant

Pete Cullers' schooner *Gallant* was designed and built for Richard Tilghman in 1966, who cruised her on the East Coast until 1983, at which time she was donated to the Chesapeake Bay Maritime Museum. In 1986 the present owners, Tuck and Anne Elfman, purchased her from the museum and put her back into service sailing the Chesapeake Bay and coastal waters, participating in the Great Chesapeake Bay Schooner Races in 1994 and 1997 and the 1986 salute to the Statue of Liberty. She is based on a Chesapeake Bay pilot schooner with quite a bit of coaster influence. Her designer described her as being a "main topmast flying jibboomer."

Gallant is built unusually rugged by today's standards, using very traditional construction features such as standing rigging of iron cable, tarred, parceled and severed, maintained with pine tar, and fastened to lignum vitae deadeyes. She has plenty of deck area to enjoy a stable sail. *Gallant* is privately owned and maintained, offering guests day trips down the Sassafras River into the Chesapeake Bay, teaching the workings of the schooner rig, safety, and traditional maintenance, among other subjects. Donations are made to area maritime museums and the Chesapeake Bay Foundation. *Gallant* carries a 10-gauge cannon for saluting notable vessels.

Flag:	USA
Rig:	Main topsail schooner, two-masted
Homeport/waters:	Georgetown, Maryland: Chesapeake Bay and East Coast
Who sails?	Individuals of all ages and families
Program type:	Sail training for volunteer crew or trainees. Informal, in-house programming in vessel maintenance. Dockside interpretation while in homeport.

Specifications:	Sparred length: 62'	Draft: 6' 6"	Sail area: 1,450 sq. ft.
	LOD: 40' 6"	Beam: 12' 6"	Tons: 20 GRT
	LOA: 43' 8"	Rig height: 62'	Power: 68 HP diesel
	LWL: 35'	Freeboard: 2'	Hull: wood

Designer:	Pete Culler
Built:	1966; South Dartmouth, Massachusetts, Concordia – Waldo Howland
Coast Guard certification:	Uninspected Vessel
Crew:	1. **Trainees/passengers:** 6
Contact:	A. Tuck Elfman, Owner
	51 Elfman Drive
	Doylestown, PA 18901
	Tel: 215-348-2731: Fax: 215-348-4178

Gazela of Phil...

The *Gazela of Philadelphia* is the oldest wooden square-rigged sailing vessel still in operation. Built as a Grand Banks fishing vessel, she is one of many Portuguese ships that fished for cod there for hundreds of years. She is currently owned and operated by the Philadelphia Ship Preservation Guild, a private, nonprofit organization, and sails as a goodwill ambassador for the City of Philadelphia, the Commonwealth of Pennsylvania, and the Ports of Philadelphia and Camden (New Jersey) at significant events worldwide. *Gazela of Philadelphia* is open to the public on weekends when at Penn's Landing, from May 15 to September 15.

Gazela of Philadelphia is maintained

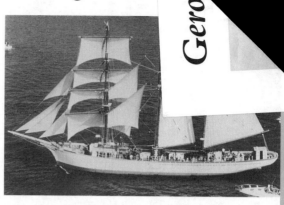

and sailed by a very active and knowledgeable volunteer group who participate in sail training activities throughout the year. After 25 hours of work on the vessel, a volunteer is eligible for a crew position on the next available cruise. An educational grant permits the teaching of young people 16 years and older, many of who become volunteer crew.

Flag:	USA
Rig:	Barquetine, three-masted
Homeport/waters:	Philadelphia, Pennsylvania: Delaware River and Atlantic Coast
Who sails?	Volunteers who support the maintenance of the ship. Dockside visitors include school groups from elementary school through college, as well as individuals and families.
Program type:	Sail training for crew and apprentices. Sea education based on informal, in-house programming. Dockside interpretation during outport visits.

Specifications:	Sparred length: 178'	Draft: 17'	Sail area: 8,910 sq. ft.
	LOD: 140'	Beam: 27' 9"	Tons: 299 GRT
	LOA: 150'	Rig height: 100'	Power: diesel
	LWL: 133'	Hull: wood	

Built:	1883; Cacilhas, Portugal
Coast Guard certification:	Attraction Vessel and Uninspected Vessel
Crew:	35 (volunteer)
Contact:	Karen H. Love, Executive Vice President
	Philadelphia Ship Preservation Guild
	Pier 36 South, 801 S. Columbus Blvd., 2nd floor
	Philadelphia, PA 19147-4306
	Tel: 215-218-0110; Fax: 215-463-1875
	E-mail: gazela@usa.net
	Web site: http://www.gazela.org

GERONIMO

Bahamas and northern Caribbean.

Geronimo's marine biology research has always included tagging sharks and collecting biological samples for the Apex Predator Investigation of the National Marine Fisheries Service. *Geronimo* also tags sea turtles in cooperation with the Center for Sea Turtle Research of the University of Florida. Their recent work has included the use of satellite transmitters on loggerhead turtles in Bahamian waters.

Geronimo makes three six-to-eight week trips during the school year, carrying students from St. George's School. Marine biology and English are taught on board, and the students continue their other courses by correspondence with the faculty at St. George's. Students receive full academic credit for their time on board. These cruises usually include operations along the eastern seaboard and in the waters of the

In the summer, *Geronimo* makes two three-week cruises, usually to the waters south of New England, to Bermuda, or to the Bahamas. Each summer cruise includes a series of lectures on marine biology and fisheries management as well as sail training, snorkeling, and the collecting of data on turtles and/or sharks.

Flag:	USA
Rig:	Sloop
Homeport/waters:	Newport, Rhode Island: North Atlantic and Caribbean
Who sails?	Enrolled students at St. George's School.
Season:	Year-round
Cost:	Regular school tuition (winter); inquire for summer 2000 cruise
Program type:	Full curriculum academics, marine biology, and environmental studies for high school students.

Specifications:			
	Sparred length: 69' 8"	Draft: 6' 8" 13' 5",	Sail area: 2,091 sq. ft.
	LOD: 68'	Beam: 18' 7"	Tons: 53 GRT
	LOA: 69' 8"	Rig height: 85' 6"	Power: diesel
	LWL: 53' 11"	Freeboard: 5'	Hull: fiberglass

Designer:	Ted Hood Design Group
Built:	1998; Portsmouth, Rhode Island, New England Boatworks
Coast Guard certification:	Sailing School Vessel (Subchapter R)
Crew:	2. Trainees: 8
Contact:	Captain Stephen Connett, St. George's School
	372 Purgatory Road, PO Box 1910
	Newport, RI 02840
	Tel: 401-847-7565; Fax: 401-842-6696
	Web site: http://www.stgeorges.edu

Gleam

The eleventh 12-meter vessel built for the United States, *Gleam* is beautifully restored and has her original pre-World War II interior. She has been painstakingly maintained by the same owner for 25 years. Together with her near sister ship *Northern Light, Gleam* offers a unique team-building program called "Your Own America's Cup Regatta." Each boat accommodates 13 guests plus three crewmembers. No previous sailing experience is necessary to participate. Group and corporate outings are available in Newport, Rhode Island, and other New England ports.

GLEAM

Flag:	USA
Rig:	Sloop
Homeport/waters:	Newport, Rhode Island: Narragansett Bay
Who sails?	Corporations who charter the vessel for team building and client entertaining.
Program type:	Sail training with paying trainees. Passenger day sails.

Specifications:			
	Sparred length: 67' 11"	Draft: 9'	Sail area: 1,900 sq. ft.
	LOD: 67' 11"	Beam: 12'	Tons: 30 GRT
	LOA: 67' 11"	Rig height: 90'	Power: diesel
	LWL: 46' 11"	Freeboard: 3'	Hull: wood

Designer:	Clinton Crane and Olin Stephens
Built:	1937; City Island, New York, Henry Nevins
Coast Guard certification:	Passenger Vessel (Subchapter T)
Crew:	3. **Trainees:** 14
Contact:	Elizabeth Tiedemann, Director of Sales and Marketing
	Seascope Systems, Inc.
	103 Ruggles Ave.
	Newport, RI 02840
	Tel: 401-847-5007; Fax: 401-849-6140
	E-mail: aboard@earthlink.net
	Web site: http://www.seascopenewport.com

Glenn L. Swetman

The *Glenn L. Swetman* is the first of two replica Biloxi oyster schooners built by the Biloxi Schooner Project under the auspices of the Maritime and Seafood Industry Museum. She is available for charter trips in the Mississippi Sound and to the barrier islands, Cat Island, Horn Island, and Ship Island. Walk-up day sailing trips are made when she is not under charter. Groups can learn about the maritime and seafood heritage of the Gulf Coast and about the vessels that began Biloxi's seafood industry. The *Glenn L. Swetman* is an integral part of the museum's Sea and Sail Summer Camp, and sailing classes are also offered through local colleges. *Glenn L. Swetman* also accommodates weddings, parties, and Elderhostel and school groups.

Money for construction and equipping the *Glenn L. Swetman* and her sister ship, *Mike Sekul*, has come from donations by interested individuals, businesses, civic groups, and a variety of museum-sponsored fundraising events.

Flag:	USA
Rig:	Gaff topsail schooner, two-masted
Homeport/waters:	Biloxi, Mississippi: northern Gulf of Mexico
Who sails?	Individuals and groups of all ages. Affiliated institutions include William Carey College, Mississippi State University, J.L. Scott Marine Education Center, and Seashore Methodist Assembly.
Season:	Year-round
Cost:	$15 per adult or $10 per child (2-1/2 hours), $750 per day group rate, $500 for half-day
Program type:	Sail training for volunteer and paying trainees. Sea education in maritime history, marine science, and ecology for college students and adults in cooperation with accredited institutions, organized groups, and as informal, in-house programming. Children's summer camp and private charters.

Specifications:	Sparred length: 76'	Draft: 4' 10"	Sail area: 2,400 sq. ft.
	LOD: 50'	Beam: 17'	Tons: 21 GRT
	LOA: 65'	Freeboard: 4' 6"	Power: 4-71 Detroit diesel
	LWL: 47'	Hull: Juniper	

Designer:	William Holland
Built:	1989; Biloxi, Mississippi, William T. Holland
Coast Guard certification:	Passenger Vessel (Subchapter T)
Crew:	3. **Trainees:** 49 (day sails)
Contact:	Robin Krohn, Executive Director
	Maritime and Seafood Industry Museum
	PO Box 1907
	Biloxi, MS 39533
	Tel: 228-435-6320; Fax: 228-435-6309
	E-mail: schooner@maritimemuseum.org
	Web site: http://www.maritimemuseum.org

Gloria

PHOTO BY THAD KOZA

Built in Bilbao, Spain, and purchased in 1966 by the Colombian Navy, the three-masted barque *Gloria* is used today as a school ship for the Colombian Navy. She has proudly served for 33 years training more than 700 officers and 4,500 enlisted men and women.

Annual cruises have taken *Gloria* to many ports around the world. In 1999 she participated in the San Francisco Gold Rush Race; in 2000 she will travel east to Tall Ships 2000®, logging an average of 150 days underway for each cadet cruise.

Gloria carries a complement of 150 men and women, ranging from enlisted to midshipmen and officers. The cruise is aimed at training officers, in their third year at the Naval Academy, to implement their academic knowledge in the areas of navigation, seamanship, leadership, and teambuilding. *Gloria* is a proud goodwill ambassador of the Colombian Navy.

GLORIA

Flag:	Colombia			
Rig:	Barque			
Homeport/waters:	Cartegena, Colombia			
Who sails?	Colombian Naval Academy cadets and officers of the Colombian Navy.			
Season:	Year-round			
Program type:	Sail training for Colombian Naval Academy cadets.			
Specifications:	Sparred length: 249' 4"	Draft: 14' 9"	Sail area: 15,075 sq. ft.	
	LOD: 189'	Beam: 34' 9"	Tons: 934 GRT	
	LOA: 212'	Rig height: 126' 4"	Power: twin 256 KV	
	LWL: 184'	Freeboard: 21' 7"	Hull: steel	
Designer:	Sener			
Built:	1968; Bilbao, Spain, Celaga S. A. Shipyards			
Certification:	Colombian Naval vessel			
Crew:	160			
Contact:	Naval Attaché, Colombia			
	2118 Leroy Place NW			
	Washington, DC 20008			
	Tel: 202-387-1979; Fax: 202-234-7220			
	E-mail: arcgloria@yahoo.com			

Governor Stone

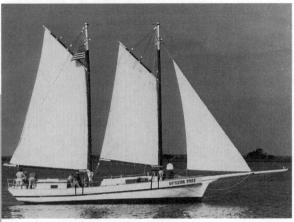

PHOTO BY ROSEMARY M.K. WYMAN

after the Civil War. This gaff-rigged, shallow draft schooner represents a class of sailing vessels unique to the Gulf Coast and is the oldest vessel of the American south afloat. Possibly the last of her type, the *Governor Stone* has seen service from an oyster buy-boat to yacht club committee boat to pleasure craft. The vessel has been declared a National Historic Landmark by the National Park Service.

The *Governor Stone* was built for Charles Greiner in Pascagoula, Mississippi, in 1877 as a cargo freighter and named for John Marshall Stone, the first elected Governor of Mississippi

Governor Stone sails year-round. Sailing times vary. Reservations are suggested and can be obtained by calling the Apalachicola Maritime Museum.

Flag:	USA
Rig:	Gaff schooner, two-masted
Homeport/waters:	Apalachicola, Florida: Gulf of Mexico, upper coast
Who sails?	School groups from elementary school through college as well as individuals and families. Affiliated institutions include Gulf Coast Community College, Panama City, Florida.
Season:	Year-round
Cost:	$20 per person per day; $900 group rate; $450 half day. Overnight trips by special arrangements.
Program type:	Sea education in marine science, maritime history, and ecology based on informal, in-house programming, with special attention given to at-risk students. Passenger day sails and overnight passages. Dockside interpretation.

Specifications:			
	Sparred length: 68'	Draft: 2' 6"	Sail area: 1,400 sq. ft.
	LOD: 42'	Beam: 13' 6"	Tons: 12 GRT
	LOA: 44'	Rig height: 52'	Power: 80 HP diesel
	LWL: 38'	Freeboard: 5'	Hull: wood

Built:	1877; Pascagoula, Mississippi
Coast Guard certification:	Passenger Vessel (Subchapter T)
Crew:	3, 1 instructor. **Trainees:** 6
Contact:	Joe Terrell, Assistant Administrator
	Apalachicola Maritime Museum, Inc.
	268 Water Street, PO Box 625
	Apalachicola, FL 32329-0625
	Tel: 850-653-8700

Guayas

Guyas was built in the Celaya Shipyard in Bilbao, Spain, with construction beginning in 1974. She is named after the Chief of Huancavilcas, a native culture in the Ecuadorian coastal region. The general arrangement was the same as *Gloria* of Colombia. *Simon Bolivar* of Venezuela and *Cuahtemoc* of Mexico were also built using the same design. *Guyas* was commissioned on July 23, 1977, and since that date has proudly served for more than 20 years training more than 500 officers and 3,000 enlisted men.

Guayas has participated in many tall ship events over the years. This representation has led her to be referred to as Ecuador's Afloat Embassy. The ship carries a complement of 16 officers, 43 midshipmen, and 94 enlisted men, including the ship's band. During a cruise, considered one semester at the Ecuadorian Naval Academy, midshipmen apply—in a very challenging environment—theoretical principles of navigation, seamanship, and other subjects learned in the classroom.

Flag:	Ecuador
Rig:	Barque
Homeport/waters:	Guayquil, Ecuador: cruises to various destinations worldwide
Who sails?	Ecuadorian Naval Academy cadets.
Season:	Year-round
Program type:	Sail training for Ecuadorian Naval Academy cadets.

Specifications:			
	Sparred length: 257' 1"	Draft: 15' 4"	Sail area: 15,784 sq. ft.
	LOD: 218'	Beam: 34' 9"	
	LOA: 221'	Power: diesel	
	LWL: 184'	Hull: steel	

Designer:	Celaya
Built:	1976; Celaya Shipyard, Bilbao, Spain
Certification:	Ecuadorian Naval Vessel
Crew:	76
Contact:	Naval Attaché, Ecuador and Captain, "Buque Escuela Guyas"
	2535 15th St. NW
	Washington, DC 20009
	Tel: 202-328-6958; Fax: 202-332-7954
	E-mail: Aembassyec@aol.com

GUAYAS

Gyrfalcon

Gyrfalcon is a copy of the faering buried with the Gokstad ship in Norway in the 9th century. She was built by the boat building program at the Hampton Mariner's Museum (now the North Carolina Maritime Museum) in Beaufort, North Carolina under the direction of Geoffrey Scofield.

Gyrfalcon is often seen at cultural, water, community, and boat festivals, historic reenactment events, and school demonstrations. She also participates in living history demonstrations in concert with the Markland Medieval Mercenary Militia's Viking reenactment camps, where the public enjoys the spectacle of crews dressed in historic costume and armor, offering historic interpretation.

As an enticement to school children and adults to discover more about the Viking Age, *Gyrfalcon* spends off-season time on display at area libraries and schools. *Gyrfalcon* and her consort, *Fyrdraca*, are both owned and operated by The Longship Company, Ltd., a member-supported nonprofit educational organization.

PHOTO BY JANET M. D'AGNOSTINO-TONEY

Flag:	USA
Rig:	Viking faering boat
Homeport/waters:	Avenue, Maryland: East Coast and Chesapeake Bay
Season:	March to November
Who sails?	School groups from elementary school through college as well as individuals of all ages.
Season:	March to November
Program type:	Sail training for crew and apprentices. Sea education in maritime history as well as informal, in-house programming. Dockside interpretation at outport visits.

Specifications:	Sparred length: 21'	Draft: 1'	Sail area: 80 sq. ft.
	LOA: 21'	Beam: 5'	Tons: 200 lbs.
	Freeboard: 1'	Rig height: 10'	Hull: wood

Built:	1981; Hampton Mariner's Museum (now the North Carolina Maritime Museum), Beaufort, North Carolina
Coast Guard certification:	Uninspected Vessel
Crew:	4. Trainees: 1-3
Contact:	Bruce E. Blackistone, Registered Agent
	Longship Company, Ltd.
	21924 Oakley Road
	Avenue, MD 20609
	Tel: 301-390-4089
	E-mail: longshipco@hotmail.com
	Web site: http://www.wam.umd.edu/~eowyn/longship

Half Moon (Halve Maen)

The replica ship *Half Moon (Halve Maen)* was launched on June 20, 1989, to draw attention to the exploration and colonization of the Mid-Atlantic States. The 1609 voyage of the original *Halve Maen*, under the command of Henry Hudson, led to the first European settlements by the Dutch in what are now the States of New York, New Jersey, Connecticut, Delaware, and Pennsylvania. In 1614, the Dutch named the area "Nieu Nederlandt."

Since her launch, the replica *Half Moon* has visited over 40 ports along the eastern seaboard and the Great Lakes. She has been boarded by over 100,000 visitors and participated in port festivals and a yearly New Netherland Festival. The *Half Moon* is featured in the 1994 Walt Disney movie, *Squanto: An Indian Warrior's Tale.*

The ship's design is based on original Dutch East India Company documents, including the resolution of 1608 ordering the original ship's construction and *Juet's Journal.* Hudson sailed the *Halve Maen* up the Hudson River as far as present-day Albany in 1609.

The *Half Moon*'s program offers the public both an active sail training program and instruction on the history of New Netherland. Thus, the crew is trained in both historical presentation and ship handling.

HALF MOON (HALVE MAEN)

Flag:	USA			
Rig:	Full-rigged ship			
Homeport/waters:	Croton-on-Hudson, New York: East Coast and Great Lakes			
Who sails?	School groups from elementary school through high school, individuals and adults.			
Program type:	Sail training and maritime history based on informal programs. Dockside interpretation.			
Specifications:	Sparred length: 95'	Draft: 8' 5"	Sail area: 2,757 sq. ft.	
	LOD: 64' 3"	Beam: 17' 6"	Tons: 112 GRT	
	LOA: 65'	Rig height: 78'	Power: diesel	
	LWL: 84'	Freeboard: 10' 5"	Hull: wood	
Designer:	Nicholas S. Benton			
Built:	1989; Albany, New York, New Netherland Museum			
Coast Guard certification:	Attraction Vessel			
Crew:	7-12 (day sails), 8-15 (overnight)			
Contact:	Dr. Andrew Hendricks, Chairman			
	New Netherland Museum, 103 Rosewood Drive			
	Lumberton, NC 28358			
	Tel: 910-738-7154; Fax: 910-738-4455			
	or New Netherland Museum, 181 South Riverside Avenue			
	Croton-on-Hudson, NY 10520			
	Tel: 914-413-9924			
	Web site: http://www.newnetherland.org			

Harvey Gamage *← Sinking Slowly*

The schooner *Harvey Gamage* offers an array of sea education programs, ranging from high school semesters-at-sea to special programs performed in partnership with schools and youth groups. All programs use the power of the sea and the challenge of traditional seafaring as the basis for the educational curriculum taught on board.

Ocean Classroom, a fully accredited semester-at-sea, is a true voyage of discovery for qualified sophomores, juniors, and seniors in high school. Young people come from all over the US to join the ship for its outstanding learning adventure. The voyage covers more than 4,000 nautical miles, connecting South American shores to the Canadian Maritimes. The students live and work as sailors, and take full courses in maritime history, literature, science, applied mathematics, writing, and navigation.

The *Harvey Gamage* will sail in the fleet of international tall ships for summer term 2000.

Other programs include Seafaring Camp for teens and the Mariners program for high school and college students. Financial aid is available for most *Harvey Gamage* programs.

Flag:	USA
Rig:	Gaff topsail schooner, two-masted
Homeport/waters:	Islesboro, Maine: Eastern US and Canada (summer), Caribbean and South America (winter)
Who sails?	School groups from middle school through college, as well as adult individuals and families. Affiliated institutions include Proctor Academy, Long Island University, Franklin Pierce College, and other schools.
Season:	Year-round
Cost:	Varies with program
Program type:	Sail training with paying trainees. Fully accredited sea education in marine science, maritime history, and ecology.

Specifications:	Sparred length: 131'	Draft: 9' 7"	Sail area: 4,200 sq ft.
	LOD: 90'	Beam: 23' 7"	Tons: 94 GRT
	LOA: 95'	Rig height: 91'	Power: 220 HP diesel
	LWL: 85'	Hull: wood	

Designer:	McCurdy & Rhodes
Built:	1973; South Bristol, Maine, Harvey Gamage Shipyard
Coast Guard certification:	Sailing School Vessel (Subchapter R), Passenger Vessel (Subchapter T)
Crew:	7-10, including instructors. **Trainees:** 69 (day sails), 27 (overnight)
Contact:	Bert Rogers, Director
	Schooner Harvey Gamage/Ocean Classroom Foundation, Inc.
	PO Box 446
	Cornwall, NY 12518
	Tel: 800-724-7245, 914-615-1412; Fax: 914-615-1414
	E-mail: mail@sailgamage.org
	Web site: http://www.sailgamage.org

Schooner Harvey Gamage Foundation Schooner Project

(Work in Progress)

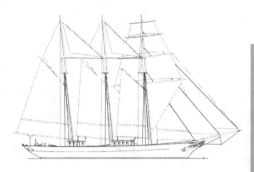

The Schooner Harvey Gamage Foundation is proud to announce its plans to build a new steel ship to meet the growing demand for the Ocean Classroom program. TriCoastal Marine is designing the vessel (as yet unnamed), to be a superb platform for teaching as well as an excellent sailer for major voyages. The new ship's preliminary design is complete, and the building yard is being selected. Keel laying and launch dates to be announced.

Ocean Classroom is a fully accredited semester-at-sea for high school students. Young people come from all parts of the US to join this award-winning program, and gain an unparalleled learning and growth experience. The new ship, conceived specifically to fulfill the mission of Ocean Classroom, will allow more worthy students to be included, to teach them better, and to increase the amount of financial aid that can be awarded each semester.

As a nonprofit organization, the Schooner Harvey Gamage Foundation gratefully accepts contributions of equipment, materials, or funds for this project or the Scholarship Endowment. For information about Ocean Classroom, or to make a contribution, contact their office.

Flag:	USA
Rig:	Square topsail schooner, three masted
Homeport/waters:	Islesboro, Maine: Eastern US and Canada (summer), Caribbean and South America (winter)
Who sails?	High school students. Affiliated institutions include Proctor Academy, Long Island University, Franklin Pierce College, and other schools.
Season:	Year-round
Cost:	Varies with term
Program type:	Sail training for paying trainees. Fully accredited sea education in marine science, maritime history, and ecology.

Specifications:	Sparred length: 158'	Draft: 12' 6"	Sail area: 8,000 sq. ft.
	LOD: 112' 6"	Beam: 27'	Tons: 99 GRT
	LOA: 124'	Rig height: 108'	Power: 500 HP diesel
	LWL: 100'	Hull: steel	

Designer:	TriCoastal Marine
Coast Guard certification:	(planned) Sailing School Vessel (Subchapter R), Passenger Vessel (Subchapter T)
Crew:	10-15, including instructors. **Trainees:** 30 (overnight)
Contact:	Bert Rogers, Director
	Schooner Harvey Gamage/Ocean Classroom Foundation, Inc.
	PO Box 446
	Cornwall, NY 12518
	Tel: 800-724-7245, 914-615-1412; Fax: 914-615-1414
	E-mail: mail@sailgamage.org
	Web site: http://www.sailgamage.org

Hawaiian Chieftain

PHOTO BY BENSON LEE

The *Hawaiian Chieftain* is a 103-foot square topsail ketch. A replica of an 18th-century European trading vessel, she was built in Hawaii in 1988. She is a contemporary interpretation of traditional design and is an excellent classroom for the teaching of traditional sailing skills.

The hands-on history program, "Voyages of Rediscovery", teaches 4th and 5th-grade students about the exploration of the West Coast during the 1790s. A summertime, weeklong day camp, "Buccaneers and Explorers Camp", is offered for youth from 9 to 12. A Longboat Program for at-risk-youth utilizing a 23-foot Royal Navy launch and two 25-foot pinkies is planned. For the past four winters *Hawaiian Chieftain* has toured Californian ports in company with the *Lady Washington* providing the "Voyages of Rediscovery" sailing and dockside educational programs.

Hawaiian Chieftain coordinates with many organizations to develop self-esteem for youth in a challenging environment. *Hawaiian Chieftain* also offers sail training and team building for adults, private charters, natural history cruises, and naval battle reenactments with visiting vessels.

Flag:	USA
Rig:	Square topsail ketch
Homeport/waters:	Sausalito, California: San Francisco Bay (summer), southern California coast (winter)
Who sails?	Elementary and middle school groups, as well as individuals under 25 and families. Affiliated institutions include National Maritime Museum Association and the Grays Harbor Historical Seaport.
Season:	Year-round
Cost:	$35 to $100 per person per day, $1,050-$2,400 group rate per day
Program type:	Sail training for volunteer or paying trainees. Sea education in maritime history in cooperation with accredited schools and colleges. Passenger day sails. Dockside interpretation during port visits.

Specifications:			
	Sparred length: 103'	Draft: 6'	Sail area: 4,200 sq. ft.
	LOD: 65'	Beam: 22'	Tons: 64 GRT
	Rig height: 75'	Freeboard: 3'	Power: twin diesels
	LWL: 62'	Hull: steel	

Designer:	Raymond R. Richards
Built:	1988; Lahaina, Maui, Hawaii, Lahaina Welding Co.
Coast Guard certification:	Passenger Vessel (Subchapter T)
Crew:	8. **Trainees:** 47
Contact:	Captain Ian McIntyre, Hawaiian Chieftain Inc.
	Suite #266, 3020 Bridgeway
	Sausalito, CA 94965
	Tel: 415-331-3214; Fax: 415-331-9415
	E-mail: tallship@hawaiianchieftain.com
	Web site: http://www.hawaiianchieftain.com

Heritage

The beautiful varnished-hulled *Heritage* was built in 1970, the last year of the wooden twelve-meters. Designed, built, and sailed by Charlie Morgan, her tank tests showed her to be a technological breakthrough. However, by the end of the summer's racing, the redesigned *Intrepid* won the right to defend the Cup.

Heritage avenged her earlier defeat to *Intrepid* when they met on the Great Lakes in the 1980s. There she dominated the Great Lakes racing circuit, scoring multiple wins in the Chicago to Mackinac, Port Huron to Mackinac, Trans-Superior, and Queen's Cup races. In 1988 she sailed from the Lakes to California and in 1991 returned to New England. She is now part of the America's Cup Charters twelve-meter fleet in Newport, Rhode Island.

Heritage is available for charter in New England and New York and is a perfect

platform for family outings and corporate entertaining or team building.

HERITAGE

Flag:	USA
Rig:	Sloop
Homeport/waters:	Newport, Rhode Island: New England and Chesapeake Bay
Who sails?	Individuals of all ages.
Cost:	$1,800 group rate per day, $60 per person evening sail
Program type:	Sail training for volunteer or paying trainees. Sea education based on informal, in-house programming. Passenger day sails.

Specifications:	LOD: 65'	Draft: 10'	Sail area: 1,700 sq. ft.
	LOA: 65'	Beam: 12'	Power: diesel
	LWL: 46'	Rig height: 90'	Hull: wood

Designer:	Charles Morgan
Built:	1970; Clearwater, Florida, Morgan Custom Yachts
Coast Guard certification:	Passenger Vessel (Subchapter T)
Crew:	3. **Trainees:** 14
Contact:	George Hill/Herb Marshall
	America's Cup Charters
	PO Box 51
	Newport, RI 02840
	Tel: 401-849-5868; Fax: 401-849-3098
	Web site: http://www.americascupcharters.com

Heritage of Miami II

The *Heritage of Miami II* is an 85-foot square topsail schooner that is modern in materials and construction but traditional in style. Built specifically for crossing wide expanses of open water, she has a wide, spacious deck that provides ample room for working the sails, lounging in the sun, and sleeping in the evening. Her shoal draft makes even small islands accessible while her long bowsprit, topmasts, and yards allow extra sails for speed between them.

Heritage of Miami II's travels take her to Garden Key and the famous Fort Jefferson in the Dry Tortugas, the coral reefs of the Florida Keys, and Key West. Sea Explorer cruises last for six days and five nights. Her professional captain and crew help the Explorers experience the life of the sea: setting and furling sails, manning the helm, and even catching, cleaning, and cooking fish. The program offers a unique opportunity to explore a part of the Florida Keys while enjoying a hands-on sailing experience.

Flag:	USA
Rig:	Square topsail schooner, two-masted
Homeport/waters:	Miami, Florida: Biscayne Bay, Florida Keys, Gulf of Mexico
Who sails?	School groups from elementary school through college as well as individuals. Affiliated institutions include Dade County Schools, Broward County Schools, area private schools, and the Boy Scouts of America.
Season:	Year-round
Cost:	$75 per person per day; $1,000 group rate per day
Program type:	Sail training for crew, apprentices, and paying trainees. Sea education in maritime history and ecology in cooperation with accredited schools and colleges and other organized groups. Passenger day sails and overnight passages. Dockside interpretation.

Specifications:			
	Sparred length: 85'	Draft: 6'	Sail area: 2,200 sq. ft.
	LOD: 65'	Beam: 17' 9"	Tons: 47 GRT
	LOA: 68'	Rig height: 64'	Power: 140 HP diesel
	LWL: 62'	Freeboard: 8'	Hull: steel

Designer:	Merritt Walters
Built:	1988; Norfolk, Virginia, Howdy Bailey
Coast Guard certification:	Passenger Vessel (Subchapter T)
Contact:	Captain Joseph A. Maggio
	The Schooner Heritage of Miami, Inc.
	3145 Virginia St.
	Coconut Grove, FL 33133
	Tel: 305-442-9697; Fax: 305-442-0119
	E-mail: heritage2@mindspring.com
	Web site: http://www.heritageschooner.com

On May 12, 1792 Captain Robert Gray sailed his ship, *Columbia Rediviva*, over the bar of the "Great River of the West" and named it Columbia's River in honor of his ship. Robert Gray never would have entered that river had it not been for the information he received from the first American vessel to enter the river, *Columbia*'s longboat.

Unnamed and unheralded, ship's boats were the workhorses of the 16th to 19th century. Powered by either oars or sails, these versatile seaworthy craft carried all manner of cargo from ship to shore and back again.

Grays Harbor Historical Seaport Authority built two 18th-century ship's longboat reproductions in 1993. The design for the Seaport longboats was painstakingly researched by noted maritime historian and artist Hewitt R. Jackson, who worked closely with naval architect Stuart Hoagland and Seaport Director Les Bolton to ensure both historical accuracy and the meeting of specific program needs.

Powered by ten oars or up to a three-masted dipping lugsail rig, these versatile vessels are ideal for exploring the protected inland waterways of Washington. Programs are customized to the needs and interests of specific groups. Half-day, full-day, and weeklong programs are available to organized groups as well as to individuals.

HEWITT R. JACKSON

Flag:	USA
Rig:	Dipping lug
Homeport/waters:	Aberdeen, Washington: Western Washington, Grays Harbor, Washington
Who sails?	School groups from middle school through college, individuals under 25.
Program type:	Sail training for volunteer and paying trainees. Sea education in marine science, maritime history, ecology, and team building in cooperation with accredited institutions and as part of informal, in-house programming. Passenger day sails, dockside interpretation.
Cost:	$95 per person per day, $600 group rate per day. Residential programs, $55 per person per day (five-day minimum).

Specifications:	Sparred length: 36'		Draft: 20"		Sail area: 310 sq. ft.
	LOD: 25'		Beam: 7'		Tons: 3,800 lbs. (dsp)
	LOA: 26'		Rig height: 16'		Hull: wood
	LWL: 26'		Freeboard: 20"		

Designer:	Stuart Hoagsland/Hewitt Jackson
Built:	1993; Aberdeen, Washington, Grays Harbor Historical Seaport Authority
Coast Guard certification:	Sailing School Vessel (Subchapter R)
Crew:	2. **Trainees:** 8-13
Contact:	James H. "Flagg" Locke, Operations Director
	Grays Harbor Historical Seaport
	PO Box 2019
	Aberdeen, WA 98520
	Tel: 800-200-LADY (5239); Fax: 360-533-9384
	E-mail: ghhsa@techline.com
	Web site: http://www.histseaport.org

...nder HOT

The crew consists of six professionals, accompanied by 9-12 deck cadets. Some cadets have already been trained at various nautical institutions, others are looking to gain some sea experience before committing to gaining the education required to start a career in this industry. The goal of this program is to seek out and prepare cadets who are suitable for work offshore. Serving as a cadet on the *Highlander* acts as an extended interview for the Human Resources Department and allows them to evaluate his or her seafaring skills and adaptability to the offshore. It also allows cadets who have already begun their training to earn valuable sea time, thus helping them to progress with their career.

Highlander was welcomed to the Secunda fleet in 1998. Along with being an ambassador for Secunda Marine Services, Ltd., she is used primarily as a sail training vessel. Various programs have been created to provide marine career awareness training for high school and college students.

HIGHLANDER

Flag:	Canada
Rig:	Gaff topsail schooner
Homeport/waters:	Halifax, Nova Scotia, Canada: Eastern Seaboard including Atlantic Provinces (summer), Caribbean (winter)
Who sails?	High school and college students, individuals of all ages, and marine institute students.
Season:	Year-round
Program type:	Sail training for volunteer trainees. Informal, in-house sea education. Dockside interpretation during port visits and in homeport.

Specifications:			
	Sparred length: 154'	Draft: 14'	Sail area: 10,000 sq. ft.
	LOD: 124'	Beam: 25' 8"	Tons: 140 GRT
	LOA: 126'	Rig height: 109'	Power: twin 380 HP
	LWL: 116'	Hull: wood	

Designer:	Sterling Burgess
Built:	1924; Essex, Massachusetts, F.W. James & Son
Certification:	Canadian Coast Guard certified
Crew:	6. **Trainees:** 12-14
Contact:	Stephen G. Widmeyer, Human Resources
	Secunda Marine Services, Ltd,
	1 Canal St.
	Dartmouth, NS B2Y 2W1, CANADA
	Tel: 902-465-3400: Fax: 902-463-7678
	E-mail: stevew@secunda.com
	Web site: http://www.secunda.com

SAIL TALL SHIPS!

Hindu

Hindu was designed by William Hand, Jr. and built as a private yacht in 1925 in East Boothbay, Maine, by the Hodgdon Brothers. She is a 79-foot wooden vessel designed as a half-scale model of a 19th-century Grand Banks fishing schooner. In her long career she has been a private yacht, a cargo ship transporting spice from India, and as a US Navy U-boat tracker in World War II on the Eastern Seaboard. *Hindu* has also participated in many blue water races, including two of the Newport-Bermuda classics.

Hindu is Coast Guard inspected for coastwise navigation, carrying 49 passengers for day sails and six passengers overnight. She is privately owned and available for private charter for any aspect of the Tall Ships 2000® schedule from Newport, Rhode Island to Halifax, Nova Scotia. In the last 36 months *Hindu* has called in the following ports: Bermuda; Port Antonio, Jamaica; Grand Cayman; Havana, Cuba; Porta Plata, Dominican Republic; and Key West, Florida. *Hindu* has been conducting four two-hour day sails out of Provincetown Harbor for over fifty years.

HINDU

Flag:	USA
Rig:	Gaff schooner
Homeport/waters:	Provincetown, Massachusetts: Provincetown, Massachusetts (summer), Caribbean (winter)
Who sails?	Elementary and middle school students, and individuals of all ages.
Season:	Year-round
Cost:	$60 per person per day, $1,500 group rate per day
Program type:	Sail training for paying trainees. Sea education as informal, in-house programming.

Specifications:			
	Sparred length: 73'	Draft: 9'	Sail area: 2,500 sq. ft.
	LOD: 61' 3"	Beam: 15'	Tons: 29 GRT
	LOA: 64'	Rig height: 60'	Power: 90 HP diesel
	LWL: 47'	Freeboard: 4'	Hull: wood

Designer:	William Hand, Jr.
Built:	1925; Boothbay Harbor, Maine, Hodgdon Brothers
Coast Guard certification:	Passenger Vessel (Subchapter T)
Crew:	3. **Trainees/passengers:** 49 (day sails), 6 (overnight)
Contact:	John Bennett, President
	Hindu of Provincetown, Inc.,
	333 Commercial St
	Barnstable, MA 02657
	Tel: 508-487-3000; Fax: 208-723-1002
	E-mail: jbennett1@capecod.net
	Web site: http://www.schoonerhindu.com

Hjørdis

The schooner *Hjørdis* was acquired for the Freshwater Studies at North House Folk School in 1997. This gaff-rigged vessel serves as an educational platform for youth, college groups, and the general public. With the *Hjørdis*, North House seeks to apply its unique and skills-based philosophy to a program based in the physical, biological, cultural, and historical elements of Lake Superior. Coursework on the *Hjørdis* focuses on nautical science, maritime history, limnology, environmental stud-

ies, and personal growth. North House Folk School's Freshwater Studies offers two-hour, half-day, and multi-day programs from Grand Marais Harbor to the near coastal waters and as far as Grand Portage National Monument and Isle Royal National Park. Each sail is limited to six trainees, with two crewmembers affording each personal attention and experiences.

Special programs include The Craft of Sail, The Great Lakes Schooner Trade, Navigation and Weather Studies, and two teacher programs; Experiential Lake Studies for Teachers, and Ten-Day Experiential Lake Studies for Teachers and Wilderness Education Experience. Fall Color Tours give participants the opportunity to experience the spectacular nature of the North Shore of Lake Superior as it changes from the green of summer to the reds, oranges, and yellows of autumn from offshore.

Flag:	USA
Rig:	Gaff schooner, two-masted
Homeport/waters:	Grand Marais, Minnesota
Who sails?	Students of all ages, individuals, and groups.
Program type:	Sail training for paying trainees. Sea education in nautical science and maritime history.

Specifications:			
	Sparred length: 50'	Draft: 3' 10"	Sail area: 1,100 sq. ft.
	LOD: 42' 2"	Beam: 11' 4"	
	LOA: 42' 2"	Rig height: 42'	Power: 36 HP diesel
	LWL: 33'	Hull: steel	

Designer:	Thomas Colvin
Built:	1978; Mt. Clement, Michigan, Kenneth R. Woodward
Coast Guard certification:	Uninspected Vessel
Contact:	Captain Matthew Brown or Peter Barsness, Curriculum Director
	North House Folk School/Freshwater Studies
	PO Box 759
	Grand Marais, MN 55612
	Tel: 218-387-9762 (office), 218-370-0675 (vessel); Fax: 218-387-9760
	E-mail: info@northhouse.org
	Web site: http://www.northhouse.org

Howard Blackburn

Howard Blackburn is a fine example of a classic John G. Alden design. Built in 1951 in Cristobal, Panama, her hull design and construction are reminiscent of the fishing vessels that sailed from New England in the 1900s. She is a very able and seaworthy vessel. Originally built as a private yacht, *Howard Blackburn* also spent some time in the charter trade, sailing in waters from South America to New England. She also did some campaigns for the Greenpeace organization.

In 1995 Mark Roesner and Terry Westhead took ownership and brought her to the Chesapeake Bay area. Mark and Terry both have years of experience sailing and teaching aboard sail training vessels. *Howard Blackburn* can take up to six trainees on day and overnight trips. During the summer camp pro-

gram, youths between the ages of 13-18 come aboard to learn all aspects of seamanship, marine science, and ecology of the Chesapeake Bay. The vessel is also available for individual, family, and group charters.

Flag:	USA
Rig:	Ketch
Homeport/waters:	Baltimore, Maryland: Chesapeake Bay, New England
Who sails?	Students from elementary school through college, individuals, and families.
Cost:	$100 per person per day
Program type:	Sail training for volunteer and paying trainees. Informal, in-house sea education in marine science and ecology.

Specifications:			
	Sparred length: 58'	Draft: 6' 6"	Sail area: 1,100 sq. ft.
	LOD: 45'	Beam: 14'	Tons: 22'
	LOA: 58'	Rig height: 57'	Power: 80 HP diesel
	LWL: 36' 6"	Freeboard: 4'	Hull: wood

Designer:	John G. Alden
Built:	1951; Cristobal, Panama Canal Zone
Crew:	1. **Trainees: 6**
Contact:	Captain Mark Roesner, Owner
	925 Bowleys Quarters Rd.
	Baltimore, MD 21220
	Tel: 410-335-7357

Hurricane (#1-22)

Hurricane Island Outward Bound® School

For 35 years The Hurricane Island Outward Bound School's sailing expeditions aboard unique 30-foot ketch-rigged pulling boats modeled after traditional whaling vessels have challenged both novice and seasoned sailors. Students experience open-ocean adventure and island living sailing the coast of Maine, one of the world's greatest cruising grounds. Nearly 3,000 islands and 3,500 miles of shoreline make this one of the last intact coastal wildernesses in America. As trainees navigate rugged shores they rotate responsibilities, learning sail handling, navigation, and boat handling.

Founded in 1964, the Hurricane Island Outward Bound School is the largest Outward Bound School in the United States. From its headquarters in Rockland, Maine, the school operates in 14 locations stretching from Maine through Maryland and Philadelphia, all the way to the Florida Keys. The school is a nonprofit educational organization whose mission is to conduct safe, adventure-based courses structured to encourage growth and discovery, and to inspire confidence, self-reliance, concern for others, and care for the environment.

By combining the school's mission with Outward Bound's motto, "To serve, to strive, and not to yield," the school hopes to better society by providing people with positive experiences that can change their outlook, their attitudes, and their lives.

Flag:	USA
Rig:	Ketch-rigged pulling boat
Waters:	Maine Coast, Chesapeake Bay, and Florida Keys.
Who sails?	Students and individuals (age 14+, coed), corporations, educational, and civic organizations.
Program type:	Sail training and seamanship taught to impel students into confidence-building, life-enhancing experiences.

Specifications:	LOA: 30'	Draft: 18"	Sail area: 366 sq. ft.
	LWL: 28'	Beam: 8'	Freeboard: 2'
	Rig height: 20'	Hull: wood	

Designer:	Cyrus Hamlin, Kennebunk, Maine
Built:	1965-1988; Maine Coast and Maryland
Crew:	2. Trainees: up to 13
Contact:	Admissions/Hurricane Island Outward Bound School
	75 Mechanic Street
	Rockland, ME 04841
	Tel: 800-341-1744; Fax: 207-594-8202
	E-mail: admissions@hurricaneisland.org
	Web site: http://www.hurricaneisland.org

Idea Due

Launched in 1986, *Idea Due* is a custom-built schooner able to accommodate 12 passengers for overnight voyages and 25 for day sails. The design guarantees a high level of safety and comfort. *Idea Due* is operated by a specialized company as a school and charter vessel in the Mediterranean Sea. She participated in the 1992 Columbus Regatta and other international events. Fully certified by R.I.Na. (Registro Italiano Navale), *Idea Due* has been mentioned in the official publication for the celebration of "A Hundred Years of Lega Navale Italiana".

Flag:	Italy
Rig:	Schooner
Homeport/waters:	Otrano, Italy: Mediterranean Sea
Who sails?	High school and college students, individuals of all ages, and families.
Cost:	$1,000 - $1,500 group rate per day
Program type:	Sail training for volunteer crew and trainees. Sea education in marine science and ecology in cooperation with accredited institutions. Dockside interpretation while in homeport.

Specifications:			
	Sparred length: 78'	Draft: 10'	Sail area: 4,130 sq. ft.
	LOD: 73'	Beam: 15'	Tons: 49 GRT
	LOA: 75'	Rig height: 85'	Power: twin 145 HP
	LWL: 63'	Freeboard: 6'	Hull: steel

Designer:	Stefano Rossi
Built:	1986; Fano (Pesaro), Italy, Bugari
Certification:	R.I.Na. (Registro Italiano Navale)
Crew:	4. **Trainees/passengers:** 12
Contact:	Captain Pantaleo Coluccia
	Otranto Navigazione s.a.s.,
	Via G. Galilei, n. 2, Casamassella, Lecce 73020, ITALY
	Tel/Fax: 39-337-701451

IDEA DUE

Imagine...!

The 76-foot schooner *Imagine...!* was built and put into service in 1997 to provide high quality leadership and team performance training programs to corporate executives and managers. Using two to five-day cruises, clients are challenged with a variety of "dock to destination" exercises, where their success is contingent upon operating individually as effective leaders and collectively as an efficient team. Ultimately the participants are expected to master the skills necessary to safely operate the vessel from point to point, using one another as resources. Facilitated debriefing sessions by professional corporate trainers transfer the experience from the "boat to the boardroom."

Imagine...! also operates educational sails for school groups, adjudicated youth, special need students, and other young people. These programs provide a wide spectrum of learning experiences, ranging from pure science-based curriculum to a full-fledged sail training offering. Cruises range from several hours to several days in duration.

Imagine...! operates primarily in the Baltimore/Annapolis, Maryland area, but throughout a March-November season travels as far north as Philadelphia, Pennsylvania and as far south as Norfolk, Virginia.

Flag:	USA		
Rig:	Gaff schooner		
Homeport/waters:	Annapolis, Maryland: Chesapeake Bay, eastern US		
Who sails?	School groups, individuals, and corporate groups.		
Program type:	Sail training for paying trainees. Corporate team building.		
Specifications:	LOD: 65'	Draft: 7' 9"	Sail area: 1,900 sq. ft.
	LOA: 76'	Beam: 16'	Power: twin 50 HP diesels
	LWL: 55'	Hull: cedar	
Built:	1997; Port of Albany, New York, Scarano Boat Building		
Coast Guard certification:	Passenger Vessel (Subchapter T)		
Contact:	Captain Michael Bagley		
	Imagine Yacht, LLC		
	PO Box 1469		
	Annapolis, MD 21404		
	Tel: 410-626-0900; Fax: 888-252-6639		
	E-mail: Captimagine@aol.com		
	Web site: http://www.schoonerimagine.com		

Inland Seas

The Inland Seas Education Association's schooner *Inland Seas* was launched in 1994 to be a hands-on laboratory for students to learn about the Great Lakes. The schooner is steel hulled with detailing similar to traditional tall ships. The vessel is equipped with scientific gear for studying the Great Lakes ecosystem. ISEA's popular Schoolship Program, which began in 1989, offers half-day Great Lakes educational opportunities for students aboard *Inland Seas* and chartered schooners *Malabar* and *Manitou*. A variety of summer shipboard programs are offered for students and adults aboard *Inland Seas*, all of which foster an appreciation for and a commitment to the natural and cultural heritage of the Great Lakes.

INLAND SEAS

Flag:	USA
Rig:	Gaff schooner, two-masted
Homeport/waters:	Suttons Bay, Michigan: Grand Traverse Bay, Lake Michigan
Who sails?	Schools groups and individuals of all ages. Affiliated institutions include the Great Lakes Maritime Academy and Eastern Michigan University.
Season:	Spring and summer
Program type:	Sail training for volunteer and paying trainees. Sea education in marine science, maritime history, and ecology for students from elementary school through college, adults, and at-risk-youth. Dockside interpretation during port visits.

Specifications:

Sparred length: 77'	Draft: 7'	Sail area: 1,800 sq. ft.
LOD: 61' 6"	Beam: 17'	Tons: 41 GRT
LWL: 53'	Rig height: 66'	Power: 130 HP
Freeboard: 4'	Hull: steel	

Designer:	Charles W. Wittholz, Woodin & Marean
Built:	1994; Palm Coast, Florida, Treworgy Yachts
Coast Guard certification:	Passenger Vessel (Subchapter T)
Crew:	5. **Trainees:** 30 (day sails), 11 (overnight)
Contact:	Thomas M. Kelly, Executive Director
	Inland Seas Education Association
	PO Box 218
	Suttons Bay, MI 49682
	Tel: 231-271-3077; Fax: 231-271-3088
	E-mail: isea@traverse.com
	Web site: http://www.schoolship.org

Internet Explorer

the definition of a bad idea.

(Work in Progress)

The aircraft industry makes giant wings of over 2,600 square feet that must be retired after 18,000 flights. These used 747 wings will become the wing-masts of the 270-foot aluminum catamaran, *Internet Explorer*. Using industrial crane bearings to support and rotate the wings, a highly engineered and reliable mechanism will be built. A vessel of this size and weight will make a very impressive package indeed—the naval architects have indicated that the vessel is capable of reaching speeds of 40 knots in 20 knots of wind.

A ferry boat with these hulls could carry more than 150 cars and 800 passengers at 50 knots, so how fast is this wing ship capable of going, and perhaps more importantly, what is she capable of being? This question is why Aeronautics joined ASTA. These hulls are capable of so much more than speed records—they can be classrooms and research labs. Aeronautics plans to use *Internet Explorer* as a sail training vessel, carrying 150 trainees and 50 faculty. The vessel will be 270 feet long, 74 feet wide, and have as much as 19,980 square feet of deck space.

Flag:	USA
Rig:	Schooner, three-masted
Waters:	Worldwide
Who sails?	College students and other groups.
Program type:	Sail training for paying trainees. Sea education in marine science and ecology. Passenger sails overnight. Dockside interpretation during port visits.

Specifications:			
	Sparred length: 270'	Draft: 3' (hull), 18' (centerboard)	
	Sail area: 15,000 sq. ft. (upwind), 48,000 sq. ft. (downwind)		
	LOD: 270'	Beam: 72'	
	LOA: 270'	Rig height: 136'	
	LWL: 244'	Freeboard: 21'	Hull: aluminum

Designer:	Aeronautics, LLC
Crew:	10. **Trainees:** 150
Contact:	Brad Cavanagh, Project Manager
	Aeronautics
	195 West Long Pond Rd.
	Plymouth, MA 02360
	Tel/Fax: 508-224-9416
	E-mail: b.s.c@worldnet.att.net

In

INTREPID

The incomparable two-time America's Cup winner *Intrepid* is close to the hearts of all sailors. Designed by Sparkman and Stephens and built by Minneford's in City Island, New York in 1967, *Intrepid* represents a tremendous breakthrough in twelve-meter design. She was the first twelve to separate the rudder from the keel, include a "bustle" or "kicker" and use a trim tab. *Intrepid*'s underbody type, with relatively minor refinements, was used on every subsequent Cup boat until *Australia II*'s winged keel of 1983.

After 32 years of hard sailing she has been rebuilt to "as new" condition. America's Cup Charters' George Hill and Herb Marshal worked with Sparkman and Stephens, Brewer's Cove Haven Marina, and master shipwright Louis Sauzedde to restore this landmark yacht. *Intrepid* proudly joins the twelve-meter fleet at America's Cup Charters, offering leisure sails, racing, and corpo-rate team building charters from any port between Maine and the Chesapeake.

Flag:	USA
Rig:	Sloop
Homeport/waters:	Newport, Rhode Island: New England and Chesapeake Bay
Who sails?	Individuals of all ages
Cost:	$1,800 group rate per day, $60 per person for evening sails.
Program type:	Sail training for volunteer or paying trainees. Sea education based on informal, in-house programming. Passenger day sails.

Specifications:			
	Sparred length: 69'	Draft: 9'	Sail area: 1,850 sq. ft.
	LOD: 65'	Beam: 12'	Tons: 28 GRT
	LOA: 65'	Rig height: 90'	Power: diesel
	LWL: 46'	Hull: wood	

Designer:	Sparkman and Stephens
Built:	1967; City Island, New York, Minneford
Coast Guard certification:	Passenger Vessel (Subchapter T)
Crew:	3. **Trainees/passengers: 12**
Contact:	George Hill/Herb Marshall America's Cup Charters PO Box 51 Newport, RI 02840 Tel: 401-849-5868; Fax: 401-849-3098 Web site: http://www.americascupcharters.com

ohnson

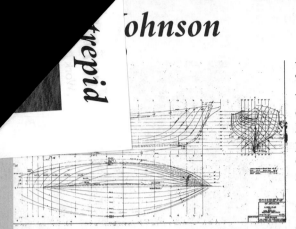

The Los Angeles Maritime Institute is building two 90-foot brigantines to be named *Irving Johnson* and *Exy Johnson* in honor of the Johnsons and their life-long commitments to character-building sail training.

Irving McClure Johnson began training for a sailor's life as a teenager. In 1929 he sailed around Cape Horn on the four-masted barque *Peking*, a voyage he documented in a film entitled "Around Cape Horn."

Captain Johnson met Electa on his next voyage aboard the *Wander Bird*. The Johnsons sailed around the world seven times in three different *Yankee*s, sharing their skill and knowledge of the sea with a hand-picked crew generally composed of four young women, 16 young men, a doctor, a cook, and a mate.

Construction will take place at the Los Angeles Maritime Museum in John Gibson Park, San Pedro. The brigantine design is based on one from the 1930s that has been adapted by W.I.B. Crealock to meet Coast Guard and LAMI program requirements.

The shipyard will be visitor friendly, set up as a living history exhibit of the museum. Construction will be carried out by professional, paid shipwrights working with trained volunteers. Funding for the project will come from private donations, corporate sponsorships, and foundation grants.

Flag:	USA
Rig:	Brigantine
Homeport/waters:	Los Angeles, California: Southern California and offshore islands
Who sails?	Referred youth-at-risk and groups catering to students and adults.
Season:	Year-round
Cost:	Based on ability to pay
Program type:	Educational sailing adventures for youth and adult groups.

Specifications:			
Sparred length: 110' 8"	Draft: 11'	Sail area: 4,540 sq. ft.
LOA: 90'	Beam: 21' 9"	Tons: 99 GRT
LWL: 72' 6"	Rig height: 87' 8"	Power: diesel

Coast Guard certification:	Sailing School Vessel (Subchapter R), Passenger Vessel (Subchapter T)
Contact:	Captain Jim Gladson, President
	Los Angeles Maritime Institute
	Berth 84, Foot of Sixth Street
	San Pedro, CA 90731
	Tel: 310-833-6055; Fax: 310-548-2055

WATCH THIS MOVIE, ITS AWESOME!

Isabelle

Isabelle is a classic yacht built and designed in 1924 by the renowned William Fife. Her construction is teak over sawn-oak frames. *Isabelle* is a beautiful reminder of the glamour and romance of the "Golden Age" of yachting.

Since 1978 *Isabelle* has been owned and operated as a day and term charter vessel out of Newport, Rhode Island. Her crew includes a master and two deckhands who are fully involved in the maintenance and upkeep of this classic vessel. *Isabelle* is available for port and maritime festivals throughout Southern New England.

ISABELLE

Flag:	USA
Rig:	Ketch
Homeport/waters:	Newport, Rhode Island: Southern New England
Who sails?	Adults and families.
Cost:	$1,400 per day group rate
Program type:	Sail training for crew and apprentices. Sea education in marine science as informal, in-house programming. Passenger day sails and dockside interpretation during port visits.

Specifications:			
	Sparred length: 83'	Draft: 10' 5"	Sail area: 3,000 sq. ft.
	LOD: 83'	Beam: 18'	Tons: 96 GRT
	LOA: 83'	Rig height: 105'	Hull: wood
	LWL: 65'	Freeboard: 4'	

Designer:	William Fife & Sons
Built:	1924; Scotland, William Fife
Coast Guard certification:	Passenger Vessel (Subchapter T)
Crew:	3 (day sails), 6 (overnight). **Trainees:** 25 (day sails), 8 (overnight)
Contact:	Captain Steve Vaitses
	Katama Yachts, Inc.
	119 Grove Street
	Clinton, CT 06413
	Tel: 860-669-5921; Fax: 860-669-6143
	E-mail: katama@uconect.net

John E. Pfriem

The *John E. Pfriem* is a classic
Chesapeake Bay bugeye ketch design
built in Gloucester, Massachusetts in
1964. She operates as a marine environmental education vessel sailing the
waters of Long Island Sound from April
through November.

Flag:	USA
Rig:	Chesapeake Bay bugeye ketch
Homeport/waters:	Bridgeport, Connecticut: Long Island Sound
Who sails?	Affiliated institutions include the University of Bridgeport, Housatonic Community College, and seven Connecticut school districts.
Season:	April to November
Program type:	Sail training for crew and apprentices. Sea education in marine science and ecology in cooperation with accredited institutions. Dockside interpretation.

Specifications:

Sparred length: 65'	Draft: 3'	Sail area: 1,200 sq. ft.
LOA: 55'	Beam: 14' 6"	Tons: 14 GRT
LWL: 47'	Rig height: 49'	Hull: wood
Freeboard: 2' 6"		

Designer:	Russell Grinnell
Built:	1964; Gloucester, Massachusetts, Russell Grinnell
Coast Guard certification:	Research Vessel (Subchapter U)
Crew:	2-3. **Trainees:** 22
Contact:	Edwin T. Merritt, Executive Director
	The Aquaculture Foundation
	525 Antelope Dr.
	Shelton, CT 06484
	Tel: 203-372-4406; Fax: 203-372-4407
	E-mail: tmerritt@pcnet.com
	Web site: http://www.tallshipblackpearl.org

Jolie Brise

Dauntsey's School Sailing Club was established in the mid-1970s by the boys and girls at Dauntsey's School. The Sailing Club operates *Jolie Brise*, a 1913 Le Havre Pilot Cutter in conjunction with the Exeter Maritime Museum. *Jolie Brise* became famous in 1925 when she won the first ever Fastnet Race. She again won the Fastnet Race in 1929 and 1930. In 1932 she rescued thirty crew from the American yacht *Adriana*, which had caught fire during the Bermuda Race, earning her the Blue Water Medal. *Jolie Brise* was also the last vessel to carry the Royal Mail under sail.

Jolie Brise sails with up to ten trainees, aged 13 and up, throughout northern Europe, with a different program each summer. In the year 2000 she will be coming to Bermuda, Boston, and Halifax as part of Tall Ships 2000®, then back across the Atlantic to Amsterdam. *Jolie Brise* is available for charter for both corporate outings and longer sail training trips. Traditionally rigged, sailing her is very much a hands-on experience, requiring everyone to be involved. The atmosphere is very friendly, informal, and relaxed.

Flag:	UK
Rig:	Cutter
Homeport/waters:	Southampton, England: Northern Hemisphere, British South Coast
Who sails?	School groups from high school through college, as well as individuals of all ages.
Program type:	Sail training for volunteer and paying trainees. Dockside interpretation during port visits.

Specifications:			
	Sparred length: 76'	Draft: 11'	Sail area: 3,750 sq. ft.
	LOD: 56'	Beam: 15'	Tons: 44 GRT
	LOA: 60'	Rig height: 77'	Power: 60 HP
	LWL: 50'	Freeboard: 4'	Hull: oak

Designer:	Paumelle
Built:	1913; LeHavre, France, Paumelle
Certification:	British MCA Cat. '0' - Sail Training
Crew:	3. **Trainees:** 15 (day sails), 10 (overnight)
Contact:	Captain T.R. Marris, Head of Sailing
	Dauntsey's School Sailing Club
	West Lavington, Near Devizes
	Wiltshire, SN10 4HE, UNITED KINGDOM
	Tel: 44-1380-818-216; Fax: 44-1380-818-216
	E-mail: marris@dauntsey's.wilts.sch.uk

Jolly II Rover

tional program working primarily with inner city youth of Philadelphia. The "*Rover*" serves as an educational platform to introduce students to sailing, maritime history, and the marine sciences. While on board the *Jolly II Rover*, students will set sail and get the chance to explore the world of plankton, study the water quality of the Delaware River, and learn about the past, present, and future of the Philadelphia waterfront.

The *Jolly II Rover* is a 73-foot topsail schooner operated by Philadelphia City Sail, and conducts educational sails and group charters out of the Philadelphia, Pennsylvania waterfront. Philadelphia City Sail is a nonprofit maritime educa-

Philadelphia City Sail works closely with The School District of Philadelphia, The Franklin Institute, and the New Jersey State Aquarium, serving over 3,000 students each year.

Flag:	USA
Rig:	Square topsail schooner
Homeport/waters:	Philadelphia, Pennsylvania: Delaware River and Chesapeake Bay
Who sails?	Middle and high school students and families.
Cost:	$750 group rate per day
Program type:	Sail training for volunteer trainees. Sea education in marine science and maritime history in cooperation with accredited institutions and as part of informal, in-house programming.

Specifications:			
	Sparred length: 73'	Draft: 5' 6"	Sail area: 1,770 sq. ft.
	LOD: 61'	Beam: 15' 6"	Tons: 34 GRT
	LOA: 61'	Rig height: 65'	Power: 130 HP
	Hull: steel		

Designer:	Merrit Walter
Built:	1993; Beaufort, North Carolina, Rover Marine Lines, Inc.
Coast Guard certification:	Passenger Vessel (Subchapter T)
Crew:	3. Trainees: 49
Contact:	Matthew Burke, Education Director
	Philadelphia City Sail,
	PO Box 43235
	Philadelphia, PA 19129
	Tel: 215-574-1200; Fax: 215-574-8360
	E-mail: Phcitysail@aol.com
	Web site: http://www.phillyfriend.com/citysail.htm

Joseph Conrad

Mystic Seaport's Sail Education Program offers young people the rare experience of living aboard a square-rigged ship as they learn sailing in Dyer Dhows and JY-14s, rowing, and the arts of the sailor. The emphasis is on learning by doing and working together and teamwork while living aboard this famous ship, which is permanently berthed at Mystic Seaport.

The *Joseph Conrad* program is open to individual boys and girls and organized groups ages 10 through 15. Groups must have one adult leader per 10 participants. No prior experience is required for beginner sessions, only a desire to participate and learn. Intermediate sessions are for those who have attended a previous beginner session or have had sailing experience. All must hold current Red Cross swimmers certification or its equivalent.

JOSEPH CONRAD

Flag:	USA
Rig:	Ship, three-masted
Homeport:	Mystic, Connecticut
Who sails?	Individuals and organized groups ages 10 through 15.
Season:	June through August
Cost:	$485 per person for six-day program
Program type:	Sail training. Dockside visitation for school groups and individuals.

Specifications:			
	Sparred length: 118' 6"	Draft: 12'	Tons: 213 GRT
	LOA: 100' 8"	Beam: 25' 3"	Hull: iron
	Rig height: 98' 6"		

Designer:	Burmeister and Wain
Built:	1882; Copenhagen, Denmark, Burmeister & Wain
Trainees:	32-50
Contact:	Museum Education Department
	Mystic Seaport
	PO Box 6000
	Mystic, CT 06355-0990
	Tel: 860-572-0711; Fax: 860-572-5395
	Web site: http://www.mysticseaport.org/sailing

Ka'iulani

Ka'iulani is a modern luxury replica of an 1850s Pacific Coast gaff topsail schooner. Designed for long distance, deep ocean cruising and to sail around Cape Horn in the greatest safety and comfort, she was deliberately overbuilt to the highest possible standards. *Ka'iulani* features a mahogany hull, traditional teak decks, rig, and hardware, and lots of varnish and polished bronze in her cabins and state-rooms. Originally launched in 1984 as a private family yacht, she has sailed over 60,000 ocean miles under the command of her original captain.

In conjunction with the non-profit Coloma Outdoor Discovery School, *Ka'iulani* offers sail training programs for grades 4 through 12. These half-day programs may combine a visit to the neighboring Bay Model, operated by the Army Corps of Engineers, or a visit to the nearby Marine Mammal Center.

Ka'iulani is also available for a wide variety of corporate and private adventures and celebrations, and ticketed Sunday morning cruises. Weddings are performed on board by the captain. Catering and beverage packages are also available.

Flag:	USA
Rig:	Gaff topsail schooner
Homeport/waters:	Sausalito, California: San Francisco Bay
Who sails?	School groups from middle school through high school. Affiliated with the Coloma Outdoor Discovery School.
Cost:	$45 per person for three-hour sail; $425 group rate per hour
Program type:	Sail training for paying trainees. Sea education as informal, in-house programming. Passenger day sails.

Specifications:			
	Sparred length: 86'	Draft: 7' 6"	Sail area: 1,436 sq. ft.
	LOD: 65'	Beam: 18'	Tons: 63 GRT
	LOA: 67'	Rig height: 75'	Power: GM 671 diesel
	LWL: 53'	Freeboard: 4'	Hull: mahogany

Designer:	W.I.B. Crealock
Built:	1984; San Diego, California, Coast
Coast Guard certification:	Passenger Vessel (Subchapter T)
Crew:	4. **Trainees:** 49 (day sails)
Contact:	Captain Robert Michaan, President
	Discovery Yacht Charters
	PO Box 1145
	Sausalito, CA 94966
	Tel: 415-331-1333; Fax: 415-331-6190
	E-mail: sail@sfyacht.com
	Web site: http://www.sfyacht.com

Kajama

Nazi Schooner

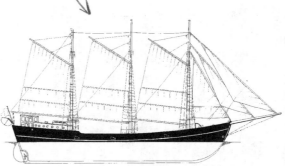

The Great Lakes Schooner Company of Toronto is currently engaged in the restoration and re-fit of the 1930 three-masted schooner *Kajama* (kai-ama). Representing one of the few remaining Nobiskrug coastal trading schooners, *Kajama* had a long and successful career as a cargo-carrying sailing ship. After years of successful trading she was converted for use as a strictly diesel-powered trader. Stripped of sails, neglected, and plodding anonymously between small European ports, *Kajama* was likely only a few years from being retired and broken up like so many sailing ships before her.

The Great Lakes Schooner Company located *Kajama* in a small Danish port and brought her to Toronto in the summer of 1999. The restoration and re-fit began with guidance from historic drawings, photographs, and information from former crew, as well as architect's drawings and construction details provided by the original builders.

The project commenced with the removal of the freighter superstructure and the installation of new masts and rigging. Below deck new bulkheads, systems, and an interior suited for passengers are being constructed. An impressive re-launching is planned for the spring of 2000 followed by an inaugural sail along the Toronto waterfront. Sailing from her berth at Harbourfront, *Kajama* will be available daily for public sails and charters.

Flag:	Canada
Rig:	Gaff rig schooner, three-masted
Homeport/waters:	Toronto, Ontario, Canada: Lake Ontario
Who sails?	Individuals and groups of all ages. Kajama operates a day sail training program in conjunction with The Pier - Toronto's Waterfront Museum.
Season:	April to October
Program type:	Day sail training program, passenger voyages, corporate, charter, maritime events.

Specifications:

Sparred length: 165'	Draft: 9'	Sail area: 7000 sq. ft.
LOD: 142'	Beam: 24'	Tons: 263 GRT
Rig height: 100'	Hull: steel	Power: 400 HP
Freeboard: 7'		

Designer:	Nobiskrug
Built:	1930; Rendsburg, Germany, Nobiskrug Shipyard
Certification:	Transport Canada Certified Passenger Vessel
Crew:	8. **Trainees/passengers:** 225 (day sails)
Contact:	Captain Doug Prothero, President
	Great Lakes Schooner Company
	249 Queen's Quay West, Suite 111
	Toronto, ON M5J 2N5, CANADA
	Tel: 416-260-6355; Fax: 416-260-6377
	E-mail: doug@greatlakesschooner.com
	Web site: http://www.greatlakesschooner.com

Kalaha

1975. Her cruising area is the Bahamas in the summer with the Sea Base program (Boy Scouts). Trainees learn sail handling, how to use ground tackle, prepare meals, and basic coastal navigation. *Kalaha* also travels to the Tortugas, Key West, and the Florida Keys. She day sails on the Gulf of Mexico and Pine Island Sound, and is available for charter for special events and overnight trips.

Designed by W.I.B. Crealock to be a world cruiser, the ketch *Kalaha* was built by the Westsail Corporation in

Flag:	USA				
Rig:	Ketch				
Homeport/waters:	Bokeelia, Florida: Bahamas (summer), Caribbean (winter)				
Who sails?	Individuals and families of all ages. Affiliated groups include the Boy Scouts of America.				
Season:	Year-round				
Cost:	$80 per person per day, $480 group rate (charter)				
Program type:	Sail training for paying trainees. Sea education in cooperation with Boy Scouts of America.				
Specifications:	Sparred length: 47'		Draft: 6'		Sail area: 990 sq. ft.
	LOD: 42' 11"		Beam: 13'		Tons: 3 GRT
	LOA: 47'		Rig height: 56'		Power: 85 HP diesel
	LWL: 33' 4"		Freeboard: 6'		Hull: fiberglass
Designer:	W.I.B. Crealock				
Built:	1975; California, Westsail				
Coast Guard certification:	Uninspected Vessel				
Crew:	1				
Contact:	Captain Bill Masenheimer				
	Pine Island Yacht Service				
	11943 Oakland Dr.				
	Bokeelia, FL 33922				
	Tel/Fax: 941-283-7129				

SAIL TALL SHIPS!

Kalmar

Built in Wilmington, Delaware and commissioned in May 1998, the *Kalmar Nyckel* is a replica of the first Swedish ship to arrive in America, at what is now Delaware, in 1638. Based on a Dutch pinnace design, she acts as Delaware's tall ship ambassador, functions as an educational tool, and draws attention to the shipbuilding history on Wilmington's Christina River.

The *Kalmar Nyckel* is manned by a professional captain, mates, and volunteer crew. Initial sail training has been for the staff and volunteers, and will expand to other groups as the ship's operations develop and grow. While current operations focus on the mid-Atlantic region, a trip to Europe is planned for the future. The *Kalmar Nyckel* is available for school group tours as well as corporate and private functions, and is available for charter.

KALMAR NYCKEL

Flag:	USA
Rig:	Full-rigged ship
Homeport/waters:	Wilmington, Delaware: Mid-Atlantic
Who sails?	School groups from elementary through college, as well as individuals and families. Affiliated institutions include the Challenge Program.
Program type:	Sail training for volunteer or paying trainees. Dockside interpretation during port visits.

Specifications:			
	Sparred length: 139'	Draft: 12' 2"	Sail area: 7,600 sq. ft.
	LOD: 93'	Beam: 24' 11"	Tons: 160 GRT
	LOA: 97' 4"	Rig height: 65'	Power: diesel
	LWL: 89' 2"	Freeboard: 8'	Hull: wood

Built:	1997; Wilmington, Delaware, Allen C. Rawl
Coast Guard certification:	Sailing School Vessel (Subchapter R), Passenger Vessel (Subchapter T)
Contact:	Captain Robert Glover, Executive Director
	Kalmar Nyckel Foundation
	1124 East 7th St.
	Wilmington, DE 19801
	Tel: 302-429-7447; Fax: 302-429-0350
	Web site: http://www.kalnyc.org

elot

Greenland Trading Company, *Kaskelot* supplied the remote East Greenland coastal settlements. In the late 1960s *Kaskelot* then worked as a fisheries support vessel in The Faroes. Square Sail purchased her in 1981 and totally redesigned and re-rigged her to replicate the *Terra Nova*, returning to East Greenland to make a film about Captain Scott's ill-fated expedition to the South Pole.

All of Square Sail's ships are fully commissioned and work throughout the year. When not filming, they have a regular sailing program, giving people the chance to experience traditional square-rig sailing first-hand. These voyages typically run between four and seven days, and occasionally longer. They are either based from Square Sail's homeport of Charlestown, Cornwall, UK, or they work around the annual schedule offering voyages between the various ports.

Square Sail runs an annual course from February to October where trainees are given the opportunity to learn the skills associated with sailing these ships, and in addition to maintenance and shore-based instruction, they form part of the regular crew throughout the season.

The flagship of the Square Sail fleet, *Kaskelot* is a three-masted barque and one of the largest remaining wooden ships in commission. Built by J. Ring Andersen in 1948 for the Royal

Flag:	UK
Rig:	Barque, three-masted
Homeport/waters:	Charlestown, Cornwall, UK: UK and Europe
Who sails?	Individuals of all ages and families. Affiliated institutions include Falmouth Marine School and Cornwall College.
Cost:	$180 per person per day, $8,000 per day group rate (corporate charter)
Program type:	Sail training for professional crew and volunteer and paying trainees. Sea education in maritime history in cooperation with accredited institutions and as informal, in-house programming. Worldwide film work and corporate charters.

Specifications:					
Sparred length: 153'		Draft: 12'		Sail area: 9,500 sq. ft.	
LOD: 120'		Beam: 28'		Tons: 226 GRT	
LOA: 124'		Rig height: 105'		Power: 375 HP diesel	
LWL: 115'		Freeboard: 9'		Hull: oak on oak	

Built:	1948; Denmark, J. Ring Anderson
Certification:	Bureau Veritas and MCA Class VI certificate (UK)
Crew:	14. Trainees/passengers: 50 (day sails), 12 (overnight)
Contact:	Chris Wilson, Marketing Manager, Square Sail, Charlestown Harbour, St. Austell, Cornwall PL25 3NJ, UNITED KINGDOM
	Tel: 44-1720-70241; Fax: 44-1726-01839, E-mail: sextant@cwcom.net
	Web site: http://www.square-sail.com

Kathryn B.

A brand-new classic, the *Kathryn B.* is a rugged, ocean-going, steel-hulled 105-foot, three-masted, gaff-rigged topsail schooner. Her huge sails propel her with grace and swiftness, and when the winds refuse to cooperate, her powerful engine carries her comfortably to her next port.

Most cabins have queen-size berths, writing desks, and their own private heads with hot shower.

Relax on a tufted-velvet settee with a good book or take tea on the afterdeck and dine on delicious dishes carefully prepared using the best local seafoods and other fresh ingredients. Accommodations are available for ten passengers in queen cabins, all with hot and cold running water. Skylights and dorades in every cabin offer plenty of

light and air. Launched in 1995, the *Kathryn B.* meets or exceeds all U.S. Coast Guard safety requirements. She is operated by a fully qualified, licensed professional captain and crew. The *Kathryn B.* is also available for charter for weddings, reunions, corporate retreats, and other memorable times.

KATHRYN B.

Flag:	USA
Rig:	Gaff schooner, three-masted
Homeport/waters:	Hope, Maine: Maine (summer), St. Vincent and Virgin Islands (winter)
Who sails?	Adult individuals and groups.
Season:	Year-round
Cost:	$3,600 group rate (charter)
Program type:	Sail training for professional crew. Sea education as informal, in-house programming.

Specifications:					
	Sparred length: 105'	Draft: 8'	Sail area: 3,000 sq. ft.
	LOD: 80'	Beam: 20'	Tons: 80 GRT
	LOA: 105'	Rig height: 64'	Power: 135 HP diesel
	LWL: 65'	Freeboard: 8'	Hull: steel

Designer:	Tom Colvin
Built:	1995; Palm Coast, Florida, Treworgy Yachts
Coast Guard certification:	Passenger Vessel (Subchapter T)
Crew:	4. **Trainees/passengers:** 60
Contact:	Kathryn Baxter, Owner, Schooner Kathryn B.
	391 Hatchet Mt. Rd.
	Hope, ME 04847
	Tel/Fax: 207-763-4255
	E-mail: kathrynb@midcoast.com
	Web site: http://www.kathrynb.com

Kruzenshtern

Biggest boot ever (handwritten)

KRUZENSHTERN

Kruzenshtern was built as *Padua* in 1927 in Bremerhaven, Germany. The sister ship to *Peking*, she is the last of the "Flying P" liners still under sail. These vessels were engaged in the grain trade from Australia to Europe. In 1933 *Kruzenshtern* sailed from her homeport of Hamburg to Port Lincoln in Australia in only 67 days. At the end of World War II she was handed to the USSR and converted into a sail training ship.

Since 1990, up to 40 trainees of all ages have been welcomed on board to sail along with the Russian students of the Baltic Academy in Kalingrad, Russia, learning the ropes, manning the helm, or climbing the rigging to set more than 30,000 square feet of sail. No previous experience is necessary.

Kruzenshtern is supported by Tall Ship Friends, a nonprofit organization in Hamburg, Germany. The goals of Tall Ship Friends are to promote sail training on square-riggers, to contribute to the further existence of these beautiful ships, and to provide an unforgettable experience for the participants. Members of Tall Ship Friends receive the quarterly *Tall Ships News* (English/German) and a personal sailing log.

Flag:	Russia
Rig:	Barque, four-masted
Homeport/waters:	Kalingrad, Russia: Western European waters (summer), Southern European waters (winter)
Who sails?	Individuals and groups of all ages.
Cost:	$50-$100 per person per day. Group charters by appointment
Program type:	Sail training for paying trainees. Fully accredited sea education in traditional seamanship.

Specifications:			
	Sparred length: 376'	Draft: 19'	Sail area: 36,380 sq. ft.
	LOA: 346'	Beam: 46'	Power: twin 600 HP
	LOD: 329'	Rig height: 176'	Hull: steel
	LWL: 311' 6"	Freeboard: 27' 9"	

Built:	1927; Bremerhaven, Germany, J.C. Tecklenborg
Certification:	Special Purpose (School Vessel), Russia
Crew:	45-70. **Trainees:** 250 (day sails), 60 (overnight)
Contact:	Wulf Marquard, Managing Director
	Tall Ship Friends Germany, Schweriner Str. 17
	Hamburg, D22143, GERMANY
	Tel: 49-40-675 635 97; Fax: 49-40-675 635 99
	E-mail: tallship1@aol.com
	Web site: http://www.tallship-friends.de

SAIL TALL SHIPS!

Lady Maryland is an authentic pungy schooner, an elegant boat designed to haul cargo, fish, dredge for oysters, and carry luxury items quickly from port to port on Chesapeake Bay and along the Atlantic Coast. Instead of carrying watermelons and oysters, her mission today is to provide students with the opportunity to experience sailing a historic vessel while studying history, sailing, seamanship, marine science, and ecology on her traditional waters from Maryland to Maine.

The Living Classrooms Foundation has developed a flexible educational program that can fit the needs of a variety of school and community groups. More than 50,000 students participate in LCF programs each year. The *Lady Maryland* operates educational day experiences for 32 trainees and extended live-aboard sail training and marine science programs for up to 14 people.

LADY MARYLAND

Flag:	USA
Rig:	Pungy schooner (gaff rigged), two-masted
Homeport/waters:	Baltimore, Maryland: Chesapeake and Delaware Bays, East Coast between Maryland and Maine
Who sails?	Student and other organized groups, individuals, and families.
Season:	March through November
Cost:	Rates vary depending on program, please call
Program type:	Sail training with paying trainees. Sea education in marine science, maritime history, and ecology for school groups from elementary school through colleges as well as adults.

Specifications:	Sparred length: 104'	Draft: 7'	Sail area: 2,994 sq. ft.
	LOD: 72'	Beam: 22'	Tons: 60 GRT
	LWL: 64' 3"	Rig height: 85'	Power: twin 80 HP diesels
	Freeboard: 3'		

Designer:	Thomas Gilmer
Built:	1986; Baltimore, Maryland, G. Peter Boudreau
Coast Guard certification:	Passenger Vessel (Subchapter T)
Crew:	6 (day sails), 8 (overnight). **Trainees:** 32 (day sails), 12-14 (overnight)
Contact:	Steve Bountress
	Living Classrooms Foundation
	802 South Caroline Street
	Baltimore, MD 21231-3311
	Tel: 410-685-0295; Fax: 410-752-8433
	Web site: http://www.livingclassrooms.org

...shington pretty, pretty, pretty

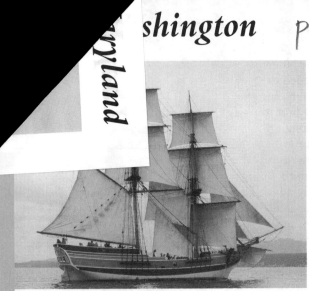

PHOTO BY TED PARRISH

Built at Grays Harbor Historical Seaport in Aberdeen, Washington and launched in 1989 as a Washington State Centennial project, the reproduction *Lady Washington* sails the waters of Washington State and the West Coast of North America as the tall ship ambassador for the state of Washington. With a busy year-round sailing schedule, *Lady Washington* regularly tours the West Coast, providing shipboard education programs for schools in 89 port communities in Washington, Oregon, California, British Columbia, and Alaska. More than 15,000 school children visit *Lady Washington* each year to learn about the rich and colorful maritime heritage of our nation.

As a privateer during the American Revolution, the original *Lady Washington* fought to help the colonies gain their independence from England. In 1788 she became the first American vessel to visit the West Coast of North America, opening trade between the colonies and the native peoples of the Northwest Coast. As the first American vessel to visit Honolulu, Hong Kong, and Japan, she played a key role in developing American involvement in Asian Pacific trade.

Crew are both paid professionals and volunteer trainees. The Historical Seaport regularly partners with a number of entities to provide unique shipboard education opportunities for trainees with independent learning contracts.

Flag:	USA
Rig:	Brig
Homeport/waters:	Aberdeen, Washington: Grays Harbor, Washington, West Coast of North America
Who sails?	School groups from elementary school through college, individuals and families.
Season:	March to January
Cost:	$35 per person for three-hour sail, $105 per person per day, $3,000 for full-day charter
Program type:	Sail training for crew, apprentices, and paying trainees. Sea education in maritime history in cooperation with accredited institutions and based on informal, in-house programming. Passenger day sails and overnight passages. Dockside interpretation.

Specifications:			
	Sparred length: 112'	Draft: 11'	Sail area: 4,400 sq. ft.
	LOD: 66' 9"	Beam: 24'	Tons: 99 GRT
	LOA: 87'	Rig height: 89'	Power: diesel
	LWL: 58'	Freeboard: 6'	Hull: wood

Designer:	Ray Wallace
Built:	1989; Aberdeen, Washington, Grays Harbor Historical Seaport Authority
Coast Guard certification:	Passenger Vessel (Subchapter T)
Crew:	12. **Trainees:** 48 (day sails), 8 (overnight)
Contact:	James H. "Flagg" Locke, Operations Director, Grays Harbor Historical Seaport
	PO Box 2019, Aberdeen, WA 98520
	Tel: 800-200-LADY (5239); Fax: 360-533-9384
	E-mail: ghhsa@techline.com, Web site: http://www.histseaport.org

162   **SAIL TALL SHIPS!**

Larinda

SANK in hurricane Juan (handwritten)

Designed and built as a modified replica of a 1767 Boston schooner, *Larinda* is a unique sailing vessel with modern safety features yet she retains traditional wood appointments and museum quality. Much of her construction is done with recycled 100-year-old hard pine. A restored seven-ton 1928 Wolverine 100 HP diesel provides auxiliary power. 300-pound bronze cannons add period excitement.

Featured in publications worldwide, *Larinda* has also starred in several documentaries shown on national and local television. Awards have been won at boat shows including the 1997 Wooden Boat Show and the 1998 Boston Antique and Classic Boat Show. Private charters are welcomed and *Larinda* is available for special events. Seaport festivals and other maritime gatherings have enjoyed her unique presence.

Flag:	USA
Rig:	Schooner
Homeport/waters:	Cape Cod, Massachusetts: New England
Who sails?	School groups from elementary through college and individuals of all ages
Cost:	Varies with program
Program type:	Sail training for volunteer and paying trainees. Sea education in marine science, maritime history, and ecology in cooperation with organized groups and as informal, in-house programming.

Specifications:			
	Sparred length: 76'	Draft: 8'	Sail area: 2,000 sq. ft.
	LOD: 56'	Beam: 16' 6"	Tons: 46 GRT
	LOA: 64'	Rig height: 62'	Power: 100 HP diesel
	LWL: 52'	Freeboard: 5'	Hull: wood and ferrocement

Designer:	Hallowell/Mahan
Built:	1996; Marstons Mills, Massachusetts, Wolverine Motor Works and Shipyard, LLC
Coast Guard certification:	Attraction Vessel
Crew:	6-8
Contact:	Captain Lawrence Mahan, President
	Schooner Larinda – Wolverine Motor Works and Shipyard LLC
	163 Walnut Street
	Marstons Mills, MA 02648
	Tel: 508-428-8728; Fax: 508-428-8728
	E-mail: tslarinda@capecod.net

Lark

LARK

Forbes family and was kept in Hadley Harbor at Naushon Island in Vineyard Sound.

Over the years, *Lark* fell into disrepair. She was purchased in 1971 by Captain Eric Little of Woods Hole, Massachusetts, who painstakingly restored her over the next 10 years to her original splendor.

Since then, *Lark* has sailed the East Coast from Marblehead to Miami, competing in classic yacht regattas and antique boat shows. Distinguished by her tanbark sails and gaff rig, *Lark* has been a successful racer and elegant cruising boat for more than 60 years, and is available for day and weekend charter. *Lark* plans to participate in Tall Ships 2000®.

Lark is a gaff-rigged cutter built in 1932 by F.D. Lawley for John Alden. She was designed as a day sailer for the

Flag:	USA
Rig:	Cutter
Homeport/waters:	Woods Hole, Massachusetts: Marblehead, Massachusetts to New York City
Who sails?	Individuals and adults.
Program type:	Sail training for volunteer trainees. Sea education as informal, in-house programming. Passenger day sails.

Specifications:			
	Sparred length: 52'	Draft: 5' 5"	Sail area: 1,200 sq. ft.
	LOD: 44' 10"	Beam: 10' 9"	Tons: 18 GRT
	LOA: 52'	Rig height: 55'	Power: 44 HP diesel
	LWL: 30'	Freeboard: 4'	Hull: mahogany over oak

Designer:	John Alden
Built:	1932; Quincy, Massachusetts, F.D. Lawley
Crew:	5
Contact:	Captain Eric Little
	2 Huettner Road
	Woods Hole, MA 02543-1506
	Tel: 508-540-7987, 508-548-9207; Fax: 508-540-5710
	E-mail: caplittle@aol.com

Lettie G. Howard

The *Lettie G. Howard* is a Fredonia model fishing schooner, a type of vessel once widely used along the Atlantic seaboard from Maine to Texas. She was built in 1893 at Essex, Massachusetts, where the majority of the schooners for the fishing fleets of Gloucester, Boston, and New York were produced. She operated out of Gloucester for her first eight years. The fishing would have been done with hand lines set either from the vessel's deck or from small boats called dories. The *Howard* was similar to the schooners that carried their Long Island and New Jersey catches to New York City's Fulton Fish Market.

In 1901 the *Howard* was purchased by Pensacola, Florida owners for use off Mexico's Yucatan Peninsula. Completely rebuilt in 1923, she was fitted with her first auxiliary engine a year later. She remained in the Gulf of Mexico until

1968, when she was sold to the South Street Seaport Museum.

The *Lettie G. Howard* was designated a National Historic Landmark in 1988. Between 1991 and 1993 the museum completely restored her to her original 1893 appearance, while outfitting her to accommodate trainees on educational cruises.

Flag:	USA
Rig:	Gaff topsail schooner, two-masted
Homeport/waters:	New York City: Northeast United States
Who sails?	School groups, Elderhostel, individual adults, and families.
Program type:	Sail training for volunteer and paying trainees. Sea education in marine science, maritime history, and ecology in cooperation with accredited institutions and other groups.

Specifications:			
	Sparred length: 129'	Draft: 11'	Sail area: 5,017 sq. ft.
	LOD: 83'	Beam: 21'	Tons: 52 GRT
	LWL: 71'	Rig height: 91'	Power: twin 85 HP diesels
	Hull: wood		

Built:	1893; Essex, Massachusetts, A.D. Story (restored at South Street Seaport Museum in 1993).
Coast Guard certification:	Sailing School Vessel (Subchapter R)
Crew:	7. **Trainees:** 14 (overnight)
Contact:	Captain Stefan Edick, Marine Education
	South Street Seaport Museum
	207 Front Street, New York, NY 10038
	Tel: 212-748-8596; Fax: 212-748-8610
	Web site: http://www.southstseaport.org

Liberty

only Coast Guard-licensed tall ship carrying passengers for harbor cruises regularly, *Liberty* is kept "shipshape and Bristol fashion" and is available for charter for special events. *Liberty* travels to New England ports for special maritime festivals.

In the fall, *Liberty* makes the two-week passage to Key West with passengers and begins her winter schedule of day sails and charters.

Liberty is modeled on early 1800s coastal schooners used by New England fishermen and as cargo vessels. Boston's

Flag:	USA
Rig:	Gaff topsail schooner
Homeport/waters:	Boston, Massachusetts (summer), Key West, Florida (winter): East Coast US
Who sails?	School groups from elementary through high school, individuals and families.
Cost:	$25 per person per two-hour harbor cruise, $175 per person per day; $3,600 group rate charter per day
Program type:	Passenger day sails and overnight passages. Corporate and private charters.

Specifications:			
	Sparred length: 80'	Draft: 7'	Sail area: 1,744 sq. ft.
	LOD: 61'	Beam: 17'	Tons: 50 GRT
	LOA: 64'	Rig height: 65'	Power: diesel
	LWL: 53'	Freeboard: 5'	Hull: steel

Designer:	Charles Wittholz
Built:	1993; Palm Coast, Florida, Treworgy Yachts
Coast Guard certification:	Passenger Vessel (Subchapter T).
Crew:	3 (day sails), 4 (overnight). **Trainees:** 49 (day sails), 8 (overnight)
Contact:	Gregory E. Muzzy, President
	The Liberty Fleet of Tall Ships
	67 Long Wharf
	Boston, MA 02110
	Tel: 617-742-0333; Fax: 617-742-1322

Liberty Clipper

The *Liberty Clipper* is a replica of the mid-19th century Baltimore clippers, famous for their fast passages around Cape Horn on their way to California and Pacific ports. The schooner *Liberty Clipper* joined *Liberty* in Boston in the summer of 1996. She is available for charter, with up to 110 passengers, in Boston Harbor and Key West for day and evening cruises. Her spacious decks and on-board hospitality create an ambiance under sail that will meet the expectation of most discriminating charter clients. Guests are invited to join in hoisting the sails, steering the boat, and otherwise joining in the fun. *Liberty Clipper* will also make several three and five-day trips from Boston to other New England ports such as Provincetown, Martha's Vineyard, and the Maine coast, and a winter program will include a trip south and a Key West itinerary.

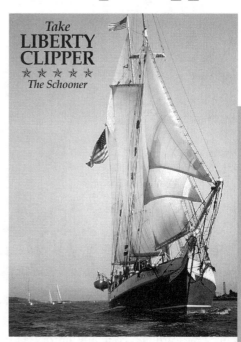

Take
LIBERTY
CLIPPER
★ ★ ★ ★ ★
The Schooner

Flag:	USA
Rig:	Gaff topsail schooner
Homeport/waters:	Boston, Massachusetts: East Coast
Who sails?	School groups from elementary through high school, individuals, and families.
Cost:	$175 per person per day; $6,500 group rate charter per day
Program type:	Passenger day sails and overnight passages. Corporate and private charters.

Specifications:			
	Sparred length: 125'	Draft: 8' (min.), 13' (max.)	Sail area: 4,300 sq. ft.
	LOD: 86'	Beam: 25'	Tons: 99 GRT
	LWL: 76'	Rig height: 78'	Power: diesel
	Freeboard: 5'	Hull: steel	

Designer:	Charles Wittholz
Built:	1983; Warren, Rhode Island, Blount Marine Corporation
Coast Guard certification:	Passenger Vessel (Subchapter T)
Crew:	5 (day sails), 10 (overnight). **Trainees/passengers:** 115 (day sails), 24 (overnight)
Contact:	Gregory E. Muzzy, President
	The Liberty Fleet of Tall Ships
	67 Long Wharf
	Boston, MA 02110
	Tel: 617-742-0333; Fax: 617-742-1322

Lisa

The brig *Lisa* offers teenagers the opportunity to sail before the mast in a new brig. Students can spend an academic year learning geography, history, and math by direct experience, all while experiencing the disciplines of life at sea and the thrill of manning a traditional vessel.

Flag:	USA
Rig:	Brig
Homeport/waters:	Wilmington, Delaware: worldwide
Season:	Year-round
Program type:	Full academic curriculum and special education programs for high school students and youth-at-risk.

Specifications:	Sparred length: 72'	Draft: 6' 3"	Sail area: 3,000 sq. ft.
	LOA: 55'	Beam: 18'	Tons: 40 GRT
	LWL: 45'	Rig height: 55'	Hull: steel
	Freeboard: 5'		

Coast Guard certification:	Uninspected Vessel
Crew:	4. Trainees: 6
Contact:	Mrs. Leibolt
	P.O. Box 161510
	Altamont Springs, FL 32716
	Tel: 407-884-8333

Little Jennie

Built in 1884, the *Little Jennie* is one of the oldest surviving examples of a Chesapeake Bay Bugeye. Built for oystering and freighting, the *Little Jennie* in now listed on the National Register of Historic Places. Acquired by Captain Pagels in the summer of 1999, work has already begun on this historic vessel to restore her back to sailing condition.

The *Little Jennie* will be based in Bar Harbor, Maine, during summers, where she will offer both overnight and day sail educational and sail training trips. Falls and winters may find her in the Chesapeake Bay once again.

Flag:	USA
Rig:	Bugeye
Homeport/waters:	Bar Harbor, Maine: Bar Harbor, Maine (summer), Chesapeake Bay (winter)
Program type:	Sail training for volunteer or paying trainees. Dockside interpretation during port visits

Specifications:	Sparred length: 86'	Draft: 4' 6"	Sail area: 1,600 sq. ft.
	LOA: 61'	Beam: 17'	Tons: 22'
	LWL: 57'	Rig height: 60'	Power: 100 HP diesel

Designer:	J.T. Marsh
Built:	1884; Solomons, Maryland, J.T. Marsh
Coast Guard	
certification:	Passenger Vessel (Subchapter T)
Contact:	Captain Steven F. Pagels, Owner
	Downeast Windjammer Cruises
	PO Box 28
	Cherryfield, ME 04622
	Tel: 207-546-2927; Fax: 207-546-2023
	E-mail: decruise@midmaine.com
	Web site: http://downeastwindjammer.com

Lord Nelson

Wheelchair accesable. Also ugly.

LORD NELSON

The 180-foot, three-masted barque *Lord Nelson* was built in 1986 for the Jubilee Sailing Trust to encourage integration between able-bodied and physi-cally disabled people by offering them the opportunity to experience the excitement of tall ship sailing together.

Voyages last from 4 to 11 days, departing from a wide variety of ports and sailing in the English Channel and the North and Irish Seas. A winter season of voyages based in the Canary Islands is also available.

Above deck the ship's equipment enables physically disabled crew to work alongside their able-bodied crewmates. Features include power steering, wide decks to accommodate wheelchairs, a speaking compass, powered lifts between decks, and Braille marking. Below are specially designed wheelchair-accessible cabins, showers, and heads.

Voyages are open to anyone between 16 to 70+ with or without sailing experience. 20 people with physical disabilities, including eight wheelchair users, serve alongside an equal number of able-bodied people. There is a permanent crew of 10, including a medically trained person and a cook.

Flag:	UK
Rig:	Barque, three-masted
Homeport/waters:	Southampton, United Kingdom: United Kingdom (summer), Canary Islands (winter)
Who sails?	Physically disabled and able-bodied people, aged 16 to 70+.
Cost:	Ranges from $65 to $133 per person per day, plus insurance
Program type:	Sail training for paying trainees. Integration of physically disabled and able-bodied people through the medium of tall ship sailing.

Specifications:			
	Sparred length: 180'	Draft: 13' 6"	Sail area: 11,030 sq. ft.
	LOD: 133'	Beam: 29' 6"	Tons: 368 GRT
	LOA: 140' 5"	Rig height: 108'	Power: twin 260 hp
	LWL: 121' 5"	Freeboard: 6' 8"	Hull: steel

Designer:	Colin Mudie
Built:	1986; Wivenhoe, UK, James W. Cook & Co., Ltd.
Certification:	Lloyds 100A1
Crew:	10. Trainees: 40
Contact:	Mrs. Lindsey Neve, Jubilee Sailing Trust
	Jubilee Yard, Hazel Road, Woolston
	Southampton, Hampshire SO19 7GB, UNITED KINGDOM
	Tel: 44-23-8044-9108; Fax: 44-23-8044-9145
	E-mail: jst@jst.org.uk
	Web site: http://www.jst.org.uk

Mabel Stevens

The ketch *Mabel Stevens* offers charter services in the Washington, DC, and Chesapeake Bay areas. Sail training cruises, group and individual charters, and other tailored sailing and maritime education programs are offered by Captain Chalker aboard the *Mabel Stevens.*

Built by Captain Dick Hartge of Galesville, Maryland, the *Mabel Stevens* holds a special place in the Washington metropolitan area. During the 1980s, the *Mabel Stevens* officially represented the District of Columbia at the tall ships events in Boston (350th anniversary) and New York (Statue of Liberty centennial), and in 1992 in New York at the Christopher Columbus Quincentennial Celebrations. She is the District of Columbia's goodwill ambassador vessel at major historic events. The *Mabel Stevens* competes in ASTA rallies and has in the past raced with the best of the Class C tall ships. In 1986, she led the fleet of sail training vessels engaged in friendly competition en route to New

York's Statue of Liberty festivities and participated in Philadelphia and Tall Ships® Newport '92.

Flag:	USA
Rig:	Ketch
Homeport/waters:	Cobb Island, Maryland: Lower Potomac River, Chesapeake Bay.
Who sails?	Individuals and groups
Season:	April to October
Cost:	$70 per person per day; inquire for group rates
Program type:	Maritime history and environmental studies.

Specifications:			
	Sparred length: 47' 6"	Draft: 4' 6"	Sail area: 1,200 sq. ft.
	LOA: 35'	Beam: 11' 6"	Sail number: TS-US 159
	LWL: 31' 9"	Rig height: 45'	Tons: 17 GRT
	Freeboard: 3'	Hull: wood	Power: 52 HP diesel

Built:	1935; Galesville, Maryland, Ernest H. Hartge
Coast Guard certification:	Uninspected Vessel
Crew:	1. Trainees: 4
Contact:	Captain Ned Chalker, Ketch Mabel Stevens
	119 Fifth St. NE, Washington, DC 20002
	Tel: 202-543-0110, 301-259-4458; Fax: 202-554-3949
	E-mail: Nchalker@aol.com

Madeline

The *Madeline* is a reconstruction of a mid-19th-century schooner, typical of the trading schooners that once sailed the upper Great Lakes. The original *Madeline* was once the first Euro-American school in the Grand Traverse region and for a short time served as a lightship in the Straits of Mackinac.

The modern *Madeline*, launched in 1990, was built over a period of five years by volunteers of the Maritime Heritage Alliance (MHA), using traditional methods and materials. From her homeport, Traverse City, Michigan, she has sailed with her volunteer crew on all five Great Lakes, visiting over 60 ports with dockside tours and historical interpretation. *Madeline* is the State of Michigan's official tall ship and is designated as the City of Traverse City's goodwill ambassador.

Madeline's dockside programs bring visitors on board to learn about schooners and Great Lakes history first-hand. Crewmembers, trained as historical interpreters, share their knowledge of history, marlinespike skills, and wooden boat building. School programs with special hand-on activities are also available.

The Maritime Heritage Alliance, a nonprofit organization, fosters the study and practice of upper Great Lakes's maritime history. MHA programs, focusing on building and operating indigenous crafts, include crew training, traditional boat carpentry, and other wooden boat maintenance skills.

Flag:	USA
Rig:	Gaff topsail schooner, two-masted
Homeport/waters:	Traverse City, Michigan: upper Great Lakes
Who sails?	Trained crewmembers of the Maritime Heritage Alliance. *Madeline* is associated with the Association for Great Lakes history.
Program type:	Adult sail training and maritime history.

Specifications:			
Sparred length: 92'	Draft: 7' 7"	Sail area: 2,270 sq. ft.
LOA: 55' 6"	Beam: 16' 2"	Tons: 42 GRT
LWL: 52'	Rig height: 65'	Freeboard: 2' 2"

Designer:	Robert Core
Built:	1990; Traverse City, Michigan, Maritime Heritage Alliance
Coast Guard certification:	Uninspected Vessel
Crew:	9
Contact:	Laura Quackenbush, *Madeline* Coordinator
	PO Box 1108
	Traverse City, MI 49685
	Tel: 231-946-2647; Fax: 231-946-6750
	E-mail: MHA.TC@juno.com
	Web site: http://www.traverse.com/maritime/

Maine

Maine's design and construction was conceived by Lance Lee at the Maine Maritime Museum. Master builders Dave Foster, Will Ansel, and Phil Shelton guided her construction by Museum apprentices between keel laying in 1981 and launching in 1986. She evolved as a project employing many skilled and experienced maritime historians, boat designers, and builders. Her lines were taken by Jim Stevens of Goudy & Stevens from a half-model dating from 1832 in East Boothbay, Maine. Marine draftsman Sam Manning drew the plans. The deck layout and rig are based on Howard Chapelle's research, with input from, among others, Maynard Bray and naval architect Jay Paris. A fast and able sailor, *Maine* serves the Museum as a floating exhibition, a sail training vessel, and a roving ambassador. *Maine* travels along the Maine coast in the summer from Portland to Penobscot Bay.

MAINE

Flag:	USA		
Rig:	Pinky schooner, two-masted (gaff-rigged)		
Homeport/waters:	Bath, Maine: coastal Maine and southern New England.		
Program type:	Sea education in maritime history.		
Specifications:	Sparred length: 56'	Draft: 8'	Tons: 14 GRT
	LOD: 40'	Beam: 12'	Power: diesel
	LOA: 43'	Freeboard: 2' 6"	Hull: wood
Built:	1985; Bath, Maine, Maine Maritime Museum		
Coast Guard certification:	Uninspected Vessel		
Contact:	Tom Wilcox/Will West		
	Maine Maritime Museum		
	243 Washington Street		
	Bath, ME 04530		
	Tel: 207-443-1316; Fax: 207-443-1665		

Malabar

the vessel in the Great Lakes before bringing her to her new homeport of Bar Harbor, Maine.

Once restoration of *Malabar*'s hull is complete this summer, Captain Steve Pagels hopes to begin a sail training program involving both day sails and overnight voyages. Captain Pagels also plans to use the vessel for oceanographic research.

Downeast Windjammer Cruises has recently acquired the schooner *Malabar* and is planning to begin restoration of

Flag:	USA
Rig:	Gaff topsail schooner, two-masted
Homeport/waters:	Bar Harbor, Maine: East Coast US
Who sails?	Individuals and groups.
Program type:	Sail training for crew and apprentices. Passenger day sails and overnight passages.

Specifications:					
	Sparred length: 105'		Draft: 8' 6"		Sail area: 3,000 sq. ft.
	LOD: 65'		Beam: 21'		Tons: 73 GRT
	LWL: 60'		Rig height: 75'		Power: 136 HP diesel
	Freeboard: 6'		Hull: ferro/steel		

Designer:	M.D. Lee
Built:	1975; Bath, Maine, Long Beach Shipyard
Coast Guard **certification:**	Passenger Vessel (Subchapter T)
Crew:	6. Trainees: 49 (day), 21 (overnight)
Contact:	Captain Steve F. Pagels, Owner
	Downeast Windjammer Cruises
	PO Box 28
	Cherryfield, ME 04622
	Tel: 207-546-2927; Fax: 207-546-2023
	E-mail: decruise@midmaine.com
	Web site: http://www.downeastwindjammer.com

Mallory Todd

Named for Captain Mallory Todd, who served as master on American vessels during the Revolutionary War, the *Mallory Todd* is a modern 65-foot schooner built in the classic style with fireplaces and exceptionally fine woodwork. Designed for long distance voyages, she has sailed the West Coast from Mexico to Alaska for 18 years. When at homeport in Seattle, she relieves the tedium of long term cancer treatment with recreational outings for hospital patients and their caregivers under the auspices of the nonprofit Sailing Heritage Foundation.

Sail training trips to the San Juan Islands, Canada, and Alaska via the Inside Passage are blessed with the full bounty of nature. Humpback whales, Orcas, sea lions, dolphins, and sea otters cavort while bears forage ashore, eagles soar the winds, and fjord hillsides entice the naturalist with breathtaking wildflowers. These trips are open to anyone between 18 and 80 with or without sailing experience. Together, part time volunteers, trainees, and professionals get the job done. Hands on tending the

sails, steering, scrubbing, navigating, fishing, or clamming, each contributes where a need fits their abilities.

Schooner *Mallory Todd* also offers corporate and private charters that provide a unique and delightful venue for business or recreational activities—be it exclusive executive meeting or picnic outing.

Flag:	USA
Rig:	Staysail schooner
Homeport/waters:	Seattle, Washington: Pacific Northwest, Canada, and Alaska
Who sails?	All ages for volunteers, paying trainees, and apprentices.
Program type:	Sail training for crew volunteers, trainees, and apprentices. Sea education based on programmed and day to day events. Passenger day sails for corporate team building or recreational events.

Specifications:		
Sparred length: 65'	Draft: 5' (min.), 8' (max.)	Sail area: 1,545 sq. ft.
LOD: 65'	Beam: 16'	Tons: 38 GRT
LOA: 60'	Rig Height: 65'	Power: diesel
LWL: 50'	Freeboard: 5'	Hull: composite

Designer:	Perry & Todd
Built:	1981; Seattle, Washington
Coast Guard certification:	Passenger Vessel (Subchapter T).
Crew:	2. **Trainees:** 6 (overnight), 25 (day sails)
Contact:	Captain George Todd, Sailing Heritage Foundation
	10042 NE 13th Street
	Bellevue, WA 98004
	Tel: 425-451-8160; Fax: 425-451-8119
	E-mail: mallorytodd@msn.com
	Web site: http://www.sailseattle.com

Manitou

sels on the Great Lakes. She can accommodate 24 overnight guests and 60 passengers for day excursions. *Manitou* is fully certified by the US Coast Guard and offers three, five, and six-day windjammer cruises to islands, bays, and coastal villages of Lake Michigan, Lake Huron, and the North Channel.

In conjunction with the Inland Seas Education Association, *Manitou* offers the Schoolship Program, which provides an environmental, historical, and sail training education for students during the spring and fall. Separate three-day family packages for adventurous adults and their children are also available on two separate cruises during the regular season. Primarily offered as an adult vacation, the windjammer season runs from Memorial Day through October 3.

Owned and operated by the Traverse Tall Ship Company, the schooner *Manitou* is one of the largest sailing ves-

Flag:	USA
Rig:	Gaff topsail schooner, two-masted
Homeport/waters:	Northport, Michigan: Great Lakes
Who sails?	Science and marine biology student groups from elementary school through junior high for educational programs. Also individual, family, and corporate groups for multi-day windjammer cruises.
Season:	May to October
Program type:	Sail training for crew and apprentices. Sea education in marine science, maritime history, ecology, and corporate team-building workshops. Individual and group windjammer cruises.

Specifications:

Sparred length: 114'	Draft: 7' (min.), 11' (max.)	Sail area: 3,000 sq. ft.
LOD: 77'	Beam: 22'	Tons: 82 GRT
LWL: 65'	Rig height: 80'	Power: 150 HP diesel
Freeboard: 6'	Hull: steel	

Designer:	Woodin & Marean.
Built:	1982; Portsmouth, New Hampshire, Roger Gagnon Steel Ship Company
Coast Guard certification:	Passenger Vessel (Subchapter T)
Crew:	6, 6 instructors. **Trainees:** 56 (day sails), 24 (overnight). **Age:** 12-60
Contact:	Richard W. Budinger, President, Traverse Tall Ship Company 13390 West Bay Shore Dr. Traverse City, MI 49684 Tel: 231-941-2000; Fax: 231-941-0520 E-mail: tallship@traverse.com Web site: http://www.traverse.com/tallship

Margaret Todd

The first four-masted schooner to operate in New England waters in over half a century, the *Margaret Todd* sails from Bar Harbor, Maine in the summer. This 151-foot, four-masted topsail schooner primarily offers day sails along the spectacular Acadia coastline. Built new in 1998, the *Margaret Todd* was inspired by the New England multi-masted schooners of the turn of the century.

Get the feel of a tall ship on an operational four-masted schooner with enough sail area to give her a good turn of speed. With her distinctive tanbark sails and rig, the *Margaret Todd* stands out along the Maine coast. Because of her shallow draft centerboard design, the *Margaret Todd* also sails southern waters during the winter season. Groups are encouraged to contact Downeast Windjammer Cruises for both educational sails, sail training, and harbor visits as an attraction vessel.

Flag:	USA
Rig:	Schooner, four-masted
Homeport/waters:	Bar Harbor, Maine: East Coast between Maine and Florida
Program type:	Sail training for paid or volunteer crew or trainees. Passenger day sails. Dockside interpretation during port visits.

Specifications:	Sparred length: 151'	Draft: 5' 9"	Sail area: 4,800 sq. ft.
	LOD: 121'	Beam: 23'	Tons: 99 GRT
	LOA: 121'	Hull: steel	Power: diesel

Designer:	Woodin and Marean
Built:	1998; St. Augustine, Florida, Schreiber Boats
Coast Guard certification:	Passenger Vessel (Subchapter T)
Trainees/passengers:	150
Contact:	Captain Steve F. Pagels, Owner
	Downeast Windjammer Cruises
	PO Box 28
	Cherryfield, ME 04622
	Tel: 207-546-2927; Fax: 207-546-2023
	E-mail: decruise@midmaine.com
	Web site: http://www.downeastwindjammer.com

Mary Day

with modern design thinking. *Mary Day* operates out of Camden, Maine, in the windjammer trade from late May to early October. She carries 30 passengers on weeklong vacation cruises in mid-coast Maine. *Mary Day* is a pure sailing vessel. She has no engine and depends on a small yawl boat when winds fail. She has a large and powerful rig and exhibits outstanding sailing abilities.

Mary Day carries a professional crew of six, including captain, mate, cook, two deckhands, and one galley hand. The galley and one deck position are considered entry-level positions, and a great many sailing professionals have started out or gained valuable experience on board the schooner *Mary Day*.

Built in 1962 by Harvey Gamage, *Mary Day* combines the best aspects of the New England centerboard coaster

Flag:	USA
Rig:	Gaff topsail schooner, two-masted
Homeport/waters:	Camden, Maine: Mid-Coast and Downeast Maine
Who sails?	Individuals and families.
Season:	May to October
Cost:	$129 per person per day
Program type:	Sail training for crew and apprentices. Passenger overnight passages. Dockside interpretation in homeport.

Specifications:	Sparred length: 125'	Draft: 7' 6"	Sail area: 5,000 sq. ft.
	LOD: 90'	Beam: 22'	Tons: 86 GRT
	LOA: 92'	Rig height: 102'	Hull: wood
	LWL: 81'	Freeboard: 5'	

Designer:	H. Hawkins
Built:	1962; South Bristol, Maine, Harvey Gamage
Coast Guard certification:	Passenger Vessel (Subchapter T)
Crew:	7. **Trainees:** 49 (day sails), 29 (overnight)
Contact:	Captains Barry King and Jen Martin
	Penobscot Windjammer Company
	PO Box 798
	Camden, ME 04843
	Tel: 800-992-2218
	E-mail: captains@schoonermaryday.com
	Web site: http://www.schoonermaryday.com

Mike Sekul

The *Mike Sekul* is one of the two Biloxi oyster schooner replicas built as part of the Biloxi Schooner Project under the auspices of the Maritime and Seafood Industry Museum. She was launched in April of 1994 as part of the effort to preserve the maritime and seafood industry of the Mississippi Gulf Coast. Money for construction and fitting out of the *Mike Sekul* and her sister ship, *Glenn L. Swetman*, has come from donations and fundraising events.

The *Mike Sekul* is available for charter for two-and-a-half hours, half-day, and full-day trips in the Mississippi Sound and to the barrier islands, Cat Island, Horn Island, and Ship Island. Walkup day sailing trips are made when she is not under charter. Groups of up to 45 passengers learn about the maritime and seafood heritage

of the Gulf Coast and about the vessels working in Biloxi's seafood industry.

Sailing classes are offered through local colleges and the museum's Sea and Sail Adventure summer camp. Wedding parties, Elderhostel, and school groups are also accommodated.

Flag:	USA
Rig:	Gaff topsail schooner, two-masted
Homeport/waters:	Biloxi, Mississippi: coastwise Gulf of Mexico
Who sails?	Elementary students through college age, adults, and families. Affiliated institutions include William Carey College, Seashore Methodist Assembly, J.L. Scott Marine Education Center, and Mississippi State University
Season:	Year-round
Cost:	$15 per adult or $10 per child (2 hour sail). Group rate (up to 45 people) $500 for half-day, $750 per day.
Program type:	Sail training for paying and volunteer trainees. Sea education in marine science, maritime history, and ecology in cooperation with accredited institutions and organized groups and as informal, in-house programming.

Specifications:	Sparred length: 78'	Draft: 5' 10"	Sail area: 2,499 sq. ft.
	LOD: 50'	Beam: 17'	Tons: 24 GRT
	LOA: 78'	Hull: wood	Power: 4-71 Detroit diesel
	LWL: 43'		

Designer:	Neil Covacevich
Built:	1993; Biloxi, Mississippi, Neil Covacevich
Coast Guard certification:	Passenger Vessel (Subchapter T)
Crew:	3. **Trainees**: 45 (day). **Age**: 15+
Contact:	Robin Krohn, Executive Director
	Maritime and Seafood Industry Museum
	PO Box 1907
	Biloxi, MS 39533
	Tel: 228-435-6320; Fax: 228-435-6309
	E-mail: schooner@maritimemuseum.org
	Web site: http://www.maritimemuseum.org

Minnie V.

MINNIE V.

The skipjack *Minnie V.*, built in Wenona, Maryland, was used to dredge oysters on the Chesapeake Bay for many years. The vessel was rebuilt by the City of Baltimore in 1981 and is now owned and operated by the Living Classrooms Foundation. The Foundation uses the vessel for educational programs and as a tourist attraction offering interpretive tours of the historic port of Baltimore. While on board the *Minnie V.*, students learn about the oyster trade, its importance to the economy of Maryland, and the hard life of a waterman as they relive history by raising the sails on one of the Chesapeake's few remaining skipjacks.

Flag:	USA
Rig:	Sloop
Homeport/waters:	Baltimore, Maryland: Baltimore Harbor
Who sails?	School groups from middle school through college as well as individuals and families.
Season:	April through October
Cost:	Rates vary depending on program. Please call for more information.
Program type:	Sea education in marine science, maritime history, and ecology in cooperation with accredited schools, colleges, and other organized groups. Passenger day sails. Dockside interpretation.

Specifications:			
	Sparred length: 69'	Draft: 3'	Sail area: 1,450 sq. ft.
	LOD: 45' 3"	Beam: 15' 7"	Tons: 10 GRT
	Rig height: 58'	Freeboard: 2'	Hull: wood

Built:	1906; Wenona, Maryland, Vetra
Coast Guard certification:	Passenger Vessel (Subchapter T)
Crew:	2. **Trainees:** 24
Contact:	Steve Bountress, Living Classrooms Foundation
	802 South Caroline Street
	Baltimore, MD 21231-3311
	Tel: 410-685-0295; Fax: 410-752-8433
	Web site: http://www.livingclassrooms.org/facilities/minniev.html

Beautiful, yes?

Misty I

MIR

Mir is regarded by many as the fastest Class A sail training ship in the world. She was the overall winner of the 1992 Columbus Race and the winner of the Cutty Sark Tall Ship Races in 1996, 1997, and 1998 under the command of Captain Victor Antonov. *Mir* was launched in 1989 at the Lenin shipyard in Gdansk, Poland, the builders of five more of the M 108 type ships: *Dar Mlodziezy, Pallada, Khersones, Druzhba,* and *Nadezhda.*

Mir is the school ship of the Makarov Maritime Academy in St. Petersburg, Russia, training future navigators and engineers for the Russian merchant fleet. Since 1990 up to 60 trainees of all ages are welcomed on board to sail along with the Russian students, learning the ropes, manning the helm, or climbing the rigging to set the sails. No previous experience is necessary.

Mir is supported by Tall Ship Friends, a nonprofit organization in Hamburg, Germany. The goals of Tall Ship Friends are to promote sail training on square-riggers, to contribute to the further exis-tence of these beautiful ships, and to provide an unforgettable experience for the participants. Members of Tall Ship Friends receive the quarterly *Tall Ships News* (English/German) and a personal sailing log.

Flag:	Russia
Rig:	Full-rigged ship
Homeport/waters:	St. Petersburg, Russia: west and southwest European waters
Who sails?	Students and individuals of all ages. Affiliated with Tall Ship Friends clubs in France, UK, Switzerland, Austria, Ireland, and Italy.
Cost:	$50-$100 per person per day
Program type:	Sail training for paying trainees. Fully accredited sea education in traditional seamanship. Dockside interpretation during port visits.

Specifications:			
	Sparred length: 345' 9"	Draft: 18'	Sail area: 29,997 sq. ft.
	LOA: 328'	Beam: 44' 9"	Tons: 2,856 GRT
	LOD: 300' 9"	Rig height: 149'	Power: twin 570 HP diesels
	LWL: 254'	Freeboard: 34' 6"	Hull: steel

Designer:	Z. Choren
Built:	1987; Gdansk, Poland, Stocznia Gdanska
Certification:	Russian registered Sailing School Vessel
Crew:	45-70. **Trainees/passengers:** up to 250 (day sails), 60 (overnight)
Contact:	Wulf Marquard, Managing Director, Tall Ship Friends Germany
	Schweriner Str. 17, Hamburg, D22 143, GERMANY
	Tel: 49-40-675 635 97; Fax: 49-40-675 635 99
	E-mail: tallship1@aol.com
	Web site: http://tallship-friends.de

The 1915 gaff-rigged ketch *Misty Isles* operates from Hampton Roads, Virginia during the school year and plans to move to New England waters during the summers. Her motto is "Serving Fishers of Men", and services are offered primarily to Christian organizations. The only cost to sail on the *Misty Isles* is that of bringing your own food, drink, and snorkel gear. Preparation and serving food underway is part of the teamwork on board, as are sail handling, naviga-tion, anchoring, and standing watches.

Two new masts, a new keel, rudder, and bow, as well as much work on deck and in the rigging kept her crew busy from 1990 to 1997 in south-ern California. During her first year in Key West, Florida, the *Misty Isles* was host to many Boat Breakfasters, helped start a local chapter of Fellowship of Christian Adult Singles (FOCAS), and signed up for a reef research project, monitor-ing selected fish and urchin populations within the Ecological Reserve at the Western Sambos.

1999 saw a trip from Key West to Boston to deliver services to the Lewis School, a middle school in Roxbury, Massachusetts, and Essex County church groups. The *Misty Isles* has recently relocated to Hampton Roads, Virginia.

Flag:	USA
Rig:	Gaff ketch
Homeport/waters:	Hampton Roads, Virginia (fall through spring): Rings Island, Salisbury, Massachusetts (summer)
Who sails?	Affiliated institutions include church youth groups.
Season:	Year-round
Program type:	Sail training for crew and apprentices.

Specifications:			
Sparred length: 60'	Draft: 9'	Sail area: 1,500 sq. ft.
LOD: 49'	Beam: 12'	Tons: 30 GRT
LOA: 50'	Rig height: 60'	Power: 80 HP diesel
LWL: 44'	Hull: wood	

Built:	1915
Crew:	3 (day sails), 6 (overnight). **Trainees:** 20 (day sails), 12 (overnight)
Contact:	Ray and Wendy Pike, Owners
	PO Box 7707
	Hampton, VA 23666
	Tel: 978-465-1976 (Pam McKay)
	E-mail: Raymond.Pike@langley.af.mil

Mystic Whaler

Built in 1967 and rebuilt in 1994, the *Mystic Whaler* carries passengers and trainees on a variety of cruises, ranging from one day to one week. In April and May, the schooner will be on the Hudson River, conducting environmental education programs in conjunction with the *Clearwater*. Sailing from Mystic, Connecticut, in the summer months, the *Mystic Whaler* will visit New York and Boston on one-week cruises with trainees, then finish the season with Elderhostel programs in September and October. Some of the two or three-day cruises during the season focus on specific topics, such as lighthouses, sea music, art, and photography. Lobster cruises are popular during the summer. Two-week apprenticeship programs run throughout the season.

Flag:	USA
Rig:	Gaff-rigged schooner
Homeport/waters:	Mystic, Connecticut: southeast New England
Who sails?	School groups from elementary school through college, as well as individuals and families.
Program type:	Sail training for crew and apprentices. Sea education in maritime history and ecology based on informal programming with organized groups such as Scouts. Passenger day sails and overnight passages.

Specifications:	Sparred length: 110'	Draft: 7' 6" (min.), 13' (max.)	Sail area: 3,000 sq. ft.
	LOD: 83'	Beam: 25'	Tons: 97 GRT
	LOA: 83'	Rig height: 90'	Power: 6-71 diesel, 175 HP
	LWL: 78'	Freeboard: 7'	Hull: steel

Designer:	"Chub" Crockett
Built:	1967; Tarpon Springs, Florida, George Sutton
Coast Guard certification:	Passenger Vessel (Subchapter T)
Crew:	5. **Trainees:** 65 (day), 36 (overnight)
Contact:	Captain John Eginton, Mystic Whaler Cruises, Inc.
	PO Box 189
	Mystic, CT 06355-0189
	Tel: 860-536-4218; Fax: 860-536-4219
	E-mail: mysticwhaler@bigplanet.com
	Web site: http://www.mysticwhaler.com

MYSTIC WHALER

Nefertiti

PHOTO BY LAURA SAWALL

Nefertiti was built for the Ross Anderson Boston Yacht Club Syndicate at the Graves yard in Marblehead, Massachusetts for the 1962 America's Cup. She was designed and skippered by Ted Hood, who ousted both *Easterner* and *Columbia* before being eliminated by Bus Mosbacher's *Weatherly* in the defender's finals.

Following her Cup challenge, *Nefertiti* was converted for cruising and traversed the globe. She crossed the Atlantic to the Mediterranean and chartered out of Greece for several years. By 1983 she was back in Newport as a spectator of the last America's Cup series held in Newport. *Nefertiti* then traveled down to the West Indies, to Fremantle, Australia in 1987, and crossed the Indian Ocean to South Africa where she remained until September 1997. She has been restored to racing trim by America's Cup Charters.

The 1962 12-meter class sloop *Nefertiti* has returned to Newport, Rhode Island from South Africa, following a ten-year worldwide voyage. Brought back by America's Cup Charters' George Hill and Herb Marshall, owners of the America's Cup defender *Weatherly* and Ted Turner's former *American Eagle*, *Nefertiti* is part of their charter fleet of former cup contenders.

Flag:	USA
Rig:	Sloop
Homeport/waters:	Newport, Rhode Island: New England and Chesapeake Bay
Who sails?	Individuals of all ages.
Cost:	$1,800 group rate per day, $60 per person for evening sails
Program type:	Sail training for volunteer and paying trainees. Sea education based on informal, in-house programming. Passenger day sails.

Specifications:			
	Sparred length: 69'	Draft: 9'	Sail area: 1,850 sq. ft.
	LOD: 67'	Beam: 13' 6"	Tons: 28 GRT
	LOA: 67'	Rig height: 90'	Power: diesel
	LWL: 46'	Freeboard: 4'	Hull: wood

Designer:	Ted Hood
Built:	1962; Marblehead, Massachusetts, Graves
Coast Guard certification:	Passenger Vessel (Subchapter T)
Crew:	3. **Trainees/passengers:** 14
Contact:	George Hill/Herb Marshall, America's Cup Charters
	PO Box 51
	Newport, RI 02840
	Tel: 401-849-5868; Fax: 401-849-3098
	Web site: http://www.americascupcharters.com

Crosscurrent Voyages is a sail training program operated onboard the Class C tall ship *Nehemiah*. Emulating the training style used on such vessels as the USCG Barque *Eagle*, the program attempts to awaken and cultivate leadership skills by challenging students to learn various disciplines and to manage different types of information and technical matters. Traditional knowledge and skills are used to integrate educational disciplines such as math, reasoning, English, and history. The object is to utilize the pace and style of administering a large sailing vessel as a tool for equipping trainees to develop personal styles for dealing with the sea of information, knowledge, and options which saturate their daily lives. The program rounds out the training by enhancing personal character development in the areas of family and community values.

The primary target age is 12 through 18. The training personnel often come from the USCG and professional maritime fields. The sailing vessel *Nehemiah* has circumnavigated the globe a number of times under previous ownership, thus adding a context to the learning.

Flag:	USA
Rig:	Ketch
Homeport/waters:	Richmond, California: San Francisco Bay and Pacific Coast
Who sails?	Groups from elementary school through college, youth organizations, individuals, and families. Court referrals are also accepted. Emphasis is on at-risk youth.
Program type:	Sail training emphasizing character and community building. Sea education in marine science, maritime history, and ecology. Passenger day sails and overnight passages.

Specifications:			
	Sparred length: 57'	Draft: 6' 5"	Tons: 23 GRT
	LOD: 46' 8"	Beam: 14' 3"	Power: Perkins 4-236
	LOA: 50'	Rig height: 58'	Hull: wood
	LWL: 39'	Freeboard: 5'	

Designer:	William Garden (modified)
Built:	1971; Santa Barbara, California, Joseph Meyr
Coast Guard certification:	Passenger Vessel (Subchapter T)
Crew:	2. **Trainees:** 25 (day sails), 12 (overnight)
Contact:	Captain Rod Phillips, Crosscurrent Voyages
	92 Seabreeze Drive
	Richmond, CA 94804-7410
	Tel: 510-234-5054; Fax: 510-234-5054
	E-mail: RodPhillips@compuserve.com

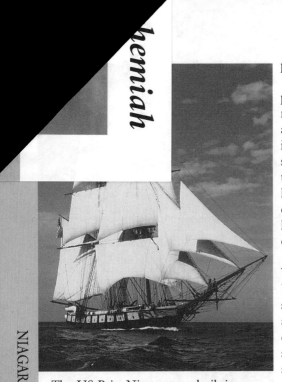

hemiah

NIAGARA

The US Brig *Niagara* was built in 1988 as a reconstruction of the warship aboard which Oliver Hazard Perry won the Battle of Lake Erie in 1813 during the War of 1812. Her mission is to interpret War of 1812 history, promote the Commonwealth of Pennsylvania, and preserve the skills of square-rig seafaring.

The present *Niagara* has auxiliary power and modern navigation equipment, but lacks modern amenities such as warm water, showers, and privacy. She is sailed by a crew of 18-20 professionals supplemented by 20 volunteers willing to live under spartan conditions such as hammock berthing and living out of a duffel bag. Volunteers do not need to have experience, but a minimum sign-on of three weeks is required.

Niagara is inspected as an Attraction Vessel in port, and sails as an Uninspected Vessel. During "home summers" (odd numbered years) there are typically two day sails per week from early May to late September, with a short voyage of three or four weeks sometime in the season. In even years the ship is away from seven to eighteen weeks on voyages to ports in the Great Lakes, US East Coast, and Canadian Maritimes. A typical schedule is public visitation in port for three days and a four-day passage between ports. 2000 will be an East Coast touring year.

Flag:	USA
Rig:	Brig
Homeport/waters:	Erie, Pennsylvania: Coastwise and Great Lakes
Who sails?	School groups from middle school through college, as well as individuals and families.
Program type:	Sail training for crew and apprentices. Sea education based on informal, in-house programming. Dockside interpretation.

Specifications:	Sparred length: 198'	Draft: 11'	Sail area: 12,600 sq. ft.
	LOD: 116'	Beam: 32' 6"	Tons: 162 GRT
	LOA: 123'	Rig height: 121'	Power: twin 180 HP diesels
	LWL: 110'	Hull: wood	

Designer:	Melbourne Smith
Built:	1988; Erie, Pennsylvania
Coast Guard certification:	Uninspected Vessel and Attraction Vessel
Crew:	40
Contact:	Captain Walter P. Rybka
	Pennsylvania Historical and Museum Commission
	150 East Front Street, Suite 100
	Erie, PA 16507
	Tel: 814-452-2744; Fax: 814-455-6760
	E-mail: sail@brigniagara.org
	Web site: http://www.brigniagara.org

Nighthawk

Built in 1980 as a replica of a 19th-century coastal schooner, *Nighthawk* sails the waters of the Chesapeake Bay and its tributaries from April 1 through November 1 each season. She voyaged to the Caribbean, Mexico, and South America prior to arriving in Baltimore in 1986.

Nighthawk operates as a private charter vessel as well as offering basic sail training to local school and scout groups. Docked in the historic Fells Point section of Baltimore's Inner Harbor, the *Nighthawk* and her captain and crew provide an ideal opportunity for character and team building through hands-on exploration.

Nighthawk is also available for a wide variety of corporate and private charters and celebrations, as well as public excursions. "Murder Mystery" and other theme cruises are featured. Weddings are performed aboard by the captain and catering is available.

NIGHTHAWK

Flag:	USA
Rig:	Schooner
Homeport/waters:	Baltimore, Maryland: Chesapeake Bay
Who sails?	Students from middle school through college. Affiliated institutions include Girl Scouts and church and youth organizations.
Season:	April through November
Program type:	Sail training for paying trainees based on informal, in-house programming.

Specifications:			
	Sparred length: 82'	Draft: 5'	Sail area: 2,000 sq. ft.
	LOD: 65'	Beam:20'	Tons: 45 GRT
	LWL: 60'	Rig height: 55'	Power: twin diesels
	Freeboard: 6'	Hull: steel	

Designer:	Haglund
Built:	1980; Florida, Haglund Schooner Company
Coast Guard certification:	Passenger Vessel (Subchapter T)
Crew:	4. **Trainees/passengers:** 49 (day sails), 6 (overnight)
Contact:	Captain Martin D. Weiss, President
	Schooner Nighthawk Cruises, Inc.
	1715 Thames St., Box 38153
	Baltimore, MD 21231
	Tel: 410-276-7447; Fax: 410-327-7245
	E-mail: schoonernighthawk@erols.com
	Web site: http://www.a1nighthawkcruises.com

Niña

Niña, Pinta, and Santa Maria are the three replica ships built by the Spanish government to commemorate the 500th anniversary of Christopher Columbus' voyage from Spain to the Bahamas in 1492. Niña is certified as a Sailing School Vessel. The three vessels are berthed adjacent to the Corpus Christi Museum of Science and History, which houses artifacts from one of the oldest known Spanish shipwrecks in the Americas. The museum also houses the Smithsonian Institution's "Seeds of Change" exhibit, which traces the impact of the European "discovery" on the indigenous peoples of the Americas and on Europe, including the exchange of flora, fauna, technology, and disease.

Flag:	Spain
Rig:	15th-century caravel, three-masted
Homeport/waters:	Corpus Christi, Texas: Corpus Christi Bay
Who sails?	School groups from elementary through college. Adults and families. Court referrals in some cases.
Program type:	Sail training for crew and apprentices. Sea education in cooperation with other organized groups and based on informal, in-house programming. Dockside interpretation in port. Affiliated institutions include Corpus Christi Museum of Science and History.

Specifications:			
	Sparred length: 93'	Draft: 7'	Sail area: 1,507 sq. ft.
	LOD: 64'	Beam: 21'	Tons: 49 GRT
	LOA: 72'	Rig height: 57'	Power: diesel
	LWL: 59'	Freeboard: 5'	Hull: wood

Designer:	Dr. José Maria Martinez Hidalgo, Barcelona Maritime Museum
Built:	1989; Spain, Cartagena Naval Shipyard
Coast Guard certification:	Sailing School Vessel (Subchapter R)
Crew:	3. Trainees: 15-20. Age: 14-70
Contact:	José Antonio Barrera, Director/Ships' Operations
	Columbus Fleet Association
	1900 North Chaparral Street
	Corpus Christi, TX 78401
	Tel: 512-882-1232; Fax: 512-882-1261

Norseman

The Leif Ericson Viking Ship, Inc. is preparing to celebrate the millennium anniversary of the first European to set foot on the North American continent. In late summer 2000, the *Norseman*, in company of approximately 16 other Viking ship replicas from the US and Europe, will sail from the only known site of Viking habitation, L'anse aux Meadows, Newfoundland and down the East Coast of Canada and the US, stopping at selected cities as a part of "Viking Sail 2000."

Built in 1992, *Norseman* offers people a glimpse of Viking culture and reminds everyone of the first discovery of North America by Europeans; Leif Ericson and his fellow Vikings, who sailed from Greenland in about the year 1000 to explore new lands to the west.

Crewmembers appear in full Viking costume, share their interests in Viking culture and their Scandinavian heritage, and practice their sailing and rowing skills. *Norseman* has appeared in sailing events on the East Coast of the US and in Sweden. In 1995 she appeared in productions shown on the History Channel and A & E cable channels. The 1999 season was spent in preparation for the voyage from Newfoundland, developing a training manual from crewmembers, and training on board the ship.

Flag:	USA
Rig:	Viking longship (single square sail)
Homeport/waters:	Wilmington, Delaware: Chesapeake Bay, Delaware River, Jersey Shore, New York Bay, Hudson River, and Long Island Sound
Who sails?	Students and individuals of all ages.
Program type:	Sail training for volunteer crew and apprentices. Sea education in maritime history relevant to Viking period. Dockside interpretation during port visits.

Specifications:			
	Sparred length: 42'	Draft: 3'	Sail area: 297 sq. ft.
	LOD: 32'	Beam: 9'	Tons: 2 GRT
	LOA: 40'	Rig height: 30'	Power: 25 HP outboard
	LWL: 30'	Freeboard: 3'	Hull: fiberglass

Designer:	Applecraft, Inc.
Built:	1992; Isle of Man, UK, Applecraft, Inc.
Crew:	7-12. **Trainees:** 7-12
Contact:	Dennis Johnson, President
	Leif Ericson Viking Ship, Inc.
	15 West Highland Ave.
	Philadelphia, PA 19118
	Tel: 215-242-3063; Fax: 215-242-3119
	E-mail: viking@libertynet.org
	Web site: http://www.libertynet.org/viking

Northern Light

the beautiful *Northern Light* sank at the dock in Lake Michigan after her Cup service. She was bought and raised by Bob Tiedemann 15 years ago, after which she underwent extensive renovation before returning to Newport. Together, *Gleam* and *Northern Light* offer a unique team building program called "Your Own

Northern Light, a 12-meter sloop, was built in 1938 as a gift to young Lee Loomis from his father. She was later owned by the Greek shipping tycoon Steven Niarchos, during her involvement in the America's Cup under the name of *Nereus*.

A long-time racing rival of *Gleam*, America's Cup Regatta", created over 12 years ago. Each boat accommodates thirteen guests plus three crewmembers. No previous sailing experience is necessary to participate. Group and corporate outings are available in Newport, Rhode Island and other New England ports.

Flag:	USA
Rig:	Sloop (12-meter)
Homeport/waters:	Newport, Rhode Island: Narragansett Bay
Who sails?	Corporations who charter the vessels for team building and client entertaining.
Program type:	Sail training with paying trainees. Passenger day sails.

Specifications:			
	Sparred length: 70'	Draft: 9'	Sail area: 1,900 sq. ft.
	LOD: 70'	Beam: 12'	Tons: 30 GRT
	LOA: 70'	Rig height: 90'	Power: diesel
	LWL: 45' 6"	Freeboard: 3'	Hull: wood

Designer:	Clinton Crane and Olin Stephens
Built:	1938; City Island, New York, Henry Nevins
Coast Guard certification:	Passenger Vessel (Subchapter T)
Crew:	3. **Trainees:** 14
Contact:	Elizabeth Tiedemann, Director of Sales & Marketing Seascope Systems, Inc., 103 Ruggles Avenue Newport, RI 02840 Tel: 401-847-5007; Fax: 401-849-6140 E-mail: aboard@earthlink.net Web site: http://www.seascopenewport.com

Ocean Star

Launched in 1991 as the school ship for *Ocean Navigator* magazine, *Ocean Star* now sails under the banner of Argo Academy as a nine-month high school afloat. Argo Academy offers a full school year of study, combining nautical training and travel. The program meets the needs of students looking for an individualized curriculum integrated with dynamic experiential education.

Accredited academics offered in cooperation with the high school distance learning division of the University of Nebraska-Lincoln allow students to complete their curriculum as they pilot *Ocean Star* throughout the Eastern Caribbean basin under the guidance of professional staff and teachers. Argo Academy's distinctive curriculum offers a dimension well beyond academics. As equals, the shipmates learn by doing in every aspect of life aboard. Every shipmate plays an integral role in daily life, whether as chef

of the day or designated skipper. A rotation of positions on board provides shipmates with the chance to diversify their skills and foster a true atmosphere of teamwork. Diverse island destinations offer a wealth of opportunity of exploration. In addition to achieving academic goals, shipmates accomplish certifications in sailing and scuba diving, with training in all aspects of seamanship.

Flag:	UK
Rig:	Schooner, two-masted
Waters:	Eastern Caribbean
Who sails?	High school students (school year), high school graduates and college-aged students (summer).
Season:	Year-round
Program type:	Nine-month academic high school afloat. In summer, marine and nautical science mini-semesters.

Specifications:			
	LOA: 88'	Draft: 9'	Sail area: 4,600 sq. ft.
	LOD: 73'	Beam: 20'	Tons: 70 GRT
	LWL: 65'	Rig height: 92'	Power: 210 HP diesel
	Freeboard: 5'	Hull: steel	

Designer:	Bill Peterson
Built:	1991; Norfolk, Virginia, Marine Metals
Crew:	4. **Trainees:** 14
Contact:	Argo Academy/Sea-mester Programs
	PO Box 5477
	Sarasota, FL 34277
	Tel: 941-924-6789; Fax: 941-924-6075
	E-mail: seamester@msn.com
	Web site: http://www.argoacademy.com

OCEAN STAR

Odyssey

The *Odyssey* is owned and operated by the Whale Conservation Institute/Ocean Alliance (WCI/OA), a nonprofit organization dedicated to the conservation of whales and their environment through research and education. Dr. Payne, President of WCI/OA and internationally acclaimed marine scientist, is best known for his pioneering research on humpback whale songs and his unparalleled long-term research on the right whale. Under Dr. Payne's leadership, WCI/OA has continually expanded benign whale research techniques. The Institute combines rigorous science with a commitment to the welfare of whales and the ocean environment, and has helped people, regardless of their ideology, to better understand and appreciate the natural world.

WCI/OA's Voyage of the *Odyssey* Program, an assessment of the baseline levels of bio-persistent toxins in the oceans, will be conducted from the *Odyssey*. In 1995 the *Odyssey* was featured in PBS's "New Explorers series", Discovery Channel's "Finite Oceans", BBC's "Paradise in Peril", and in 1996, the IMAX production "Whales".

Flag:	USA
Rig:	Ketch
Homeport/waters:	Key West, Florida and San Diego, California: Global
Who sails?	High school and college students and adults.
Program type:	WCI/OA is developing sea education programs in cooperation with accredited schools and colleges in marine science, including marine mammal research, education, and conservation programs. Dockside interpretation during port visits.

Specifications:			
	Sparred length: 94'	Draft: 11'	Sail area: 4,500 sq. ft.
	LOD: 85'	Beam: 18' 6"	Tons: 100 GRT
	LOA: 85'	Rig height: 89'	Power: Detroit diesel
	LWL: 69'	Freeboard: 6'	Hull: steel

Designer:	WECO/Whangarei, New Zealand
Built:	1976; New Zealand, WECO/Whangarei
Crew:	4, 1 instructor. **Trainees:** 6
Contact:	Iain Kerr, Vice President
	Ocean Whale Conservation Institute/Ocean Alliance
	191 Weston Road
	Lincoln, MA 01773
	Tel: 781-259-0423; Fax: 781-259-0288
	E-mail: interns@oceanalliance.org
	Web site: http://www.oceanalliance.org

OMF Ontario

(Work in Progress)

On July 2, 1994, the hull of the schooner *OMF Ontario* was launched amidst the cheers of over 2,500 people from as far away as Florida and California. They came to applaud a six-year commitment by an all-volunteer crew to stimulate interest in and awareness of the Great Lakes. In 1998 all welding was completed, the final ballast in place, and spar construction begun. By early 2000 the *OMF Ontario* is expected to be ready for sea trials. She will resemble many of the ships built at this location in the 19th century, except that she is built of welded steel to modern standards and will have backup diesel power. When complete, the schooner will serve as a

floating classroom for the Education through Involvement program. Participants of all ages will have a hands-on learning experience about the history, heritage, resources, ecology, and the future of the Great Lakes.

OMF ONTARIO

Flag:	USA
Rig:	Topsail schooner
Homeport/waters:	Oswego, New York: Great Lakes
Who sails?	School children, community groups, and senior citizens.
Program type:	Passenger day sails for organized groups such as schools, community organizations, and businesses. Dockside interpretation.

Specifications:			
	Sparred length: 85'	Draft: 8'	Sail area: 2,000 sq. ft.
	LOD: 60'	Beam: 16'	Power: 100 HP diesel
	LOA: 65'	Rig height: 70'	Tons: 42 GRT
	Freeboard: 6'	Hull: steel	

Designer:	Francis MacLachlan
Built:	1994; Oswego, New York
Coast Guard certification:	Passenger Vessel (Subchapter T)
Crew:	2, 4 instructors. **Trainees:** 25
Contact:	Dr. Henry Spang, Director
	Education Through Involvement Program
	Oswego Maritime Foundation
	41 Lake Street
	Oswego, NY 13126
	Tel: 315-342-5753

One and All

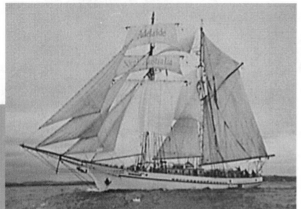

ONE AND ALL

One and All was built to fulfill the dream of a dedicated group of South Australians to provide sail training in South Australia. This dream came to fruition on April 5, 1987 on her commissioning day. Since her commissioning, *One and All* has carried many thousands of trainees from South Australia and further afield from all states and territories of Australia and overseas.

One and All also caters to many other groups, including half and full-day educational trips for school groups, recreational day trips to the public, and adventure voyages of two to ten days for those who wish to experience the wonders of sailing on a square-rigged vessel.

One and All has participated in three Sydney to Hobart Races, a Darwin to Ambon Yacht Race, has been chartered to carry out scientific studies on the East Coast of Australia, and has participated in a number of tall ship events in Australia. *One and All* spends her time sailing the Australian coastline, but is equipped and certified to the highest Australian survey standard, which has allowed her to sail internationally in the past. No previous experience is needed to sail on board *One and All*, only a desire to experience sailing a square-rigger in Australian waters.

Flag:	Australia
Rig:	Brigantine
Homeport/waters:	Port Adelaide, Adelaide, South Australia, Australia: East Coast of Australia (summer), Gulfs of South Australia (winter)
Who sails?	High school students and individuals of all ages.
Season:	Year-round
Cost:	$3,000 AUS group rate per day, $120 AUS per person per day on extended voyages
Program type:	Sail training for paying trainees. Sea education based on informal, in-house programming. Dockside interpretation during port visits.

Specifications:			
	Sparred length: 140'	Draft: 9' 4"	Sail area: 6,251 sq. ft.
	LOD: 98' 7"	Beam: 26' 11"	Tons: 121 GRT
	LWL: 86' 11"	Rig height: 88' 7"	Power: 380 HP diesel
	Hull: wood		

Designer:	Kell Steinman
Built:	1985, North Haven, South Australia, Australia, W.G. Porter and Sons Pty. Ltd.
Certification:	Australian Maritime Safety Authority Certificate for Australian and International Waters
Crew:	10. **Trainees:** 50 (day sails), 24 (overnight)
Contact:	Captain Ian Kuhl, CEO
	Sailing Trust of South Australia, Inc.
	PO Box 222, Port Adelaide, South Australia, 5015, AUSTRALIA
	Tel: 61-8-8447-5144; Fax: 61-8-8341-1-0167
	E-mail: tallship@oneandall.org.au
	Web site: http://www.oneandall.org.au

Oosterschelde is a Dutch three-masted schooner, built in 1918. Owned by a family that also sailed her, the ship remained Dutch until the late 1930s. *Oosterschelde* was then Danish-owned and later Swedish-owned. Modernization took away the sailing power and the engine got bigger. In the 1980s she became a motor coaster, with no sails left.

In 1988, *Oosterschelde* was purchased by the current owners, who were interested in restoring her to her original condition. Many companies, private individuals, and governmental institutions supported the foundation "The Rotterdam Tall Ship" with a $1.7 million budget. Since the restoration (1988-1992), the ship has been run by a company established for that purpose. Voyages are sailed with a professional crew of eight, with berths for 24 passengers. Day sail trips are also available. *Oosterschelde* made a world voyage from 1996-1998.

Flag:	The Netherlands
Rig:	Schooner, three-masted
Homeport/waters:	Rotterdam, The Netherlands: Worldwide
Who sails?	High school students, adults, and families.
Cost:	$100-$200 per person per day
Program type:	Sail training for crew, volunteer, and paying trainees. Passenger day sails and overnight passages. Sea education based on informal, in-house programming.

Specifications:			
	Sparred length: 164'	Draft: 9' 8"	Sail area: 8,000 sq. ft.
	LOD: 121'	Beam: 24' 7"	Tons: 400 GRT
	LOA: 131'	Rig height: 115'	Power: 360 HP
	LWL: 115'	Freeboard: 4' 4"	Hull: steel

Built:	1918; The Netherlands, Apollo
Crew:	8. **Trainees:** 36 (day sails), 24 (overnight)
Contact:	Captain Dick van Andel
	BV Reederij Oosterschelde
	PO Box 23429
	3001 KK Rotterdam, THE NETHERLANDS
	Tel: 31-184-653182; Fax: 31-184-653182
	E-mail: oosterschelde@planet.nl
	Web site: http://www.oosterschelde.nl

OOSTERSCHELDE

Grace Really nice boats,

(...ogress)

been carefully copied and a new replica vessel is well underway. Construction is of double-sawn fir frames, and she is the largest wooden sailing vessel presently being built in Canada using traditional methods. The boat building team consists largely of skippers and crewmembers of other SALTS vessels, ably assisted by volunteers and past trainees.

The maiden voyage is scheduled to take place upon completion with a 22-month world circumnavigation. The *Pacific Grace* will join the *Pacific Swift* in providing both coastal and offshore sail training voyages for approximately 1,000 young people each year.

Since the retirement of SALTS flagship, the *Robertson II*, at the end of the 1995 sail training season, *Pacific Grace* has been taking shape at the SALTS Heritage Shipyard and was launched in the harbor of Victoria, British Columbia on October 9, 1999. The lines of the old ship, one of Canada's last original Grand Banks fishing schooners, have

Flag:	Canada
Rig:	Gaff topsail schooner, two-masted
Homeport/waters:	Victoria, British Columbia, Canada: Pacific Northwest, Pacific Ocean
Who sails?	Students and young adults aged 13-25
Season:	March to October
Cost:	$85 CDN per 24 hours per trainee
Program type:	Sail training.

Specifications:			
	Sparred length: 130'	Draft: 11'	Sail area: 5,637 sq. ft.
	LOD: 105'	Beam: 22' 2"	Tons: 170 GRT
	LOA: 107' 10"	Rig height: 105'	Power: twin diesels
	LWL: 93'	Freeboard: 5'	Hull: wood

Built:	Under construction; Victoria, British Columbia, SALTS
Canadian Coast Guard	
certification:	Passenger Vessel, Sailing School Vessel
Crew:	5, 3 instructors. **Trainees:** 40 (day), 30 (overnight)
Contact:	Executive Director, Sail and Life Training Society (SALTS)
	PO Box 5014, Station B
	Victoria, British Columbia V8R 6N3, CANADA
	Tel: 250-383-6811; Fax: 250-383-7781

PACIFIC GRACE

Pacific Swift

(handwritten: but also crazy Christian sily cult.)

Built as a working exhibit at Expo '86 in Vancouver, British Columbia, the *Pacific Swift* has sailed over 100,000 deep-sea miles on training voyages for young crewmembers. Her offshore travels have taken her to Australia and Europe, to remote communities on Easter and Pitcairn Islands, and to many other unusual and far-flung ports of call.

When not offshore, the *Swift* provides coastal sail training programs among the cruising grounds of the Pacific Northwest which include shorter school programs in the spring and fall and 10-day summer trips open to anyone aged 13 to 25.

Each year over one thousand young people participate in an experience which combines all aspects of shipboard life, from galley chores to helmsmanship, with formal instruction in navigation, pilotage, seamanship, and small boat handling. Rooted in Christian values, SALTS believes that training under sail provides the human spirit a real chance to develop and mature. SALTS received the 1998 Sail Training Program of the Year Award from the American Sail Training Association.

Flag:	Canada
Rig:	Square topsail schooner, two-masted
Homeport/waters:	Victoria, British Columbia, Canada: Pacific Northwest, North and South Pacific, Caribbean, and Atlantic
Who sails?	Individuals and groups.
Season:	Year-round
Cost:	$80 CDN per 24 hours per trainee
Program type:	Offshore and coastal sail training.

Specifications:			
	Sparred length: 111'	Draft: 10' 8"	Sail area: 4,111 sq. ft.
	LOD: 78'	Beam: 20' 6"	Tons: 98 GRT
	LOA: 83'	Rig height: 92'	Power: 220 HP diesel
	LWL: 65'	Freeboard: 3' 6"	Hull: wood

Built:	1986; Vancouver, British Columbia, Canada, SALTS
Canadian Coast Guard certification:	Passenger vessel, Sailing School Vessel
Crew:	5. **Trainees:** 30. **Age:** 13-25
Contact:	Executive Director, Sail and Life Training Society (SALTS)
	Box 5014, Station B
	Victoria, British Columbia V8R 6N3, CANADA
	Tel: 250-383-6811; Fax: 250-383-7781

Palawan

Designed and built in 1965 as an ocean racer under the old Cruising Club of America rule, *Palawan* achieved a number of firsts. An early aluminum yacht, she was the first offshore boat to use the fin keel. Although she could not keep up with the newer hulls encouraged by the IOR rule, everyone spoke highly of the boat, and designer Olin Stephens declared her "perhaps the easiest steering boat I ever drew." Her racing career has been an active one, and she was used by the Maine Maritime Academy for over 10 years as a sail training vessel.

Palawan has operated as a passenger vessel since 1988 in Portland, Maine, serving both individuals and groups, and she is a popular vehicle for fundraising events for groups such as Friends of Casco Bay, Maine Island Trails, and others. A winter season may be spent as a yacht in warmer waters with up to six crew aboard.

Flag:	USA				
Rig:	Cutter				
Homeport/waters:	Portland, Maine: Casco Bay, Caribbean				
Who sails?	Students, adults, and groups.				
Cost:	$125 per person per day, $950 group rate				
Program type:	Sail training with team-building activities for paying trainees. Passenger day sails and overnight passages.				
Specifications:	Sparred length: 58'		Draft: 8' 1"		Sail area: 1,308 sq. ft.
	LOD: 58'		Beam: 12' 4"		Tons: 24 GRT
	LOA: 58'		Rig height: 68'		Power: 60 HP
	LWL: 40'		Freeboard: 4' 4"		Hull: aluminum
Designer:	Olin Stephens				
Built:	1965; New York, New York, Derecktor				
Coast Guard certification:	Passenger Vessel (Subchapter T)				
Crew:	2 (day sails), 3 (overnight). **Trainees:** 24 (day sails), 6 (overnight)				
Contact:	Captain Tom Woodruff				
	Palawan Services, Inc.				
	PO Box 9715-240				
	Portland, ME 04104				
	Tel: 207-773-2163; Fax: 207-781-5530				
	E-mail: palawan@nlis.net				
	Web site: http://www.sailpalawan.com				

My favorite little boat in the universe

Tall Ship Adventures conducts sail training on board *Pathfinder*, a square-rigged ship designed specifically for youth sail training on the Great Lakes. Since 1964 over 15,000 young people have lived and worked aboard *Pathfinder* and her sister ship, *Playfair*.

Youth between the ages of 14 and 18 become the working crew on one or two-week adventures, making 24-hour passages from ports all over the Great Lakes. The program is delivered by youth officers between the ages of 15 and 18, trained and qualified during Tall Ship Adventures' Winter Training Programs. The captain and first mate are the only adults on board.

Every year each ship sails over 4,000 miles, spends over 40 nights at sea, and introduces 300 trainees to the tall ship experience. *Pathfinder* is owned and operated by Toronto Brigantine, Inc., a registered charity.

Flag:	Canada
Rig:	Brigantine
Homeport/waters:	Toronto, Ontario, Canada: Great Lakes
Who sails?	In July and August, youth programs for ages 14-18; in May, June, and September, school groups from middle school through college, and interested adult groups.
Cost:	$675 CDN for one week, $1,175 CDN for two weeks. Call for spring and fall group rates.
Program type:	Sail training for paying trainees, including seamanship and leadership training based on informal, in-house programming. Shoreside winter program. Dockside interpretation. Affiliated institutions include the Canadian Sail Training Association and the Ontario Camping Association.

Specifications:				
	Sparred length: 72'	Draft: 8'	Sail area: 2,600 sq. ft.	
	LOD: 58'	Beam: 15' 3"	Tons: 31.63 GRT	
	LOA: 60'	Rig height: 54'	Power: 150 HP diesel	
	LWL: 45'	Freeboard: 4'	Hull: steel	

Designer:	Francis A. Maclachlan
Built:	1963; Kingston, Ontario, Canada, Kingston Shipyards
Crew:	10. **Trainees:** 25 (day sails), 18 (overnight)
Contact:	Catharine McLean, Executive Director
	Toronto Brigantine, Inc.
	370 Queen's Quay West, Ste. 203
	Toronto, ON, M5V 3J3, CANADA
	Tel: 416-596-7117; Fax: 416-596-9119
	E-mail: mail@tallshipadventures.on.ca
	Web site: http://www.tallshipadventures.on.ca

PATHFINDER

PHOTO BY NORMAN BROUWER

PEKING

Peking was launched in 1911 at Hamburg, Germany by the Blohm & Voss shipyard. She was owned by the F. Laeisz Company of that port, who used her to carry fuel and manufactured goods to the West Coast of South America, around Cape Horn, and return to European ports with nitrate mined in northern Chile.

With her four-masted barque rig, steel hull and masts, and mid-ship bridge deck, *Peking* represents the final generation of sailing ships built for world trade. Though a product of the 20th century, she still sailed in the traditional way, with few labor-saving devices or safety features. Her crew followed the standard sailing vessel routine of four hours on duty and four hours off duty, around the clock, seven days a week.

Peking was retired in 1933, when steamers using the Panama Canal took over what was left of the nitrate trade. She served as a nautical school for boys, moored on a British River, until she was acquired by the South Street Seaport Museum in 1974. She now serves as a floating dockside exhibit. Educational programs for children and young adults take place on board, with a wet lab on the ship interpreting the biology of New York harbor.

Flag:	USA
Rig:	Barque, four-masted
Homeport/waters:	New York, New York
Cost:	$3 per person
Program type:	Sea education in marine science, maritime history, and ecology based on informal, in-house programming.

Specifications:			
	Sparred length: 377' 6"	Draft: 16'	Sail area: 44,132 sq. ft.
	LOD: 320'	Beam: 45' 8"	Tons: 3,100 GRT
	Rig height: 170' 5"	Hull: steel	

Built:	1911; Hamburg, Germany, Blohm & Voss
Contact:	Paula Mayo, Director of Programs
	South Street Seaport Museum
	207 Front Street
	New York, NY, 10038
	Tel: 212-748-8681; Fax: 212-748-8610
	Web site: http://www.southstseaport.org

Phoenix

The coastal schooner *Phoenix* was built on Long Island, New York and launched in 1984 as a replica of the type of vessels plying the waters of Long Island Sound at the turn of the century. *Phoenix* was first used as a cargo vessel between Port Jefferson, New York and Bridgeport, Connecticut, before carrying passengers over the same route for day trip excursions. In the mid-1980s the Nassau County Board of Cooperative Services used her as a platform for their marine biology public school education program. The vessel was later sold and moved to the Bahamas.

In 1993 *Phoenix* returned to Long Island and was acquired by the Coastal Ecology Learning Program, a nonprofit educational corporation. C.E.L.P. offers shipboard environmental education programs for schoolchildren, families, and adults. *Phoenix* is the training ship for the Long Island US Naval Sea Cadets. The vessel is also available for private functions, children's birthday parties, corporate events, etc. *Phoenix* travels the length of Long Island Sound, offering programs throughout the region.

Flag:	USA
Rig:	Gaff schooner, two-masted
Homeport/waters:	Glen Cove, New York: Long Island Sound
Who sails?	Students of all ages, individuals and families.
Program type:	Sail training for volunteer and paying trainees. Sea education in marine science, ecology, and maritime history. Affiliated with the Long Island US Naval Sea Cadets.

Specifications:	Sparred length: 71'	Draft: 6'	Sail area: 1,600 sq. ft.
	LOD: 56'	Beam: 16'	Tons: 40 GRT
	LOA: 60'	Rig height: 60'	Power: diesel
	LWL: 54'	Freeboard: 4'	Hull: steel

Designer:	Walter Merrit
Built:	1984; Patchogue, New York, Greg Brazier
Coast Guard certification:	Passenger Vessel (Subchapter T)
Crew:	4. **Trainees:** 5 (day sails), 2 (overnight)
Contact:	Captain Dennis F. Watson
	Coastal Ecology Learning Program, Inc.
	PO Box 473
	Huntington, NY 11743
	Tel/Fax: 516-385-2357
	E-mail: celp@optonline.net

Phoenix

film "1492: Conquest of Paradise". In 1996 her name was changed back to *Phoenix* and she was converted into a two-masted brig.

All of Square Sail's ships are fully commissioned and work throughout the year. When not filming, they have a regular sailing program, giving people the chance to experience traditional square-rig sailing first-hand. These voyages typically run between four and seven days, and occasionally longer. They are either based from Square Sail's homeport of Charlestown, Cornwall, UK, or they work around the annual schedule offering voyages between the various ports.

Square Sail runs an annual course from February to October where trainees are given the opportunity to learn the skills associated with sailing these ships, and in addition to maintenance and shore-based instruction, they form part of the regular crew throughout the season.

Built in Denmark in 1929 as a missionary schooner, *Phoenix* retired from missionary work after 20 years and carried cargo until her engine room was damaged by fire in 1972. In 1974 she was purchased and converted into a brigantine, before being purchased by Square Sail in 1988. In 1991 she was converted into a 15th-century Caravel, to replicate the *Santa Maria*, Christopher Colombus' flagship, for Ridley Scott's

Flag:	UK
Rig:	Brig, two-masted
Homeport/waters:	Charlestown Harbour, St. Austell, Cornwall, UK: UK and Europe
Who sails?	Individuals and families of all ages.
Season:	Year-round
Cost:	$160 per person per day, $5,600 group rate per day (charter)
Program type:	Sail training for professional crew, volunteer and paying trainees. Sea education in maritime history in cooperation with accredited institutions and as informal, in-house programming. Worldwide film work and corporate charters.

Specifications:			
	Sparred length: 112'	Draft: 8' 6"	Sail area: 4,000 sq. ft.
	LOD: 76'	Beam: 21'	Tons: 79 GRT
	LOA: 86'	Rig height: 81'	Power: 235 HP diesel
	LWL: 70'	Freeboard: 6'	Hull: oak on oak

Built:	1929; Frederickshavn, Denmark, Hjorne & Jakobsen
Certification:	MCA and MECAL (UK)
Crew:	10. **Trainees:** 12
Contact:	Chris Wilson, Marketing Manager, Square Sail
	Charlestown Harbour, St. Austell
	Cornwall PL25 3NJ, UNITED KINGDOM
	Tel: 44-1720-70241; Fax: 44-1726-01839
	E-mail: sextant@cwcom.net
	Web site: http://www.square-sail.com

Picara

The Nauset Sea Scouts have just celebrated more than 50 years of sail training. This program teaches seamanship and sailing to young people between the ages of 14 and 20 through education and annual cruises along the New England Coast. While on cruises, each scout takes part in every aspect of the voyage, including planning, cooking, navigation, sail repair, and sailing the vessel. The Nauset Sea Scouts have participated in such tall ships gatherings as the New York World's Fair 1964, Montreal's Expo '67, OpSail '76, Boston's 350th

anniversary in 1980, and the Grand Regatta 1992 Columbus Quincentenary in both New York and Boston.

Flag:	USA
Rig:	Sloop
Homeport/waters:	Eastham, Massachusetts: New England coast
Who sails?	Sea Explorers, middle school and high school students.
Program type:	Sail training for crew and apprentices. Sea education in maritime history and ecology in cooperation with Sea Scouts. Dockside interpretation during outport visits.

Specifications:			
	Sparred length: 36'	Draft: 5' 6"	Sail area: 750 sq. ft.
	LOA: 36'	Beam: 12'	Tons: 15 GRT
	LWL: 28'	Rig height: 49'	Power: 4,108 diesel
	Freeboard: 4'	Hull: fiberglass	

Designer:	S-2 Yachts
Built:	1982; Holland, Michigan, S-2 Yachts
Crew:	2. **Trainees:** 20 (day sails), 11 (overnight). **Age:** 14-20
Contact:	Captain Michael F. Allard
	Nauset Sea Explorers
	PO Box 1236
	Orleans, MA 02653
	Tel: 508-255-8150
	E-mail: mallard@capecod.net

Picton Castle

(handwritten: Ship of death to douchebag captain.)

(handwritten: Also has super stumpy masts)

The 300-ton steel barque *Picton Castle* is dedicated to making square-rig sailing ship voyages around the world. In the just-completed year-and-a-half voyage, the *Picton Castle* visited 47 ports and islands in the South Pacific, the Far East, Africa, and the Caribbean. As a training ship all on board work, stand watch, and learn the way of a ship. Workshops are conducted in rigging, sailmaking, boat handling, navigation, and practical seamanship.

On her last world voyage, the *Picton Castle* served as flagship for UNESCO's "1998—Year of the Ocean" program, delivering environmental education materials provided by NOAA throughout the South Pacific. While underway, the ship conducts a Web-based distance learning program, bringing the sailing and cultural experiences of the crew and scientific information gathered at sea and ashore to schoolchildren around the world.

Rigged following Germanischer Lloyd's rules for Cape Horners and outfitted to the highest standard with safety gear, the *Picton Castle* is a strong, seaworthy home for adventurers devoted to learning the art of square-rig seafaring. The ship will be conducting a summer training cruise for 16 to 25 year-olds in conjunction with Tall Ships 2000®. The next world voyage sets sail November 1, 2000.

Flag:	Cook Islands
Rig:	Barque, three-masted
Homeport/waters:	Rarotonga, Cook Islands, South Pacific Ocean: worldwide service with refits in Lunenburg, Nova Scotia, Canada
Who sails?	Those over 18 years old on the world voyage, 16 years and up on shorter training cruises.
Program type:	Deep-water sail training for expense-sharing trainees. Maritime education in cooperation with various institutes and organized groups. Comprehensive instruction in the arts of seafaring under sail. Dockside school visits and receptions. Charitable/educational outreach and supply to isolated islands.

Specifications:	Sparred length: 176'	Draft: 14' 6"	Sail area: 12,450 sq. ft.
	LOD: 135'	Beam: 24'	Tons: 284 GRT
	LOA: 148'	Rig height: 100'	Power: 690 HP diesel
	LWL: 130'	Freeboard: 6'	Hull: steel

Designer:	Masts, rigging, decks, and layout—Daniel Moreland. Stability, calculation, and ballasting—Daniel Blachley, NA/ME Webb Institute
Certification:	Registered and certified as a Sail Training Vessel for worldwide service by the Cook Islands Department of Transportation and Tourism
Crew:	Permanent crew, 12. **Trainees:** 35
Contact:	David Robinson, Voyage Coordinator
	Barque Picton Castle Office
	1 Woodbine Lane
	Amherst, NH 03031-2102
	Tel: 603-424-0219; Fax: 603-424-1849
	E-mail: wissco@juno.com
	Web site: http://www.picton-castle.com

PICTON CASTLE

Pilgrim

The *Pilgrim* is a full-scale replica of the ship immortalized by Richard Henry Dana in his classic book *Two Years Before the Mast*. Owned and operated by the Ocean Institute, *Pilgrim* is dedicated to multidisciplinary education. During the school year, the Ocean Institute offers an 18-hour, award-winning living history program that offers a hands-on exploration of literature, California history, and group problem solving in which crewmembers recreate the challenge of shipboard life. Students live like sailors of the 1830s as they hoist barrels, row in the harbor, stand night watches, swab the decks, and learn to cope with a stern captain.

On summer evenings, audiences are treated to the sights and sounds of the sea as the *Pilgrim*'s decks come alive with theatrical and musical performances. In late summer the *Pilgrim* sails on her annual cruise with an all-volunteer crew to ports along the California coast as a goodwill ambassador for the City of Dana Point. She returns in September to lead the annual tall ship parade and festival.

PILGRIM

Flag:	USA
Rig:	Snow brig
Homeport/waters:	Dana Point, California: Point Conception to Ensenada, Mexico
Season:	Year-round
Who sails?	Student groups and individual volunteers.
Program type:	Maritime living history and volunteer sail training.

Specifications:		
Sparred length: 130'	Draft: 9'	Sail area: 7,600 sq. ft.
LOD: 98'	Beam: 24' 6"	Tons: 99 GRT
Freeboard: 8'	Rig height: 104'	Power: diesel
Hull: wood		

Designer:	Ray Wallace
Built:	1945; Holbaek, Denmark, A. Nielsen
Coast Guard certification:	Uninspected Vessel
Crew:	35. **Dockside visitors:** 50
Contact:	Daniel Stetson, Director of Maritime Affairs
	Ocean Institute
	24200 Dana Point
	Dana Point, CA 92629
	Tel: 949-496-2274; Fax: 949-496-4296
	Web site: http://www.ocean-institute.org

Pilgrim

Islands area of the St. Lawrence River. This schooner's main mission lies in creating an interest and appreciation of the Great Lakes maritime heritage and environment. The *Pilgrim* offers adult sail training, private charters, and participation in historical reenactments and festivals.

The captain and crew welcome the challenge of fulfilling your dreams through

The *Pilgrim* sails primarily the waters of Lake Ontario and the Thousand unique hands-on opportunities designed especially for you or your group.

Flag:	USA
Rig:	Gaff schooner, two-masted
Homeport/waters:	Oak Orchard River, New York: Lake Ontario, Thousand Islands area of St. Lawrence River
Who sails?	High school students, adults, and families.
Season:	May to October
Cost:	$100 per person per day, $600 group rate per day
Program type:	Sail training for paying trainees. Sea education in cooperation with organized groups and as part of informal, in-house programming.

Specifications:			
	Sparred length: 68'	Draft: 6'	Sail area: 1,850 sq. ft.
	LOD: 52'	Beam: 15'	Tons: 33 GRT
	LOA: 52'	Rig height: 58'	Power: 85 HP diesel
	LWL: 44' 3"	Freeboard: 3' 6"	Hull: steel

Designer:	William Wood
Built:	1987; Norfolk, Virginia, Marine Metals
Coast Guard certification:	Uninspected Vessel
Crew:	3. Trainees: 6
Contact:	Captain Gary Kurtz
	Pilgrim Packet Company
	PO Box 491
	Kendall, NY 14476
	Tel: 716-682-4757

SAIL TALL SHIPS!

Pilgrim of Newport

Built by one man as a lifetime dream, *Pilgrim of Newport* was constructed over 13 years to plans purchased from the Smithsonian Institution. She is a traditionally built accurate replica of a 1770s privateer used during the American Revolution. Predecessor to the Baltimore Clipper, similar vessels were known for their speed and were used for smuggling and the slave trade. *Pilgrim of Newport*'s mission in the 20th century is marine education for children of all ages.

Sailing with the Catalina Island Marine Institute, *Pilgrim of Newport* does three and five-day marine science-based programs which include snorkeling and hiking on Catalina Island. The vessel is also used by the Ocean Institute in their living history programs. Whale watching, corporate team building, and cannon battles are just some of the activities available on *Pilgrim of Newport*. The goal is to provide a platform where dreams are realized and the ocean's strength, beauty, and history are directly experienced.

Flag:	USA
Rig:	Gaff topsail schooner
Homeport/waters:	Long Beach, California: Southern California
Who sails?	School groups from elementary school through college, adult education groups, and individuals and families of all ages.
Cost:	$45-$65 per person per day, $1,000-$2,000 group rate per day
Program type:	Sail training for volunteer crew or trainees. Sea education in marine science, maritime history, and ecology based on informal, in-house programming and in cooperation with other organizations. Day sails and overnight passages. Affiliated institutions include the Ocean Institute, other school education programs, and museums.

Specifications:	Sparred length: 118'	Draft: 10'	Sail area: 5,000 sq. ft.
	LOD: 83'	Beam: 25'	Power: diesel
	LOA: 83'	Rig height: 100'	Hull: wood
	LWL: 79'		

Designer:	Records from the Smithsonian Institution, working drawings by Howard Chapelle
Built:	1983; Costa Mesa, California, Dennis Holland
Coast Guard certification:	Passenger Vessel (Subchapter T)
Crew:	9. **Trainees:** 82 (day sails), 40 (overnight)
Contact:	Wade and Susan Hall
	Pilgrim of Newport
	611 9th St.
	Coronado, CA 92118
	Tel/Fax: 714-966-0686
	E-mail: sailpilgrim@earthlink.net
	Web site: http://www.sailpilgrim.com

Pinta

anniversary of Christopher Columbus' voyage from Spain to the Bahamas in 1492. *Pinta* is certified as a Sailing School Vessel. The three vessels are berthed adjacent to the Corpus Christi Museum of Science and History, which houses artifacts from one of the oldest known Spanish shipwrecks in the Americas. The museum also houses the Smithsonian Institution's "Seeds of Change" exhibit, which traces the impact of the European "discovery" on the indigenous peoples of the Americas and on Europe, including the exchange of flora, fauna, technology, and disease.

Niña, Pinta, and *Santa María* are the three replica ships built by the Spanish government to commemorate the 500th

Flag:	Spain
Rig:	Caravel, 15th-century square-rig
Homeport/waters:	Corpus Christi, Texas
Who sails?	School groups from elementary school through college. Individuals, adults, and families.
Program type:	Sail training for crew and volunteer trainees. Sea education in cooperation with accredited institutions and other groups.

Specifications:		
Sparred length: 96'	Draft: 7'	Sail area: 2,008 sq. ft.
LOD: 53'	Beam: 24'	Tons: 52 GRT
LOA: 75'	Rig height: 60'	Power: 3208 diesel
LWL: 66'	Freeboard: 6'	Hull: wood

Designer:	Dr. José María Martinez Hildalgo
Built:	1990; Isla Cristina, Spain, Astilleros Reunidos
Coast Guard certification:	Sailing School Vessel (Subchapter R)
Crew:	n/a. **Trainees:** 25 (day sails), 20 (overnight)
Contact:	José Antonio Barrera, Director/Ships Operations
	Columbus Fleet Association
	1900 Chaparral Street
	Corpus Christi, TX 78401
	Tel: 512-882-1232; Fax: 512-882-1261

The first iron sloop built in the United States, *Pioneer* is the only surviving American iron-hulled sailing vessel. Built in 1885 by the Pioneer Iron Foundary in Chester, Pennsylvania, she sailed the Delaware River, hauling sand for use in the iron molding process. Ten years later *Pioneer* was converted to a schooner rig for ease of sail handling. In 1966, the then abandoned vessel was acquired and rebuilt by Russell Grinnell, Jr. of Gloucester, Massachusetts. In 1970 the fully restored schooner was donated to the South Street Seaport Museum.

Today historic *Pioneer* serves as a vital education platform. Students of all ages can come on board and experience New York history and other curricular subjects during the hands-on program. *Pioneer* also offers corporate and private charters, Elderhostel day programs, and public sails.

Flag:	USA
Rig:	Gaff topsail schooner, two-masted
Homeport/waters:	New York, New York: New York Harbor, Hudson River, and Atlantic Coast
Who sails?	School groups from elementary school through college, charter groups, museum members, and general public.
Season:	April through October
Program type:	Sail training for crew and volunteers, hand-on education sails designed to augment school curriculums in history, ecology, marine science, physics, and math. Corporate and private charters, Elderhostel programs, and public sails.

Specifications:		
Sparred length: 102'	Draft: 4' 8" (min.), 12' (max.)	Sail area: 2,700 sq. ft.
LOD: 65'	Beam: 21' 6"	Tons: 43 GRT
LOA: 65'	Rig height: 79'	Power: diesel
LWL: 58' 11"	Hull: steel	

Built:	1885; Marcus Hook, Pennsylvania, Pioneer Iron Works (rebuilt 1968; Somerset, Massachusetts)
Coast Guard certification:	Passenger Vessel (Subchapter T)
Crew:	3
Contact:	Captain, Schooner Pioneer
	South Street Seaport Museum
	207 Front Street
	New York, NY 10038
	Tel: 212-748-8684; Fax: 212-748-8610
	Web site: http://www.southstseaport.org

PIONEER

SAIL TALL SHIPS!

3rd favorite boat in the universe

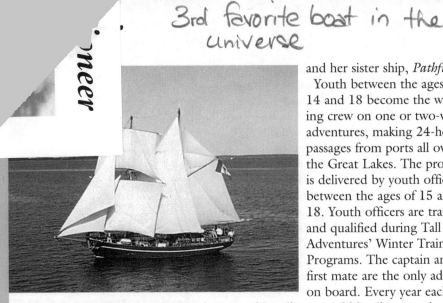

PHOTO BY CHRIS DEETH

Tall Ship Adventures conducts sail training on board *Playfair*, a square-rigged ship designed specifically for youth sail training on the Great Lakes. Since 1964 over 15,000 young people have lived and worked aboard *Playfair* and her sister ship, *Pathfinder*. Youth between the ages of 14 and 18 become the working crew on one or two-week adventures, making 24-hour passages from ports all over the Great Lakes. The program is delivered by youth officers between the ages of 15 and 18. Youth officers are trained and qualified during Tall Ship Adventures' Winter Training Programs. The captain and first mate are the only adults on board. Every year each ship sails over 4,000 miles, spends over 40 nights at sea, and introduces 300 trainees to the tall ship experience. *Playfair* is owned and operated by Toronto Brigantine, Inc., a registered charity.

Flag:	Canada
Rig:	Brigantine
Homeport/waters:	Toronto, Ontario, Canada: Great Lakes
Who sails?	In July and August, youth programs for ages 14-18; in May, June, and September, school groups from middle school through college, and interested adult groups.
Cost:	$675 CDN for one week; $1,175 CDN for two weeks (summer youth rate). Call for spring and fall group rates. Also day sails and group rates.
Program type:	Sail training for paying trainees, including seamanship and leadership training based on in-house programming. Shoreside winter program. Dockside interpretation. Affiliated institutions include the Canadian Sail Training Association and the Ontario Camping Association.

Specifications:			
	Sparred length: 72'	Draft: 7' 6"	Sail area: 2,600 sq. ft.
	LOD: 58'	Beam: 16'	Tons: 32.98 GRT
	LOA: 60'	Rig height: 54'	Power: 110 HP diesel
	LWL: 45'	Freeboard: 4'	Hull: steel

Designer:	Francis A. Maclachlan
Built:	1973; Kingston, Ontario, Canada, Canada Dredge and Dock Co.
Crew:	10. **Trainees:** 25 (day sails), 18 (overnight)
Contact:	Catharine McLean, Executive Director
	Toronto Brigantine, Inc.
	370 Queen's Quay West, Ste. 203
	Toronto, ON, M5V 3J3, CANADA
	Tel: 416-596-7117; Fax: 416-596-9119
	E-mail: mail@tallshipadventures.on.ca
	Web site: http://www.tallshipadventures.on.ca

Potomac is a dory boat, a work boat native to the Potomac River. Once these boats filled the river, oystering, fishing, and hauling cargo. Launched in 1995, the Alexandria Seaport Foundation's *Potomac* is the first sailing dory built on the river in over 50 years. Built by volunteers and apprentices of ASF's Craddock Boat Building School, the Dory Boat *Potomac* serves as a floating classroom for groups of up to 28. Students gain the experience of sailing aboard a native Potomac River watercraft while conducting on-the-water studies that reinforce lessons in environmental science and history taught in the classroom.

POTOMAC

Flag:	USA
Rig:	Leg-o-mutton, two-masted
Homeport/waters:	Alexandria, Virginia: Potomac River
Who sails?	Student groups and individuals.
Season:	Spring through fall
Program type:	Sail training and sea education in environmental studies.
Specifications:	LOD: 42' Tons: 7.2 GRT
	Draft: 2' 6" Power: diesel
	Beam: 12' 6" Hull: native yellow pine, white oak, white cedar.
Built:	1995; Alexandria, Virginia, Craddock Boat Building School
Coast Guard certification:	Passenger Vessel (Subchapter T)
Crew:	2. **Passengers:** 28
Contact:	Joe Youcha, Executive Director
	Alexandria Seaport Foundation
	1000 South Lee Street
	Jones Point, Alexandria, VA 22314
	Tel: 703-549-7078; Fax: 703-549-7615
	E-mail: asfhqs@aol.com
	Web site: http://www.capaccess.org/asf

Baltimore II

100% Sexy.
<100% badass.

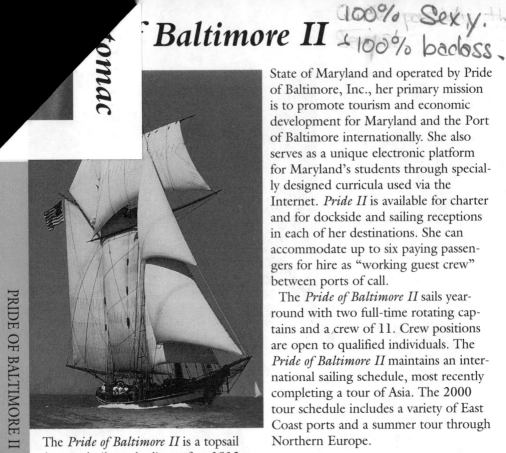

State of Maryland and operated by Pride of Baltimore, Inc., her primary mission is to promote tourism and economic development for Maryland and the Port of Baltimore internationally. She also serves as a unique electronic platform for Maryland's students through specially designed curricula used via the Internet. *Pride II* is available for charter and for dockside and sailing receptions in each of her destinations. She can accommodate up to six paying passengers for hire as "working guest crew" between ports of call.

The *Pride of Baltimore II* sails year-round with two full-time rotating captains and a crew of 11. Crew positions are open to qualified individuals. The *Pride of Baltimore II* maintains an international sailing schedule, most recently completing a tour of Asia. The 2000 tour schedule includes a variety of East Coast ports and a summer tour through Northern Europe.

The *Pride of Baltimore II* is a topsail schooner built to the lines of an 1812-era Baltimore Clipper. Owned by the

Flag:	USA
Rig:	Square topsail schooner, two-masted
Homeport/waters:	Baltimore, Maryland: Global
Who sails?	Corporate clients and residents of the State of Maryland and the City of Baltimore.
Season:	Year-round
Cost:	$150 per person per day (working guest crew); $750 per hour (dockside reception); $1,000 group rate per hour (sailing reception)
Program type:	Sea education and marketing development in cooperation with the State of Maryland. Passenger day sails and overnight passages, dockside school tours.

Specifications:			
	Sparred length: 170'	Draft: 12' 4"	Sail area: 10,442 sq. ft.
	LOD: 96' 6"	Beam: 26'	Tons: 97 GRT
	LOA: 108'	Rig height: 107'	Power: twin 165 HP diesels
	Freeboard: 6'	Hull: wood	

Designer:	Thomas C. Gillmer
Built:	1988; Baltimore, Maryland, G. Peter Boudreau
Coast Guard certification:	Passenger Vessel (Subchapter T)
Crew:	12. **Trainees:** 35 (day sails), 6 (overnight). **Age:** 18+
Contact:	Dale Hilliard, Executive Director
	Pride of Baltimore, Inc.
	401 East Pratt Street, Suite 222
	Baltimore, MD 21202
	Tel: 410-539-1151; Fax: 410-539-1190
	E-mail: pride2@pride2.org, Web site: http://www.pride2.org

Pride of MANY

The *Pride of MANY* is a 65-foot Spanish Galleon modeled after the *Pinta* of Columbus fame. Owned and operated by the Youth Services Agency of Pennsylvania, Inc., and named for the Mid-Atlantic Network of Youth and Family Services (MANY), of which YSA is a member, she also serves as part of a comprehensive program for Community Development through Youth. *Pride of MANY*'s mission is to enhance the character of youth through Adventure Challenge Therapy, perform community service projects in the region, and promote awareness of the marine environment, vocations, and heritage.

Clients of YSA can attend single-day events of exploration, fun, and an introduction to the sea and sailing, or multi-day adventures that typically provide a life-changing experience. The *Pride* and her crew provide an environment that nurtures and encourages the development of skills and attitudes necessary for the education of today's youth. Participants experience the value of communication, understanding, teamwork, and growth of awareness as well as a maturing of the

traits of patience, endurance, persistence, courage, and caution.

Marine communities can receive our assistance with creative community service projects that promote the awareness of the marine environment. These projects demonstrate the energy, talent, and desire that is our future—our youth.

Flag:	USA
Rig:	Barque, three-masted
Homeport/waters:	Georgetown, Maryland: Delaware and Chesapeake Bays, Atlantic Coast
Who sails?	School groups from middle school through college. Individuals under age 25. Trainees are from existing Youth Services Agency of Pennsylvania programs.
Program type:	Sail training for trainees and agency related volunteers with an emphasis on self-esteem and team building. Sea education in maritime vocational opportunities based on informal, in-house programming. Affiliated institutions include Youth Services of Pennsylvania and MANY (Mid-Atlantic Network of Youth and Family Services).

Specifications:			
	Sparred length: 75'	Draft: 7' 6"	Sail area: 3,700 sq. ft.
	LOD: 60'	Beam: 17'	Tons: 50 GRT
	LOA: 65'	Rig height: 70'	Power: 130 HP diesel
	LWL: 55'	Freeboard: 5'	Hull: steel

Designer:	Steve Martin
Built:	1986; Port Stanley, Canada, Steve Martin
Coast Guard certification:	Uninspected Vessel
Crew:	3. **Trainees:** 6
Contact:	Roger Dawson, Youth Services of Pennsylvania
	PO Box 508, Jamison, PA 18929
	Tel: 215-343-7800
	E-mail: roger@ysaofpa.org
	Web site: http://www.prideofmany.com

Providence

£ pretty.

career in which she sank or captured 40 British ships, she earned the nickname "Lucky Sloop." John Paul Jones said of her, "She was the first and she was the best."

The Continental Sloop *Providence* is a statewide resource administered by the Providence Maritime Heritage Foundation and the City of Providence, Rhode Island. The primary mission of the *Providence* is to inspire and educate the thousands of Rhode Islanders served each year and to keep Rhode Island's rich maritime heritage alive. As Rhode Island's Flagship, the Sloop *Providence* serves youth and adults through the "Classroom Under Sail" programs, which illuminate Rhode Island's maritime history and the importance of Providence in our nation's early development.

The *Providence* is a replica of one of the first ships of the American Navy. Built as a merchant ship in the 1760s, the *Providence* (ex-*Katy*) went on to become the first command of John Paul Jones and one of the most successful American ships to fight in the Revolutionary War. After a successful

The Sloop *Providence* also serves as the Ocean State's sailing ambassador, representing Rhode Island at waterfront festivals along the East Coast. The *Providence* is available for charter for education, special events, corporate outings, documentary and film use, and historic reenactments.

Flag:	USA
Rig:	Square topsail sloop
Homeport/waters:	Providence, Rhode Island: East Coast US
Who sails?	School groups from elementary school through college, individuals, and families.
Program type:	Sail training for crew and volunteers. Passenger day sails. Dockside interpretation at homeport and during port visits. Sea education in marine science, maritime history, and more for school groups of all ages.

Specifications:			
	Sparred length: 110'	Draft: 10'	Sail area: 3,470 sq. ft.
	LOD: 61' 1'	Beam: 20'	Tons: 59 GRT
	LOA: 65'	Rig height: 94'	Power: 170 HP diesel
	LWL: 59'	Freeboard: 8'	Hull: fiberglass and wood

Designer:	Charles W. Wittholz
Built:	1976; Melville, Rhode Island
Coast Guard certification:	Passenger vessel (Subchapter T)
Crew:	5-8. **Trainees:** 24-40 (day sails), 4-6 (overnight)
Contact:	Providence Maritime Heritage Foundation, PO Box 1261, Providence, RI 02901
	Tel: 401-274-7447; Fax: 401-274-8230
	E-mail: info@sloopprovidence.org
	Web site: http://www.sloopprovidence.org

Quinnipiack

Built in 1984 for passenger service, *Quinnipiack* now serves as the primary vessel for Schooner, Inc., an organization dedicated to teaching about the ecology of Long Island Sound. Since 1975, Schooner, Inc. has taught in classrooms, on the shores, and aboard a variety of vessels. Participants of all ages study under sail and explore the ecology of the estuary while getting an introduction to maritime heritage and seamanship. Students work alongside regular crew, learning the lessons in teamwork, self-reliance, flexibility, and interdependence that only sailing vessels can teach.

Quinnipiack programs complement traditional classroom studies in the sciences, mathematics, geography, history, literature, folklore, and social studies. Hands-on learning activities include collection, identification, and interpretation of estuarine organisms, land use, plankton study, piloting, sail handling, seamanship, sediment analysis, water chemistry, and weather.

Seafaring Scientists is a weeklong summer program in basic seamanship and marine ecology for students entering grades 5-8. In the Mates Program, high school students learn the operation and care of a traditional sailing vessel while sailing as a volunteer crew. The permanent crew consists of a licensed captain, mate, deckhands, and scientists, all of whom serve as educators in shipboard programs. Volunteers supplement paid educators and crew.

Flag:	USA
Rig:	Gaff schooner, two-masted
Homeport/waters:	New Haven, Connecticut: Long Island Sound
Who sails?	School groups from middle school through college, individuals, and families.
Season:	April to November
Program type:	Sail training for crew, apprentices, and trainees. Sea education in marine science, maritime history, and ecology in cooperation with accredited schools and colleges and as informal, in-house programming. Dockside interpretation during port visits. Passenger day sails.

Specifications:	Sparred length: 92'	Draft: 4' 6" - 11'	Sail area: 2,400 sq. ft.
	LOD: 65'	Beam: 20'	Tons: 41 GRT
	LOA: 72'	Rig height: 75'	Power: 119 HP diesel
	LWL: 58'	Freeboard: 5' 2"	Hull: wood

Designer:	Phil Sheldon
Built:	1984; Milbridge, Maine, Phil Sheldon
Coast Guard certification:	Passenger vessel (Subchapter T)
Crew:	4-8. **Trainees:** 30. **Age:** 12-18
Contact:	Beth McCabe, Executive Director, Schooner, Inc.
	60 South Water Street, New Haven, CT 06519
	Tel: 203-865-1737; Fax: 203-624-8816
	E-mail: schooner@mail.snet.net
	Web site: http://pages.cthome.net/schooner

Rachel B. Jackson

The *Rachel B. Jackson* is a one off design of an 1890s coastal schooner by Burt Frost. The keel was laid in Jonesport, Maine in 1974. She was planked and floated in Southwest Harbor where she sat unfinished at a mooring until 1979. The hull was pur- chased by George Emery and towed to Freeport, Maine. George, his brother Jim, and their father took the next three years to complete the *Rachel B. Jackson*, and launched her in 1982. George and Jim operated the boat out of Mystic Seaport as a sail training vessel. In 1984 she was sold and embarked on a three-year circumnavigation. She was sold again in 1990 and was put into the charter trade in Maine and the Virgin Islands. The *Rachel B.* was chartered by the National Geographic Society to do whale research off the coast of the Dominican Republic. The current owners, Steve and Andrew Keblinsky, just completed a two-year refit in May 1999. The *Rachel B. Jackson* now operates in Boston and Maine.

Flag:	USA
Rig:	Schooner, two-masted
Homeport/waters:	Southwest Harbor, Maine: Maine
Who sails?	School groups from elementary school through high school, individuals, and families.
Cost:	$2,000 group rate per day (charter)
Program type:	Sail training for volunteer and paying trainees. Sea education in marine science, maritime history, and ecology in cooperation with organized groups. Passenger day sails, dockside interpretation during port visits.

Specifications:			
	Sparred length: 75'	Draft: 8'	Sail area: 2,500 sq. ft.
	LOD: 52'	Beam: 17'	Tons: 52 GRT
	LOA: 52'	Rig height: 75'	Power: 108 HP diesel
	LWL: 43'	Freeboard: 4'	Hull: wood

Designer:	Burt Frost
Built:	1982; Freeport, Maine, George Emery
Coast Guard certification:	Passenger Vessel (Subchapter T)
Crew:	3. **Trainees/passengers:** 30
Contact:	Captain Steven Keblinsky
	Downeast Sailing Adventures, LLC
	PO Box 1252
	Southwest Harbor, ME 04679
	Tel: 207-244-7813
	E-mail: downeastsail@acadia.net
	Web site: http://www.downeastsail.com

Raindancer II

Raindancer II is a unique modern classic. Fashioned from rare Angelique teak, she was finely crafted in Lunenburg, Nova Scotia, in 1981. *Raindancer II* was refurbished in 1997/98 and currently sails the Caribbean (including Cuba) and the East Coast of Canada. She is comfortably appointed with private cabins to serve six guests on weekly eco-sailing adventures combining hands-on shipboard activities with shore excursions and exploration.

Flag:	Canada
Rig:	Staysail schooner
Homeport/waters:	Lunenburg, Nova Scotia, Canada
Who sails?	Individuals, families, and corporate groups.
Season:	Year-round
Program type:	Sail training for paying trainees. Passenger day sails and overnight voyages.

Specifications:	LOA: 75'	Draft: 8'	Sail area: 2,700 sq. ft.
	Rig height: 76'	Tons: 45 GRT	Power: 225 HP diesel
	Hull: teak		

Designer:	Stevens
Built:	1981; Nova Scotia, Canada, Stevens
Contact:	Captain Ron Lipscombe, Raindancer Sailing
	10 Daleview Court
	Peterborough, ON K9J 8E5, CANADA
	Tel: 613-542-6349
	E-mail: info@raindancerii.com
	Web site: http://www.raindancerii.com

Ranger
(Work in Progress)

The Ranger Foundation, Inc. was established in March 1999 to undertake one of the most exciting ventures in American maritime history—the rebuilding of John Paul Jones' famous warship, the *Ranger*. In 1777, no one expected that John Paul Jones and the Continental Sloop of War *Ranger* would help turn the tide of the American Revolution—no one but Jones himself. It was unthinkable for a lone ship to take on the world's mightiest navy in its own home waters, but that's exactly what Jones did.

It was the *Ranger* that first carried the new American flag into harm's way. When the French acknowledged that flag at Quiberon Bay off the coast of France, *Ranger* became the first ship under American colors to be recognized by a foreign power. Not long after, Jones and the *Ranger* crew initiated a guerilla naval campaign against Britain that is the subject of books and ballads to this day. The Ranger Foundation is dedicated to bringing that story alive by creating a sailing and maritime education programs around a full-size replica of the famous ship.

Flag:	USA
Rig:	Full-rigged ship, three-masted
Homeport/waters:	Portsmouth, New Hampshire: worldwide
Program type (planned):	Sail training and an extensive maritime education program integrated with other historical and maritime organizations throughout the region.
Coast Guard certification:	Undetermined
Crew (projected):	14
Contact:	Tom Cocchiaro, Chair
	The Ranger Foundation
	PO Box 6578
	Portsmouth, NH 03802-6578
	Tel: 603-436-2808; Fax: 603-436-2808
	Web site: http://www.rangerfoundation.org

Rattlesnake

The *Rattlesnake* was built in Nova Scotia during the early 1980s by Captain David May and sailed to Florida. She was built as a two-thirds wooden replica of over 81 feet. *Rattlesnake* is moored on the downtown waterfront in Jacksonville, Florida, and owned by the Maritime Heritage Foundation, Inc. A select group of the more than 200 members and volunteers of the Foundation is involved in the restoration of the vessel. These volunteers are learning boat-building skills and are preparing *Rattlesnake* to accommodate schoolchildren.

Much of Florida was originally explored and settled by people arriving in ships very similar to *Rattlesnake*. Once restoration is completed, the Foundation plans to use the vessel for excursions, nautical and environmental programs, and as a teaching aid for other programs along the Georgia and Florida coasts.

Flag:	USA
Rig:	Barque, three-masted
Homeport/waters:	Jacksonville, Florida: St. Johns River, Atlantic Ocean
Who sails?	School groups from elementary school through college, individuals, and families. Affiliated groups include Boy Scouts, Police Athletic League, Duval County Schools.
Program type:	Sail training for volunteer trainees. Sea education in marine science, maritime history, ecology, art, and music in cooperation with other organized groups.

Specifications:	Sparred length: 81' 6"	Draft: 6'	Power: diesel
	LOD: 60'	Beam: 16'	Hull: wood
	LOA: 70'	Rig height: 66'	

Designer:	May/Millar via Royal Navy Archives
Built:	1983; Toronto, Canada, David May
Coast Guard certification:	Uninspected Vessel.
Crew:	n/a. **Trainees:** 16
Contact:	Mr. Wayne Moore, President
	Maritime Heritage Foundation, Inc.
	PO Box 806
	Jacksonville, FL 32201
	Tel: 904-741-3030 ext. 109; Fax: 904-741-4209
	Web site: http://rattlesnake.daci.net

Red Witch

A living tribute to US maritime history and her designer, John G. Alden, the *Red Witch* was built in the tradition of the vessels that were the workhorses of America's 19th-century transportation system. True to her ancestors, her block and tackle, wooden hull, and gaff rig capture the romance and adventure of sail.

Built expressly for chartering, she worked in San Diego and Hawaii from 1987 through 1997. In 1997 the *Red Witch* started plying the waters of western Lake Erie. From her new home in Port Clinton, she now sails from ports in Ohio from Toledo to Cleveland, and plans to visit Detroit soon. Available for walk-on day sails or private group charters, the *Red Witch* is also designing sail training programs for 2000. The *Red Witch* offers dockside interpretations, two-hour hands-on sails, and all-day island excursions.

Flag:	USA
Rig:	Gaff schooner
Homeport/waters:	Port Clinton, Ohio: Lake Erie
Who sails?	School groups from elementary school through college, individuals, and families.
Program type:	Sail training for volunteer or paying trainees. Sea education in marine science and maritime history in cooperation with accredited institutions and organized groups. Passenger day sails.

Specifications:			
	Sparred length: 77'	Draft: 6' 6"	Sail area: 2,100 sq. ft.
	LOD: 54'	Beam: 17' 6"	Tons: 41 GRT
	LOA: 57'	Rig height: 73'	Power: 125 HP diesel
	LWL: 48'	Hull: wood	

Designer:	John Alden
Built:	1986; Bayou La Batre, Alabama, Nathaniel Zirlott
Coast Guard certification:	Passenger Vessel (Subchapter T)
Crew:	4. Trainees/passengers: 49
Contact:	Captain Karl A. Busam
	Red Witch Charters
	PO Box 386
	Port Clinton, OH 43452
	Tel: 419-798-1244; Fax: 419-798-5449
	E-mail: schooner@redwitch.com
	Web site: http://www.redwitch.com

Regina Maris

It is the goal of the Friends of Regina Maris to restore *Regina Maris* to her former status as a fully functional barquentine, certified by the US Coast Guard. During her restoration, the *Regina Maris* will be used for on-the-job training, teaching shipbuilding, rigging, carpentry, and related trades. People from a wide range of economic and cultural groups will be asked to participate in the restoration process. In conjunction with her rebuilding, educational exhibits detailing the *Regina Maris'* history will be displayed at the restoration site.

Upon completion of the restoration, the vessel will be used for a variety of purposes, including sail training for adults, a dockside attraction, and participation in tall ship events.

Flag:	USA
Rig:	Barquentine, three-masted
Homeport/waters:	Glen Cove, New York
Who will sail?	High school and college students, and adult individuals.
Proposed program type:	Sail training for paying trainees. Sea education in maritime history and ecology in cooperation with accredited institutions and other groups.

Specifications:	Sparred length: 144'	Draft: 10' 10"	Sail area: 7,000 sq. ft.
	LOD: 114' 4"	Beam: 25'	Tons: 400 GRT
	LOA: 139' 5"	Rig height: 108' 3"	Hull: wood

Designer:	J. Ring-Anderson
Built:	1908; Svendborg, Denmark, J. Ring-Anderson
Contact:	Ms. Sunny Seitler
	Save the Regina Maris Ltd.
	PO Box 152
	Glen Cove, NY 11542
	Tel: 516-656-4704; Fax: 516-242-4306

REGINA MARIS

Resolute

Resolute was built in 1939 for the US Naval Academy at Annapolis, Maryland. She was the third of twelve Luders yawls built for the Navy, and over the course of twenty years it is estimated that some seventy thousand midshipmen trained aboard these yawls. During this time

Resolute was an active participant in intercollegiate and club racing circuits on the East Coast.

Resolute now finds her home on the West Coast. Purchased for one dollar by the Evergreen State College in 1972, she currently provides sail training opportunities and access to Pacific Northwest waters for students and volunteers. *Resolute* and her companion vessel *Sea Wulff* are used to teach a wide range of interdisciplinary programs, which vary from year to year. All of these classes are built around the fundamentals of sailing, seamanship, and navigation. Previous programs include Wooden Boat Building and Repair, Marine Biology and Field Work Methods, Native American Culture Studies, Pacific Northwest History and Development, and Maritime Literature.

Academic programs are available to students enrolled at Evergreen only, though outside charters are considered on a case by case basis. Student and community volunteers assist in maintaining *Resolute* and *Sea Wulff* in exchange for sailing opportunities.

Flag:	USA
Rig:	Yawl
Homeport/waters:	Olympia, Washington: Puget Sound and inland waters of British Columbia
Who sails?	Enrolled students at Evergreen State College. Outside charters on a case by case basis.
Cost:	$225 group rate per day
Program type:	Sail training for volunteer trainees. Fully accredited sea education in marine science, maritime history, and ecology.

Specifications:

Sparred length: 44'	Draft: 6'	Sail area: 1,050 sq. ft.
LOD: 44'	Beam: 11'	Tons: 12 GRT
LOA: 44'	Rig height: 60'	Power: diesel
LWL: 30'	Freeboard: 3'	Hull: wood

Designer:	Luders
Built:	1939; Stamford, Connecticut, Luders Marine Construction Company
Coast Guard certification:	Passenger Vessel (Subchapter T)
Crew:	2. **Trainees:** 10 (day sails), 5 (overnight)
Contact:	Greg Buikema, Marine Operations Manager The Evergreen State College 2700 Evergreen Parkway Olympia, WA 98505 Tel: 360-866-6000; Fax: 360-866-6794

Roald A...

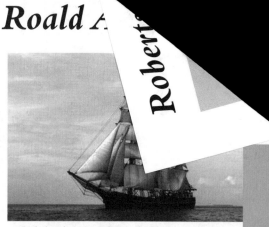

From Germany, Sails everywhere

The brig *Roald Amundsen* was originally built in 1952 as a motor-tanker for the East German Navy. After the German reunification she was bought and transformed into her present shape and is now run by the nonprofit association LebenlernenaufSegelschiffen (Learn to Live on Sailing Ships), under the direction of Detlev Löll.

Since 1993, *Roald Amundsen* has sailed between Iceland, St. Petersburg, and the Canary Islands on voyages mainly dedicated to the education and understanding of young people. She has participated in several Cutty Sark Tall Ships Races.

Roald Amundsen is designed so that she will only sail with all hands onboard helping to sail the ship. Her permanent crew (well trained volunteers) undertakes the challenge of forming the new trainees into a group of enthusiastic young sailors.

While the rig of *Roald Amundsen* is designed like it was in the 19th century, the interior is built to high standards, with wood paneling and private heads. The vessel was built under the surveillance of Germanischer Lloyd and fully complies with the German "Traditionsschiffsverordnung" (safety standards for traditional sail training vessels). Her safety standards are the highest available and she is licensed for worldwide voyaging.

ROALD AMUNDSEN

Flag:	Germany		
Rig:	Brig		
Homeport/waters:	Wolgast, Germany: Baltic Sea, Canary Islands, Caribbean Sea		
Who sails?	Youth trainees, school groups, families, and individuals over 16.		
Cost:	Youth trainees, $70 per person per day; trainees over 26, $110 per person per day		
Program type:	Sail training for apprentices and paying trainees. Accredited sea education. Day sails and overnight passages.		
Specifications:	Sparred length: 165'	Draft: 15'	Sail area: 9,265 sq. ft.
	LOD: 139'	Beam: 25'	Tons: 252 GRT
	LOA: 140'	Rig height: 112'	Power: 300 HP
	LWL: 130'	Freeboard: 8' 6"	Hull: steel
Designer:	Detlev Löll		
Built:	1952; Rorlau, Germany, Learn to Live on Sailing Ships		
Certification:	German Lloyd Traditionsschiffsverordung		
Crew:	14. **Trainees:** 65 (day sails), 32 (overnight)		
Contact:	*North Americans*: HANSA Foundation, PO Box 69, North Reading, MA 01864		
	Tel: 781-944-0304; Fax: 781-944-2469;		
	E-mail: info@hansafoundation.org		
	Web site: http://www.hansafoundation.org		
	Others: Captain Ben Lodemann, Learn to Live on Sailing Ships		
	Friederich-Voß-Ufer 24, D-24159 Kiel, GERMANY		
	Tel: 49-431-364-9558; Fax: 49-431-364-9559		
	E-mail: office@sailtraining.de		
	Web site: http://www.segel.de/windjammer		

...son II

The most beautiful boat to sink last year. (handwritten)

1974, she was brought through the Panama Canal to Victoria, British Columbia, where for the past 20 years she has provided sail training programs for young people.

Officially retired in 1995 from active service, the *Robertson II* continues to provide dockside programs for younger trainees of elementary school age and is open to the general public from May until September. The City of Victoria has provided a permanent dock in the inner harbor where the historic schooner is prominently exhibited.

One of the last original Canadian Grand Banks fishermen built, the *Robertson II* was launched at Shelburne, Nova Scotia in 1940. Fishing up to

ROBERTSON II

Flag:	Canada
Rig:	Gaff schooner, two-masted
Homeport:	Victoria, British Columbia, Canada
Program type:	Dockside training and interpretive programs.

Specifications:		
Sparred length: 130'	Draft: 11' 1"	Sail area: 5,500 sq. ft.
LOD: 105'	Beam: 22' 1"	Tons: 170 GRT
Rig height: 105'	Hull: wood	Power: GM diesel

Built:	1940; Sherburne, Nova Scotia, Canada, McKay and Sons
Contact:	Executive Director
	Sail and Life Training Society (SALTS)
	Box 5014, Station B
	Victoria, BC V8R 6N3, CANADA
	Tel: 250-383-6811; Fax: 250-383-7781

Ros

St. Law

ROSE, "HMS"

The tall ship *Rose* is a three-masted full-rigged ship designed after an 18th-century colonial-era British frigate of the same name. She is currently the only Class A size ship certified by the US Coast Guard as a Sailing School Vessel, and may carry groups as large as 100 for day sailing or as many as 49 for overnight passages and live-aboard programs.

Carrying 19 professional crew and educators, *Rose* specializes in adventure-under-sail, experience-based education for youth groups, but also includes a number of sessions in her itinerary each year that are open to the public for general admission. Most educational sessions are approximately one week long, but special arrangements may also be made for longer or shorter programs. Corporate training, civic events, and other private functions may also be scheduled by groups or individuals.

Rose has sailed the waters of the US East Coast and Canada for many years, and has recently expanded her territory to include the Caribbean and western Europe, with special extended sail training programs during her transatlantic passages. A comprehensive sailing schedule is published several times each year. Starting in August 2000 *Rose* will offer several two-week-long summer term courses in maritime history accredited by Boston University.

PHOTO BY PHILIP PLISSON

Flag:	USA
Rig:	Full-rigged ship, three-masted
Homeport/waters:	Bridgeport, Connecticut: East Coast of North America (summer), overseas
Who sails?	Individuals and groups of all ages.
Season:	Year-round
Program type:	Fundamental sail training with additional education modules tailored for specific programs for middle and high school, college and university, adults and families, corporate team building, and more.

Specifications:	Sparred length: 179'	Draft: 13'	Sail area: 13,000 sq. ft.
	LOD: 125'	Beam: 32'	Tons: 500 GRT
	LOA: 135'	Rig height: 130'	Power: twin diesels
	LWL: 105'	Freeboard: 13'	Hull: wood

Designer:	Original design by Hugh Blades, British Admiralty, in 1757; revised by Phil Bolger in 1970
Built:	1969/70; Lunenberg, Nova Scotia, Canada, Smith & Rhuland (rebuilt: 1985-87; Bridgeport, Connecticut and Fairhaven, Massachuetts)
Coast Guard certification:	Sailing School Vessel (Subchapter R) and Attraction Vessel
Crew:	18. Trainees: 85 (day sails), 31 (overnight). Age: junior high school to adult.
Contact:	"HMS" Rose Foundation, Inc., One Bostwick Avenue, Bridgeport, CT 06605
	Tel: 203-335-0932, 203-335-1433; Fax: 203-335-6793
	E-mail: sailrose@aol.com or onboard@tallshiprose.org
	Web site: http://www.tallshiprose.org

SAIL TALL SHIPS!

My Second Favorite / First Love

The *St. Lawrence II* is a purpose-built sail training vessel in operation since 1957, primarily on the Great Lakes. She was designed to be manageable by a young crew, yet complex enough with her brigantine rig to introduce teenagers to the challenge of square-rig sailing.

The ship is owned and operated by Brigantine, Inc., a nonprofit charity staffed by local volunteers who share the conviction that the lessons of responsibility, self-reliance, and teamwork pro-vided by sail training are especially applicable to teenagers. With 41 years of operation, Brigantine, Inc. is one of the pioneering sail training programs in North America.

Cruises in this hands-on program range from four to ten days or more in length. *St. Lawrence II*'s crew complement of 28 comprises 18 new trainees, plus a crew of watch officers, petty officers, cook, and bosun, all aged 13 to 18. The captain is usually the only adult onboard.

The ship's teenage officers are graduates of Brigantine, Inc.'s winter training program, involving lessons in seamanship, navigation, and ship's systems, as well as the ongoing maintenance of the ship. Every year the *St. Lawrence II* sails over 4,000 miles, spends more than 40 nights at sea, and introduces over 300 trainees to the rigors of life aboard ship on the Great Lakes.

Flag:	Canada
Rig:	Brigantine
Homeport/waters:	Kingston, Ontario, Canada: Lake Ontario and adjacent waters
Who sails?	Any youth, age 13-18, plus elementary and private school groups.
Season:	April to November (sailing); October to March (winter program)
Cost:	$55 CDN per person per day. Scholarships available.
Program type:	Sail training with paying trainees.

Specifications:			
	Sparred length: 72'	Draft: 8' 6"	Sail area: 2,560 sq. ft.
	LOD: 57'	Beam: 15'	Tons: 34 GRT
	LOA: 60'	Rig height: 54'	Power: 165 HP diesel
	LWL: 46'	Freeboard: 4' 6"	Hull: steel

Designer:	Francis McLachlan/Michael Eames
Built:	1953; Kingston, Ontario, Canada, Kingston Shipyards
Crew:	10. Trainees: 29 (day sails), 18 (overnight)
Contact:	Carol Jeffrey, Office Manager
	Brigantine, Inc.
	...nge Street
	...on, Ontario K7M 6G4, CANADA
	...13-544-5175; Fax: 613-544-5175
	...l: briginc@kos.net
	...site: http://web.ctsolutions.com/brigantine

Samana

The School of Ocean Sailing operates in the North Atlantic Ocean off the coast of Maine, offering courses in offshore ocean sailing and ocean navigation in a live-aboard setting. *Samana* is a modern, well-found, romantic, beautiful, fast, and very seakindly vessel. Built in 1975 in The Netherlands, she has circumnavigated the globe and completed several noteworthy offshore passages.

Captain Larry Wheeler and Letty Wheeler are professional teachers with more than 25 years of classroom teaching experience and over 10 years of sail training experience. Based in Portland, Maine, courses span the Maine coast and reach the coastline of Nova Scotia. The curriculum is a rich blend of technical skills, confidence building, and common sense coupled with a spirit of adventure and romance.

The school offers courses in Advanced Ocean Sailing and Navigation, Celestial Navigation, and Offshore Passage Making. In each course, the trainees handle all offshore sailing operations. All instruction is delivered by mature, professional, Coast Guard-licensed teachers.

Flag:	USA				
Rig:	Ketch				
Homeport/waters:	Portland, Maine: Gulf of Maine to Nova Scotia (summer), Caribbean (winter)				
Who sails?	Individuals of all ages				
Cost:	$200 per person per day, $995 per person per five days				
Program type:	Sail training for paying trainees. Ocean sailing, celestial navigation, offshore passage making.				
Specifications:	Sparred length: 63'		Draft: 7'		Sail area: 1,500 sq. ft.
	LOD: 53'		Beam: 16'		Tons: 34 GRT
	LOA: 63'		Rig height: 85'		Power: Ford Lehman 135
	LWL: 45'		Freeboard: 4'		Hull: steel
Designer:	Van de Wiele				
Built:	1975; The Netherlands				
Crew:	3. **Trainees:** 6				
Contact:	Captain Larry Wheeler				
	School of Ocean Sailing				
	PO Box 7359				
	Portland, ME 04110				
	Tel: 207-871-1315, 888-626-3557; Fax: 207-871-1315				
	E-mail: svsamana@nlis.net				
	Web site: http://www.sailingschool.com				

Santa Maria

Niña, *Pinta*, and *Santa Maria* are the three replica ships built by the Spanish government to commemorate the 500th anniversary of Christopher Columbus' voyage from Spain to the Bahamas in 1492. *Santa Maria* is certified as a Sailing School Vessel. The three vessels are berthed adjacent to the Corpus Christi Museum of Science and History, which houses artifacts from one of the oldest known Spanish shipwrecks in the Americas. The museum also houses the Smithsonian Institution's "Seeds of Change" exhibit, which traces the impact of the European "discovery" on the indigenous peoples of the Americas and on Europe, including the exchange of flora, fauna, technology, and disease.

Flag:	Spain
Rig:	Nao, 15th-century, square rig
Homeport/waters:	Corpus Christi, Texas
Who sails?	School groups from elementary school through college, individuals and families.
Program type:	Sail training for crew and volunteer trainees. Dockside sea education in ecology in cooperation with accredited institutions and other groups.

Specifications:

Sparred length: 102'	Draft: 10'	Sail area: 2,512 sq. ft.
LOD: 53'	Beam: 27'	Tons: 105 GRT
LOA: 87'	Rig height: 82'	Power: twin diesels
LWL: 73'	Freeboard: 8'	Hull: wood

Designer:	Dr. José María Martinez Hildalgo
Built:	1990; Barcelona, Spain, Villdes Shipyard
Trainees:	35 (day sails), 30 (overnight)
Contact:	José Antonio Barrera, Director/Ships Operations
	Columbus Fleet Association,
	1900 N. Chaparral
	Corpus Christi, TX 78401
	Tel: 512-882-1232; Fax: 512-882-1261

Sarah Abbot

Built as an example of classic Nova Scotian schooner construction by master shipwright David Stevens in 1966, *Sarah Abbot* was a major player on the Nova Scotian schooner racing circuit until she moved to Massachusetts and began her career working for Phillips Academy in Andover, Massachusetts. For the last fifteen years *Sarah Abbot* has sailed the coast of Massachusetts, carrying Andover Summer Session students on summer research cruises. Highlights of the "Oceans" program include on-going studies of the Buzzards Bay ecosystem, a scallop restoration project in the Westport River, nonfiction writing instruction, and observation and tracking of whales on Stellwagen Bank. Experienced field biologists sail as faculty on *Sarah Abbot* and aim to give their students an experience akin to Charles Darwin's cruise on the *HMS Beagle*. Each

cruise carries six high school students, a scientist, mate, and licensed captain.

Flag:	USA
Rig:	Gaff schooner, two-masted
Homeport/waters:	Marion, Massachusetts: Coastal Massachusetts/Cape Cod
Who sails?	High school marine science students who attend Phillips Academy/ Andover's Summer Session.
Season:	Summer
Cost:	$4,200 for six-week "Oceans" marine biology course which includes four weeks at Andover's campus and 11-day research cruise aboard *Sarah Abbot*.
Program type:	Academically challenging marine biology course which includes a major cruise project, labs, extensive field collection, and paper writing.

Specifications:	Sparred length: 55'	Draft: 6' 6"	Tons: 15 GRT
	LOD: 47' 6"	Beam: 11' 6"	Power: 36 HP diesel
	Rig height: 61'	Hull: wood	

Designer:	David Stevens
Built:	1966, Lunenburg, Nova Scotia, Canada
Coast Guard certification:	Research Vessel (Subchapter U)
Crew:	3. **Trainees:** 6 (overnight). **Age:** 15-19
Contact:	Captain Randall Peffer, Program Coordinator
	Phillips Academy
	180 Main St.
	Andover, MA 01810
	Tel: 978-475-5967,
	E-mail: rpeffer@andover.edu

SeaWulff

The *SeaWulff* was originally conceived in 1974 by the faculty of The Evergreen State College as a sailing fishing vessel. Three years into its construction the vessel burned to the ground. Tremendous community support resulted in the project beginning anew. The design of the second vessel, launched in 1980, was revised to more fully meet the mission of the college. The fish hold was turned into laboratory space and sampling equipment was added. This gear enables the *SeaWulff* to provide all the teaching opportunities afforded by a sailing vessel and to be used as a platform for marine research and education.

The *SeaWulff* and her companion vessel *Resolute* are fundamental to a full range of academic programs at Evergreen. Previous classes have included Wooden Boat Design, Building, and Repair, Marine Biology and Fieldwork Methods, Native American Culture Studies, Pacific Northwest History, and Maritime Literature. Regardless of the focus of the class, students are always involved in all aspects of outfitting, operating, maintaining, and living aboard the college's sailing vessels.

Academic programs using the *SeaWulff* and *Resolute* change from year to year and are available to Evergreen State College students only. Student and community volunteers help maintain the vessels in exchange for sailing opportunities.

Flag:	USA
Rig:	Sloop
Homeport/waters:	Olympia, Washington: Puget Sound and inland waters of British Columbia
Who sails?	Evergreen State College students. Outside charters considered on a case by case basis.
Cost:	$225 group rate per day
Program type:	Sail training for volunteer trainees. Fully accredited sea education in marine science, maritime history, and ecology. Passenger day sails and overnight passages.

Specifications:					
	Sparred length: 39'		Draft: 6'		Sail area: 800 sq. ft.
	LOD: 36'		Beam: 12'		Tons: 12.5 GRT
	LOA: 36'		Rig height: 56'		Power: diesel
	LWL: 31'		Freeboard: 4'		Hull: wood

Designer:	Robert Perry and The Evergreen State College
Built:	1980; Olympia Washington, The Evergreen State College
Coast Guard certification:	Passenger Vessel (Subchapter T)
Crew:	2. **Trainees:** 10 (day sails), 4 (overnight)
Contact:	Greg Buikema, Marine Operations Manager
	The Evergreen State College
	2700 Evergreen Parkway
	Olympia, WA 98505
	Tel: 360-866-6000; FAX 360-866-6794

Shamr...

Shamrock V has been acquired by the Newport Shamrock V Corporation, which plans to charter her in the Caribbean for the winter of 1999-2000. J-Class Management has been hired to assist the new owners with a refit, which will include the addition of water makers, air conditioning, ice maker, and washer/dryer.

Today, *Shamrock V* is the sum of 69 years of meticulous maintenance and thoughtful improvement. The comfort and luxury below are made all the more wonderful by the improved safety and ease of sail handling on deck. *Shamrock V* is ready to give more years of service as one of yachting's great queens.

Flag:	USA		
Rig:	Sloop		
Homeport/waters:	Newport, Rhode Island: Newport, Rhode Island (summer), Caribbean (winter)		
Who sails?	Individuals and groups		
Cost:	$9,000 group rate per day		
Specifications:	Sparred length: 120'	Draft: 15' 6"	Sail area: 8,500 sq. ft.
	LOD: 120'	Beam: 19' 9"	Tons: 146 GRT
	LOA: 120'	Rig height: 155'	Power: twin 181 HP diesels
	LWL: 87'	Hull: teak planks over steel frames	
Designer:	Charles Nicholson		
Built:	1930; England, Camper and Nicholson		
Crew:	9		
Contact:	Marcia Whitney, Manager		
	Newport Shamrock V Corporation		
	28 Church Street		
	Newport, RI 02840		
	Tel: 401-849-3060; Fax: 401-849-1642		
	E-mail: info@jclass.com		
	Web site: http://www.jclass.com		

...doah No Engine. ...ck V

painted white, but she now wears the black and white checkerboard paint scheme of the 19th-century Revenue Service. Every summer *Shenandoah* plies the waters of southern New England and Long Island Sound, visiting the haunts of pirates and the homeports of whaling ships. *Shenandoah*'s economic bottom line is paying passengers. That reality includes sharing one's world with weekly passengers, which can be a satisfying and sometimes challenging endeavor.

While the *Shenandoah* is not a replica, the vessel's design bears a strong resemblance to that of the US Revenue Cutter *Joe Lane* of 1851. For her first 25 years, the rakish square topsail schooner was

Flag:	USA
Rig:	Square topsail schooner, two-masted
Homeport/waters:	Vineyard Haven, Massachusetts: Southern New England
Who sails?	Elementary and middle school students, adult individuals.
Season:	June to September
Cost:	$100 per person per day
Program type:	Sail training for paying trainees. Sea education in cooperation with accredited institutions and as part of informal, in-house programming.

Specifications:

Sparred length: 152'	Draft: 11'	Sail area: 7,000 sq. ft.
LOA: 108'	Beam: 23'	Tons: 85 GRT
LWL: 101'	Rig height: 94'	
Freeboard: 3' (amidships)		

Coast Guard certification: Passenger Vessel (Subchapter T)
Crew: 9. **Trainees:** 35 (day sails), 30 (overnight). **Age:** 12-20
Contact: Captain Robert S. Douglas
Coastwise Packet Co., Inc.
PO Box 429
Vineyard Haven, MA 02568
Tel: 508-693-1699

The skipjack *Sigsbee* was built in 1901 in Deale Island, Maryland and worked as an oyster dredge boat until the early 1990s. She was named after Charles D. Sigsbee, who was the Commanding Officer of the battleship *Maine*. The vessel was rebuilt by the Living Classrooms Foundation in 1994, and now sails Chesapeake Bay with students on board. While sailing on board the *Sigsbee*, students learn the history of skipjacks and the oyster industry, marine and nautical science, and gain an appreciation of Chesapeake Bay and the hard work of the watermen of a bygone era.

SIGSBEE

Flag:	USA
Rig:	Sloop
Homeport/waters:	Baltimore, Maryland: Chesapeake Bay and the Delaware River
Who sails?	Students and other organized groups, individuals, and families.
Season:	March through September
Program type:	Sail training with paying trainees. Sea education in marine and nautical science, maritime history, and ecology for school groups from elementary through college.

Specifications:	Sparred length: 76'	Draft: 3' 5"	Sail area: 1,767 sq. ft.
	LOD: 50'	Beam: 16'	Tons: 14 GRT
	Rig height: 68'	Freeboard: 2' 5"	Power: 150 HP diesel

Built:	1901; Deale Island, Maryland
Coast Guard certification:	Passenger Vessel (Subchapter T)
Crew:	4. **Trainees:** 30 (day sails), 15 (overnight). **Age:** 13+. **Dockside visitors:** 30
Contact:	Steve Bountress
	Living Classrooms Foundation
	802 South Caroline Street
	Baltimore, MD 21231-3311
	Tel: 410-685-0295; Fax: 410-752-8433
	Web site: http://www.livingclassrooms.org

skipjacks are sweet

SOREN LARSEN

...arsen

...osbee

in the late 1970s, she initially starred in a number of films which helped to raise funds to fit her out to the high standards required by the British Maritime Coastguard Agency (MCA).

In 1982 the Davies realized their dream of taking people of all ages to sea under a three-year charter with the British Jubilee Sailing Trust, pioneering sailing for the disabled. In 1986 *Soren Larsen* embarked on a circumnavigation, rounding Cape Horn in 1991 and visiting New York and Boston for the Columbus Regatta.

In 1993 *Soren Larsen* sailed on a second world voyage to New Zealand via the Panama Canal. In 1999 she cruised the Pacific islands and will be in New Zealand for millennial celebrations and the America's Cup races. In April 2000, *Soren Larsen* will depart for Europe via the Pacific, Panama Canal, Caribbean, US, and Canada to participate in Tall Ships 2000® and OpSail events. Berths are available for these voyages. Please contact the *Soren Larsen* office for information.

Soren Larsen is one of the last wooden sailing ships built in Denmark. Restored by Captain Tony Davies and his family

PHOTO BY MAX

Flag:	United Kingdom
Rig:	Brigantine
Homeport/waters:	Auckland, New Zealand: New Zealand coastal waters (summer), southwest Pacific islands (winter)
Who sails?	Families and individuals of all ages.
Cost:	$100 per person per day for overnight voyages.
Program type:	Sail training for paying trainees. Sea education in marine science, maritime history, and ecology as informal, in-house programming.

Specifications:			
	Sparred length: 140'	Draft: 11'	Sail area: 6,500 sq. ft.
	LOD: 98'	Beam: 25' 6"	Tons: 125 GRT
	LOA: 105' 6"	Rig height: 100'	Power: 240 HP diesel
	LWL: 90'	Freeboard: 3' 7"	Hull: wood

Designer:	Soren Larsen
Built:	1949; Denmark, Soren Larsen and Sons
Certification:	UK Maritime and CG Agency Loadline; Bureau Veritas Class Certificate.
Crew:	12. **Trainees:** 80 (day sails), 22 (overnight)
Contact:	Fleur Davies, Director
	Square Sail Pacific, Ltd.
	PO Box 310~Kumeu
	Auckland 1250, NEW ZEALAND
	Tel: 64-0-9-411-8755; Fax: 64-0-9-411-8484
	E-mail: sorenlarsen@voyager.co.nz
	Web site: http://squaresail.q.co.nz

SAIL TALL SHIPS!

SoundWaters

SoundWaters is a nonprofit organization dedicated to protecting Long Island Sound and its watershed through education. Each year, SoundWaters offers shipboard and land-based programs to 15,000 children and adults from Fairfield County, Connecticut, Westchester County, New York, and Long Island, New York. The schooner *SoundWaters* features a hands-on learning experience that weaves marine science, art, history, and literature to emphasize the interconnectedness between human life and the environment. The schooner also offers sail training and marine ecology study during weeklong summer camps for children ages 11-14. Instruction includes basic seamanship, navigation, knot tying, and field explorations of salt marshes and beaches.

The public may attend Public or Lecture Sails, offered several times each month from April through October. During these two-hour sails, passengers participate in sailing a traditional vessel and learn about the wonders of Long Island Sound. The schooner is also avail-

able for evening or weekend charters for private groups and corporations.

SoundWaters' staff includes environmental educators, crew, and a licensed captain. College graduates with expertise in marine science, ecology, or sailing may apply for seasonal jobs.

SoundWaters also conducts land-based programs, offered through public and private schools, and community and senior centers.

SOUNDWATERS

Flag:	USA
Rig:	Gaff schooner, three-masted
Homeport/waters:	Stamford, Connecticut: Long Island Sound
Who sails?	School groups from elementary through college, individuals and families.
Season:	April to November
Cost:	$25 per person per two-hour sail, $700-$2,000 group rate for three-hour sail
Program type:	Sea education in marine science and ecology in cooperation with accredited institutions and other groups, and as informal, in-house programming.

Specifications:	Sparred length: 80'	Draft: 3'-8'	Sail area: 1,510 sq. ft.
	LOD: 65'	Beam: 14'	Tons: 32 GRT
	Rig height: 60'	Hull: steel	Power: diesel
	Freeboard: 3' 6"		

Designer:	William Ward
Built:	1986; Norfolk, Virginia, Marine Metals, Inc.
Coast Guard certification:	Passenger Vessel (Subchapter T)
Crew:	3, 5 instructors. **Trainees:** 42 (day sails). **Age:** 8+
Contact:	SoundWaters, Inc., Brewers Yacht Haven Marina
	69 Dyke Lane, Box 13, Stamford, CT 06902-7312
	Tel: 203-323-1978; Fax: 203-967-8306
	E-mail: swaters@soundwaters.org
	Web site: http://www.soundwaters.org

Spirit of Gloucester

was purposely sunk in a river so the Germans could not use her. Raised after the war, this Baltic trader continued to haul logs, lumber, salt, salt fish, and grain in bulk.

The *Spirit of Gloucester* was brought to the US in the late sixties, along with other Baltic Traders, to be converted into yachts. She was made over in the seventies in Maine, and brought to Gloucester in the late eighties to be used as a home.

The *Spirit of Gloucester* was originally built as a log carrier and still retains the log door in the bow. She later carried lumber to Iceland and salt fish on the return voyage. During World War II she

Purchased by the Spirit of Gloucester Foundation in the summer of 1999, the *Spirit of Gloucester* is currently being restored, with a new interior designed for sail training and maritime education.

Flag:	USA
Rig:	Ketch
Homeport/waters:	Gloucester, Massachusetts: New England
Who sails?	School groups from elementary school through high school, individuals, and families.
Cost:	$30 per person per day, $300 per person per week, $1,000 group rate per day
Program type:	Sail training for volunteer and paying trainees. Informal, in-house sea education in marine science.

Specifications:			
	Sparred length: 74'	Draft: 7' 8"	Sail area: 3,750 sq. ft.
	LOD: 74'	Beam: 21' 2"	Tons: 65 GRT
	LOA: 76' 9"	Rig height: 90'	Power: 6-71 Detroit diesel
	LWL: 68'	Freeboard: 4' 6"	Hull: wood

Built:	1914; Vejle, Denmark
Coast Guard certification:	Sailing School Vessel (Subchapter R)
Crew:	4. **Trainees:** 40 (day sails), 20 (overnight)
Contact:	Graham Bell, Executive Director
	Spirit of Gloucester Foundation
	PO Box 281
	Gloucester, MA 01931-0281
	Tel: 978-283-3351

Spirit of Massachusetts

The *Spirit of Massachusetts* is modeled after the fishing schooner *Fredonia*, which was designed by Edward Burgess in 1889 and was popular for its beautiful appearance and speed. The design is typical of the Gloucester fishing schooners of the late 19th and early 20th centuries; the "fast and able" vessels that plied the rich Grand Banks and Georges Bank. The *Spirit of Massachusetts* was launched in 1984, and while traditional in design and construction, conforms to all current US Coast Guard safety requirements. She is operated by Schools for Children, Inc.

Aboard *Spirit of Massachusetts*, students participate in its operation and learn skills, including basic seamanship and navigation, with an introduction to the ocean's resources. Each program has a unique historical, marine science, or environmental theme. Personal skills

acquired from sea experience are leadership, self-esteem, confidence, and the flexibility needed to meet life's challenges.

Flag:	USA
Rig:	Gaff topsail schooner, two-masted
Homeport/waters:	Boston, Massachusetts: Atlantic Ocean and Caribbean
Who sails?	Student and other groups and individuals.
Season:	Year-round
Program type:	Sail training, character building, and sea education in marine science, maritime history, and ecology in cooperation with accredited schools and colleges and other groups such as scouts and youth community centers. Special three-week intervention program for at-risk students.

Specifications:	Sparred length: 125'	Draft: 10' 6"	Sail area: 7,000 sq. ft.
	LOD: 100'	Beam: 24'	Tons: 90 GRT
	LOA: 103'	Rig height: 103'	Power: 235 HP diesel
	LWL: 80'	Freeboard: 7'	Hull: wood

Designer:	Melbourne Smith and Andrew Davis
Built:	1984; Boston, Massachusetts, Schools for Children, Inc.
Coast Guard certification:	Sailing School Vessel (Subchapter R), Passenger Vessel (Subchapter T)
Crew:	7, 2 instructors. **Trainees:** 50 (day sails), 22 (overnight). **Age:** 15+
Contact:	David Whitney, Port Captain
	c/o Schools for Children, Inc.
	20 Academy Street, Suite 200
	Arlington, MA 02476
	Tel: 617-242-1414; Fax: 617-641-2713

Star of India

engine. Built as the full-rigged ship *Euterpe*, this former merchant ship has survived countless perils of the sea to survive as a fully restored square-rigger and National Historic Landmark. She embodies the term "tall ship" both in looks and spirit.

Star of India is the flagship of the San Diego Maritime Museum fleet. She sails on an annual basis. *Star* is host to thousands of schoolchildren each year, many of whom participate in overnight living history programs on board. *Star*'s decks are also used for highly acclaimed cultural events from theatrical performances of *Two Years Before the Mast* and sea chantey festivals, to Gilbert & Sullivan comic operas and "Movies Before the Mast." Volunteer sail handling is held every other Sunday, with the best sailors being selected to sail the tall ship when she goes to sea.

The oldest active square-rigger in the world, *Star of India* has been around the globe 21 times and has never had an

PHOTO BY BOB GRIESER

Flag:	USA
Rig:	Barque, three-masted
Homeport/waters:	San Diego, California: Coastal waters between San Diego, California, and northern Baja California, Mexico
Who sails?	Selected volunteers, permanent crew, and invited passengers.
Program type:	Sail training for crew and apprentices. Sea education in maritime history based on informal, in-house programming. Dockside interpretation.

Specifications:	Sparred length: 278'	Draft: 21' 6"	Sail area: 18,000 sq. ft.
	LOD: 210'	Beam: 35'	Tons: 1,197 GRT
	LWL: 200'	Freeboard: 15'	Hull: iron
	Rig height: 140'		

Designer:	Edward Arnold
Built:	1863; Ramsey, Isle of Man, United Kingdom, Gibson, McDonald & Arnold
Coast Guard certification:	Museum Attraction Vessel
Trainees:	50. **Dockside visitors:** 300
Contact:	Erninia Taranto, Office Manager
	San Diego Maritime Museum
	1306 North Harbor Dr.
	San Diego, CA 92101
	Tel: 619-234-9153; Fax: 619-234-8345
	E-mail: info@sdmaritime.com
	Web site: http://www.sdmaritime.com/ourfleet/star.html

European boats are the most sexy, (handwritten)

Statsraad L[ehmkuhl]

Statsraad Lehmkuhl is a three-masted steel barque, built by Johann C. Tecklenborg in Bremerhaven Geestemünde in 1914 as a training ship for the German merchant marine. During most of World War I she was used as a stationary training ship in Germany, and after the war was taken as a prize of war by the British.

In 1923 the ship was purchased by the Norwegian Shipowners Association, who named her *Statsraad Lemhkuhl* in honor of Minister Kristoffer Lehmkuhl in appreciation of his work on sail training ship regulations. She was used as a sail training ship from 1923 to 1966, except from 1940-1945, when she was captured by the Germans during World War II.

In 1966 the ship was purchased by Hilmar Reksten, who was intent on continuing to use the vessel as a training ship. From 1968-1972, he operated *Statsraad Lehmkuhl* as a sail training vessel at his own expense, donating her to the Statraad Lehmkuhl Foundation in 1978. She is now chartered to schools, corporations, and other organizations.

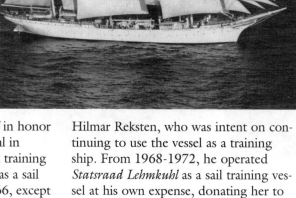

Flag:	Norway
Rig:	Barque, three-masted
Homeport/waters:	Bergen, Norway: Northern Europe
Who sails?	Individuals and families
Cost:	$85 per person per day
Program type:	Sail training for paying trainees. Sea education as informal, in-house programming.

Specifications:			
	Sparred length: 321' 6"	Draft: 17'	Sail area: 21,800 sq. ft.
	LOD: 256'	Beam: 41' 6"	Tons: 1,516 GRT
	LOA: 256'	Rig height: 170'	Power: 1,125 HP diesel
	LWL: 239' 6"	Hull: steel	

Designer:	Georg W. Clausen
Built:	1914; Bremerhaven, Germany, Johan C. Tecklenborg
Certification:	Certified by Det Norske Veritas and Norwegian Maritime Directorate
Crew:	22. **Trainees:** 350 (day sails), 140 (overnight)
Contact:	Stiftelsen Seilskipet Statsraad Lehmkuhl
	Skur 7, Bradbenken
	N-5003 Bergen, NORWAY
	Tel: 47-55-30-1700; Fax: 47-55-30-1701
	E-mail: lehmkuhl@lehmkuhl.no
	Web site: http://www.lehmkuhl.no

Sultana
(in progress)

SULTANA

Sultana Project will be a full-sized reproduction of the 1767 schooner *Sultana*. The new *Sultana* is currently under construction at the Sultana Shipyard in Chestertown and is scheduled to be launched and operational by the summer of 2001. The Sultana Shipyard is located at 346 Cannon Street and is open to the public from 10 AM – 4 PM, Tuesday through Saturday, except for major holidays.

The Schooner Sultana Project is an undertaking of Chester River Craft and Art, Inc., a nonprofit organization based in the historic port of Chestertown, on Maryland's Eastern Shore. The mission of the Sultana Project is to provide unique, hands-on educational opportunities for children and adults that focus on the history and natural environment of the Chesapeake Bay and its watershed. The principal classroom for the

In 1999 the Sultana Project provided over 2000 student days of educational programming, ranging from interactive shipyard experiences for elementary school students to long-term shipbuilding classes and apprenticeships for high school students and adults. Schools or individuals interested in learning more about the diverse variety of shipbuilding-based educational programming offered at the Sultana Shipyard are encouraged to contact the Project's offices for a catalog. Educational programming on board the completed *Sultana* will begin in July of 2001.

Flag:	USA
Rig:	Square topsail schooner, two-masted
Homeport/waters:	Chestertown, Maryland: Chesapeake Bay
Who sails?	Students, individuals, and families of all ages.
Season:	Year-round
Program type (planned):	Sail training for paying trainees. Passenger day sails and overnight passages. Dockside interpretation during port visits. Sea education in maritime history and ecology.

Specifications:			
	Sparred length: 97'	Draft: 7' 6"	Tons: 50 GRT
	LOD: 53'	Beam: 17'	Power: diesel
	LOA: 56'	Rig height: 72'	Hull: wood
	LWL: 53'	Freeboard: 5'	

Designer:	Benford Design Group
Built:	Under construction; Chestertown, Maryland, Swain Boatbuilders
Coast Guard certification:	Passenger Vessel (Subchapter T)
Crew:	5. **Trainees:** 31 (day sails), 11 (overnight)
Contact:	Drew McMullen, Director, Schooner Sultana Project, Schooner Sultana Shipyard 346 Cannon Street, PO Box 524, Chestertown, MD 21620 Tel: 410-778-6461; Fax: 410-778-4531 E-mail: dmcmullen@skipjack.bluecrab.org Web site: http://www.chesterriver.com/sultana

SAIL TALL SHIPS!

Susan Constant

Susan Constant is a full-scale re-creation of the flagship of a small fleet that brought America's first permanent English colonists to Virginia in 1607. Together with the smaller *Godspeed* and *Discovery*, *Susan Constant* is on exhibit at Jamestown Settlement, a living history museum of 17th-century Virginia, and hosts nearly a half-million visitors every year. Jamestown Settlement is administered by the Jamestown-Yorktown Foundation, an agency of the Commonwealth of Virginia.

Built on the museum grounds and commissioned in 1991, *Susan Constant* replaced a vessel built for the 1957 Jamestown Festival commemorating the 350th anniversary of the colony's founding. While no plans or renderings of the original *Susan Constant*, *Godspeed*, and *Discovery* have ever been located, the replicas are based on the documented tonnages of the 17th-century ships, and *Susan Constant*'s design incorporates research information that emerged after

the first replicas were built.

With a crew of staff and volunteers, *Susan Constant* and *Godspeed* periodically sail to other ports in the Chesapeake Bay region to participate in commemorative and community events and host educational programs. A volunteer sail training program is offered to individuals of all ages. Participants are trained in sailing a 17th-century merchant vessel, including handling square sails, marlinespike seamanship, navigation, safety procedures, watch standing, and maritime history.

SUSAN CONSTANT

Flag:	USA
Rig:	Barque, three-masted (lateen mizzen)
Homeport/waters:	Jamestown Settlement, Virginia: Chesapeake Bay
Who sails?	Crew consisting of Jamestown Settlement staff and volunteers.
Program type:	Sail training for crew and apprentices. Dockside interpretation.

Specifications:			
	Sparred length: 116'	Draft: 11' 6"	Sail area: 3,902 sq. ft.
	LOD: 83'	Beam: 24' 10'	Tons: 180 GRT
	LOA: 96'	Rig height: 95'	Power: twin diesels
	LWL: 77'	Freeboard: 11'	Hull: wood

Designer:	Stanley Potter
Built:	1991; Jamestown Settlement, Virginia, Allen C. Rawl
Crew:	25
Contact:	Eric Speth, Maritime Program Manager
	Jamestown Settlement
	PO Box 1607
	Williamsburg, VA 23187
	Tel: 757-229-1607; Fax: 757-253-7350

Svanen

both coastal and inshore waters. She maintains a yearly program to suit corporate sail training, general charter, and harbor commitments.

Sail training aboard *Svanen* provides team spirit, problem solving, coordination, and initiative opportunities, increasing self-confidence, self-worth, personal goals, and creating new horizons. Equally popular are offshore day sails, weekend packages and adventure holidays, and harbor cruises. *Svanen* will tailor programs to the client's voyage requirements.

Svanen is fully surveyed by the Maritime Service Board in conjunction with the Uniform Shipping Laws of Australia, which enables *Svanen* to operate as a charter and sail training vessel in

Flag:	Australia
Rig:	Barquentine, three-masted
Homeport/waters:	Port Jackson, Sydney, New South Wales, Australia: New South Wales and Queensland, Australia coast
Who sails?	Middle school students and individuals of all ages. Affiliated with organizations serving disadvantaged children.
Season:	Year-round
Cost:	$120 per person per day
Program type:	Sail training for professional crew and paying trainees. Sea education in cooperation with accredited institutions and organized groups. Passenger day sails and overnight passages.

Specifications:		
Sparred length: 130'	Draft: 10' 1"	Sail area: 3,385 sq. ft.
LOD: 130'	Beam: 22' 4"	Tons: 119 GRT
LOA: 98' 4"	Rig height: 87' 3"	Power: diesel
LWL: 120'	Freeboard: 3'	Hull: Danish oak

Built:	1922; Frederikssund, Denmark
Certification:	Waterways Authority, New South Wales, Australia – 1E & 2C Survey
Crew:	5. Trainees: 25 (day sails), 30 (overnight)
Contact:	Laurence Nash Kalnin, Managing Director
	Svanen Charters Pty. Ltd.
	148-152 Regent St.
	Redfern, NSW 2016, AUSTRALIA
	Tel: 61-2-9698-4456; Fax: 61-2-9699-3399
	E-mail: medind@fl.net.au
	http://www.charterguide.com.au/main/search/boat/default.asp

Swift of Ipswich

The Los Angeles Maritime Institute (LAMI), the educational affiliate of the Los Angeles Maritime Museum, operates the square topsail schooner *Swift of Ipswich* and the gaff topsail schooner *Bill of Rights*. LAMI staff use the ship to teach trainees how to sail and how to develop personal and "human skills" such as communication, cooperation, teamwork, persistence, self-reliance, and leadership in three different programs.

Topsail is the basic outreach program, with participants recommended by people who work with youth, including educators, youth leaders, and clergy. Cost is on an ability-to-pay basis. The program begins with a five-day series of day sails followed by a five-day voyage planned and organized by the participants. Participants are encouraged to continue as active members of the "*Swift* Family."

Swift Expeditions are more advanced and challenging voyages with specific purposes, goals, and durations. Cooperative programs afford organizations such as youth, church, school, and community groups to voyage on *Swift of Ipswich*. The Los Angeles Maritime Museum and its affiliates take pleasure in offering assistance to visiting tall ships and other "educationally significant" vessels.

Flag:	USA
Rig:	Square topsail schooner, two-masted
Homeport/waters:	Los Angeles, California: Coastal California and offshore islands
Who sails?	Referred youth-at-risk and groups catering to students and adults.
Season:	Year-round
Program type:	Educational sailing adventures for "at-risk" youth and other youth or adult groups.

Specifications:			
	Sparred length: 90'	Draft: 10'	Sail area: 5,166 sq. ft.
	LOD: 66'	Beam: 18'	Tons: 46 GRT
	LOA: 70'	Rig height: 74'	Power: diesel
	LWL: 62'	Freeboard: 5'	Hull: wood

Designer:	Howard I. Chappelle
Built:	1938; Ipswich, Massachusetts, William A. Robinson
Coast Guard certification:	Passenger Vessel (Subchapter T)
Crew:	6. **Trainees:** 49 (day sails), 31 (overnight). **Age:** 12+
Contact:	Captain Jim Gladson
	Los Angeles Maritime Institute
	Berth 84, Foot of Sixth Street
	San Pedro, CA 90731
	Tel: 310-833-6055; Fax: 310-548-2055
	Web site: http://www.tollway.com/swift/

Sylvina W. Beal

The schooner *Sylvina W. Beal* is once again sailing in downeast waters. Built as a fishing vessel in 1911, this classic and historic schooner sails coastal Maine waters with passengers and trainees where she once worked under sail. Set up for day and overnight cruises, the *Sylvina W. Beal* offers groups the opportunity to charter the vessel for educational, vacation, or sail training programs. With her coal stove in the forecastle galley and her small but cozy cabins, this schooner is an enjoyable home away from home.

Groups are encouraged to contact Downeast Windjammer Cruises regarding their charter needs, whether it be extended overnight programs or shorter day sails on the coast. Trainees can step aboard an authentic downeast-built wooden vessel, working for a living since 1911.

Flag:	USA
Rig:	Gaff schooner, two-masted
Homeport/waters:	Bar Harbor, Maine: New England (summer), Chesapeake Bay (winter)
Who sails?	Individuals and groups.
Program type:	Sail training for volunteer and paying trainees. Passenger day sails and overnight passages.

Specifications:					
	Sparred length: 84'		Draft: 8'		Sail area: 2,200 sq. ft.
	LOA: 80'		Beam: 17'		Tons: 46 GRT
	LWL: 70'		Rig height: 56'		Hull: wood
	Freeboard: 4'				

Built:	1911; East Boothbay, Maine, Frank J. Adams Yard
Coast Guard certification:	Passenger Vessel (Subchapter T)
Contact:	Captain Steven F. Pagels, Owner
	Downeast Windjammer Cruises
	PO Box 28
	Cherryfield, ME 04622
	Tel: 207-546-2927; Fax: 207-546-2023
	E-mail: decruise@midmaine.com
	Web site: http://downeastwindjammer.com

Tabor Boy

Tabor Boy has been engaged in sail training as a seagoing classroom for Tabor Academy students since 1954. Offshore voyaging and oceanographic studies go together in the curriculum, with cruises to destinations as distant as Mexico and Panama adding adventure to the experience. Many Tabor Academy graduates go on to the US Merchant Marine, Naval, or Coast Guard academies.

The schooner also offers seven summer orientation voyages for newly enrolled freshmen and sophomore students. During this time, trainees are fully involved in sail handling while studying Gulf of Maine marine wildlife and ecology. Winter programs feature sailing and snorkeling in the US and British Virgin Islands to observe and study coral reef ecosystems.

Flag:	USA
Rig:	Gaff schooner, two-masted
Homeport/waters:	Marion, Massachusetts: Coastal New England (summer), offshore Atlantic Ocean (school year)
Who sails?	Enrolled students at Tabor Academy.
Program type:	Seamanship and oceanography for high school students.

Specifications:			
	Sparred length: 115'	Draft: 10' 4"	Sail area: 3,540 sq. ft.
	LOD: 84' 6"	Beam: 21' 8"	Tons: 99.9 GRT
	LOA: 92' 10"	Rig height: 95'	Power: 295 HP diesel
	LWL: 78' 8"	Hull: iron	

Built:	1914; Amsterdam, The Netherlands, Scheepswerven & Machinefabrik
Coast Guard certification:	Sailing School Vessel (Subchapter R)
Crew:	6. **Trainees:** 23. **Age:** 14-18
Contact:	Captain James F. Geil, Master
	Tabor Boy, Tabor Academy
	66 Spring St.
	Marion, MA 02738-1599
	Tel: 508-748-2000; Fax: 508-748-0353
	E-mail: jgeil@tabor.pvt.k12.ma.us
	Web site: http://www.taboracademy.org

Tango

interior provides comfortable accommodations for overnight trips.

From June through September, Captain Tim Bogle provides learning experiences for students, corporate team building, and private charters for up to 12 people. *Tango* is a familiar sight on the beautiful waters of Casco Bay, Maine. Since 1991 she has transported people through the many islands and passages of southern Maine.

Tango is a 56-foot Bruce Roberts ketch. Her 16-foot beam makes her an ideal platform for day sails and her spacious

Flag:	USA
Rig:	Ketch
Homeport/waters:	Peaks Island, Maine: Portland, Maine, Casco Bay, coastal Maine (summer), Caribbean (winter)
Who sails?	High school and college students, adult individuals, and families.
Cost:	$80 per person per day
Program type:	Sail training for paying trainees. Sea education as informal, in-house programming. Passenger day sails and overnight passages.

Specifications:					
	Sparred length: 56'		Draft: 7' 6"		Sail area: 1,200 sq. ft.
	LOD: 56'		Beam: 15' 10"		Tons: 24 GRT
	LOA: 56'		Rig height: 63'		Power: 90 HP diesel
	LWL: 45' 10"		Freeboard: 4' 5"		Hull: fiberglass

Designer:	Bruce Roberts
Built:	1981; Durban, South Africa, Brown Bros.
Coast Guard certification:	Uninspected Vessel
Crew:	1. **Trainees:** 12 (day sails), 6 (overnight)
Contact:	Captain Tim Bogle
	Tango Charters
	108 Upper A Street
	Peaks Island, ME 04108
	Tel: 207-766-2751; Fax: 207-233-7687
	E-mail: tangochart@aol.com

HMS *Tecumseth*

Tecumseth is a replica of the 19th-century British war schooner *Tecumseth*, which served with the Royal Naval Establishment (now Discovery Harbour) at Penetanguishene. Used for defense and transport from the Royal Navy base, she was active on Lake Huron after the War of 1812 and eventually put into Ordinary. Today's replica was designed from the original British Admiralty plans and has been built to appear as close as possible to the original ship.

Although the replica is a modern ship with up-to-date safety features, *Tecumseth* is the mirror of her namesake and takes visitors back to the days of Nelson's Navy and England's "wooden walls." Officers and crew are in historic uniform and participants join in making the ship come alive during *Tecumseth*'s sail training programs. An extended season is planned for 2000 including three, five, and seven-day journeys on Georgian Bay.

HMS TECUMSETH

Flag:	Canada
Rig:	Square topsail schooner, two-masted
Homeport/waters:	Discovery Harbour, Penetanguishene, Ontario, Canada: Georgian Bay, Lake Huron
Who sails?	Individuals and groups.
Season:	May to October
Cost:	$26 CDN per person per two-hour sail
Program type:	Sail training for crew and apprentices.

Specifications:			
	Sparred length: 125'	Draft: 8'	Sail area: 4,700 sq. ft.
	LOD: 70'	Beam: 29'	Tons: 146 GRT
	LOA: 80'	Rig height: 90'	Power: 360 HP diesel
	LWL: 63'	Hull: steel	

Designer:	Bob Johnston
Built:	1992; St. Thomas, Ontario, Canada, Kanter Yachts
Crew:	12. **Trainees:** 45 (day sails). **Age:** 10+ (ages 10-16 must be accompanied by an adult)
Contact:	Bill Brodeur, Information Officer
	Discovery Harbour
	93 Jury Drive
	Penetanguishene, Ontario L9M 1G1, CANADA
	Tel: 705-549-8064; Fax: 705-549-4858
	Web site: http://www.discoveryharbour.on.ca

SAIL TALL SHIPS!247

Tenacious

Bringing the ethos of integration ashore, the JST has developed the concept of Shorewatch, weeklong shipbuilding holidays. Professional shipwrights and mixed-ability volunteers have worked side-by-side as part of this amazing project.

Like the *Lord Nelson*, *Tenacious* enables all members of her crew to sail together on equal terms. Features include signs in Braille, power-assisted hydraulic steering, and points throughout the ship that enable wheelchairs to be secured during rough weather.

The 213-foot, three-masted barque *Tenacious* is the Jubilee Sailing Trust's (JST) new, second ship. She is the largest wooden tall ship of her kind to be built in Great Britain this century.

JST promotes the integration of able-bodied and disabled people though the mediums of tall ship sailing and building. Such has been the success of the JST's first ship, *Lord Nelson*, that that JST decided to build *Tenacious*.

Voyages are open to anyone between 16 – 70+ and no previous experience is required. The crew of 40 is split 50/50 between able-bodied and physically disabled people, with eight wheelchair users. There is a permanent crew of 10, including a medical purser and cook. The ship's maiden voyage will take place in early summer 2000.

Flag:	United Kingdom
Rig:	Barque, three-masted
Homeport/waters:	Southampton, United Kingdom: Northern Europe (summer), Canary Islands and Southern Europe (winter)
Who sails?	Physically disabled and able-bodied people, aged 16 to 70+.
Season:	Year-round
Cost:	$135 per person per day
Program type:	Sail training for paying trainees. Integration of physically disabled and able-bodied people through the medium of tall ship sailing.

Specifications:		
Sparred length: 213' 3"	Draft: 14' 9"	Sail area: 12,956 sq. ft.
LOD: 163' 6"	Beam: 34' 9"	Rig height: 129' 9"
LOA: 177' 3"	Hull: wood/epoxy	Power: twin 400 HP
LWL: 151' 3"	Freeboard: 7' 3"	

Designer:	Tony Castro, Ltd.
Built:	1996-2000; Woolston, Southampton, United Kingdom
Crew:	8. **Trainees:** 40
Contact:	Mrs. Lindsey Neve, Jubilee Sailing Trust
	Jubilee Yard, Hazel Road, Woolston
	Southampton, Hampshire, SO19 7GB, UNITED KINDDOM
	Tel: 44-23-8044-9108; Fax: 44-23-8044-9145
	E-mail: jst@jst.org.uk,
	Web site: http://www.jst.org.uk

Thomas E. Lannon

Over 4,000 schooners were built in the town of Essex, Massachusetts from the mid-1600s to 1948. Tom Ellis' dream of continuing that tradition came true when the sawn-framed trunnel-fastened schooner *Thomas E. Lannon* was launched at the Essex Shipbuilding Museum Shipyard in June 1997, just six months after her keel was laid. The *Lannon*, a fine new addition to the long line of Essex-built Gloucester fishing schooners, is similar to the schooner *Nokomis*, built in Essex by Mel McClain in 1903. The *Lannon* is named for Tom Ellis' grandfather, who came from Newfoundland and fished out of Gloucester from 1901-1943.

The schooner *Thomas E. Lannon* is berthed at Seven Seas Wharf at the Gloucester House Restaurant in Gloucester, Massachusetts, the oldest fishing port in America. The *Lannon* carries passengers on a variety of two-hour harbor sails from May to October. She is also available for charter to corpo- rations, individuals, school groups, etc. for corporate outings, family gatherings, weddings, parties, field trips, and other special events.

THOMAS E. LANNON

Flag:	USA
Rig:	Gaff topsail schooner, two-masted
Homeport/waters:	Gloucester, Massachusetts: Cape Ann, Massachusetts
Who sails?	Individuals, groups, and families of all ages.
Season:	May to October
Cost:	$29 per person per two-hour sail, $400-$550 group rate per day (charter)
Program type:	Sail training for paying trainees. Sea education in marine science and maritime history based on informal, in-house programming. Passenger day sails.

Specifications:			
	Sparred length: 93'	Draft: 9'	Sail area: 2,000 sq. ft.
	LOD: 65'	Beam: 17' 6"	Tons: 51 GRT
	LOA: 83'	Rig height: 70'	Power: diesel
	LWL: 55'	Freeboard: 4'	Hull: wood

Designer:	Harold A. Burnham
Built:	1997; Essex, Massachusetts, Harold A. Burnham
Coast Guard certification:	Passenger Vessel (Subchapter T)
Contact:	Kay M. Ellis, President
	Thomas E. Lannon, Inc.
	5 Old Bray St.
	Gloucester, MA 01930
	Tel: 978-281-6634; Fax: 978-281-0369
	E-mail: k@schooner.org
	Web site: http://www.schooner.org

Three Hierarchs

(Work in Progress)

" ТРИ СВЯТИТИЛЯ "

On the island of Kodiak in the North Pacific the construction of a ship is underway. The *Three Hierarchs* is a replica of the ship that brought the first Russian settlers to America. In 1785 she landed on Kodiak Island to begin Russian life in the New World. These new pioneers relied on her to bring them supplies from Russia every year. After 10 years of sailing the treacherous waters of the North Pacific she was sent back to Russia on her most famous voyage. Before leaving port in Russia she picked up ten Russian Orthodox monks and brought them to Kodiak. These monks became the first Christian missionaries of the great land of Alaska.

Although the *Three Hierarchs* is little known, her importance is great. She is a legend in her own right, going down in history as the ship that brought two different worlds and peoples together, forming one unique heritage. This legendary ship, the *Three Hierarchs*, will always be remembered as the ship that connected Russia with America.

Now, 200 years later, the *Three Hierarchs* is rising again, being built by the at-risk youth of Alaska and, believe it or not, by monks.

Flag:	USA
Rig:	Galiot
Homeport/waters:	Kodiak, Alaska: North Pacific
Who sails?	School groups from elementary school through college, adults, and families. Affiliated with St. Innocent's Academy.
Program type:	Sail training for volunteer and paying trainees. Sea education in maritime history in cooperation with accredited schools. Dockside interpretation during port visits.
Specifications:	LOD: 78'
Designer:	Stuart Hoagland
Built:	Under construction; Kodiak, Alaska, St. Innocent's Academy
Coast Guard certification:	Sailing School Vessel (Subchapter R), Passenger Vessel (Subchapter T)
Contact:	Father John Marler, Manager
	Three Hierarchs
	St. Innocent's Academy
	PO Box 1517
	Kodiak, AK 99615
	Tel: 907-486-4376; Fax: 907-486-1758
	E-mail: innocent@ptialaska.net

Tole Mour

Built in 1988 to support primary health care and educational programs in Micronesia, *Tole Mour* ("gift of life and health") was named by the school children of the Marshall Islands. From 1988 through 1992, *Tole Mour* made regular teaching and medical "rounds" through the remote atolls of the Marshalls, serving 15,000 men, women, and children in 58 far-flung communities. She carried multinational teams of educators and health care professionals, most of whom served as volunteers. By the end of 1992, the volunteer professional health teams had been replaced entirely by Marshallese counterparts using powered patrol craft, which allowed Marimed to phase out support and bring *Tole Mour* home.

Since 1992 *Tole Mour* has been used to support programs for special needs adolescents, including youth referred by juvenile courts and mental health agencies. The ship currently supports a 6 to 12-month residential treatment program for Hawaiian youth who live, work, and attend school on board while receiving group, individual, and family therapy from a multidisciplinary treatment team.

Flag:	USA
Rig:	Square topsail schooner, three-masted
Homeport/waters:	Honolulu, Hawaii: South Pacific
Who sails?	Trainees include emotionally impaired youth referred by the Hawaiian Department of Health, Child, and Adolescent Mental Health Division.
Season:	Year-round
Program type:	Long-term residential treatment and education (including special education) for emotionally impaired male adolescents; vocational training leading to AB Sail MMD.

Specifications:

Sparred length: 156'	Draft: 13' 6"	Sail area: 8,500 sq. ft.
LOD: 123'	Beam: 31'	Tons: 229 GRT
LWL: 101'	Rig height: 110'	Power: 575 HP diesel
Freeboard: 6'	Hull: steel	

Designer:	Ewbank, Brooke & Associates
Built:	1988; Seattle, Washington, Nichols Bros.
Coast Guard certification:	Sailing School Vessel (Subchapter R), Freight and Miscellaneous (Subchapter I)
Crew:	11, 10 instructors. **Trainees:** 80 (day sails), 28 (overnight). **Age:** 13-25
Contact:	David D. Higgins, Marimed Foundation
	45-021 Likeke Place
	Kanehoa, HI 96744
	Tel: 808-236-2288; Fax: 808-235-1074
	E-mail: Kailana@pixi.com
	Web site: http://www.pixi.com/~kailana

Tree of Life

The schooner *Tree of Life*, launched in 1991, was built in Nova Scotia, Canada and Jacksonville, Florida. She sleeps 12 in three cabins and the foc'sle. Powered by 4,500 square feet of sail, she cruises at 8 to 10 knots. Her hull is a composite of strip planked clear fir and kevlar saturated in epoxy and sheathed in fiber-glass. Her deck is fir, spars are spruce, and brightwork is Honduran mahogany. The interior is paneled in koa and teak.

In the past seven years, more than 200 trainees have crewed the *Tree* around the world, completing her first circumnavigation. The winter of 1998-1999 was spent in Spain, refitting for the 1999 Cutty Sark Tall Ships Race. The *Tree*'s crew roster has berths for the skipper and three permanent crew, plus six to eight trainees. Permanent crew includes skipper, first mate, provisioner, and engineer. All crewmembers share the cooking, cleaning, and navigation.

Tree of Life was chosen as one of the top ten yachts in North America by *Sail* magazine (1993), and in 1997 won the Bay of Islands Race.

Flag:	USA
Rig:	Gaff schooner
Homeport/waters:	Alexandria, Virginia
Who sails?	Adult individuals and families.
Program type:	Sail training for volunteer and paying trainees. Sea education in marine science and maritime history.

Specifications:			
	Sparred length: 93'	Draft: 8' 5"	Sail area: 4,200 sq. ft.
	LOD: 70'	Beam: 18' 6"	Tons: 70 GRT
	LOA: 70'	Rig height: 85'	Power: diesel
	LWL: 58'	Freeboard: 4' 5"	Hull: wood/epoxy

Designer:	Ted Brewer
Built:	1991; Covey Island, Canada
Crew:	4. Trainees: 6
Contact:	Captain Kelly Kellogg
	1015 Oronoco Street
	Alexandria, VA 22314
	Tel: 703-548-8810; Fax: 703-548-0511
	E-mail: kellykellogg@hotmail.com
	Web site: http://www.schoonertreeoflife.com

True North of Toronto

True North of Toronto was built in 1947 as a North Sea Trawler. She was converted to sail in 1979 and has spent her years since then world voyaging for sail training and charter. *True North* is dedicated to promoting the preservation of traditional maritime life. This is accomplished by creating opportunities for people of all ages to participate in sail training voyages, fulfill professional crew positions, dockside visitations, and film work. *True North* was the proud recipient of the overall 1st place ranking for the 1998 ASTA Great Lakes Tall Ships® Race. Her crew is looking forward to representing Canada during Tall Ships 2000®.

Flag:	Canada
Rig:	Topsail schooner
Homeport/waters:	Toronto, Canada: Great Lakes, Atlantic, Caribbean
Who sails?	Individuals of all ages.
Program type:	Sail training for groups and individuals. Nautical curriculum, waterfront festivals, and film work.

Specifications:

Sparred length: 118'	Draft: 10'	Sail area: 9,688 sq. ft.
LOD: 90'	Beam: 22'	Tons: 98 GRT
LWL: 83'	Freeboard: 3' 6"	Power: 350 HP diesel
Rig height: 90'	Hull: steel	

Built:	1947; Alphen, The Netherlands, Gouwsluis
Crew:	8. **Trainees:** 50 (day sails), 25 (overnight)
Contact:	Captain Doug Prothero, President
	True North of Toronto, Ltd.
	249 Queen's Quay West, Suite 111
	Toronto, Ontario M5J 2N5, CANADA
	Tel: 416-260-6355, 416-918-0137; Fax: 416-260-6377
	E-mail: doug@greatlakesschooner.com
	Web site: http://www.greatlakesschooner.com

Now Unicorn, owned by douchebags... Probably sinking...

Victory Chimes

Built in Bethel, Delaware, in 1900, the schooner *Victory Chimes* is the largest commercial sailing vessel under the American flag and the only original three-master still working in America. Recently nominated for National Historic Landmark status, the *Victory Chimes* has been quietly supporting herself and a succession of private owners for the past 100 years. She has never been supported by foundations, grants, or endowments, and continues to be a well-maintained working vessel. Her current caretakers/owners, Captain Kip Files and Captain Paul DeGaeta, offer Windjammer style vacations on Penobscot Bay. At over 200 gross tons, the *Victory Chimes* attracts career-minded professional crew and carries a crew of nine.

Flag:	USA
Rig:	Gaff schooner, three-masted
Homeport/waters:	Rockland, Maine: Coastal Maine
Who sails?	High school and college groups as well as individuals and adults of all ages. Affiliated institutions include Baylor Academy.
Season:	June through September
Cost:	$100 per person per day
Program type:	Sail training for crew, apprentices, and paying trainees. Sea education in marine science, maritime history, and ecology based on informal, in-house programming. Paying passengers on overnight passages.

Specifications:			
	Sparred length: 170'	Draft: 7' 5" (min.)	Sail area: 7,100 sq. ft.
	LOD: 132'	Beam: 25'	Tons: 208 GRT
	LOA: 140'	Rig height: 87'	Power: yawl boat with engine
	LWL: 127'	Freeboard: 11'	Hull: wood

Designer:	J.M.C. Moore
Built:	1900; Bethel, Delaware, Phillips & Co.
Coast Guard certification:	Passenger Vessel (Subchapter T)
Crew:	10. **Trainees: 44. Age:** 16-75
Contact:	Captain Kip Files Victory Chimes, Inc. PO Box 1401 Rockland, ME 04841 Tel: 207-265-5671, 800-745-5651 E-mail: kip@somtel.com Web site: http://www.midcoast.com/victorychimes

Viking

Viking is a sailing whaleboat, an open boat designed to be launched from a larger ship while at sea, and was built at Puget Sound Naval Shipyard in 1939 for use in the Navy's fleet sailing program. As the US prepared for war, the Navy stripped its ships and whaleboats were sent ashore. The sailing program was never reinstated, and surplus Navy whaleboats found their way to Sea Scout units around the country, offering thousands of youth the opportunity to learn sailing, seamanship, and teamwork on the water. Of those boats, only a handful remain.

The Sea Scout Ship *Viking* has been serving the youth of the Bay Area for over 60 years, offering programs that teach sailing, seamanship, and leadership to young women aged 14-21. Her sister ship, *Corsair*, offers similar programs for young men. The two ships participate in many joint activities. In addition to the annual two-week summer cruise in the

VIKING

Sacramento Delta, the Sea Scouts organize day sails, races, weekend outings, dances, and regattas. New members are always welcome, both young and adult.

Flag:	USA
Rig:	Cutter
Homeport/waters:	San Francisco, California: San Francisco Bay and tributaries
Who sails?	High school students and individuals. Affiliated institutions include Sea Exploring, Boy Scouts of America, San Francisco Bay Area Council.
Program type:	Sail training for female trainees, aged 14-21. Sea education in marine science and maritime history in cooperation with other groups.

Specifications:	Sparred length: 30'	Draft: 4' 6"	Sail area: 600 sq. ft.
	LOD: 30'	Beam: 8'	Tons: 8 GRT
	LOA: 30'	Rig height: 35'	Hull: wood
	LWL: 28'	Freeboard: 2'	

Designer:	US Navy
Built:	1939; US Navy, Puget Sound Naval Shipyard
Coast Guard certification:	Uninspected Vessel
Crew:	6-18
Contact:	Nick Tarlson
	220 Sansome Street, Ste. 900
	San Francisco, CA 94104
	Tel: 415-956-5700; Fax: 415-982-2528
	E-mail: seascouts@dictyon.com
	Web site: http://www.tbw.net/~chriss/scouts

Virginia

the convoy movements transiting in and out of Chesapeake Bay.

The Schooner Virginia Project, a 501(c) (3) not-for-profit corporation, seeks to build a replica of this historic ship along the Norfolk, Virginia waterfront. *Virginia*'s "living shipyard" will provide a unique educational experience, focusing on traditional wood ship construction, maritime history, and the vital role ship pilots and their vessels played throughout the history of the Commonwealth of Virginia.

A topsail schooner, *Virginia* will accommodate up to ten passengers in addition to eight full-time crew on overnight voyages. Day excursions will be limited to 35 passengers. In her mission as a goodwill ambassador for the Commonwealth, *Virginia* will maintain an international sailing schedule with crew positions open to qualified individuals.

The last of the great pilot schooners, the 118-foot *Virginia* served the Virginia Pilot Association from 1917 to 1926. Fast and seaworthy, *Virginia* remained in service long into an age where power vessels became the preferred platform for pilot station ships. *Virginia* was recognized in WWI for outstanding piloting services rendered to

Flag:	USA
Rig:	Gaff topsail schooner, two-masted
Homeport/waters:	Hampton Roads, Virginia: worldwide
Who sails?	Students from elementary through college and individuals of all ages.
Season:	Year-round
Program type:	Sail training for crew and volunteer trainees. Sea education in marine science, maritime history, and ecology in cooperation with accredited institutions. Overnight passenger voyages. Dockside interpretation during port visits.

Specifications:	Sparred length: 126'	Draft: 13'	Sail area: 7,000 sq. ft.
	LOD: 115'	Beam: 22'	Tons: 97 GRT
	LOA: 118'	Rig height: 105' 4"	Power: twin diesels
	LWL: 80'	Freeboard: 6'	Hull: wood

Built:	Under construction
Coast Guard **certification:**	Passenger Vessel (Subchapter T)
Crew:	8. **Trainees:** 35 (day sails), 10 (overnight)
Contact:	Rick Boesch, Executive Director
	Schooner Virginia Project
	PO Box 3126
	Norfolk, VA 23514
	Tel: 757-496-4110; Fax: 757-481-6003
	E-mail: schoonerva@aol.com

Wavertree
(Work in Progress)

Check it out at South St. Seaport in NYC

Wavertree was built in Southampton, England in 1885. She was first employed to carry jute for use in making rope and burlap bags, voyaging between India and Scotland. Within two years, she entered the tramp trade, taking cargoes anywhere in the world. After 25 years, she limped into the Falkland Islands in 1911, having been almost dismasted in a gale off Cape Horn. Rather than re-rigging her, her owners sold her for use as a floating warehouse at Punta Arenas, Chile.

Wavertree was converted into a sand barge at Buenos Aires, Argentina in 1947, and was acquired there by the South Street Seaport Museum in 1968 for eventual restoration to her appearance as a sailing vessel. By the time *Wavertree* was built, she was nearly obsolete, being replaced by ocean-crossing steam ships. At the same time, iron—long the choice of shipbuilders in iron-producing countries such as England—was giving way to steel. *Wavertree* was one of the last large sailing ships built of wrought iron, and today is the largest afloat. Currently undergoing restoration, the *Wavertree* is expected to begin a limited sail training program in 2000.

WAVERTREE

Flag:	USA
Rig:	Full-rigged ship
Homeport/waters:	New York, New York
Program type:	Sea education in marine science, maritime history, and ecology in cooperation with accredited schools and other groups. Other education programs focused toward restoration.

Specifications:	Sparred length: 325'	Draft: 11' (min.), 22' (max.)	Sail area: 31,495 sq. ft.
	LOD: 263'	Beam: 40'	Tons: 2,170 GRT
	Rig height: 167'	Hull: iron	

Built:	1885; Southampton, England, Oswald Mordaunt & Co.
Contact:	Paula Mayo, Director of Programs
	South Street Seaport Museum
	207 Front Street
	New York, NY 10038
	Tel: 212-748-8681; Fax: 212-748-8610
	Web site: http://www.southstseaport.org

Weatherly

PHOTO BY LINDSEY SMITH-HILL

The legendary Emil "Bus" Mosbacher bought her back in 1962 and in very close racing she defeated the first Australian challenger, *Gretel*, and won the Cup.

Weatherly is a classic; her mahogany hull has been restored by owner George Hill to her original lines and her varnished interior makes her a beauty. She is part of America's Cup Charters' 12-meter fleet in Newport, Rhode Island,

The fast and beautiful *Weatherly* is the only yacht in history to win the America's Cup without doing so when new. She was built for the 1958 campaign in which she raced well, but *Columbia* went on to defend the Cup. and is available for racing, corporate team building, and casual sails at the port of your choice from Maine down to the Chesapeake. Sail aboard an America's Cup winner—no sailing experience is necessary.

Flag:	USA
Rig:	Sloop
Homeport/waters:	Newport, Rhode Island: New England and Chesapeake Bay
Who sails?	Individuals of all ages.
Cost:	$1,800 group rate per day, $60 per person for evening sail
Program type:	Sail training for volunteer or paying trainees. Sea education based on informal, in-house programming. Passenger day sails.

Specifications:			
Sparred length: 69'	Draft: 9'	Sail area: 1,850 sq. ft.
LOD: 69'	Beam: 12'	Tons: 28 GRT
LOA: 69'	Rig height: 90'	Power: diesel
LWL: 60'	Freeboard: 4'	Hull: wood

Designer:	P. Rhodes
Built:	1958; Stamford, Connecticut, Luders
Coast Guard certification:	Passenger Vessel (Subchapter T)
Crew:	3. **Passengers/trainees:** 12
Contact:	George Hill/Herb Marshall
	America's Cup Charters
	PO Box 51
	Newport, RI 02840
	Tel: 401-849-5868; Fax: 401-849-3098
	Web site: http://www.americascupcharters.com

Welcome

The *Welcome* is a 55-foot sloop, a replica of the original *Welcome* built in 1775 at Fort Michimackinac during the Revolutionary War, which later became a British military vessel. The current *Welcome* is under reconstruction on a pier at the Great Lakes Maritime Academy in Traverse City, Michigan.

The Mackinac Island State Park Commission built the *Welcome* for the 200th anniversary of Independence Day. The vessel sailed the Great Lakes for a number of years before serving as a dockside museum in Mackinac City. In December of 1992, the Maritime Heritage Alliance (MHA), a nonprofit organization located in Traverse City, Michigan, was awarded the vessel for reconstruction.

Volunteers of the MHA, having built

the schooner *Madeline*, are using their traditional boat building skills to restore this magnificent vessel. A target date for launching has been set for August 2000. When completed, the *Welcome* will again serve as a living museum of Michigan's maritime tradition, from the era of the American Revolution.

Flag:	USA
Rig:	Square topsail sloop
Homeport/waters:	Traverse City, Michigan: Upper Great Lakes
Who sails?	Students from elementary school through high school and adult individuals.
Program Type:	Sail training for volunteer trainees. Dockside sea education in maritime history during port visits.

Specifications:	Sparred length: 90'	Draft: 8'	Tons: 45 GRT
	LOA: 56'	Beam: 16'	Power: diesel
	LWL: 49'	Rig height: 96'	Hull: wood
	Freeboard: 6'		

Designer:	Ted McCutcheon
Built:	1976; Mackinaw City, Michigan, State of Michigan
Coast Guard certification:	Attraction Vessel
Crew:	5. **Trainees:** 11. **Age:** 13+
Contact:	Carol Hale, Office Manager
	Maritime Heritage Alliance
	232 East Front Street
	Traverse City, MI 49684
	Tel: 231-946-2647; Fax: 231-946-6750
	E-mail: mha.tc@juno.com
	Web site: http://www.traverse.com/maritime/

WELCOME

Western Union

The *Western Union* is patterned after the schooners of the turn of the century that once roamed the high seas in the age of sail. Constructed of long leaf yellow pine with a Spanish Madeira mahogany-framed hull, the ship was built in Key West by the order of the Thompson Fish Company for operations they conducted on behalf of the Western Union Telegraph Company.

When launched in 1939, *Western Union* was among the last "working schooners" to be built in the United States. She was homeported in Key West during her 35 years of active service for Western Union as a cable repair vessel. In 1974 she was about to be converted into a barge when she was purchased by Captain John Krause and put into passenger service. *Western Union* was acquired by Vision Quest in 1984 and renamed *New Way* for the important role she would play in redirecting troubled youth.

In February 1997 the *Western Union* returned to Key West and was designated the flagship of the city. Already a national landmark, plans are underway to create a museum recalling the vessel's origins. She is now available for dockside tours, day sails, and special charters.

Flag:	USA
Rig:	Gaff topsail schooner, two-masted
Homeport/waters:	Key West, Florida
Who sails?	School groups from elementary school through high school and individuals of all ages.
Season:	Year-round
Program type:	Passenger day sails. Dockside interpretation while in port.

Specifications:			
	Sparred length: 130'	Draft: 7' 9"	Sail area: 5,000 sq. ft.
	LOD: 92'	Beam: 23'	Tons: 91 GRT
	LWL: 85'	Rig height: 103'	Power: twin diesels
	Hull: wood		

Built:	1939; Key West, Florida, Herbert Elroy Arch
Coast Guard certification:	Passenger Vessel (Subchapter T)
Contact:	Harry Bowman, General Manager
	202 (R) William Street
	Key West, FL 33040
	Tel: 305-292-9830; Fax: 305-292-1727
	E-mail: keywu@ibm.net
	Web site: http://www.historictours.com/keywest/wunion.htm

Westward

Westward was built in 1961 as a private yacht for around-the-world service. She is modeled after the North Sea pilot schooners, which sailed offshore in rough seas to await incoming cargo vessels. She is owned and operated by the Sea Education Association (SEA) of Woods Hole, Massachusetts. SEA's founders located *Westward* through the late Captain Irving Johnson and purchased her to found SEA in 1971. During the last 28 years, SEA has refitted *Westward* several times to make her suitable as a seagoing classroom and research platform. Bunks were added below and the on-deck scientific laboratory was significantly upgraded in 1988. *Westward* also houses a small computer room/library

and an impressive array of oceanographic sampling gear, plus navigational and safety equipment. From 1971 to 1988, *Westward* sailed as a Research Vessel; she now meets the USCG specifications for Sailing School Vessels. See also: *Corwith Cramer*.

Flag:	USA
Rig:	Staysail schooner, two-masted
Homeport/waters:	Woods Hole, Massachusetts: Worldwide
Who sails?	SEA educational programs attract outstanding educators and a variety of motivated and adventuresome students who are admitted by competitive selection. More than 150 colleges and universities award full credit for SEA Semester.
Season:	Year-round
Program type:	Marine and maritime studies including oceanography, nautical science, history, literature, and contemporary maritime affairs. SEA programs include SEA Semester (college level, 12 weeks long), SEA Summer Session (college level, 8 weeks long), and SEA Seminars for high school students and K-12 teachers. All programs include a seagoing component on board the Sailing School Vessels *Westward* and/or *Corwith Cramer*.

Specifications:	LOA: 125'	Draft: 12'	Sail area: 7,000 sq. ft.
	LWL: 82'	Beam: 22'	Tons: 138 GRT
	Hull: steel	Power: 350 HP diesel	

Designer:	Eldridge McInnis
Built:	1961; Lemwerder, Germany, Abeking & Rasmussen
Coast Guard certification:	Sailing School Vessel (Subchapter R)
Crew:	10 instructors (6 professional mariners; 4 scientists). **Students/trainees:** up to 24.
Age:	Primarily college-age students, with some high school and postgraduate students.
Contact:	Sea Education Association (SEA) Inc.
	PO Box 6
	Woods Hole, MA 02543
	Tel: 508-540-3954; 800-552-3633; Fax: 508-457-4673
	E-mail: admission@sea.edu
	Web site: http://www.sea.edu

WESTWARD

When and If

in 1939. Built in Wicasset, Maine, *When and If*, as she was named, was perhaps the strongest Alden built. General Patton's dream was not to be, however—he was killed in an automobile accident shortly after the end of the war.

When and If remained in the Patton family until the 1970s, when Patton's nephew made a gift of her to the Landmark School in Pride's Crossing, Massachusetts, where she was the centerpiece of a sail training program for dyslexic children. In a storm in 1990, her mooring pennant broke and she was driven onto the rocks. Although the damage was extensive, the structural integrity of the boat was unaffected. She passed into private ownership, was rebuilt over the next three years, and relaunched in 1994.

When and If can now be seen cruising up and down the East Coast. With her majestic black hull and powerful rig, she turns heads wherever she goes.

"*When* the next war is over, *and if* I live through it, Bea and I are going to sail her around the world." So said George S. Patton about the 63-foot Alden schooner he had commissioned

Flag:	USA
Rig:	Schooner
Homeport/waters:	Vineyard Haven, Massachusetts: New England
Who sails?	School groups from elementary school through college, individuals, and families.
Program type:	Sail training for paying trainees. Sea education in cooperation with accredited schools and other groups. Special education arrangements are available. Dockside interpretation during port visits.

Specifications:			
	Sparred length: 85'	Draft: 9'	Power: GM 4-71
	LOD: 63' 5"	Beam: 15'	Hull: wood
	LOA: 63' 5"	LWL: 43' 3"	

Designer:	John G. Alden
Built:	1939; Wicasset, Maine, F.F. Pendleton. Rebuilt by Gannon and Benjamin, Vineyard Haven, Massachusetts.
Coast Guard certification:	Passenger Vessel (Subchapter T)
Crew:	3. **Passengers/trainees:** 15 (day sails), 6 (overnight)
Contact:	Virgina C. Jones, Gannon and Benjamin Marine Railway PO Box 1095 Vineyard Haven, MA 02568 Tel: 508-693-4658; Fax: 508-693-1818 E-mail: gandb@gannonandbenjamin.com Web site: http://www.gannonandbenjamin.com

William H. Albury

In an era when the Atlantic crossing is measured in hours rather than weeks and most people's occupations anchor them to a desk, counter, or workbench, Sea Exploring offers a learning-by-doing environment. Lessons of character building and teamwork apply to all facets of one's life. The Sea Explorer program requires that each trainee exert and extend him or herself physically, morally, and mentally to perform duties which contribute to the ship. The reward, over and above the experience of a world of beauty and challenge, is the satisfaction and self-assurance that contributes to self-discipline. The *William H. Albury*'s Sea Explorer Program offers lessons in ecology and international cooperation, as well as history, science, literature, and art. Subject to the dictates of nature, the Sea Explorer program is adventuresome while also a developer of character and a molder of lives. The *William H. Albury* is now in its 26th year of sail training.

Flag:	USA
Rig:	Gaff topsail schooner, two-masted
Homeport/waters:	Miami, Florida: Biscayne Bay, Florida Keys, and Bahamas
Who sails?	School and other groups and individuals. Affiliated institutions include Boy Scouts and schools in Dade County, Broward County and Abaco, Bahamas.
Cost:	$75 per person per day; $600 group rate
Program type:	Sail training with crew, apprentices, and paying trainees. Sea education in maritime history and ecology in cooperation with accredited schools and colleges and other groups. Passenger day sails and overnight passages.

Specifications:		
Sparred length: 70'	Draft: 6'	Sail area: 2,100 sq. ft.
LOD: 56'	Beam: 14'	Tons: 24 GRT
LOA: 60'	Rig height: 64'	Power: 150 diesel
LWL: 49'	Freeboard: 6'	Hull: wood

Built:	1964; Man o' War Cay, Abaco, Bahamas, William H. Albury
Coast Guard certification:	Uninspected Vessel
Crew:	3. **Trainees:** 30 (day sails), 14 (overnight)
Contact:	Captain Joseph A. Maggio, Marine Superintendent
	Inter-Island Schooner
	3145 Virginia St.
	Coconut Grove, FL 33133
	Tel: 305-442-9697; Fax: 305-442-0119
	E-mail: heritage2@mindspring.com
	Web site: http://www.heritageschooner.com

William H. Thorndike

ing the "Most Photogenic" at the 1994 Antigua Wooden Boat Regatta. Current voyaging plans include a revisit to Antigua in 1999/2000 and participation in Tall Ships 2000®. Formerly the schooner *Tyrone*, the *William H. Thorndike* was named as the fourth ship for Dr. William H. Thorndike of Boston. Voyages feature traditional sailing with a spirit of lighthearted competition and camaraderie.

The schooner *William H. Throndike* sails the coast of Maine in the summer. She has received several awards, includ-

Flag:	USA				
Rig:	Gaff schooner, two-masted				
Homeport/waters:	Maine				
Who sails?	Individuals and families				
Season:	Year-round				
Program type:	Sail training and seamanship for trainees of all ages.				
Specifications:	Sparred length: 75'		Draft: 8' 6"		Sail area: 2,200 sq. ft.
	LOD: 65'		Beam: 15'		Tons: 43 GRT
	LOA: 65'		Rig height: 80'		Power: diesel
	LWL: 50'		Hull: wood		
Designer:	Sam Crocker				
Built:	1939; Sims Brothers				
Coast Guard certification:	Uninspected Vessel				
Crew:	2. Trainees: 4				
Contact:	Townsend D. Thorndike				
	222 Whiteface Intervale				
	North Sandwich, NH 03259				
	Tel: 603-284-7174; Fax: 603-284-9258				

What happens when 3 ugly boats collide? Possibly the most disgusting thing afloat.

Windy

Built in 1996, *Windy* was the first four-masted schooner built in the US since 1921. During the summer months she sails daily out of Navy Pier near downtown Chicago, offering hands-on sailing experiences to the public. During the off-season she sets an educational course through the Great Lakes, Erie Canal, eastern seaboard, and Caribbean. She is a unique blend of the best traditions, modern materials, and safety features. She has many features not found on older tall ships, including 10 private cabins, a bunk room for 12, a great cabin, as well as a bow thruster, shoal draft, and wing keel.

Windy's sail training programs focus on maritime heritage and nautical science and are designed for groups up to 150 for day sails and 26 on overnight passages. Programs are adapted to the needs of schools, seniors, corporations, churches, scouts, and other groups.

Windy is also ideal for private charters, corporate functions, team building, weddings, and other celebrations. A new sister ship to *Windy* is planned to be launched in time to participate in Tall Ships 2000®. *Windy II* will serve in a new summer sail training program based in Chicago and will offer two-month fall and spring voyages through the Great Lakes and eastern seaboard.

WINDY

Flag:	USA
Rig:	Gaff topsail schooner, four-masted
Homeport/waters:	Chicago, Illinois: Great Lakes, East Coast, and Caribbean
Who sails?	Individuals high school age and older.
Cost:	$10 and up for student groups, $25 for adults for 1.5-hour introductory sail, $3,800 for fall and spring voyages.
Season:	June-September, Chicago; October-May, East Coast.
Program type:	Maritime heritage and nautical science education programs, public recreation cruises, and private charters.

Specifications:	Sparred length: 148'	Draft: 8' 6"	Sail area: 5,000 sq. ft.
	LOD: 109'	Beam: 25'	Tons: 140 (displacement)
	LOA: 109'	Rig height: 85'	Power: 300 HP diesel
	LWL: 95'	Freeboard: 7'	Hull: steel

Designer:	R. Marthai
Built:	1996; Detyens Shipyard/Southern Windjammer, Ltd.
Coast Guard certification:	Passenger Vessel (Subchapter T)
Trainees:	150 (day cruises), 26 (overnight)
Contact:	Captain Robert Marthai
	Windy of Chicago, Ltd.
	600 East Grand Ave.
	Chicago, IL 60611
	Tel: 312-595-5472
	Off-season: 2044 Wappoo Hall Rd., Charleston, SC 29412; Tel: 803-762-1342

Wolf

The *Wolf* is a classic 74-foot topsail schooner built in 1982-1983 in Panama City, Florida by Master Builder Willis Ray and Finbar Gittleman. Designed by Merrit Walter, the *Wolf* is a Norfolk Rover class steel-hulled schooner.

Homeported in Key West, Florida, the vessel is owned and operated by Captain Finbar Gittleman of Key West Packet Lines, Inc. She is patterned after the blockade runners that plied the waters of the Florida Straits, Caribbean Sea, and Atlantic Ocean in the 19th century. The *Wolf* provides an ideal setting for dockside receptions, day sails, and sunset cruises.

The *Wolf* has been operating in Key West for more than 16 years and has come to symbolize the essence of that "island spirit" which draws visitors from all parts of the world. She often serves as the lead vessel in local harbor parades and traditional events.

With Captain Gittleman at the helm, the *Wolf* has sailed extensively the waters of the Caribbean, Bahamas, and Gulf of Mexico, and is known for her humanitarian missions. She is showcased in many films and documentaries and is available for private charters, long-term voyages, and special events, including overnight Boy Scout excursions, weddings, and fundraising events..

Flag:	USA
Rig:	Square topsail schooner
Homeport/waters:	Key West, Florida: Caribbean, Atlantic, Gulf of Mexico
Who sails?	Elementary and middle school groups, individuals, and families.
Cost:	$25 per person for two-hour sail, $800-$1,900 group rate per day
Program type:	Sail training for crew and volunteer trainees. Sea education in cooperation with organized groups and as informal, in-house programming. Passenger day sails and overnight passages. Dockside interpretation at home and during port visits.

Specifications:	Sparred length: 74'	Draft: 7'	Sail area: 2,500 sq. ft.
	LOD: 63'	Beam: 15'	Tons: 37 GRT
	LOA: 63'	Rig height: 56'	Power: 216 HP diesel
	LWL: 49'	Freeboard: 5'	Hull: steel

Designer:	Merrit Walter
Built:	1983; Panama City, Florida, Willis Ray/Captain Finbar Gittleman
Coast Guard certification:	Passenger Vessel (Subchapter T)
Crew:	4-5. **Trainees:** 44 (day sails), 6 (overnight)
Contact:	Captain Finbar Gittleman
	Wolf/Key West Packet Lines, Inc.
	PO Box 1153
	Key West, FL 33041
	Tel: 305-296-9653; Fax: 305-294-8388
	Web site: http://www.schoonerwolf.com

By the late 1980s, *Zebu*, a lovely brigantine originally built in the Baltic, had become one of the most internationally distinguished of windjammers. Following a trading career as a High Canvas Merchantman carrying timber around Northern Europe, she was comprehensively rebuilt (to present as a vessel of the 1850s) for a four-year circumnavigation of the world as Adventure Flagship of Operation Raleigh, the International Youth Expedition. During this she was crewed by young adventurers from 23 nations, visited 41 countries, and sailed 69,000 miles.

In 1988 *Zebu* returned to a new homeport, the historic seaport of Liverpool, England. In 1996 a new Master, Susan Hanley-Place, was appointed to rebuild *Zebu* as a traditional adventure sailing ship for the 21st century, and return her to a role of international prominence as Heritage Flagship of the City of Liverpool.

As Liverpool's flagship, *Zebu* is undertaking a series of international Youth Expeditions. SeaChallenge 2000 employs the challenges and life-changing experiences of adventure at sea in a program to

develop youth leaders. SeaChallenge works with youth development agencies on a local, national, and international basis. During SeaChallenge, *Zebu* will visit the East Coast of the US. This beautiful ship is also available for private charter and film work.

Flag:	UK
Rig:	Brigantine, rigged to circa 1850
Homeport/waters:	Liverpool, England: UK and international
Who sails?	Young people in training for youth leadership selected through youth organizations and individuals of all ages (group bookings preferred).
Season:	Sailing, April to October; education, year-round
Program type:	Personal development/adventure sailing. Dockside education while in port.

Specifications:			
	Sparred length: 110'	Draft: 8' 7"	Sail area: 4,800 sq. ft.
	LOD: 72'	Beam: 22'	Tons: 123 GRT
	LOA: 75'	Rig height: 87'	Power: 150 HP diesel
	LWL: 64'	Freeboard: 6'	Hull: Kalmar pine on oak

Built:	1938; Holms Shipyard, Raa, Sweden
Certification:	UK Loadline
Crew:	8. Trainees: 16
Contact:	Captain Susan Hanley-Place
	SeaChallenge Shorebase
	11 Greenbank Drive
	Liverpool L17 1AN, UNITED KINGDOM
	Tel/Fax: +44 (0) 151-733-0699
	Email: seachallenge@btinternet.com

Zodiac

schooner ever operated by the Bar Pilots. She was bought in 1975 by a group of young craftsmen experienced in wooden boat restoration and was renamed *Zodiac*.

In 1982 she was placed on the National Register of Historic Places. Certified by the Coast Guard as a Passenger Vessel, she sails Puget Sound, the San Juan Islands, and the Canadian Gulf Coast. *Zodiac*'s spaciousness and amenities make her the ideal boat for sail training and education programs enjoyed by a wide range of people.

Designed to reflect the highest achievement of naval architecture under working sail, *Zodiac* was fundamentally a yacht. Built in 1924 for the Johnson & Johnson Pharmaceutical Company, she raced the Atlantic from Sandy Hook, New Jersey to Spain in 1928. The crash of 1929 forced her sale to the San Francisco Pilots Association in 1931.

Renamed *California*, she served forty years off the Golden Gate as the largest

In early spring and late fall *Zodiac* hosts Elderhostel sessions, offering courses on sailing, navigation, Northwest Native American culture, legends of the Pig War Island, and geology and natural resources of the San Juan Islands. Summer sessions are open to sailing enthusiasts sixteen years and older.

Flag:	USA
Rig:	Gaff schooner, two-masted
Homeport/waters:	Seattle, Washington: Puget Sound, San Juan Islands, Canadian Gulf Islands
Who sails?	High school through college age students, adults, and families.
Season:	March to November
Cost:	$2,300 per day group rate
Program type:	Sail training for trainees sixteen and older, learning by standing watches on the helm, on sailing stations, and in the chart house.

Specifications:			
	Sparred length: 160'	Draft: 16'	Sail area: 7,000 sq. ft.
	LOD: 127'	Beam: 26'	Tons: 147 GRT
	LOA: 127'	Rig height: 101'	Power: diesel
	LWL: 101'	Freeboard: 5'	Hull: wood

Designer:	William Hand, Jr.
Built:	1924; East Boothbay, Maine, Hodgdon Brothers
Coast Guard certification:	Passenger Vessel (Subchapter T)
Crew:	8. Trainees: 49
Contact:	June Mehrer, Vice President
	Vessel Zodiac Corporation
	PO Box 322
	Snohomish, WA 98291-0322
	Tel: 425-483-4088; Fax: 360-563-2469
	Web site: http://www.nwschooner.org

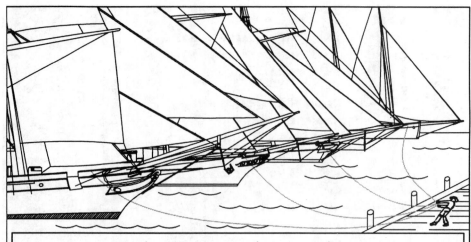

☆ Tri-Coastal Marine ☆

Creating traditional sailing ships for the 21st century

145' **Prime Meridian**

120' **Great Circle**

85' **Amistad**

Sailing Ship Design
Ship Construction
Project Management and Planning
USCG Licensing

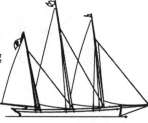

90' **Bermudian**

Find out how we can help your organization:

Andy Davis (andy@tricoastal.com)
Peter Boudreau (peter@tricoastal.com)
tel: 510.235.7770   fax: 510.236.3980
www.tricoastal.com

CHICAGO, CHICAGO,

THAT TODDLIN TOWN

Romance?

Drank a bottle of Goslings here and watched the sun come up.

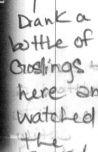

Your Port for AT&T Tall Ships®
Chicago, Labor Day 2000

NAVY PIER LABOR DAY 2000

Bet your bottom dollar you'll lose the blues as you settle into your slip on our historic pier. Located in the heart of the city, Navy Pier is within walking distance of lakefront parks, museums, restaurants, shops and State Street... that great street. Marine services are readily available from local professionals. Land and air transportation are conveniently located (car rentals within 1 mile, commercial flights - 12 miles).

You'll have the time of your life... In Chicago, our hometown.

- Magnificent Mile Shopping
- Lakefront Museum Campus
- Downtown Art Galleries
- Sports
- World-class Night Life

Navy Pier®
600 East Grand Avenue
Chicago, Illinois 60611
(312) 595-PIER
plock@mpea.com · www.navypier.com

1998 ASTA Port City of the Year

Photo by Vito Palmisano

Thank you for choosing...

South Haven

Photo by John Davidson

...as one of the ports on the American Sail Training Association's 1998 Great Lakes Tall Ships® Race. Our quaint, Michigan community will remember this event for a long time. You're welcome to berth with us anytime!

Come see why we were named ASTA "Port of the Year"!

MICHIGAN MARITIME MUSEUM

(800) 747-3810

South Haven • Van Buren County
LAKESHORE
CONVENTION & VISITORS BUREAU

(800) SO-HAVEN

City of South Haven

(616) 637-0700

SAIL TALL SHIPS!

Affiliate Members

ORGANIZATIONS WHICH DO NOT OPERATE
VESSELS BUT DO OFFER SAIL TRAINING
OR SEA EDUCATION PROGRAMS

ActionQuest

ActionQuest summer adventure programs offer teenagers the excitement of yachting while living aboard, developing new friendships through teamwork, and acquiring valuable, lifelong leadership skills. Shipmates gain certifications in sailing, scuba diving, marine science, water skiing, and windsurfing during their three weeks on board. Most shipmates arrive with no previous experience, yet the first time they set sail from the dock, it will be a shipmate who takes the helm under the guidance of licensed sailing masters. Programs operate in the Caribbean, Mediterranean, Galapagos, Australia, and South Pacific. Attracting over 450 teens from 37 states and 18 countries, ActionQuest creates an environment in which teens can discover the extraordinary in their lives and expand both geographical and personal horizons. ActionQuest also offers a nine-month high school afloat (Argo Academy) and 80-day college-level programs (Sea-mester Programs).

>Contact: ActionQuest Programs
>PO Box 5517
>Sarasota, FL 34277
>Tel: 941-924-6789, 800-317-6789; Fax: 941-924-6075
>E-mail: actionquest@msn.com
>Web site: http://www.actionquest.com

Boy Scout Sea Base

The Orange County Boy Scout Sea Base uses the topsail ketch *Argus* as a sail training vessel for its members. Laid down and launched as a merchant vessel for work in the Baltic and Scandinavian waters, *Argus* probably began life as a salt fish carrier, but later carried a variety of cargoes including grain. In 1968 she was sailed from the Baltic to Spain, Canary Islands, then across the Atlantic to the Caribbean, through the Panama Canal, and north to Newport Beach, California. She has been used and loved by Sea Scouts ever since. *Argus* has a large diesel engine and a full component of working sails, which include three jibs, main, mizzen, and main topsail and course. She is supported by the "Friends of Argus," who enlist and train crewmembers, and the Orange County Council of the BSA, who bear the burden of financial support and arranging Sea Scout high adventure sails. *Argus* takes five-day and two-day trips at sea to Catalina Island and coastal ports for a working sail training cruise with trainees climbing the rigging, learning helmsmanship and small boat handling, snorkeling, swimming, beach hikes, and having the experience of night watches.

>Contact: William Mountford, Sea Base Manager
>Boy Scout Sea Base, 1931 West Pacific Coast Highway
>Newport Beach, CA 92663
>Tel: 714-642-5031; Fax: 714-650-5407

Buffalo Maritime Heritage Foundation, Inc.

The Buffalo Maritime Heritage Foundation was founded to promote visits of sail training vessels to the Great Lakes and City of Buffalo. The Foundation promotes and supports sail training in the area. Visiting ships are berthed in the beautiful park setting of the Erie Basin Marina. Tall ships from around the world have visited, including *Christian Radich*, *Pride of Baltimore II*, *America*, and *Bounty*. Potable water, electricity, telephone service, showers, and waste disposal facilities are available. Stores are located close by in the downtown area. Buffalo is the western terminus of the Erie Canal, which made the city prosperous and famous. The canal is used today for yachts transiting from Albany on the Hudson River, and for recreational boating and barge traffic.

Contact: RADM J. Edmund Castro, NYNM, President
120 Delaware Ave., Suite 100
Buffalo, NY 14202-2704
Tel: 716-847-2900; Fax: 716-856-6100
E-mail: jdecastro@jdecastro.com
Web site: http://www.transportationlaw.jdecastro.com

CIMI Tall Ship Expeditions

CIMI Tall Ship Expeditions is a nonprofit organization dedicated to making a difference in the lives of children, taking youth and their teachers to sea in order to build character and minds. The focus is marine science embedded in sail training. Students sail three and five-day liveaboard expeditions to Catalina Island on board the *Pilgrim of Newport* in which they sail, snorkel, hike, kayak, sing, and work together to keep the vessel shipshape. All instruction, equipment, and meals are provided. Topics covered on each expedition range from marlinespike seamanship and GPS navigation to plankton study, electronic oceanography, and much more. Topics for each expedition are selected by the teacher in charge of the participating school. Live specimens are temporarily brought on board for study. Through sail training and hands-on marine science, CIMI Tall Ship Expeditions teaches students self-reliance and discovery.

Contact: *For information, brochures, and bookings:*
CIMI Tall Ship Expeditions Coordinator
PO Box 1360
Claremont, CA 91771
Tel: 800-645-1423; Fax: 909-625-7305
Web site: http://www.guideddiscoveries.org
For program specifics:
Tim Hatler, Program Director
PO Box 1716
Sunset Beach, CA 90742
Tel: 310-508-0748; Fax: 562-592-1250
E-mail: thatler@guideddiscoveries.org

Coloma Outdoor Discovery School

The Coloma Outdoor Discovery School has added a California Gold Rush History and Science and Awareness program on board the 86-foot gaff-rigger schooner *Ka'iulani* to their well-established list of student educational adventures. With an experienced crew, talented naturalists, and a lot of enthusiasm, children will experience the voyage of a lifetime. Students engage in meaningful, dynamic, hands-on learning experiences while sailing on San Francisco Bay. The age-appropriate curriculum features social studies, science, math, history, and language arts. The experiential approach invites and maintains a high level of attention and enthusiasm throughout the program.

Contact: Coloma Outdoor Discovery School

PO Box 484
Coloma, CA 95613
Tel: 530-621-2298; Fax: 530-621-4960
E-mail: info@cods.org
Web site: http://www.cods.org

Dirigo Cruises, Ltd.

Since 1973, offering educational voyages for all ages: celestial navigation, nature
expeditions, sail training, and midshipman programs. Operating in New England,
Canada, Caribbean, and the South Pacific.

     Contact: Captain Eben M. Whitcomb, Jr.
     39 Waterside Lane
     Clinton, CT 06413
     Tel: 860-669-7068; Fax: 860-669-2297

East End Seaport Museum and Marine Foundation

The mission of the East End Seaport Museum and Marine Foundation is to pre-
serve the maritime history of Eastern Long Island. The Foundation operates the
Seaport Museum, maintains the Long Beach "Bug" lighthouse at the entrance to
Peconic Bay, runs educational sail training programs for Long Island school chil-
dren, and produces the Maritime Festival the last weekend in September. The muse-
um features exhibits on aids to navigation, yacht racing (including the America's
Cup), whaling, Revolutionary War, the Hooligan Navy (sailing yachts used to detect
U Boats off the East Coast in World War II), and the history of local ship building.

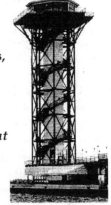

The museum has on display a clock works fourth-order lens from Plum Island and a second-order lens from Little Gull Island. The museum is located on the waterfront at the foot of Third Street.

Contact: East End Seaport Museum and Marine Foundation
PO Box 2095
Greenport, NY 11944
Tel: 516-477-0004; Fax: 516-477-3422
Web site: http://www.greenport.com/seaport

El Viento

El Viento will provide children and young adults with opportunities for success in life as responsible citizens through a long-term relationship based on leadership, mutual trust and respect, teamwork, learning, and skills building. Sea-related activities will be focused through partnerships with schools, colleges, development organizations, and other community constituencies. By using the sea and sailing as a metaphor for life, El Viento will introduce young people to their greater role in the environment while providing the tools and skills needed to create opportunities in life.

Contact: Ellen K. Shockro, Ph.D., Executive Director
El Viento Fund
PO Box 3369
Newport Beach, CA 92659
Tel: 949-673-1654; Fax: 949-675-1794
Web site: http://www.elviento.org

Girl Scouts of the USA

2000 brings new opportunities for Girl Scouts sailing with GirlSports. Every council will be getting a copy of ASTA's *Sail Tall Ships!* as a part of a new national collaboration with ASTA. A sailing ship is a superb "camp-of-the-sea", where Girl Scouts can focus on environmental action, international friendship, heritage, arts, technology, science, or careers. Girl Scouts can sail through handbooks, badges, and interest projects with a progression of activities for every age level. Starting with basic safety for the youngest Daisy Girl Scouts who are in kindergarten through sailing adventures for Senior Girl Scouts in high school, Girl Scout girls and volunteers are always eager for more local and national opportunities like ASTA Tall Ships® Races and Rallies.

Girl Scouts and sail training have a long tradition, going back to 1935 with Girl Scout Mariners sailing the Johnson's *Yankee*. The Mystic Seaport Mariner Program was originally named for the Girl Scouts for whom the program was designed. Mariner Girl Scouts has been a special interest option for thousands of girls, with some troops continuously active for over 60 years! If you or someone you know is or wants to sail with Girl Scouts or to come aboard for possible Girl Scout and Mariner reunions in tall ships ports of call, contact Nancy Richardson.

  Contact: Nancy H. Richardson
  Girl Scouts of the USA
  420 Fifth Avenue
  New York, NY 10018-2798
  Tel: 800-223-0624, ext. 8554; Fax: 212-852-6515
  E-mail: nrichardson@girlscouts.org

HANSA Foundation

The HANSA Foundation's goals are: to provide a sail training-based opportunity for North American and European young people, aged 15-25, principally from the Gulf of Maine community and the Hanseatic cities of the North Sea and the Baltic; to join an intercultural exchange with internationally mixed crews of trainees; to place North American trainees aboard Hanseatic sail training ships, and reciprocally European youth aboard North American ASTA ships; to provide programs on and in association with their partners, all of who are ASTA members; to make sail training opportunities available to all youth through need-blind scholarships, bridging the gap between the ASTA Sail Training Scholarship Program (which is restricted to USCG-inspected vessels), and STAG (Sail Training Association of Germany), whose trainee scholarships are restricted to German citizens or residents; and to build cultural and economic bridges with our largest European trading partner, Germany.

HANSA is the North American trainee coordinators for ASTA members *Esprit* and *Roald Amundsen*. They work actively with ASTA members *Amara Zee* and the Hurricane Island Outward Bound School, and work broadly in the German sailing community and with the German bluewater cruising club TRANS-OCEAN on Gulf of Maine awareness-raising issues.

  Contact: David Schurman, Executive Director
  HANSA Foundation
  PO Box 69
  North Reading, MA 01864
  Tel: 781-944-0304; Fax: 781-944-2469

E-mail: info@hansafoundation.org
Web site: http://www.hansafoundation.org

Headwaters to Ocean (H$_2$O), Inc.

The only boat program of its kind in the Columbia River Basin, H$_2$O is dedicated to fostering community-based stewardship of these awe-inspiring rivers through boat-based learning and hands-on experiences. Founded in 1995 by veterans of sail training programs world-wide, H$_2$O uses the vintage 65-foot tugboat *Captain Conner*, stoutly built of timbers by prisoners at McNeil Island Penitentiary during World War II, to carry out its education-to-action mission. To date, H$_2$O has inspired 10,000 people to make small changes in their behavior to create healthier watersheds and stronger communities. H$_2$O uses its floating platform to provide a great variety of on-water educational experiences for all ages, including: decision-maker briefings; teen overnight navigation voyages; youth field trips; tug and kayak two-day adventures, and the popular "Shanghai" free boat rides for the general public. With all eyes on the Pacific Northwest as it grapples with some of the most challenging environmental issues of our time, H$_2$O is redefining boat-based education and environmentalism to meet the needs of a new era. H$_2$O enjoys a diverse base of support from private grants, businesses, public agencies, individuals, and volunteers.

Contact: Angela Borden Jackson, President
Headwaters to Ocean (H$_2$O), Inc.
3945 SE Hawthorne Blvd.
Portland, OR 97214
Tel: 971-228-9600
E-mail: h2ocean@teleport.com
Web site: http://www.h2ocean.org

Independence Seaport Museum

The Independence Seaport Museum is located on the Delaware River at Penn's Landing in downtown Philadelphia. The Museum is a private, nonprofit institution dedicated to the collection, preservation, and interpretation of materials relating to maritime history, with a particular emphasis on the Delaware Bay and River.

Located in a newly renovated, multi-million dollar facility, the Museum houses permanent and changing exhibit galleries, classrooms, an active boat building shop, and a specialized maritime library. Museum visitors can tour the 1944 US Navy submarine BECUNA and the cruiser OLYMPIA, launched in 1895. The 1934 Trumpy motor yacht *Enticer* is maintained and operated in the charter trade.

The Museum regularly provides berths for visiting vessels and has jointly offered educational programs with sail training vessels such as *Niagara*, *A.J. Meerwald* and *Pioneer*.

Contact: Paul DeOrsay, Assistant Director
Independence Seaport Museum
211 South Columbus Boulevard
Philadelphia, PA 19106
Tel: 215-925-5439; Fax: 215-925-6713
E-mail: seaport@libertynet.org
Web site: http://www.libertynet.org/~seaport

Maryland School of Sailing and Seamanship

The Maryland School of Sailing and Seamanship has conducted sail training courses from the basic through the advanced levels since 1991 and offshore sail training
cruises since 1993 using Island Packet cruising yachts. Graduates of their courses
earn certification from the American Sailing Association. This year's courses include
Basic and Intermediate Sailing courses taught in the US Virgin Islands and the
Chesapeake Bay; Intermediate Sailing/Cruising courses taught in coastal waters
along the Atlantic Coast from Norfolk to Nantucket; Ocean Training Courses
between Norfolk, Bermuda, and the US Virgin Islands; and classroom instruction
including Coastal and Celestial Navigation and Offshore Passage Preparation.

> Contact: The Maryland School of Sailing and Seamanship, Inc.
> PO Box 609
> Rock Hall, MD 21661
> Tel: 410-639-7030; Fax: 410-639-7038
> E-mail: office@mdschool.com

Mercy High School's Tall Ship Semester for Girls

Sponsored by Mercy High School in San Francisco, California, the Tall Ship
Semester is the only extended academic sail training program for high school girls.
This semester-long outreach program is designed to foster self-esteem and to offer
young women life skills, a sense of opportunity, and a tangible community. Active
both as crewmembers and as scholars, each of the participants will stand watch and
perform the duties of a deck hand. Classes are taught in Oceanography, Maritime
Literature, Coastal History, the Mathematics of Navigation, and Seamanship.

The semester offers young women a chance to test themselves, to accomplish real
feats, and, in the process, to discover new capabilities. The program begins ashore in
San Francisco, with the students then embarking on an eight-week voyage to the
Sea of Cortez aboard the *Californian*. Following the voyage, the students complete
their academics for five weeks on land. As the students learn to take risks and accept
challenges, they discover new cultures, new possibilities, and new personal horizons.
These lessons will serve them throughout their lives.

> Contact: Caitlin Schwarzman
> Mercy High School's Tall Ship Semester for Girls
> 3250 19th Ave.
> San Francisco, CA 94132
> Tel: 415-334-0525, ext. 311; Fax: 415-334-9726
> E-mail: caitlin@infinex.com
> Web site: http://www.mercyhs.org

National Outdoor Leadership School (NOLS)

The National Outdoor Leadership School (NOLS) has a 30-year history of excellence in outdoor education and leadership. Today, NOLS runs eight branch schools
around the world and courses on five continents. Sail training is available on open
boats in Baja California, Mexico, on keel boats in Desolation Sound, British
Columbia, and as a cultural experience aboard dhows in Kenya, East Africa. These
courses are run as self-reliant sailing expeditions. Training in a multitude of other
skill areas is available from sea kayaking to mountaineering, hiking, horse packing,
and more. Leadership, safety and judgment, and minimum-impact camping are cen-

tral themes throughout every NOLS experience. College credit is available on most courses through the University of Utah. NOLS is a private, nonprofit educational corporation.

Contact: Nathan Steele
288 Main Street
Lander, WY 82520-3128
Tel: 307-332-8800; Fax: 307-332-8811
E-mail: nate_steele@nols.edu
Web site: http://www.nols.edu

Northern S.T.A.R. (Sail Training and Renewal)

The Northern S.T.A.R. programs offers academic programs focused on maritime history and ecological marine biology, with particular emphasis on crew experience, expeditionary learning, and early intervention.

Contact: David Smith, Executive Director
1010 Stroud Court
Charlevoix, MI 49720
Tel: 616-547-1817
E-mail: dsmith@sunny.ncmc.cc.mi.us

North Star Adventures

North Star Adventures specializes in travel by sea kayak, raft, canoe, or on foot to the best wilderness areas of Alaska and Baja California. For the past 20 years they have been dedicated to making your trip the finest possible experience. North Star Adventures offers a large selection of adventures, offering state-of-the-art equipment, excellent camp cuisine, smooth trip logistics, skilled guides, and a fun and supportive atmosphere where your needs and enjoyment are truly cared for. All ages are welcomed.

Contact: North Star Adventures
PO Box 1724
Flagstaff, AZ 86002
Tel: 800-258-8434, 520-773-9917; Fax: 520-773-9965
Web site: http://www.Adventuretrip.com

Northwest Schooner Society

Seattle's Northwest Schooner Society (NWSS) provides a unique opportunity for teens and adults to experience a piece of American history aboard fully restored "floating classrooms." The Society is a nonprofit, tax-exempt organization, founded in 1994 to allow more people to experience the excitement and challenge of old-fashioned seamanship, twenty-four hours a day.

The Northwest Schooner Society sponsors voyages of different lengths on historic ships through their own multidisciplinary educational program. Under billowing canvas, schools and youth groups experience real-life application of science, math, history, and geography. Programs are designed to bring out the best in teenagers, introducing youngsters to an inner strength they never knew they had while they haul sail to harness the elements. From their homeports in Bellingham and Seattle, they sail the stunning and protected waters of Washington State and British Columbia. The Society organizes environmental cruises on the 1924 schooner

Zodiac, the largest sailing ship on the West Coast. The Society also owns and operates the 87-foot steel power yacht *Rebecca*, built in 1947.

     Contact: Bill Vonk
     Northwest Schooner Society
     PO Box 9504
     Seattle, WA 98109
     Tel: 800-551-6977; Fax: 206-633-2784
     E-mail: bvonk@nwschooner.org
     Web site: http://www.nwschooner.org

Ocean Navigator School of Seamanship

The Ocean Navigator School of Seamanship offers the following seminars for offshore sailors in approximately ten locations around the country:
- Introduction to Celestial Navigation
- Predicting Marine Weather I & II
- The Basics of Offshore Seamanship
- Introduction to Offshore Emergency Medicine
- Integrated Navigation Techniques
- Using Weather & Ocean Currents to Win
- Marine Diesel Engine Operation and Maintenance
- Ancillary Marine Systems Operation and Maintenance
- Marine Electrical Systems Operation and Maintenance
- The On Board Computer
- Marine Communication Systems and Operations
- Introduction to Yacht Design

The seminars are fast-paced and fairly intense, designed for experienced sailors. A knowledge of basic skills is assumed although most seminars begin with a review of those skills. In many cases the subject is too broad to produce experts overnight, but in every case you will go away with a full appreciation for the subject and the ability to go on learning from that day forward. The school's mission is to teach present and future offshore sailors important knowledge and techniques that will make them better voyagers and navigators.

     Contact: Ocean Navigator School of Seamanship
     PO Box 418
     Rockport, ME 04856
     Tel/Fax: 207-230-0385
     E-mail: education@oceannavigator.com
     Web site: http://www.oceannavigator.com

Ocean Voyages

Ocean Voyages was founded 20 years ago to provide participatory educational sailing programs throughout the world. Programs are open to sailing enthusiasts of all ages. Most programs run from one to four weeks in length. Ocean Voyages works with educators and institutions to design customized programs for youth participation for "youth of all ages." Ocean Voyages also has extensive experience in scientific research projects and documentary and feature films.

Ocean Voyages works toward preserving our maritime heritage and sailing arts, and providing opportunities for people to gain sailing education and seafaring experience. Coastal and inter-island programs are available in addition to offshore passage-making and around-the-world voyaging opportunities. Program areas include: Hawaii, California, the Pacific Northwest, Galapagos Islands, Aegean Sea, Caribbean, French Polynesia, and New Zealand, as well as Pacific and Atlantic Ocean crossings. Many of the international vessels that Ocean Voyages works with are preparing to participate in Tall Ships 2000® and OpSail 2000.

Contact: Mary Crowley, Director
Ocean Voyages
1709 Bridgeway
Sausalito, CA 94965
Tel: 415-332-4681, 800-299-4444; Fax: 415-332-7460
E-mail: sail@voyages.com *or* voyages@ix.netcom.com

Project HMS Detroit

As a nonprofit registered charity, the aim of Project HMS Detroit is to build and maintain a full-sized sailing replica of the *HMS Detroit*. Built in 1813, the *HMS Detroit* was the last ship constructed in Amherstburg's King's Navy Yard. The largest warship on the Great Lakes at the time, she served as the British Flagship, a three-masted, square-rigged vessel. Moored at King's Navy Yard Park, the replica *Detroit* will be available for cruises, charters, sail training, festivals, and tall ship events on both sides of the border.

Contact: Project HMS Detroit
PO Box 1812
Amherstburg, ON N9V 2Z2
CANADA
Tel: 519-736-1133; Fax: 519-736-0640
Web site: http://www.hmsdetroit.org

Project Link, Ltd.

Project Link was founded in 1984 to facilitate the incorporation of special-needs students into regular classroom settings. Project Link recently expanded the scope of its mission to include all students both before and after graduation. The new focus of the organization relates directly to the maritime world, taking special advantage of the coastal opportunities of Boston Harbor and vicinity.

Project Link is working with a number of Boston area schools to develop a program that will allow students to interact with personnel aboard several sailing vessels, providing real-life, real-time elements to issues and problems being discussed in class. Two such Internet links have been established with the *Picton Castle* and the USCG Barque *Eagle*. The study course will culminate with a sail aboard *Firebird*, a 47-foot Alden yawl. In addition to this program, Project Link helps students discover meaningful careers in the maritime field following high school graduation.

Contact: John V. Henderson, Executive Director
Project Link, Ltd.
PO Box 167
Manchester, MA 01944
Tel: 978-768-7469; Fax: 617-357-5834
E-mail: projlink@ma.ultranet.com

Sail America

Sail America was founded in 1990 by members of the US sailing industry who wanted to play a very active role in growing sailing as a sport, an industry, and a way of life. Its nearly 500 members represent every segment of the industry, from manufacturers to sailing schools, charter companies to publications. It is the only nonprofit industry association exclusively working to promote the growth of sailing businesses. Sail America's mission statement is: "To promote the growth of the sailing industry." To achieve this, they have developed programs and events which will significantly increase participation in sailing. Sail Expo St. Petersburg, Sail Expo Atlantic City, and Pacific Sail Expo not only boost sales for the businesses involved, but serve to educate sailors and nonsailors. Over 300 seminars and special events take place during the three Sail Expo events. These seminars are a compilation of the best technical, safety, and entertainment presentations offered to the sailing public.

> Contact: Karen Kelly, Executive Director
> 850 Aquidneck Ave., Unit B-4
> Middletown, RI 02842-7201
> Tel: 401-841-0900; Fax: 401-847-2044
> Web site: http://www.sailamerica.com

Sail Martha's Vineyard

Sail Martha's Vineyard is a 501(c)(3) nonprofit organization dedicated to celebrating and perpetuating Martha's Vineyard's maritime heritage and culture. Its activities encourage island children to be comfortable on the water by offering boat handling and sailing instruction free of charge, adult sailing classes, and support for the high school sailing team for competitive sailors.

Sail Martha's Vineyard supports educational programs in the public elementary schools that familiarize island children with the maritime traditions of Martha's Vineyard, such as their wooden boat project. It attracts interesting and historic vessels to the island, supports such local vessels, and serves as a clearinghouse for other maritime-related organizations and initiatives on the island.

Sail Martha's Vineyard depends entirely on its volunteers and is funded through individual and community contributions and grant support.

> Contact: Matthew Stackpole, President or Noreen Baker, Coordinator
> Sail Martha's Vineyard
> PO Box 1998
> Vineyard Haven, MA 02568
> Tel: 508-696-7644; Fax: 508-696-8819

Sausalito Tall Ships Society

The Sausalito Tall Ships Society (STSS) is a California nonprofit organization dedicated to educating people in nautical skills and supporting the preservation and operation of traditional sailing vessels, particularly tall ships.

Goals and Strategies:
• Provide opportunities for sail training experiences for young people.
• Provide sails and shipboard education for members.
• Support shore-side education.
• Replenish the Cadet Scholarship Fund.
• Promote tall ships visits in San Francisco Bay.

- Increase the size and visibility of the organization.

STSS supported Mercy High School's Tall Ship Semester for Girls aboard the *Californian* in 1999. This is a first for high school girls in San Francisco.

Contact: Alice Cochran, President
Sausalito Tall Ships Society
PO Box 926
Sausalito, CA 94966
Tel: 415-331-1009
E-mail: info@stss.org
Web site: http://www.stss.org

Sail Training Association of Taiwan

Contact: Al Scalabrin
208 Jong Shiaw 1st Road
Kaohsiung, Taiwan
Tel: 886-7-221-336; Fax: 886-7-216-6585

Seattle Area Sea Scouts

Contact: Captain John Kelly
5271 45th Avenue SW
Seattle, WA 98136
Tel: 206-932-0971

SeaQuest Studio

SeaQuest Studio represents three generations of sailors passing on the seafaring arts as an integral discipline of maritime education. Through junior sailing outreach, scouts, teacher workshops, flotillas, and festival demonstrations, they are actively promoting the past and future of seafaring artistry.

For two years, the "Seafaring Artisan" crew has sailed the coast of North Carolina, involving sailors and educators in meaningful, practical, and decorative art forms of seamanship; i.e. wayfinding arts, logs/illustration, cartography, carving/scrimshaw, graphics, marlinespike, textiles, etc.

Training artists for the marine industry involves understanding dynamic innovation as a tradition, and it is this creative force that our sailors come to find within themselves. By exploring our artistic heritage under sail, they hope to nurture a genuine concern for our water planet.

Contact: Susan R. Wallace, Director
SeaQuest Studio
PO Box 5375
#10 Osprey Ridge Drive
Emerald Isle, North Carolina 28594
Tel: 252-354-8833

United States Merchant Marine Academy

The United States Merchant Marine Academy is located on Long Island Sound at Kings Point, New York. The USMMA, founded in 1943, is the fourth of the five federal service academies. Its mission is to train young men and women for civilian and military careers in the nation's maritime and intermodal transportation system.

During a four-year course of study, midshipmen spend one year at sea as cadets aboard commercial merchant ships, where they gain valuable practical experience. The remaining three years are spent at the Academy. Upon graduation, individuals receive a Bachelor of Science degree, a US Coast Guard license as deck or engineer officer, and a commission as an Ensign in the US Naval Reserve. Tuition, room, and board are provided by the federal government, in exchange for a 5-8 year service obligation in the civilian transportation industry, active duty military, or Naval Reserve.

The Academy has long recognized the leadership and seamanship skills gained through sail training, and supports an extensive waterfront program. This includes a five-boat offshore sailing team, an inter-collegiate sailing team, and an extensive instructional and recreational fleet. All midshipmen are required to learn to sail, and nearly 20% participate in the extracurricular programs. Midshipmen operate and maintain all small craft and serve in all billets, from skippers to watch captains and navigators.

Contact: CDR Eric Wallischeck, USMS, Sailing Master
Yocum Sailing Center
US Merchant Marine Academy
Kings Point, NY 11024-1699
Tel: 516-773-5396
E-mail: wallischecke@usmma.edu
Web site: http://www.usmma.edu

Urban Harbors Institute

The Urban Harbors Institute conducts multidisciplinary research on urban harbor issues ranging from water quality to waterfront development. The Institute sponsors workshops, symposia, and educational programs. It publishes reports and proceedings, provides technical assistance to community and business leaders and the general public, and maintains a resource library. It also cosponsors an annual expedition aboard the schooner *Ernestina* (for six geography credits), and day programs are offered aboard various schooners from the New England region.

The Institute is associated with the University of Massachusetts' programs in environmental sciences, geography, and management. Its core staff, senior associates, and researchers have expertise in public policy, coastal resource management, marine law, economics, waterfront planning, international coastal zone management, and education.

> Contact: Madeleine Walsh
> Urban Harbors Institute
> University of Massachusetts-Boston
> 100 Morrissey Blvd.
> Boston, MA 02125
> Tel: 617-287-5570; Fax: 617-287-5575

Ventura County Maritime Museum

The Ventura County Maritime Museum is located at Channel Islands Harbor in Oxnard, California, about 50 miles "upcoast" from Los Angeles. Founded in 1991,

the mission of the Museum is to provide a cultural center dedicated to the interpretation of maritime history through interactive exhibits and educational outreach.

The Museum houses displays which depict the history of Channel Islands harbor and Port Hueneme, the only deep-water port between Los Angeles and San Francisco. Ship models trace more than 3,000 years of maritime history, from reed boats used by Peruvian fisherman to modern-day car carriers, including the work of Ed Marple, one of America's foremost ship model builders. The Museum also has an extensive and world-class marine art collection, featuring works by noted artists John Stobart, Montague Dawson, David Thimgan, Roy Cross, and others. Exhibits on whaling, sailor's arts, navigation instruments, and shipwrecks round out the permanent collection.

The Student Outreach program, staffed entirely by volunteers, visits more than 30 schools each year, and conducts in-house tours for approximately 3,500 fourth and fifth-grade students from Ventura County schools.

Contact: Mark Bacin
Ventura County Maritime Museum
2731 South Victoria Avenue
Oxnard, CA 93035
Tel: 805-984-6260; Fax: 805-984-5970
E-mail: VCMM@aol.com

Williams-Mystic Maritime Studies Program

The Maritime Studies program of Williams College and Mystic Seaport offers undergraduates the opportunity to focus a semester on the study of the sea. Students take four Williams College courses at Mystic Seaport: maritime history, literature of the sea, marine science (either oceanography or marine ecology), and marine policy. Academics are enhanced by hands-on maritime skills classes in sailing, shipsmithing, celestial navigation, or sea music. There are opportunities to climb aloft on square-riggers.

Four field seminars are incorporated into the curriculum each semester. Aboard a 130-foot staysail schooner, students voyage offshore for nearly two weeks in the North Atlantic each fall and in the Caribbean each spring semester. These expeditions involve intensive student participation. Students also travel to Nantucket and the Port of New York for the Atlantic Coast Field Seminar, and out west to California and Oregon to compare and contrast the flora, fauna, history, and environmental issues of the Pacific Coast.

Students return to Mystic and apply knowledge gained in their field experiences toward research projects in history, marine science, and marine policy. A full semester of credit is granted through Williams College (equivalent to 18 transfer credits). Financial aid is available.

Contact: Rush Hambleton, Assistant Director of Admissions
Williams-Mystic Maritime Studies Program, Mystic Seaport
75 Greenmanville Avenue, PO Box 6000
Mystic, CT 06355-0990;
Tel: 860-572-5359; Fax: 860-572-5329
E-mail: williams@mysticseaport.org
Web site: http://www.williamsmystic.org

The Wooden Boat Foundation

The Wooden Boat Foundation is a nonprofit organization located in Port Townsend, Washington, committed to fostering respect for self, community, and environment by providing a center for unique educational experiences through the exploration of traditional maritime skills.

The Foundation offers its members and the community access to a maritime bookstore and library, and educational courses and events. Current maritime programs include regattas, community rowing, small boat sailing and sail training for youth and adults, and specialized charters aboard the longboat *Townshend*.

The Wooden Boat Foundation's annual fundraiser, the Wooden Boat Festival, takes place Friday, Saturday, and Sunday following Labor Day. With up to 30,000 visitors, the Festival features hundreds of finely crafted wooden boats displayed in the water and on land, demonstrations, lectures, regattas, young mariners' boat building, regional music, food, and fun for the entire family. Proceeds from the Festival support the Wooden Boat Foundation's educational mission.

> Contact: Aletia Alvarez
> Cupola House
> 380 Jefferson St.
> Port Townsend, WA 98368
> Tel: 360-385-3628; Fax: 360-385-4742
> E-mail: wbf@olympus.net
> Web site: http://www.olympus.net/edu/wbf/

WoodenBoat School

The WoodenBoat School is located on a 64-acre waterfront campus in Brooklin, Maine. Founded in 1981, the school's twin focus is on wooden boat building and seamanship taught by experienced professionals in the marine industry. Sailing courses are taught by experienced, licensed instructors on cutters, Friendship sloops, ketches, and more than 20 assorted small craft ranging from sailing prams to Herreshoff 12 ½ s. Instruction in related crafts such as lofting, marine mechanics, marine survey, painting and varnishing, marine photography, navigation, and marine art is also offered. Accommodations are available at the school. Courses are also offered at various off-site locations around the country.

> Contact: Rich Hilsinger, Director
> WoodenBoat School
> PO Box 78
> Brooklin, ME 04616
> Tel: 207-359-4651; Fax: 207-359-8920
> Web site: http://www.woodenboat.com

Youth Adventure, Inc.

Youth Adventure, Inc. is the oldest nonprofit sail training organization in the Pacific Northwest. Founded in 1959, Youth Adventure purchased the 1913 schooner *Adventuress* and began to offer a sail training program for "youth of all ages." This limited program became more active in the late 60s when stewardship of the historic schooner was assumed by Ernestine "Erni" Bennett. For the next 25 years, Erni and a dedicated group of volunteers operated sail training programs aboard the venerable ship for thousands of youth, adults, and seniors in Girl and

Boy Scout, school, environmental education, Elderhostel, and other groups.

In 1991, Youth Adventure passed ownership and stewardship of the *Adventuress* to Sound Experience, a nonprofit environmental education and sail training organization. Since then, Youth Adventure has continued to help fund regional sail training and sea education programs, youth scholarships, and related activities. Today, the 40-year-old organization envisions an expanded support role for Pacific Northwest groups that provide sea-related educational experiences aboard a variety of traditional sailcraft—from large tall ships to small longboats.

In recognition of her commitment to sail training, Erni Bennett was presented the ASTA Lifetime Achievement Award in 1998. Youth Adventure is dedicated to continuing this proud legacy, supporting and promoting sailing-based, lifelong learning opportunities for "youth of all ages."

Contact: Ernestine "Erni" Bennett, Youth Adventure, Inc.
PO Box 23
Mercer Island, WA 98040
Tel: 206-232-4024
Or
Chuck Fowler
2518 Walnut Rd. NW
Olympia, WA 98502-4110
Tel: 360-943-2858; Fax: 360-943-5411
E-mail: nwnx@olywa.net

SAIL TALL SHIPS!

SOUTH STREET SEAPORT MUSEUM
Sail Training / Marine Education Opportunities

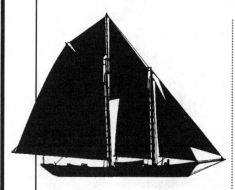

PIONEER
**1885 Iron Hulled
Cargo Schooner**

- School Trips
- Boy Scouts / Girl Scouts
- Charters
- Volunteer Opportunities

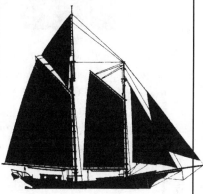

LETTIE G. HOWARD
**1893 Gloucester
Fishing Schooner**

- Elderhostel
- Seafaring Camp (with Harvey Gamage)
- Urban Waters
- Team Building

Recipient, ASTA's 1997
Sea Education Program Award

Come join us!
For information call (212) 748-8600
or write to us at
207 Front Street
New York, NY 10038

www.southstseaport.org

Brilliant 2000 Transatlantic

Mystic Seaport's schooner *Brilliant* will join the Tall Ships 2000® fleet races to Halifax and Amsterdam, followed by challenging sails in Europe and to the Caribbean.

> **July 13 - July 19** – New London to Boston to Halifax
> **July 21 - August 24** – Halifax to Amsterdam
> **September 3 - 13** – Holland to England via France
> **September 17 - 27** – England to Ireland
> **October 1 - 11** – Ireland to Lisbon via France/Spain
> **Oct. 22 - Nov. 1** – Lisbon to Canary Islands via Madeira
> **Nov. 18 - Dec. 9** – Canaries to Antigua

Each leg will have berths for six sail trainees, ages 18-25. Interviews may be required. For application forms or more information: Phone 860.572.5323; email suzanne@mysticseaport.org or visit www.mysticseaport.org/brilliant

MYSTIC SEAPORT®

www.mysticseaport.org

THE MUSEUM OF AMERICA AND THE SEA™

Supporting Members

PORTS, BUSINESSES, AND ASSOCIATES OF TALL SHIPS

Alliance Marine Risk Managers, Inc.

Alliance Marine Risk Managers, Inc. specializes in the consultation and placement of marine insurance for yacht owners and seaman worldwide. Founded and operated by lifelong sailors, Alliance Marine provides the product knowledge and insurance market experience one expects from highly regarded marine insurance professionals. Equally important to the owner of traditional and historic vessels, Alliance honors and shares the values these vessels represent to the past, present, and future of America's maritime heritage.

>Contact: Fredric A. Silberman, President
>Alliance Marine Risk Managers, Inc.
>1400 Old Country Road, Suite 307
>Westbury, NY 11590
>Tel: 516-333-7000, 800-976-2676; Fax: 516-333-9529
>Email: AMRM-NY@worldnet.att.net

Atlantic City & The Casino Reinvestment Development Authority

Atlantic City extends a warm welcome to vessels participating in Tall Ships 2000®, especially on June 29 through July 2, 2000. Plans are in place to accommodate vessels visiting Atlantic City during this period. Atlantic City offers easy access to Absecon Inlet, southern New Jersey's finest inlet to the Atlantic Ocean. Historic Gardiner's Basin, Frank Farley Marina, and Harrah's Marine have joined together to offer food, fireworks, recreation, modern berthing facilities, and more.

>Contact: Bunny Loper, Senior Project Officer
>Casino Reinvestment Development Authority
>1014 Atlantic Avenue
>Atlantic City, NJ 08401
>Tel: 609-347-0500, ext. 3118

Battle of Georgian Bay, 2001

The Battle of Georgian Bay is a fictional War of 1812 and Revolutionary War Naval and Military reenactment. It will be hosted by the historic towns of Penetanguishene, Midland, and Discovery Harbour, Canada's leading marine heritage site. Over 1,200 naval and military reenactors will stage a number of battles and skirmishes as well as open their living history encampment at Discovery Harbour to the public. The battle will feature 19th-century battle tactics, street fighting, marine assault landings, artillery duels, tall ship battles, and cavalry charges. The Battle of Georgian Bay Committee would like to extend an invitation to all tall ships to attend this unique and special event. All ships and vessels would be moored at the historic and picturesque historic site of Discovery Harbour, a reconstructed British Naval and Military base in use from 1817 to 1856. The committee, towns, and Discovery Harbour have plenty of facilities and services to help make your visit a pleasurable and memorable one. For special arrangements, financial assistance, or further information please contact:

>Contact: David J. Brunelle, Battle of Georgian Bay Chairman, 2001
>22 Fox Street
>Penetanguishene, ON L9M 1G1
>CANADA

Tel: 705-549-6850 (H), 705-549-8981 (W); Fax: 705-549-6625
E-mail: brunelle@csolve.net
Web site: http://www.battleofgeorgianbay.huronia.com

Bowen's Wharf, Newport, Rhode Island

Brick walks, granite quays, and 18th-century commercial wharf buildings bring you back to Newport's beginnings as a thriving seaport in one of the finest natural harbors in New England. Trading with all corners of the world then and now, Bowen's Wharf is central to Newport's commerce and culture. Explore unique shops and galleries carrying scrimshaw, pottery, hand-blown glass, canvas, furniture, toys, art, jewelry, clothing, and more. From the romantic ambiance of sunsets over the harbor to the colorful dynamics of a historic working waterfront, a day at Bowen's Wharf is a day well spent. The central location offers plentiful parking. Open all year, seven days a week.

Contact: Bart Dunbar
Bowen's Wharf
PO Box 814
Newport, RI 02840
Tel: 401-849-2243; Fax: 401-849-4322

Buffalo, New York Inner Harbor Waterfront Project

Buffalo, New York, "Queen City of the Great Lakes", celebrates its rich waterfront heritage with the Inner Harbor Development Project. The site was once the western terminus of the Erie Canal. The heritage of the Erie Canal is acknowledged in the site design by creating a setting where authentic maritime uses are organized along with a newly created inland slip for visitors. The new Inner Harbor will open with a grand celebration July 4, 2001. Buffalo's capacity to harbor maritime activity will dramatically increase with the addition of three boat basins. Commercial maritime activities are grouped together in the South Basin's three finger piers located adjacent to Buffalo's Marine Midland Arena. A Canal Slip, bordered by the new naval museum and canal park for Erie Canal touring vessels and visitors, is the centerpiece of harbor activity. Buffalo extends a warm invitation to visit the "Queen of the Great Lakes."

Contact: Peggy Beardsley
Buffalo Place, Inc.
671 Main Street
Buffalo, NY 14203
Tel: 716-856-3150; Fax: 716-852-8490
Web site: http://www.buffaloplace.com

Classic Galleries

Classic Galleries specializes in maritime art. The gallery offers original art, signed/numbered prints, and antiques. ASTA member vessels and their crews are welcome to visit anytime. Winthrop, Massachusetts is a peninsula between Massachusetts Bay and Boston Harbor, offering fine views of the Sail Boston Parade of Sail. The community will welcome four vessels during Tall Ships 2000®. Accessible by public transportation and minutes from Logan Airport, the marinas and yacht clubs of Winthrop offer dock space and services for those coming by sea.

Contact: Captain Jeff Esche

Classic Galleries
Winthrop, MA 02152
Tel/Fax: 888-846-6487
E-mail: aclassic@concentric.net

Clayton, New York Area Chamber of Commerce

Nestled among the Thousand Islands, Clayton, New York is a community that caters to the needs of visiting boaters. Sitting on a peninsula surrounded by the St. Lawrence River, the area provides and endless variety of recreational opportunities.

In the past, the village was home to small boat builders and large shipyards, turning out three-masted schooners that plied the Great Lakes. Clayton offers a full range of services, including marinas, ship's stores, and repair facilities. Ample dockage is available along the picturesque waterfront.

Contact: Karen Goetz
Clayton Area Chamber of Commerce
510 Riverside Drive
Clayton, NY 13624
Tel: 315-686-3771, 888-252-9806; Fax: 315-686-5564
E-mail: ccoc@gisco.net
Web site: http://thousandislands.com/claytonchamber

Colonna's Shipyard, Inc.

Colonna's Shipyard, Inc. is a full-service ship repair and shipbuilding facility strategically located in the Port of Hampton Roads, Virginia. Founded in 1875, it is the oldest family shipyard in the United States.

Colonna's has four marine railways capable of handling vessels up to 400 feet in length and up to 18 feet of draft. There is also a floating drydock for even larger vessels—17,200 tons, 640 feet long, 85 feet wide, and drawing 30 feet.

Especially important to the prudent sailing mariner is Colonna's shop capabilities, including the finest machine shop on the East Coast. A carpenter shop is available for heavy timber, deck, spar, and finish joinery repairs, as well as overhauls and conversions. Colonna's and Norseman Marine's joint-effort rigging shop is capable of designing and fabricating standing and running rigging to the largest sizes and the most rigid quality standards. Steel and aluminum repairs and new construction are carried out in Colonna's new fabrication facility. ASTA members are always welcome at Colonna's.

Contact: J. Douglas Forrest, Executive Vice President
Colonna's Shipyard
400 East Indian River Road
Norfolk, VA 23523
Tel: 757-545-2414; Fax: 757-543-2480
E-mail: colonna@series2000.com
Web site: http://www.colonnaship.com

Downtown Hampton Public Piers

Chart a course to the lovely and picturesque Hampton waterfront, the premiere boating center on the Lower Chesapeake Bay. Visit the secluded, safe, deep waters of Downtown Hampton and you'll find:

- Six downtown waterfront marinas.
- Secluded, safe harbor with deep water slips up to 13 feet.
- Two major marine supply retailers, three sailmakers, dozens of fiberglass, engine, and other marine repair services.
- Haul-out facilities for vessels from 15 to 80 feet and up to 70 tons.
- Waterfront hotel and amenities, drug store, post office, laundry, gourmet wine shop, 14 restaurants and 35 specialty shops, all within a two-block radius; hospital and dentists within 10 minutes; two international airports within 20 minutes.
- Virginia Air & Space Center, restored antique wooden carousel for adults and children, scenic parks, and waterfront promenade.
- Downtown block parties, festivals, and special events from April through November.

Showers, restrooms, laundry, dumpsters, pump-out facilities, telephones, and data ports are available through the Downtown Hampton Public Piers Dockmaster office. Visit the Downtown Hampton Public Piers, one mile from the Intracoastal Waterway, just past Old Point Comfort. Follow channel markers 13 & 14 to Hampton River. VHF Channel 16 is monitored.

> Contact: Ian Bates, Dockmaster
> Downtown Hampton Public Piers
> 762 Settlers Landing Road
> Hampton, VA 23669
> Tel: 757-727-1271; Fax: 757-727-1255

Fall River Celebrates America

The 14th annual Fall River Celebrates America Waterfront Festival, August 9-13, 2000, will be a family-oriented, alcohol-free series of events and exhibits at Battleship Cove and Heritage State Park on the historic Fall River, Massachusetts waterfront. Tall ships, Portuguese Night, multi-cultural exhibits, Country Night, three entertainment stages, fireworks, children's entertainment, sailing regattas, International Food and Desserts Fairs, Arts and Crafts, six-division parade, and waterski shows are a few of the many events available. In addition, year-round attractions such as Battleship MASSACHUSETTS, the Marine Museum at Fall River, the Old Colony and Fall River Railroad Museum, the Fall River Carousel, and the *Bounty* will be available.

The festival is produced by the Chamber of Commerce in cooperation with the City of Fall River, the Fall River Cultural Council, The FIRSTFED Charitable Foundation, and other businesses. Tall ships interested in participating and for further information please contact Donna Futoransky.

> Contact: Donna Futoransky, Executive Director
> Fall River Celebrates America
> 200 Pocasset St.
> Fall River, MA 02721
> Tel: 508-676-8226; Fax: 508-675-5932
> E-mail: donnaf@fallriverchamber.com
> Web site: http://www.frchamber.com

City of Glen Cove, New York

Glen Cove, New York is located on the north shore of Long Island and has ten miles of waterfront, bordered by Hempstead Harbor and Long Island Sound. The city's

rolling hills and natural coastline brought the Matinecock Indian Tribe, the city's founding fathers, in 1668, and affluent entrepreneurs such as J.P. Morgan, F.W. Woolworth,
and their families to Glen Cove. Today the city is home to three public beaches, a beautiful waterfront golf course, 300 acres of natural preserves, the Garvies Point Museum,
and the Nassau County Holocaust Memorial and Educational Center.

Glen Cove has three active yacht clubs and 600 slips in two marinas—Brewer
Marina and Glen Cove Marina—with lifts, knowledgeable ship outfitters, and all
types of maritime services. The three-masted barquentine *Regina Maris*, the Coastal
Ecology Learning Program aboard the gaff-rigged schooner *Phoenix*, and the paddle
wheeler *Thomas Jefferson* call Glen Cove their home. America's Sail '98 and Glen
Cove's Waterfront Festival 99 brought over 350,000 visitors to the city, which welcomes visitors June 30 through July 2, 2000, for what will be one of the outstanding celebrations of the new millennium.

Contact: Mayor Thomas R. Suozzi or Stuart Held, Executive Director
Glen Cove's Waterfront Festival 2000
City of Glen Cove, City Hall
913 Glen Street
Glen Cove, New York 11542
Tel: 516-676-2144; Fax: 516-676-0108
E-mail: stuheld@aol.com or cdwillson@aol.com
Web site: http://www.glencove-li.com

PHOTO BY MAX

Village of Greenport, New York

Located in the beautiful, deep, and superbly protected waters of the Gardiners/Peconic Bay system of eastern Long Island, Greenport Harbor has been a uniquely appealing destination for mariners since the dawn of American history. Modern-day Greenport remains true to this heritage. A seaborne visitor arriving today steps off the boat and back in time to enjoy an authentic working seaport where a car is unnecessary.

Deep-water dockage for large and small vessels is available at a municipally owned marina in the heart of a downtown listed on the National Register of Historic Places. Stores, galleries, and services, including those catering to mariners such as welding, hauling, carpentry, and marine hardware—even a hospital—are but steps away. A waterfront park upland of the marina is currently being developed with a vintage carousel, outdoor amphitheater, and a boardwalk connecting the marina to a transportation center where bus, rail, and ferry connections are available to Shelter Island, New York City, and destinations throughout Long Island.

Greenport is keenly interested in visits by tall ships and sail training vessels and will make special arrangements to attract them.

> Contact: Mayor David Kapell
> Village of Greenport
> 236 Third Street
> Greenport, NY 11944
> Tel: 516-477-3000; Fax: 516-447-2488
> Hail the Greenport Harbormaster on VHF Channel 9

Lorain, Ohio Port Authority

Lorain, Ohio is a working waterfront located at the mouth of the Black River on the southern shore of Lake Erie, midway between Cleveland and Sandusky. Phase 1 of the 1986 Strategic Development Plan for Lorain's harbor area, including marinas, retail and public open space, and recreational facilities is complete.

The new, 20-acre Black River Wharf Boat Ramp site provides six-lane public launch with commercial/retail shops and public open space. The 22-acre "Grove Site" Project will create a well-balanced mixed-use development. Proposed uses for the site include a Riverwalk, Transportation Center, Industrial Heritage Museum, and Festival Grounds.

The Lorain Port Authority also sponsors the PortFest, held annually the second weekend in June to celebrate the development occurring along the waterfront. There is continuous live entertainment on three stages and activities for all ages, including artists' displays, waterfront exhibits and demonstrations, a boat show, car show, children's rides, and fireworks.

Contact: Amit M. Pandya
Lorain Port Authority
110 Alabama Avenue
Lorain, OH 44052
Tel: 440-204-2267; Fax: 440-288-1872

Louisbourg Merchants Association

Louisbourg, Nova Scotia is the largest historical reconstruction in North America, and many visitors plan two-day visits. Fifteen years ago the local Merchants Association of Louisbourg banded together and built the Louisbourg Motorhome RV Park and Campground. The park provides employment opportunities for local students, and income from the park is reinvested in the community through donations to the local school breakfast program, Little League teams, the Railway Museum, the Louisbourg Theater, and others. Hot showers, fresh water, and garbage facilities are available for visiting vessels at the adjacent Guy M. Hiltz Pier.

Contact: Gary Peck
Louisbourg Merchants Association
PO Box 10
Louisbourg, NS B0A 1M0
CANADA
Tel: 902-733-2210; Fax: 902-733-3140
E-mail: gary.peck@ns.sympatico.ca

Mobile Tricentennial, Inc.

The city of Mobile, Alabama will be celebrating its Tricentennial, 300 Years of America, in the year 2002. As part of a yearlong celebration to commemorate the rich heritage and treasured culture of the region, one of the areas of emphasis will be to showcase the port of Mobile Bay. Since the forebears came here by way of the sea, the fair city would be a natural choice for an inaugural visit to the Gulf of Mexico. The City of Mobile would welcome this occasion with great pomp and celebration. The waterfront is visible and accessible to the public and within one block of hotels, restaurants, and the downtown entertainment district. Mobile is also host to the Dauphin Island Regatta, which is the largest one-day regatta in the United States.

The city of Mobile is using this once-in-a-lifetime occasion to celebrate our heritage and teach their children about Mobile's history and their role in its future. Come be a part of Mobile's Tricentennial!

Contact: J. Renee Eley Ellis
Mobile Tricentennial, Inc.
2900 Dauphin St.
Mobile, AL 36606
Tel: 334-470-7730; Fax: 334-470-7732
E-mail: jreellis@ci.mobile.al.us

Norfolk FestEvents

Norfolk FestEvents coordinates all aspects of Norfolk's waterfront ship visits program. Facilities in Norfolk include the new, state-of-the-art Nauticus International Pier located at the National Maritime Center. Regular ship visits scheduled include tall ships and government vessels from the Navy, Coast Guard, and the National Oceanographic and Atmospheric Administration (NOAA). It is immediately adjacent to Town Point Park, site of free weekly festivals, concerts, and special events, and the Waterside Festival Marketplace, with 150 shops and restaurants open seven days a week. The Nauticus International Pier is centrally located and within short walking distance to downtown Norfolk shopping areas, a wide variety of restaurants and nightclubs, the YMCA, harbor and dinner cruise boats, churches, cultural activities such as theater and opera, the Chrysler Museum, and the MacArthur Memorial.

Contact: Karen Scherberger, Executive Director
Norfolk FestEvents
120 West Main St.
Norfolk, VA 23510
Tel: 757-441-2345; Fax: 757-441-5198
Web site: http://www.festevents.va.org

Piscataqua Maritime Commission

The Piscataqua Maritime Commission (PMC) was formed in January 1998 to meet several needs within the community—to promote the region's rich maritime history through special programs and projects and to provide a means of organizing support for visiting ships. The organization's first project was providing support for the HM Bark *Endeavour*, a replica of Captain James Cook's 18th-century ship of discovery. The ship, which visited Portsmouth in September 1998, drew more than 60,000 visitors, including 1,500 school children, who were thrilled to get the chance to experience the age of sail first-hand. PMC continues to be committed to providing programs like the *Endeavour* to the Greater Portsmouth community and welcomes sail training organizations that would like to show off their vessels and programs in the Portsmouth, New Hampshire area (prime display season is May 30 - October 15).

PMC is made up of more than 300 volunteers and representatives from the Port of New Hampshire, Portsmouth City Council, Portsmouth Naval Shipyard, the Navy League, and other local maritime groups.

Contact: Piscataqua Maritime Commission
PO Box 545

Portsmouth, NH 03802-0545
Tel: 603-431-7447
E-mail: t.cocchiaro@rscs.net

City of Port Colborne, Ontario

The Canal Days Festival is a celebration of the Welland Canal and its further extension to Port Colborne, Ontario, Canada in 1833. The festival will run from August 4-7, 2000. More than 100,000 people are expected to visit the city to view tall ships and unique maritime vessels, a parade of lighted boats, food expo, historic West Street specialty shops, fireworks, live concerts, kite flyers, antique cars and motorcycles, arts, crafts, and more. A 20-minute drive from Niagara Falls, the City of Port Colborne has two beautiful beaches, its own marina equipped with showers, a multi-use recreational trail, and some of the best bass and Walleye fishing in the world. All tall ships are welcome as guests at Canal Days. Call Shane Sargant for inquiries regarding financial assistance or for more information.

Contact: Shane Sargant
66 Charlotte St.
Port Colborne, ON L3K 3C8
CANADA
Tel: 888-767-8386, 905-835-2900 ext. 112
E-mail: dccs@portcolborne.com
Web site: http://www.portcolborne.com

St. Lucie, Florida Chamber of Commerce

St. Lucie County is one of the fastest growing areas in the nation. At the same time, the cost of living has remained relatively low. St. Lucie County's location at the convergence of I-95 and Florida's Turnpike, combined with ongoing road improvements and relatively low land costs, reinforces the County's position as an ideal location for distribution purposes. Approximately 80% of the Florida market is within a 150-mile radius.

St. Lucie County remains a prime location for companies and families to expand or relocate. The county continues to provide a favorable quality of life and has a receptive business climate. It offers many assets and continues to make gains in many areas. The development of a port offers ideal facilities for visiting tall ships.

Contact: George Haygood
St. Lucie Chamber of Commerce
1626 SE Port St. Lucie Blvd.
Port St. Lucie, FL 34952
Tel: 561-595-9999; Fax: 561-335-4446
E-mail: georgehaygood@stluciechamber.org
Web site: http://www.stluciechamber.org

Sail Baltimore

Sail Baltimore is a nonprofit community organization dedicated to offering maritime educational experiences to the general public, visitors, local citizens, children, and disadvantaged youth. Other goals are to stimulate the economy of the City of Baltimore and surrounding communities, to increase regional tourism, provide a forum and network for encouraging business development opportunities, and to foster international cultural exchange.

This mission is accomplished through recruiting, planning, and hosting visits of various types of ships whose presence in the harbor offers an educational but non-commercial experience. Sail Baltimore also produces special events designed to attract people to the city's waterfront, including several successful tall ship events and water parades over the past 25 years.

> Contact: Laura Stevenson, Executive Director
> Sail Baltimore
> 200 West Lombard St., Suite B
> Baltimore, MD 21201-2517
> Tel: 410-752-8632; Fax: 410-385-0631
> E-mail: sailbalt@us.net
> Web site: http://www.sailbaltimore.org

Savannah Waterfront Association

In the 1970s the City of Savannah implemented a major urban renewal program to revitalize the waterfront. Today the Savannah historic waterfront is lined with more than 100 unique shops and galleries, fabulous restaurants, seductive nightspots, and elegant inns and hotels. Old cotton warehouses were transformed and the Savannah Waterfront Association hosts many exciting festivals to bring people to the river. The docking facilities were updated in the last five years and Savannah has hosted several tall ships with wonderful participation from the public. The Savannah Waterfront Association is a nonprofit organization whose purpose is to promote and attract visitors to the area.

> Contact: Carol Devine
> Savannah Waterfront Association
> PO Box 572
> Savannah, GA 31401
> Tel: 912-234-0295; Fax: 912-234-4904
> E-mail: bbtohmy@aol.com

Société du Vieux-Port de Montréal (Old Port of Montreal Corporation, Inc.)

Since May 1992, the Old Port of Montréal has been offering Montréalers, yachting tourists, and tall ships a quality marina: The Port d'Escale. Located in the Jacques Cartier Basin, the Port d'Escale is equipped with full range of up-to-date facilities to accommodate sailboats over 200 feet, docking on floating docks. Tucked into the heart of the Old Port, a few steps away from downtown Montreal, this secure facility provides a quiet haven for tall ships mooring there. Because of its varied activities and its unique atmosphere, the Old Port is an important site for recreation and tourism in Montreal. Set a heading for the Port d'Escale, and discover Montreal in style.

> Contact: Sylvain A. Deschamps, Harbourmaster
> 333 de la Commune Street West
> Montréal, QUE H2Y 2E2
> CANADA
> Tel: 514-283-5414; Fax: 514-283-8423

Tall Ships® Newport Salute 2000

Come to legendary Newport, Rhode Island where entertaining tall ships and their crews is a well-practiced tradition. Nowhere is there a tradition so rich in history, style, and culture. Often referred to as the birthplace of the American Navy, Newport's nautical history is evident everywhere. Founded in 1639 as a haven for those seeking religious freedom, today the City by the Sea is a favored spot of competitive sailors and a resort destination for those seeking an extraordinary travel experience.

Tall Ships® Newport Salute 2000 will take place from June 29 to July 2, 2000. While events such as a parade of lighted yachts, a band concert, a picnic with fireworks, a formal ball at a historic mansion, crew dances, parties, and rally events are planned around these dates, ships are welcome any time. Newport has an active ship repair and supply industry. See the advertisement in the front of this Directory for more details.

> Contact: Captain Eric J. Williams
> Tall Ships® Newport Salute 2000
> 17B Bowen's Wharf
> Newport, RI 02840
> Tel: 401-847-8206; Fax: 401-847-8508
> E-mail: talshpsnpt@aol.com
> Web site: http://www.tallshipsnewport.org

Tall Ships® Charleston

Following the first transatlantic race leg of Tall Ships 2000® and port activities in Bermuda from June 9-12, 2000, ASTA will conduct a blue water sail training race from Bermuda to Charleston, South Carolina, where visiting tall ships from around the world will be welcomed from June 16-21. The race will start during the afternoon of June 12, and participating vessels will race due west to Charleston. Organizers are planning events in Charleston that will bring trainees together in friendly competition and a relaxed social setting. Other events are planned for visitors that will highlight the role of sailing ships in history and the role of sail training today, including a wooden boat festival and family boat-building event.

The rules for the race will be the same as those for the other legs of Tall Ships 2000®: the minimum waterline length for participating vessels is 30 feet and at least half of those on board each vessel must be between the ages of 15 and 25. For visitor information about Tall Ships® Charleston call 843-853-8000 or fax to 843-853-0444. Ships interested in visiting Charleston should call Beth Bonds at 843-849-1231 or e-mail to bbonds@tallshipscharleston.com. Visit the Tall Ships® Charleston Web site: http://www.tallshipscharleston.com. For more information about the race, contact Race Director Steve Baker in the ASTA office.

> Contact: Vessels: Beth Bonds, Tall Ships® Charleston
> PO Box 975, Charleston, SC 29402
> Tel: 843-849-1231; Fax: 843-853-0444
> E-mail: bbonds@tallshipscharleston.com
> Other inquiries: Jeanne Aichele, Tall Ships® Charleston
> Tel: 843-805-3052; Fax: 843-853-0444
> E-mail: jaichele@charlestoncvb.com
> Web site: http://www.tallshipscharleston.com

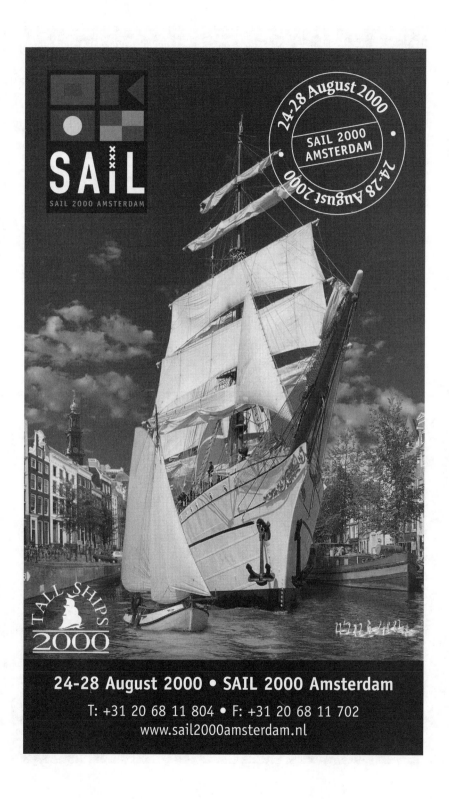

PHOTO BY MAX

SAIL TALL SHIPS!

About Sail Training

INFORMATION TO HELP YOU
PLAN YOUR SAIL TRAINING
EXPERIENCE

Take Responsibility for Your Adventure!

BY MICHAEL J. RAUWORTH

One of the most important products of sail training is the development of a sense of judgment about what and whom you can rely on, and to what degree. This applies to: the compass, the weather forecast, your shipmates, the depths on the chart, the strength of the anchor cable, the vigilance of the lookout on the other ship, and many other things. Sail training also builds a reasoned sense of self-reliance. All of this starts from the moment you begin to think about a voyage. Use the information in this Directory to begin to evaluate and decide what might be the best sail training experience for you.

Recognize who you are dealing with and what is included. When you book a sail training trip, you are dealing with the vessel owner or its representatives—ASTA is not involved. You must evaluate whether the financial and business arrangements make sense for you. If there is connecting travel involved, for example, find out if you must make the arrangements, or if it is somehow tied into those you make with the vessel. What happens if you miss your ship because your plane is delayed, or vice versa? Do you need trip insurance? Have you confirmed with the vessel owner any possible customs or immigration issues? Will you need a passport or a pre-purchased air ticket? You must seek out the answers to these questions.

PHOTO BY THAD KOZA

Make informed, responsible decisions about risk and safety, level of challenge, physical suitability and other important issues. One of the important reasons to embark on a sail training trip is to engage the world in a different, stimulating, and challenging way—if you want to stay warm and dry, you should stay at home by the fireplace. Much of the point is to come face-to-face with the elements. At the very least, this probably means that you will find yourself wet, chilled, or tired at some point in a challenging voyage. But everyone's threshold for this is different, and you need to find out what you are likely to be experiencing in order to find out if it is well matched for you.

Since the beginning of time, going to sea has been recognized as carrying an element of risk. These days, we more commonly think about risk in connection with highway travel or aviation, but the idea is the same: you get a pre-flight safety brief on an airliner, you get a lifeboat drill on a cruise ship. Part of the value of sail training is addressing these issues head on. You need to decide whether you are comfortable with the combination of risks and safety measures connected with your proposed sail training trip.

For example, will you be able to go aloft? Will trips in smaller craft be involved? Will you be expected to stand watch at night? Do the demands of the ship match your physical and health capabilities? Are you on medication that will (or may) become necessary during the voyage, or do you have a condition (for example, hemophilia or epilepsy) that may require special access to medical attention; if so, is the vessel operator aware of this? Will you be able to get up and down the ladders, in and out of your berth, and along a heeled-over deck? If there is an emergency, will you be needed to handle safety equipment or to help operate the vessel?

Remember that sail training is often not intended to be like a vacation. Some vessels, on the other hand, may offer leisurely voyages, where very little will be asked of you. You should arrive at a clear understanding of these issues prior to setting sail.

In short, you must satisfy yourself that the trip you are looking into is the right thing for you to do, considering safety, risk, suitability, challenge, comfort, convenience, educational value, cost, and any other factors you consider important.

Does the American Sail Training Association have a hand in any of this? In a word—no! ASTA is your "bulletin board" to introduce you to opportunities. However, the American Sail Training Association does not operate any vessels, and has no ability or authority to inspect, approve, or even recommend vessels or programs because programs are constantly evolving and changing.

The American Sail Training Association is a nonprofit organization with a limited staff. It serves as a forum for the sail training community, but it has no authority over what programs are offered, or how vessels are operated. The information in this Directory is supplied by the vessel operators, and ASTA can not possibly verify all the information, nor visit all the ships in order to evaluate programs. For these reasons, you must take the information in this Directory as a starting point only, subject to change and correction, and proceed directly with the vessel operator. The American Sail Training Association is not an agent or business partner for the vessel operators, and is not a travel agent.

ASTA believes in the value of sail training as a concept, but remember, from the moment you step beyond looking at this book, the decision and the resulting experiences rest with you.

Choosing a Sail Training Program

The four essential components of any sail training program are a seaworthy vessel, a competent captain and crew, qualified instructors, and a sound educational program appropriate and suited to the needs of the trainees on board.

There are as many sail training programs as there are ships, and choosing the right one depends a great deal on your personal needs and desires. Sail training differs from going on a cruise ship, in that you are expected to take part in the running of the ship by handling sail and line and standing watch, as well as working in the galley (the ship's kitchen) or performing routine cleaning or maintenance duties. To what degree depends on the sail training program you select.

Do you want a program that specializes in marine biology or adventure travel? Would you like to ship out for a day, a week, a school semester—or, for as long as it takes to circumnavigate the world? Are you interested in maritime history? In celestial navigation? Whales? Do you want the unique challenge of climbing aloft in a square-rigger? A race across the Atlantic? Maine lobster dinners aboard classic windjammers? Exotic ports of call? Will you be bringing your wheelchair? Would you like to receive academic credit?

The answers to the above questions provide a profile for just some of the options available to you. As to what sail training programs require of you—beyond an eager willingness to get the most out of your voyage—the requirements are few:

Safety First!

Take a close look at the vessel's credentials. In the US, check to see if the vessel operates under United States Coast Guard regulations. Does the vessel currently hold a USCG-issued Certificate of Inspection (see page 312, "Regulation of US Sailing Vessels") or comparable certification from the authorities of the country in which it is registered? If it is a non-US vessel you should ensure that the vessel operates in accordance with the maritime safety rules of that country. In most cases this is supervised by a government agency similar to the US Coast Guard. The resources section of the ASTA Web site lists the latest known Web sites of some of these agencies.

Talk to the program provider! Ask questions! Read the organization or company's literature; check out their Web site. Most important: visit the ship if you can. Get a sense of the professionalism of the operation and the quality of its program. Find out about the experience level of the captain and officers. How long have they served the ship you are looking into? If you will be joining the vessel in a distant port, or if it does not hold a current USCG Certificate of Inspection, be especially diligent in your research. Ask the program operator for the names of past trainees or clients and give them a call and ask about their experience. The amazingly diverse range of opportunities featured in this book provides each of us with a variety of options.

Many ships venture no more than 20 miles from a harbor and are rarely underway overnight; others offer offshore voyaging and the challenge of distant passages where severe weather and water conditions may be unavoidable. Being underway around the clock requires watch duties night and day, demanding both physical and mental stamina and perseverance.

Experience

With very few exceptions, no prior sailing experience is required of trainees. Some programs do accept non-paying volunteers as crewmembers, but typically require experience in similar vessels or a long-term commitment—or both. Paying positions typically require a license—"Able-bodied Seaman" papers document a minimum of 180 days spent underway and successfully passing an exam administered by the US Coast Guard. Licenses are awarded to crew based on additional time underway, the tonnage of vessels served in, waters sailed, technical training, and additional testing.

Swimming ability

Trainees are encouraged to have the ability to feel comfortable in and around the water; however, many programs have no formal swimming requirements.

Age

Most voyages are planned with a specific age group in mind. This varies from program to program, but many sail training programs start accepting unaccompanied trainees from the age of 14 (ninth grade). Ask what the composition of the ship's complement will be and, if you plan to send a young person on an extended voyage, what the in-port supervisory arrangements will be. Day sails and dockside education programs are readily available for elementary school students and overnight trips can be arranged for older school groups as well. There are a tremendous variety of adventure programs for adults of all ages, including "Elderhostel" voyages for seniors.

Academic credit

Some vessels are tied directly to academic institutions that grant academic credit to trainees who successfully complete sail training programs as part of a course of study or project in a wide range of subjects. Some educational institutions will also grant credit for on-board independent study.

Co-education

Just about every sail training vessel in the US sails with both male and female professional crew and programs are typically co-ed. Others are designed specifically for groups such as the Girl Scouts or in conjunction with a single-gender school or affiliated program.

Cost

Prices vary considerably, ranging from $25 to $150 per person per day, depending on the nature and the duration of the program and the type of vessel.

Financial aid

A few vessels have limited financial assistance available, and some trainees, Scouting, and school groups have successfully sought private, business, and/or community support to help defray the cost of sail training. In addition, there are a small number of independent organizations that provide financial aid to trainees, usually through matching grants. Check with the sail training program you are interested in to see what opportunities may be available.

Regulation of US Sailing Vessels

Underway operations differ from vessel to vessel depending on the type of program offered and the resulting opportunities provided. While the curriculum taught aboard any given vessel can vary from year to year or from voyage to voyage, the scope of a ship's mission is governed by regulations written and enforced by official agencies of the country in which the vessel is registered.

In the US, the United States Coast Guard (USCG) regulates the design, construction, operation, manning, sailing route, and program options for all US-owned vessels carrying more than six passengers or paying trainees. In addition, the USCG also regulates all vessels working dockside as tourist attractions or historical exhibits. Passenger trade is limited to US-flagged vessels, which means that vessels registered in other countries may not carry passengers between US ports; however, sail training vessels from outside the US may carry trainees.

Each year, the Coast Guard issues qualified US-owned vessels a Certificate of Inspection (COI) outlining what waters may be sailed, how many crew must be carried and what qualifications they must have, how many trainees or passengers may be carried, the type of safety equipment required, and so forth.

The type of COI to be issued is determined by both the size and construction of the vessel and the operating intentions of the owner. Some types of certification require the vessel to undergo annual inspection of all on-board safety equipment (required in accordance with the type of certification and the sailing route) and of the vessel itself in regular out-of-

PHOTO BY GEORGE ANCONA

the-water hull inspections. Some vessels carry dual certification.

Following is a brief description of the various types of certifications governing the operation of US-flagged vessels:

Sailing School Vessels (SSV) are certified under Title 46, Subchapter R of the Code of Federal Regulations (CFR). An SSV is a vessel of less than 500 gross tons carrying six or more sailing school students or instructors, principally propelled by sail, and operated by a nonprofit educational organization exclusively for the purpose of sailing education. Sailing School Vessels are required to pass regular inspection by the USCG in order to maintain their certification.

Passenger Vessels are certified according to size and number of passengers (not engaged in educational activities or in the operation of the vessel) carried under Title 46 of the CFR:

•**Subchapter C**—Uninspected vessels which operate with no more than six passengers.

•**Subchapter T**—Small passenger vessels of under 100 gross tons that carry more than six passengers and are required to pass regular USCG inspection of the ship and all onboard equipment.

•**Subchapter K**—Small passenger vessels of under 100 gross tons that carry more than 150 passengers and are required to pass regular USCG inspection of the ship and all onboard equiment.

•**Subchapter H**—Passenger vessels of more than 100 gross tons that carry passengers for hire and are required to pass regular USCG inspection of the ship and all onboard equipment.

Attraction Vessels are fre-

quently, although not always, stationary dockside exhibits. Although crewmembers may take the vessel from port to port, the USCG inspection certifies their safety for dockside programs only.

Oceanographic Research Vessels (ORV) are certified under Subchapter U of Title 46 of the CFR. An ORV is a vessel employed exclusively in either oceanographic (saltwater) or limnologic (freshwater) instruction and/or research, and is not necessarily equipped for passengers or other non-professionals.

For more information, access the United States Coast Guard through the link on ASTA's Web site or contact the Government Printing Office for the above listed sections of the Code of Federal Regulations.

Shipping Out

Each year, ASTA asks one of its Member Organizations for the equipment list they provide to potential trainees, for use in this Directory. This list is a general guide only. Requirements may vary from vessel to vessel. Check for specific requirements of the program you are considering. The following list was provided by Toronto Brigantine, Inc., operators of *Pathfinder* and *Playfair*.

•(Leave your treasures and valuables at home!)

•There is very limited space on board! Your personal storage space (not including your sleeping bag and rain gear) is approximately 24" x 12" x 10". Be conservative when packing! You must use soft unframed luggage (duffel bags, etc.). No suitcases or framed backpacks are allowed on board. Do not bring valuables. The gear list includes warm clothes and long underwear, etc. Even in the summer, night watches can be surprisingly cold.

•Proof of citizenship is required. Birth certificates for Canadian and American-born trainees and appropriate documentation for others (passport, immigration papers, visa, etc.)

Sun Protection
Sunglasses (with UV protection) with a solid case and neck strap, sunscreen and lip balm (minimum 12 SPF), sun hat (preferably with strap).

Clothing

[1 week]		[2 weeks]
2	pairs of long pants (cords, jeans, or sweat pants)	3
2	long-sleeved shirts	4
4	t-shirts	6
2	pairs of shorts	3
2	wool or fleece (WARM) sweaters	2
2	sweatshirts	2
	underwear	
	socks (many! mostly warm)	
1	long underwear	1
2	pair of shoes (non-skid, laced, easily dried)	2
1	rain gear (jacket with hood/hat) and pants	1
1	appropriate sleepwear	1
1	mitts/gloves and watch cap	1

Trainees are not allowed to wear sandals . . . so don't bring any. Pierced ears must be empty or studs only, no hoops, etc.

Bedding
Sleeping bag and single bed sheet

Other
Personal toiletries and shaving gear (no need for makeup, perfume, hairspray, etc.)
1 bathing suit and towel, insect repellent
If you use contact lenses, don't forget your equipment and bring a pair of glasses as a backup.

Optional
Wristwatch with secure strap, camera and film, writing materials, books for recreational reading

Trainees are not allowed to board our ships with the following:
- Electronics (portable cassette or CD players, video games, hair dryers, etc.)
- Knives (rigging knives are used only by officers)
- Alcohol and illegal substances

All medications (prescription and non-prescription), birth certificates, money, and passports must be given to the designated ship's officer for safekeeping.

Note: Labeling your clothing and belongings is a good idea. We're not responsible for your stuff . . . you are, but it's easier to find is your name is on it!

SAIL TALL SHIPS!

ASTA Activities
and Membership

INFORMATION ON ASTA
PROGRAMS, PUBLICATIONS, AND
MEMBERSHIP OPPORTUNITIES

ASTA Programs and Professional Services

STA's Annual Conference on Sail Training and Tall Ships gathers ships' masters, port representatives, public officials, marine suppliers, naval architects, program administrators, festival managers, preservationists, environmentalists, crewmembers, and educators. Topics concerning vessel operations, regulatory issues, management, educational programming, and safety at sea are addressed each year, as are sessions on media relations, marketing, funding, and communications.

The **International Sail Training Safety Forum**, initiated in 1992 in cooperation with the ISTA, expands the international dialogue among professional mariners by collecting and discussing case studies of actual incidents at sea and from these developing workable safety strategies. Professionals engaged in sail training, sea education, vessel operations, and tall ship events from throughout the world participate in this annual symposium, which take place in conjunction with ASTA's Annual Conference during odd-numbered years and in Europe during even-numbered years.

The **Henry H. Anderson, Jr. Sail Training Scholarship** and **ASTA Sailing Vessel Assistance Grant** programs were established in 1999. The first is designed to assist young people between 14 and 19 to achieve a sail training experience aboard USCG-inspected ASTA Member Vessels. Scholarships are available to both individuals and groups. The second is designed to assist ASTA Member Vessels which are not USCG-inspected in maintenance and improvement projects that will better enable them to further ASTA's missions.

http://tallships.sailtraining.org links you to the world of sail training. Links to ASTA Member Vessels make it easy to continue to learn more about opportunities under sail and the ships that can take you to sea. The ASTA Web site also provides links to Tall Ships® Events such as Tall Ships 2000® and to international sail training associations and resources around the world.

A **Billet Bank** provides notice of positions available aboard ASTA member vessels on ASTA's Web site and in quarterly issues of *Running Free*. ASTA does not endorse any specific program or vessel, but simply shares information as it becomes available.

One of ASTA's chief concerns has always been to ensure that the highest safety standards are maintained by all those who participate in sail training programs, whether as officers, crew, instructors, or trainees. ASTA's **Safety Under Sail Seminars** focus on safety and survival issues for sail training programs and provide the opportunity for captains, crew, and program developers to improve their instructional and operational skills.

The **American Sail Training Association Marine Insurance Program** provides ASTA Member Vessels the ability to secure comprehensive commercial insurance for all vessels, whether they are navigating, permanently berthed, or under construction and includes benefits such as personal effects coverage for crew and trainees, separate deductibles for theft of electronics, and extension of liability coverage for piers, docks, and ticket areas.

ASTA Scholarships and Grants

During 1999, ASTA established two new scholarship and grant programs, and began development of a third. The Henry H. Anderson, Jr. Sail Training Scholarship Fund was created to provide financial support for young people who might not otherwise be able to afford the cost of a sail training experience. Named in honor of Harry Anderson, a former Chairman of ASTA and world-renowned yachtsman, the program was launched with a highly successful fundraising event on the grounds of the International Yacht Restoration School—an ASTA member—in Newport in June, 1999. At the same time, the American Sail Training Association Sailing Vessel Assistance Grant program was announced.

The scholarships are open to youth in the 14-19 age range who wish to sail aboard an ASTA Member Vessel which is Coast Guard-inspected as either a Sailing School Vessel or a Small Passenger Vessel. Scholarships are awarded according to need, with priority given to students determined to reach beyond prior experience. Students must pay some part of their tuition, but the percentage is not fixed, nor is it a determining factor in the selection process. ASTA may fund up to 75% of the cost for an individual, to a maximum of $750, and up to 50% for a group, to a maximum of $1,500. Applications will be reviewed twice each year; application deadlines are April 1 and September 1.

Recognizing that a substantial number of ASTA's Professional Members do not operate vessels required to be inspected by the Coast Guard, and that trainees on board these vessels would therefore not be eligible for scholarship awards, ASTA has also established a Sailing Vessel Assistance Grant Program. Grants of up to $1,000 may be awarded for projects that further the mission and goals of the American Sail Training Association, or are consistent with ASTA's stated mission. These awards will be made once each year, with an application deadline of January 15.

ASTA is also developing guidelines for a third program that would support the professional development of crewmembers who regularly serve aboard ASTA Member Vessels. This program, expected to be announced in 2000, will support training courses for both individuals and groups. Complete details and application forms for these exciting new programs are available from ASTA's Web site, or by contacting the office directly.

Pride of Baltimore II

SAIL TALL SHIPS!

ASTA Publications

ail Tall Ships! A Directory of Sail Training and Adventure at Sea first appeared in 1980, and is now in its twelfth edition. The Directory provides program and contact information for member vessels and sail training associations throughout the world. To help fulfill ASTA's mission, the directory is also distributed through maritime museums and their affiliated shops, marinas, maritime events, and sail training programs, as well as bookstores, libraries, high school guidance counselors, university career resource centers, and education conferences throughout the United States and Canada.

Guidelines for Educational Programs Under Sail defines ASTA standards for sail training and sea education within the framework of the Sailing School Vessels Act. This manual defines criteria and indicators of effectiveness for the design, delivery, and evaluation of curricula, instruction, and program administration. In addition to the core of safe seamanship education, the guidelines apply to all aspects of sail training: adventure, education, environmental science, maritime heritage, and leadership development.

The ASTA Training Logbook enables trainees and crew to keep a personal log of their sea time and to document their progress in sail training, and records a progression of skill-building activities in safety, seamanship, and navigation. Completion of course work and sea time must be certified by either the instructor or the ship's master.

The International Safety Forum Proceedings, an annual publication of the International Safety Forum, is a record of the papers submitted and discussions held on various aspects of sail training safety and operations, emergency procedures, professional training and qualifications, vessel design and construction, etc. The Forum has been held each year since 1992, and copies of each year's proceedings are available on request.

A Quick Guide to the Regulations Pertaining to Sail Training Vessels Visiting US Waters gives non-US vessels a sense of the regulations governing all ships visiting ports in the United States and provides contact information for each of the federal authorities enforcing those regulations.

Tall Ships, by Thad Koza, published by TideMark Press with a foreword by ASTA's former Executive Director, Pamela Dewell Smith, is available through the ASTA office. This beautiful book features four-color photographs of 150 sail training vessels in the international fleet.

PHOTO BY GEORGE ANCONA

THE MAINE POWDER HOUSE

Your Black Powder Supplier

J.R. Worthington
Proprietor

Post Office Box 5 Peru, Maine 04290

Telephone 207-562-7499
FAX 800-701-9061

e-mail
mainepowder@ctel.net
www.mainepowderhouse.com

JODY LEXOW
YACHT CHARTERS

LUXURY SAILING &
POWER YACHTS WORLDWIDE

BARGES ON THE INLAND WATERWAYS
OF EUROPE

OVER 20 YEARS' EXPERIENCE
PLANNING CUSTOM YACHT CHARTERS

26 CODDINGTON WHARF
NEWPORT, RI 02840
PHONE   800 662-2628
FAX 401 845-8909
EMAIL JLYC@EDGENET.NET

MEMBER AYCA/CYBA

ASTA Membership Opportunities

Individual $45

(Tax-deductible value is $15)

• Complimentary copy of *Sail Tall Ships! A Directory of Sail Training and Adventure at Sea*.

• Subscription to *Running Free*, the ASTA newsletter covering tall ships news, events, and job opportunities.

• Discounts at all ASTA programs, such as ASTA's Annual Conference on Sail Training and Tall Ships and the International Safety Forum.

Junior $30

(Tax-deductible value is $0)

Open to sailors 22 years of age and younger.

• All of the benefits of Individual Membership above.

Family $75

(Tax-deductible value is $35)

Open to 2 members at the same address.

• All of the benefits of Individual Membership above plus:

• Two coffee mugs.

• Member discounts applicable to two.

Supporting $250

(Tax-deductible value is $215)

Ports, businesses, and associates of tall ships.

• All of the benefits of Individual Membership above plus:

• Listing in *Sail Tall Ships! A Directory of Sail Training and Adventure at Sea*.

• Listing in *Running Free*, the ASTA newsletter, and editorial opportunities.

• A listing on ASTA's Web site with a link to your Web site if reciprocated.

• Set of four coffee mugs.

Corporate $1,000

(Tax-deductible value is $900)

For businesses and individuals wishing to express a greater commitment to ASTA's goals.

• All of the benefits of Supporting Membership above plus:

• Two complimentary tickets to the ASTA Annual Awards Dinner.

• Choice of ASTA Necktie or Blazer Patch.

Sail Training Organizations

(Tax-deductible value is $0)

Organizations operating sail training vessels or tall ships are enrolled for the calendar year, renewable between January and May of that year. Membership fees are based on annual budget. A budget less than $250,000 results in a membership fee of $225 per year; between $250,000 and $500,000, $300 per year; and greater than $500,000, $375 per year.

- Full-page listing (including photo of your vessel) in *Sail Tall Ships! A Directory of Sail Training and Adventure at Sea.*
- 10 complimentary copies of the Directory.
- Subscription to *Running Free*, the ASTA newsletter, and editorial opportunities.
- A listing on ASTA's Web site with a link to your Web site if reciprocated.
- Publication of your ships' news/job opportunities in *Running Free.*
- Crew openings posted on ASTA's Web site and printed in *Running Free.*
- Member's Discounts for all staff to ASTA Programs, such as ASTA's Annual Conference on Sail Training and Tall Ships and the International Safety Forum.
- Access to the ASTA Marine Insurance Program.

Affiliate $150

(Tax-deductible value is $0)

Open to nonprofit organizations which do not operate vessels but do offer sail training or sea education programs (Scouts, schools, colleges, etc.).

- Listing in *Sail Tall Ships! A Directory of Sail Training and Adventure at Sea.*
- 10 complimentary copies of the Directory.
- Subscription to *Running Free*, the ASTA newsletter, and editorial opportunities.
- A listing on ASTA's Web site with a link to your Web site if reciprocated.
- Discounts for Affiliate Member staff representatives to ASTA Programs, such as ASTA's Annual Conference on Sail Training and Tall Ships and the International Safety Forum.

Membership Form

Yes, I/we want to join the American Sail Training Association!

Name_____

Organization_____

Mailing Address_____

City_____ State_____ Zip_____

Country_____

Phone_____ Fax_____

E-mail_____

Please enroll me/us in the following membership category:

Associate Memberships*
    ❑ Individual $45
    ❑ Junior $30
    ❑ Family $75
    ❑ Supporting $250
    ❑ Corporate $1,000

Professional Trade Memberships**
    ❑ Affiliate (youth groups and schools) $150

Sail Training Organizations
    ❑ Budget less than $250,000 $225
    ❑ Budget between $250,000 and $500,000 $300
    ❑ Budget greater than $500,000 $375

Associate memberships are renewable on date of anniversary.
**Professional memberships are for calendar year.*
•*Addresses in Canada/Mexico please add US $16 to cover additional postage and handling cost. Memberships outside North America please add US $24.*

    ❑ Check enclosed (US dollars drawn on US bank only)
    ❑ Visa
    ❑ MasterCard

Card number_____ Expiration date_____

Name on card_____

Mail or fax this form to: ASTA
                         PO Box 1459
                         Newport, RI 02840   USA
                         FAX: + 1 401-849-5400
                         or join via ASTA's Web site:
                         http://tallships.sailtraining.org

SAIL TALL SHIPS!

ASTA Ship's Store

Sail Tall Ships!
A Directory of Sail Training and Adventure at Sea.
12th edition. 42 new vessels! $18.00

Guidelines for Educational Programs Under Sail $14.00

1999 International Safety Forum Proceedings $20.00

1998 International Safety Forum Proceedings $20.00

1997 International Safety Forum Proceedings $8.00

ASTA Logbook - **New, revised edition!**
    A valuable aid for trainees and crew of all levels
    used to track their training progress.
1-10 copies $5.00 ea.
11-25 copies $3.50 ea. + shipping
26 or more $2.00 ea. + shipping

Tall Ships, by Thad Koza $43.45
Photographs of some of the world's great ships by the
country's premiere tall ship photographer.

By Force of Arms, signed by author James Nelson. $15.00
The first in the Revolution at Sea Saga.

The Maddest Idea, signed by author James Nelson. $17.00
The second in the Revolution at Sea Saga.

The Continental Risque, signed by author James Nelson. $17.00
The third in the Revolution at Sea Saga.

American Photographers at the Turn of the Century $22.95
Beautifully reproduced photo essays on world travel;
includes Roger Archibald's photos of experiences aboard ASTA vessels.

2000 and 2001 Tall Ships Calendar $15.00
Celebrate the new millennium with tall ship photos by Thad Koza.

ASTA polo shirt, Men's M-XL	$36.00
"Outer Banks" cotton pique, Men's M-XXL	$38.00

    Blue with white embroidered ASTA logo.
    White with blue embroidered ASTA logo.

ASTA baseball cap	$18.00

    "Adams" pre-washed cotton. Tan with gray bill and
    embroidered navy ASTA logo—one size fits all.

ASTA Ceramic Coffee Mug	$6.00
Tall Ships 2000® Ceramic Coffee Mug	$6.00
ASTA Necktie	$38.00

    Silk blend with woven ASTA logo.

ASTA Bowtie	$38.00

    Silk blend with woven ASTA logo.

ASTA Flags

    Navy with white ASTA logo. Fly from your ship, home, or office.

12" x 18"	$15.00
2' x 3'	$25.00
3' x 5'	$35.00
4' x 6'	$45.00
5' x 8'	$60.00

*All prices include shipping and handling to US addresses, except where noted.
Please inquire for shipment outside the US. Payment may be made with
US bank check, Visa, or MasterCard.*

Mail or fax order information to:

**ASTA
PO Box 1459
Newport, RI 02840 USA**

FAX: + 1 401-849-5400

or call the ASTA office: +1 401-846-1775

order via the Web: http://tallships.sailtraining.org/shipsstr.htm

Barque *Picton Castle*

SAIL TALL SHIPS!

SAIL TALL SHIPS!

Ships' Shapes

Sail training vessels are as varied as the programs operated on board them. Below are examples of the different rig configurations used by ASTA's Member Vessels. At right is a diagram of the different sails carried by a full-rigged ship.

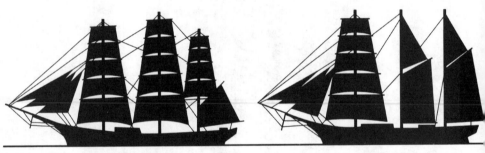

Two-Masted Schooner   Brigantine   Topsail Schooner

Full-Rigged Ship   Barquentine

Three-Masted Schooner   Brig

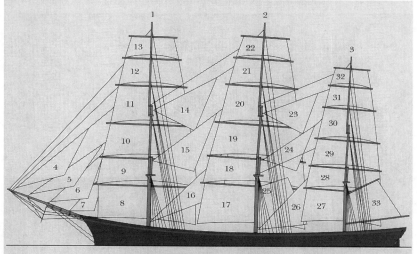

SAIL NAMES

1. Fore mast
2. Main mast
3. Mizzen mast
4. Flying jib
5. Outer jib
6. Inner jib
7. Fore topmast staysail
8. Fore sail, fore course
9. Fore lower topsail
10. Fore upper topsail
11. Fore lower topgallant sail

12. Fore upper topgallant sail
13. Fore royal
14. Main royal staysail
15. Main topgallant staysail
16. Main topmast staysail
17. Main sail, main course
18. Main lower topsail
19. Main upper topsail
20. Main lower topgallant sail
21. Main upper topgallant sail
22. Main royal

23. Mizzen royal staysail
24. Mizzen topgallant staysail
25. Mizzen topmast staysail
26. Main spencer
27. Crossjack, mizzen course
28. Mizzen lower topsail
29. Mizzen upper topsail
30. Mizzen lower topgallant sail
31. Mizzen upper topgallant sail
32. Mizzen royal
33. Spanker

If you want to come **sailing to adventure...**
SOLO or in a group, **YOUNG** or **MATURE,**
NOVICE or
EXPERIENCED

**FIRST
BUY
OUR
224
PAGE
A4
SIZE
BOOK**

Over 300 ships
discussed, half
with a page on
each, from the
UK, Europe,
and abroad...

Find a ship
Join the adventure
What's the cost?

240 SHIPS IN FULL COLOUR
Introductions by the INTERNATIONAL SAIL
TRAINING ASSOCIATION
and the ASSOCIATION OF SEA TRAINING
ORGANISATIONS

£20.00

...with 240 superb colour photos,
and forewords by the International Sail Training Association and Association of Sea Training Organisations.

Michael Burnett
Classic Yachts
and
Tall Ships
Brokerage

We are specialists in the international sale and term charter of larger classic yachts, sail training vessels, and tall ships. We have extensive experience in dealing with TV, film companies and special projects. We also offer a project management function for the construction of new vessels.

Because we don't handle modern vessels unlesss they are 'retrodesigned' or replicas, we are able to offer a well informed service to our clients. Call Mike Burnett to discuss your requirements.

Michael Burnett
Classic Yachts and Tall Ships Brokerage
2, Leonard Road, Gosport, Hants,
PO12 4TU, England
Tel: +44(0)2392-524524 fax: +44(0)2392-782594
GSM: +44-07801-52 00 00
email: classicyachts@messages.co.uk

International Sail Training Association Affiliated Organizations

The following organizations have functions corresponding to those of the American Sail Training Association. Please contact them for information about sail training opportunities in their respective countries.

AUSTRALIA

Australian Sail Training Association (AUSTA)
PO Box 196
Crows Nest, NSW 2065
AUSTRALIA
Tel and Fax: + 61 2 9498 6103

BELGIUM

Sail Training Association Belgium (STAB)
Grote Singel 6
B-2900 Schoten
BELGIUM
Tel: + 32 3 6580 006

CANADA

Canadian Sail Training Association (CSTA)
PO Box 21067
Ottawa South RPO
Ottawa, ONT K1S 5N2
CANADA
Tel: (613) 730-3243
Fax: (613) 730-2224

DENMARK

Danish Sail Training Association (DSTA)
Lodsvænget 12
DK-6710 Esbjerg V
DENMARK
Tel: + 45 7511 7581

FINLAND

Sail Training Association Finland (STAF)
Tarmonkuja 2, FIN-001180 Helsinki
FINLAND
Tel: + 358 9685 2616
Fax: + 358 9685 2615

FRANCE

Sail Training Association France (STA France)
France - Voiles - Equipages
8 rue Jean Delalande
F-35400 Saint-Malo
FRANCE
Tel: + 33 2 99 82 35 33
Fax: + 33 2 99 82 27 47

GERMANY

Sail Training Association Germany (STAG)
Hafenhaus, Columbusbahnhof
D-27568 Bremerhaven
GERMANY
Tel: + 49 471 945 5880
Fax: + 49 471 945 8845

INDONESIA

Sail Training Association of Indonesia (STA Ina)
Mabesal, Gilangkap, PO Box 7334
Jakarta TMII 13560 A
INDONESIA

ITALY

Sail Training Association Italia (STAI)
Yacht Club Italiano

Porticciolo Duca degli Abruzzi
I-16128 Genova
ITALY
Tel: + 39 10 246 1206
Fax: + 39 10 246 1213

JAPAN
Sail Training Association of Japan (STAJ)
Memorial Park Tower A
2-1-1 Minato-Mirai
Nishi-ku, Yokohama
Kanagawa 220-00 12
JAPAN
Tel: + 81 45 680 5222
Fax: + 81 45 680 5221

THE NETHERLANDS
Sail Training Association Netherlands (STAN)
Postbus 55
NL-2340 AB Oegstgeest
THE NETHERLANDS
Tel and Fax: + 31 71 515 3013

POLAND
Sail Training Association Poland (STAP)
PO Box 113
PL-81-963 Gdynia
POLAND
Tel: + 48 58 20 6580
Fax: + 48 58 20 6225

PORTUGAL
Portuguese Sail Training Association (APORVELA)
Doca do Terreiro do Trigo
P-1100 Lisbon
PORTUGAL
Tel: + 351 1 887 68 54
Fax: + 351 1 887 38 85

RUSSIA
Sail Training Association Russia (STAR)
Admiral Makarov State Maritime Academy
Kosaya Linia 15a, RU-199026
St. Petersburg
RUSSIA
Tel: + 7 812 217 1934
Fax: + 7 812 217 0682

SWEDEN
Sail Training Association of Sweden
C/o Lt. Cdr. Ragnar Westblad
MKV, Box 5155
S-426 05 V. Frölunda
SWEDEN

UNITED KINGDOM
Sail Training Association (STA)
2A The Hard
Portsmouth PO1 3PT
UNITED KINGDOM
Tel: + 44 23 92 832055
Fax: + 44 23 92 81576

National Representatives

Representatives to the International Race Committee
of the International Sail Training Association

Australia	Rear Admiral Rothesay Swan, AO, CBE
Belgium	Captain Roger Ghys
Denmark	Bo Rosbjerg
Finland	Christian Johansson
France	Philip Rousseau
Germany	Captain Manfred Hövener
Indonesia	Captain Gita Arjakusuma
Ireland	Sean Flood
Italy	Dr. Giovanni Novi
Japan	Kaoru Ogimi
The Netherlands	Bernard Heppener
Norway	Gunn von Trepka
Poland	Captain Andrzej Szleminski
Portugal	Dr. Luis de Guimarães Lobato
Russia	Prof. Alexander Pimoshenko
Russia	Ivan I. Kostylev
Spain	Rafael Iturrioz
Sweden	Lt. Cdr. Ragnar Westblad
Ukraine	Captain Oleg Vandenko
United Kingdom	John Hamilton
United States	Captain David V.V. Wood, USCG (Ret.)

PHOTO BY THAD KOZA

SAIL TALL SHIPS!

339

Indices

GEOGRAPHICAL, ADVERTISERS',
AND ALPHABETICAL INDICES

Geographical Listing of Vessels

Great Lakes, US

Bay City, Michigan: *Appledore IV*
Chicago, Illinois: *Windy*
Erie, Pennsylvania: *Niagara*
Grand Marais, Minnesota: *Hjørdis*
Kendall, New York: *Pilgrim*
Milwaukee, Wisconsin: *Denis Sullivan*
Milwaukee, Wisconsin: The Challenge
  Project
Oswego, New York: *OMF Ontario*
Port Clinton, Ohio: *Red Witch*
Suttons Bay, Michigan: *Inland Seas*
Traverse City, Michigan: *Madeline*
Traverse City, Michigan: *Manitou*
Traverse City, Michigan: *Welcome*

Great Lakes and St. Lawrence, Canada

Kingston, Ontario: *Amara Zee*
Kingston, Ontario: *Fair Jeanne*
Kingston, Ontario: *St. Lawrence II*
Ottawa, Ontario: *Black Jack*
Penetanguishene, Ontario: *HMS Bee*
Penetanguishene, Ontario: *HMS
  Tecumseth*
Toronto, Ontario: *Empire Sandy*
Toronto, Ontario: *Kajama*
Toronto, Ontario: *Challenge*
Toronto, Ontario: *Pathfinder*
Toronto, Ontario: *Playfair*
Toronto, Ontario: *True North of
  Toronto*

Canadian Maritimes

Halifax, Nova Scotia: *Dorothea*
Halifax, Nova Scotia: *Highlander*
Lunenburg, Nova Scotia: *Avon Spirit*
Lunenburg, Nova Scotia: *Bluenose II*
Lunenburg, Nova Scotia: *Raindancer
  II*

New England

Bar Harbor, Maine: *Edna Berry*
Bar Harbor, Maine: *Little Jennie*
Bar Harbor, Maine: *Malabar*
Bar Harbor, Maine: *Margaret Todd*
Bar Harbor, Maine: *Sylvina W. Beal*

Bath, Maine: *Maine*
Block Island, Rhode Island: *Danielle
  Louise*
Boothbay Harbor, Maine: *Eastwind*
Boston, Massachusetts: *America*
Boston, Massachusetts: *Liberty*
Boston, Massachusetts: *Liberty Clipper*
Boston, Massachusetts: *Spirit of
  Massachusetts*
Bridgeport, Connecticut: *Black Pearl*
Bridgeport, Connecticut: *John E.
  Pfriem*
Bridgeport, Connecticut: "HMS" *Rose*
Camden, Maine: *Appledore II*
Camden, Maine: *Mary Day*
Castine, Maine: *Bowdoin*
Charlestown, Massachusetts: *USS
  Constitution*
Fall River, Massachusetts: *Bounty*
Gloucester, Massachusetts: *Adventure*
Gloucester, Massachusetts: *Ebb Tide*
Gloucester, Massachusetts: *Spirit of
  Gloucester*
Gloucester, Massachusetts: *Thomas E.
  Lannon*
Harpswell, Maine: *Fritha*
Hope, Maine: *Kathryn B.*
Islesboro, Maine: *Harvey Gamage*
Islesboro, Maine: Harvey Gamage/
  Ocean Classroom Foundation
  Schooner Project
Marion, Massachusetts: *Sarah Abbot*
Marion, Massachusetts: *Tabor Boy*
Marstons Mills, Massachusetts:
  Larinda
Mystic, Connecticut: *Argia*
Mystic, Connecticut: *Brilliant*
Mystic, Connecticut: *Joseph Conrad*
Mystic, Connecticut: *Mystic Whaler*
New Bedford, Massachusetts:
  Ernestina
New Haven, Connecticut: *Amistad*
New Haven, Connecticut:
  Quinnipiack
New London, Connecticut: USCG
  Barque *Eagle*
Newport, Rhode Island: *Abaco*
Newport, Rhode Island: *Adirondack*

Newport, Rhode Island: *American Eagle*
Newport, Rhode Island: *Aurora*
Newport, Rhode Island: *Columbia*
Newport, Rhode Island: *Corban*
Newport, Rhode Island: *Coronet*
Newport, Rhode Island: *Endeavour*
Newport, Rhode Island: *Geronimo*
Newport, Rhode Island: *Gleam*
Newport, Rhode Island: *Heritage*
Newport, Rhode Island: *Intrepid*
Newport, Rhode Island: *Isabelle*
Newport, Rhode Island: *Nefertiti*
Newport, Rhode Island: *Northern Light*
Newport, Rhode Island: *Shamrock V*
Newport, Rhode Island: *Weatherly*
Orleans, Massachusetts: *Picara*
Peaks Island, Maine: *Tango*
Plymouth, Massachusetts: *Internet Explorer*
Portland, Maine: *Palawan*
Portland, Maine: *Samana*
Providence, Rhode Island: *Providence*
Provincetown, Massachusetts: *Hindu*
Portsmouth, New Hampshire: *Ranger*
Rockland, Maine: *Hurricane* (# 1-22)
Rockland, Maine: *Victory Chimes*
Robinhood, Maine: *William H. Thorndike*
Salem, Massachusetts: *Friendship*
Stamford, Connecticut: *SoundWaters*
Southwest Harbor, Maine: *Rachel B. Jackson*
Vineyard Haven, Massachusetts: *Alabama*
Vineyard Haven, Massachusetts: *Shenandoah*
Vineyard Haven, Massachusetts: *When and If*
Woods Hole, Massachusetts: *Corwith Cramer*
Woods Hole, Massachusetts: *Lark*
Woods Hole, Massachusetts: *Westward*

Mid-Atlantic

Alexandria, Virginia: *Federalist*
Alexandria, Virginia: *Potomac*
Alexandria, Virginia: *Tree of Life*
Annapolis, Maryland: *Imagine…!*
Baltimore, Maryland: *Clipper City*
Baltimore, Maryland: USS *Constellation*
Baltimore, Maryland: *Howard Blackburn*
Baltimore, Maryland: *Lady Maryland*
Baltimore, Maryland: *Minnie V.*
Baltimore, Maryland: *Nighthawk*
Baltimore, Maryland: *Pride of Baltimore II*
Baltimore, Maryland: *Sigsbee*
Bivalve, New Jersey: *A.J. Meerwald*
Bristol, Pennsylvania: *Pride of MANY*
Chestertown, Maryland: *Sultana*
Cobb Island, Maryland: *Mabel Stevens*
Croton-on-Hudson, New York: *Half Moon*
Georgetown, Maryland: *Gallant*
Glen Cove, New York: *Regina Maris*
Huntington, New York: *Phoenix*
Jamestown, Virginia: *Susan Constant*
New York, New York: *Adirondack*
New York, New York: *Lettie G. Howard*
New York, New York: *Peking*
New York, New York: *Pioneer*
New York, New York: *Wavertree*
Norfolk, Virginia: *American Rover*
Norfolk, Virginia: *Virginia*
Oakley, Maryland: *Fyrdraca*
Oakley, Maryland: *Gyrfalcon*
Philadelphia, Pennsylvania: *Gazela of Philadelphia*
Philadelphia, Pennsylvania: *Jolly II Rover*
Poughkeepsie, New York: *Clearwater*
Wilmington, Delaware: *Kalmar Nyckel*
Wilmington, Delaware: *Lisa*
Wilmington, Delaware: *Norseman*

Southeast and Gulf Coast

Apalachicola, Florida: *Governor Stone*
Biloxi, Mississippi: *Mike Sekul*
Biloxi, Mississippi: *Glenn L. Swetman*
Bokeelia, Florida: *Kalaha*
Charleston, South Carolina: *777* (Triple Seven)
Corpus Christi, Texas: *Niña*
Corpus Christi, Texas: *Pinta*
Corpus Christi, Texas: *Santa Maria*
Fort Lauderdale, Florida: *Compass Rose*
Galveston, Texas: *Elissa*
Hamilton, Bermuda: Bermuda Sloop

Foundation
Hilton Head, South Carolina: *Camelot*
Jacksonville, Florida: *Rattlesnake*
Key West, Florida: *Odyssey*
Key West, Florida: *Misty Isles*
Key West, Florida: *Western Union*
Key West, Florida: *Wolf*
Manteo, North Carolina: *Elizabeth II*
Miami, Florida: *Heritage of Miami II*
Miami, Florida: *William H. Albury*
Morgan City, Louisiana: *Clipper Patricia*

California and Pacific Northwest

Coupeville, Washington: *Cutty Sark*
Dana Point, California: *Pilgrim*
Grays Harbor, Washington: *Hewitt R. Jackson*
Grays Harbor, Washington: *Lady Washington*
Kodiak, Alaska: *Three Hierarchs*
Long Beach, California: *Californian*
Long Beach, California: *Pilgrim of Newport*
Los Angeles, California: *Bill of Rights*
Los Angeles, California: *Exy Johnson*
Los Angeles, California: *Irving Johnson*
Los Angeles, California: *Swift of Ipswich*
Newport Beach, California: *Alaska Eagle*
Olympia, Washington: *Resolute*
Olympia, Washington: *SeaWulff*
Port Townsend, Washington: *Adventuress*
Port Townsend, Washington: *Alcyone*
Richmond, California: *Nehemiah*
San Diego, California: *Distant Star*
San Diego, California: *Star of India*
San Francisco, California: *Alma*
San Francisco, California: *Bagheera*
San Francisco, California: *Balclutha*
San Francisco, California: *C.A. Thayer*
San Francisco, California: *Corsair*
San Francisco, California: *Viking*
Sausalito, California: *Dariabar*
Sausalito, California: *Hawaiian Chieftain*
Sausalito, California: *Ka'iulani*
Seattle, Washington: *Mallory Todd*
Seattle, Washington: *Zodiac*

Victoria, British Columbia, Canada: *Pacific Grace*
Victoria, British Columbia, Canada: *Pacific Swift*
Victoria, British Columbia, Canada: *Robertson II*

Europe and Russia

Amsterdam, The Netherlands: *Europa*
Bergen, Norway: *Statsraad Lehmkuhl*
Bremen-Vegesack, Germany: *Esprit*
Charlestown Harbour, St. Austell, Cornwall, UK: *Earl of Pembroke*
Charlestown Harbour, St. Austell, Cornwall, UK: *Kaskelot*
Charlestown Harbour, St. Austell, Cornwall, UK: *Phoenix*
Kalingrad, Russia: *Kruzenshtern*
Liverpool, UK: *Zebu*
Otrano, Italy: *Idea Due*
Rotterdam, The Netherlands: *Oosterschelde*
St. Petersburg, Russia: *Mir*
Southampton, UK: *Jolie Brise*
Southampton, UK: *Lord Nelson*
Southampton, UK: *Tenacious*
Upnor, Near Rochester, Kent, UK: *Arethusa*
Wolgast, Germany: *Roald Amundsen*

Pacific and Indian Oceans

Auckland, New Zealand: *Soren Larsen*
Avatis, Rarotonga, Cook Islands: *Picton Castle*
Honolulu, Hawaii: *Tole Mour*
Port Adelaide, Adelaide, South Australia, Australia: *One and All*
Port Jackson, Sydney, New South Wales, Australia: *Svanen*
Surabaya, Indonesia: *Dewa Ruci*
Sydney, Australia: HM Bark *Endeavour*
Vila, Republic of Vanuatu: *Alvei*

South America and Caribbean

Castries, St. Lucia: *Fantasy*
Cartegena, Colombia: *Gloria*
Guayquil, Ecuador: *Guyas*
Nassau, Bahamas: *Concordia*
Road Harbour, Tortola, British Virgin Islands: *Ocean Star*

Advertisers' Index

Index

SAIL TALL SHIPS!

SAIL TALL SHIPS!

SAIL TALL SHIPS!

PHOTO BY GEORGE ANCONA

PHOTO BY MAX

SAIL TALL SHIPS!

357

SAIL TALL SHIPS!

PHOTO BY MAX

TALL SHIPS 2000

The
Tall Ships® Race
of the Century

The Route

The first leg of the route will commence with two
separate races, both in April and both over similar
distances. One race will start from Southampton,
England, and the other from Genoa, Italy, both
finishing in Cadiz, Spain.

SOUTHAMPTON · AMSTERDAM
HALIFAX · GENOA
BOSTON · CADIZ
BERMUDA

The second leg will be a westbound transatlantic race from Cadiz to Bermuda. The Fleet will then cruise north along the eastern seaboard of the United States, visiting a number of different ports en route to Boston. From Boston, the ships will race to Halifax, Nova Scotia.

The final leg of the route will be a transatlantic race from Halifax to Amsterdam, finishing in August.

TALL SHIPS 2000®

What are *you* doing for the millennium?

If you are interested in registering a vessel for all or part of the race, taking part as a member of the crew, or just want more information, please contact:

International Sail Training Association
5 Mumby Road, Gosport, Hampshire PO12 1AA, England
Telephone: +44 (0)2392 586367
Facsimile: +44 (0)2392 584661
e-mail: tallships2000@ista.co.uk
www.tallships2000.com

American Sail Training Association
559 Thames Street, PO Box 1459
Newport, Rhode Island 02840 USA
Telephone: (401) 846-1775
Facsimile: (401) 849-5400
http://tallships.sailtraining.org

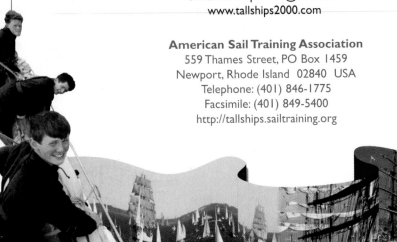